Positioning Women in Conflict Studies

How Women's Status Affects Political Violence

Positioning Women in Conflict Studies

How Women's Status Affects Political Violence

SABRINA KARIM
DANIEL W. HILL, JR.

OXFORD
UNIVERSITY PRESS

Oxford University Press is a department of the University of Oxford.
It furthers the University's objective of excellence in research, scholarship,
and education by publishing worldwide. Oxford is a registered trade mark of
Oxford University Press in the UK and in certain other countries.

Published in the United States of America by Oxford University Press
198 Madison Avenue, New York, NY 10016, United States of America.

© Oxford University Press 2024

All rights reserved. No part of this publication may be reproduced, stored in a retrieval system,
or transmitted, in any form or by any means, without the prior permission in writing of Oxford
University Press, or as expressly permitted by law, by license or under terms agreed with the
appropriate reprographics rights organization. Inquiries concerning reproduction outside the scope
of the above should be sent to the Rights Department, Oxford University Press, at the address above.

You must not circulate this work in any other form and
you must impose this same condition on any acquirer

Library of Congress Cataloging-in-Publication Data
Names: Karim, Sabrina, author. | Hill, Daniel W., Jr., author.
Title: Positioning women in conflict studies : how women's status affects
political violence / Sabrina Karim and Daniel W. Hill, Jr.
Description: New York, NY : Oxford University Press, 2024. |
Includes bibliographical references and index.
Identifiers: LCCN 2024013872 | ISBN 9780197757949 (paperback) |
ISBN 9780197757932 (hardback) | ISBN 9780197757963 (epub) |
ISBN 9780197757970
Subjects: LCSH: Women's rights—Developing countries. | Women—Developing
countries—Social conditions—21st century. | Sex discrimination against
women—Political aspects—Developing countries. | Political
violence—Social aspects.
Classification: LCC HQ1236.5.D44 K37 2024 |
DDC 323.3/4091724—dc23/eng/20240510
LC record available at https://lccn.loc.gov/2024013872

DOI: 10.1093/9780197757970.001.0001

In profound gratitude to my mother, Selina Karim, whose remarkable life journey required her to balance the roles of student, scientist, daughter, sister, wife, mother, and artist across disparate continents and cultures. It is a story that continues to inspire.

—SK

To Ezra, Alastair, and Quinn, whose natural kindness, compassion, and respect for others provide reassurance that tomorrow will be better than today.

—DH

Contents

List of Abbreviations	ix
List of Figures	xi
List of Tables	xiii
List of Boxes	xv
Acknowledgments	xvii

Introduction	1

PART I FROM "GENDER (IN)EQUALITY" TO THE STATUS OF WOMEN

1.	Solving the Concept Stretching Problem	29
2.	Solving the Measurement Invalidity Problem	51

PART II THE STATUS OF WOMEN AND POLITICAL VIOLENCE

3.	Women's Inclusion and Political Violence	81
4.	Women's Rights and Political Violence	120
5.	Harm to Women and Political Violence	147
6.	Beliefs about Women's Gender Roles and Political Violence	173
7.	Conclusion	193

Appendix	217
Notes	251
References	267
Index	293

Abbreviations

ATWS	Attitudes Toward Women Scale
CEDAW	Convention on the Elimination of All Forms of Discrimination Against Women
CCPR	Covenant on Civil and Political Rights
CESCR	Covenant on Economic, Social, and Cultural Rights
CINC	Composite Indicator of National Capability
CIRI	Cingranelli-Richards Human Rights Data Project
COW	Correlates of War
DCAF	Geneva Centre for Democratic Control of Armed Forces
DRC	Democratic Republic of the Congo
FEA	Feminist Evolutionary Analytic
FWCW	Fourth United Nations Conference on Women
GDP	Gross Domestic Product
GDI	Gender Development Index
GII	Gender Inequality Index
GTD	Global Terrorism Database
HDI	Human Development Indicator
HIV	Human Immunodeficiency Virus
IGO	Intergovernmental Organization
ILO	International Labor Organization
INGO	International Non-Governmental Organization
IO	International Organization
IR	International Relations
IRT	Item Response Theory
LGBTQ	Lesbian, Gay, Bisexual, Transgender, Queer
LRW	Sexual Assault and Rape Scale
MID	Militarized Interstate Dispute
MSS	Modern Sexism Scale
NGO	Non-Governmental Organization
OECD	Organisation for Economic Co-operation and Development
ODIHR	Office for Democratic Institutions and Human Rights
OSCE	Organization for Security and Co-operation in Europe
PRIO	Peace Research Institute Oslo
PTS	Political Terror Scale
RUF	Revolutionary United Front
SGBV	Sexual and Gender-Based Violence
SIGI	Social Institutions and Gender Index

X ABBREVIATIONS

UAE	United Arab Emirates
UDHR	Universal Declaration of Human Rights
UK	The United Kingdom
UNESCO	United Nations Educational, Scientific and Cultural Organization
UN	United Nations
UNAIDS	Joint United Nations Programme on HIV/AIDS
UNDP	United Nations Development Programme
UNICEF	United Nations Children's Fund
UNSC	United Nations Security Council
US	The United States
USAID	United States Agency for International Development
WPS	Women, Peace, and Security
WVS	World Values Survey
UCDP	Uppsala Conflict Data Program

Figures

0.1:	Number of Articles Using Quantitative Methods on Gender/Sex and Conflict	4
0.2:	Number of Articles Using Quantitative Methods on Gender/Sex and Conflict by Sex of Author	5
0.3:	Placement of Articles Using Quantitative Methods on Gender/Sex and Conflict	6
1.1:	Number of Articles Using Quantitative Methods on Gender and/or Sex	42
2.1:	Indicators used in Quantitative Scholarship on Gender and Conflict	57
2.2:	Yearly Correlation Coefficients for "Usual Suspect" Indicators	60
2.3:	Violin Plots for "Usual Suspects" for Each Value of the Relevant CIRI Scale	61
2.4:	Latent Variables over Time	72
2.5:	Correlations between Latent Variables	73
2.6:	Beliefs Estimates for Three Countries	75
3.1:	Estimates from Measurement Model for Women's Inclusion	86
3.2:	The Relationships Between Women's Inclusion and Two Continuous Indicators	87
3.3:	The Relationships Between Women's Inclusion and Two Binary Indicators	88
3.4:	Estimates from Women's Political Inclusion Model	89
3.5:	Women's and Men's (Hypothetical) Dispositions toward Violence	94
3.6:	Coefficient Estimates for Women's Inclusion from Models of Political Violence	110
4.1:	Estimates from Measurement Model for Women's Rights	130
4.2:	Coefficient Estimates for Women's Rights from Models of Political Violence	139
4.3:	Marginal Effect of Women's Rights at Different Values of Women's INGOs (WINGOs)	140
5.1:	Estimates from Measurement Model for Harm to Women	154
5.2:	Coefficient Estimates for Harm to Women from Models of Political Violence	169
6.1:	Estimates from Measurement Model for Beliefs about Women's Gender Roles	180
6.2:	Coefficient Estimates for Beliefs about Women's Gender Roles from Models of Political Violence	189

xii FIGURES

A2.1:	Average Incidence of Conflict for Every Country in the Data	218
A2.2:	Average Fatal MID Initiation Count for Every Country in the Data	220
A2.3:	Average PTS Score for Every Country in the Data	222
A2.4:	Average CIRI Score for Every Country in the Data	223
A2.5:	Median Number of Terror Attacks for Every Country in the Data	225
A3.1:	Marginal Effect of Political Inclusion on Terror Attacks	229
A3.2:	Coefficient Estimates from Models of Civil Conflict and War Onset	230
A3.3:	Coefficient Estimates from Models of International Disputes	231
A3.4:	Coefficient Estimates from Models of State Violence	232
A3.5:	Coefficient Estimates from Models of Terror Attacks	233
A4.1:	Coefficient Estimates from Models of Civil Conflict and War Onset	235
A4.2:	Coefficient Estimates from Models of International Disputes	236
A4.3:	Coefficient Estimates from Models of State Violence	236
A4.4:	Coefficient Estimates from Models of State Violence: Rights Interacted with Women's INGOs	237
A4.5:	Coefficient Estimates from Models of Terror Attacks	238
A4.6:	Coefficient Estimates from Models of State Violence with Women's Inclusion added	238
A5.1:	The Relationship between Harm to Women and One Ordinal Indicator	239
A5.2:	Marginal Effect of Harm to Women on Civil Conflict Onset	241
A5.3:	Marginal Effect of Harm to Women on Interstate Dispute Initiation	241
A5.4:	Coefficient Estimates from Models of Civil Conflict and War Onset	242
A5.5:	Coefficient Estimates from Models of International Disputes	242
A5.6:	Coefficient Estimates from Models of State Violence	243
A5.7:	Coefficient Estimates from Models of Terror Attacks	243
A5.8:	Coefficient Estimates from Models of Civil Conflict Onset with Women's Rights Added	243
A5.9:	Coefficient Estimates from Models of International Disputes with Women's Rights Added	244
A6.1:	Marginal Effect of Beliefs About Women's Gender Roles on Terror Attacks	246
A6.2:	Coefficient Estimates from Models of Civil Conflict and War Onset	247
A6.3:	Coefficient Estimates from Models of International Disputes	248
A6.4:	Coefficient Estimates from Models of State Violence	249
A6.5:	Coefficient Estimates from Models of Terror Attacks	250

Tables

0.1:	Characteristics of Concepts	14
1.1:	Gender Equality Definitions among International Organizations	44
3.1:	Indicators for Inclusion Model	85
4.1:	Indicators for Rights Model	127
5.1:	Indicators for Harm Model	152
6.1:	World Values Survey Items for Beliefs Model	179
7.1:	Summary of Results	194

Boxes

1.1:	Classical Subtypes of Gender (In)equality	33
1.2:	Classical Subtypes of Gender (In)equality: Patriarchy	34
1.3:	Classical Subtypes of Gender (In)equality: Misogyny	35
1.4:	Diminished Subtypes of Gender (In)equality: Social Inequality	36
1.5:	Diminished Subtypes of Gender (In)equality: Gender Hierarchy	36
1.6:	Women's Status	37
3.1:	Characteristics of Women's Inclusion	84
4.1:	Characteristics of Women's Rights	124
5.1:	Characteristics of Harm to Women	149
6.1:	Characteristics of Beliefs about Women's Gender Roles	175

Acknowledgments

This book started because two scholars, who were both using Bayesian latent variable models to develop measures of women's rights, met during a seminar talk. Sabrina had just taken a course on Bayesian Statistical Modeling taught by Drew Linzer, in which the final class project was to create a new item response scale. Sabrina chose to create a scale for women's rights. Danny had been working on, and receiving rejections for, a paper that used those same models to create new measures of women's rights. Instead of keeping their efforts separate, Sabrina and Danny decided to work together to write a paper, which eventually became this book.

In addition to this fortuitous meeting at the University of Georgia, other encounters inspired this book. During one International Studies Association conference, Sabrina was chatting with a scholar who mentioned that he was interested in integrating a lecture on gender and international relations into his undergraduate introduction to international relations class but did not really know how to do so. This book is intended to help scholars such as this person—scholars who are looking for an entry point into understanding how gender and women's status affect political violence globally. We hope that it helps scholars include lectures and classes on gender, women's status, and global conflict in their introductory (and seminar) courses, given the importance of the topics.

Moreover, conversations with Laura Sjoberg, Kelly Kadera, Caitlin Ryan, María Martín de Almagro, and others who have spent their careers highlighting some of the issues we bring up here also inspired the book. Conversations with them always challenged the way we thought about things and improved our thought process for the book. Many of the arguments we make are not new, but rather scholars have been writing about them in some form for decades. As such, we want to recognize the vast amount of literature on gender, women's status, and political violence that precedes this book. Without the work of pioneers such as Cynthia Enloe, Ann Tickner, Carol Cohn, V. Spike Peterson, Chandra Mohanty, and many others, this study of the effect of gender and women's status on conflict would not have been possible.

xviii ACKNOWLEDGMENTS

We are also especially indebted to Dara Cohen, Valerie Hudson, Kyle Beardsley, Dan Reiter, Matt Evangelista, Mary Katzenstein, Elisabeth Jean Wood, and Alice J. Kang, who all read different chapters or versions of the book and provided feedback and comments. We were fortunate to workshop this manuscript and versions of chapters at various conferences. Cornell's Reppy Institute for Peace and Conflict Studies program and Feminist, Gender & Sexuality Studies Program both hosted talks where the authors were able to present versions of the book. Comments by those who attended, especially Matt Evangelista, Sarah Kreps, Durba Ghosh, Peter Katzenstein, Isabel Hull, and others in the seminars were foundational for future edits. We were also fortunate to be able to present versions at conferences including the Folke Bernadote Academy research working group meeting in Oslo where comments from Elin Bjarnegård, Louise Olsson, Mimmi Söderberg Kovacs, Gudrun Østby, Zoe Marks, Karen Brounéus, Molly Melin, Ragnhild Nordås, Henrik Urdal, Jana Krause, Angela Muvumba Sellström, and others helped shape the manuscript. We also presented at the International Studies Association annual conference, where comments by Amanda Murdie, Jillienne E. Haglund, Laura Huber, Emily Ritter, Annie Watson, and others were very helpful as we made some final edits. We are also incredibly grateful to the entire WomenStats Project team for allowing us to host our data and for the invaluable comments at conferences and workshops. Finally, we are also thankful to the two anonymous reviewers who undoubtedly helped improve this manuscript.

We are enormously grateful to a number of people for making this book happen. First and foremost, Sabrina would like to thank her husband and partner, Joshua Eli Smith, for giving her the space and time to do research, whether that means traveling to some international destination every month or taking over childcare duties so that she could finish her research. Indeed, this book would not have been possible without his dedication to being such a wonderful partner. In addition to Josh, Sabrina is also indebted to her father, M. Nazmul Karim, and mother, Selina Karim, for their never wavering support and steadfast commitment to raising a daughter in the most gender equal way possible. Never did Sabrina once doubt what she was capable of achieving in her life thanks to her parents believing in her. During the course of working on this book, Sabrina became a mother to Ansel Nazmul Karim-Smith. The experience has only radicalized her into becoming even more of a feminist than before, as the institutional and cultural inequities and challenges of motherhood (as well as for those trying to become parents more generally) can only be understood by those who experience them. The experience of motherhood has made Sabrina more steadfast in working to promote gender equality globally. In this way, her son Ansel inspires her every day to make the world a better place.

Danny would like to thank his partner Jamie Hill for managing all aspects of their home and family life while he worked to complete this book and for her invaluable encouragement and support over the years. Danny would also like to thank his parents Dan and Nancy Hill for encouraging him to pursue a degree and career in political science and for their patience when he was younger. He is also grateful to his sons Ezra, Alastair, and Quinn for making every day brighter and happier and for making the world a kinder and gentler place. Finally, Danny owes a debt of gratitude to his friend and mentor Will H. Moore, whose assurance gave him the confidence to become an academic, and who was always willing to invest time and effort in his students.

We had extensive help with writing this book. Specifically, we are grateful to the research assistants who worked on this project. These include Tessa Evans and Addison Barton. The book would not have been possible without their timely assistance. Finally, we are grateful to Angela Chnapko for making our vision a reality.

Much of the first draft of this book was written during the pandemic, when there was a bright spotlight on gender inequality and women's status globally and at home. Recognizing that the status of many women declined during this time, we hope that this book continues shining a light on these important issues.

Introduction

On March 6, 2023, United Nations (UN) Secretary General Antonio Guterres (2023) warned that decades of global progress on women's status are "vanishing before our eyes." Speaking to the Commission on the Status of Women in New York, he listed examples of global rollbacks to the status of women and girls including the erasure of women from public life in Afghanistan, the backsliding on reproductive health in many countries, and the kidnapping and killing of girls. He suggested that the goal of "gender equality" is at least "300 years away."

The secretary general is not necessarily exaggerating in his statement. Progress on improving women's status globally has slowed, stalled, or even reversed (England, Levine, and Mishel 2020a; 2020b; Moyer and Birchall 2023).[1] For one, the Covid-19 global pandemic exacerbated women's conditions around the world. Domestic violence increased, job insecurity for women worsened, access to sexual and reproductive health services declined, women face higher levels of food and water insecurity than men, and girls' enrollment in schools has dropped. Amnesty International's secretary general, Agnès Callamard, sums up the grim news in this way, "events [in 2021 and 2022] have conspired to crush the rights and dignity of millions of women and girls. The world's crises do not impact equally, let alone fairly. The disproportionate impacts on women's and girls' rights are well-documented yet still neglected, when not ignored outright."[2]

However, the Covid-19 global pandemic cannot be solely responsible for these trends. There have been government rollbacks in women's rights all over the world, some predating the onset of the pandemic. Women's employment has been on the decline since 2008; women's earnings have not changed since the early 2000s; and the desegregation of the types of degrees that men and women receive have stalled (England, Levine, and Mishel 2020a). Moreover, Russia, Poland, and Turkey have backtracked on legislation related to sexual and gender-based violence. The US Supreme Court overturned Roe vs. Wade and drastically reduced women's reproductive rights. The return of Taliban rule in Afghanistan has meant restrictions on many aspects of daily life for

---

Positioning Women in Conflict Studies. Sabrina Karim and Daniel W. Hill, Jr., Oxford University Press.
© Oxford University Press 2024. DOI: 10.1093/9780197757970.003.0001

2 POSITIONING WOMEN IN CONFLICT STUDIES

women and girls: girls cannot attend secondary school or universities, hold a job, or move freely outside of their homes. South Korea has sought to abolish the Ministry of Gender Equality and Family, and Sweden has rescinded its "feminist foreign policy."

The toll of these changes on the lives of women and girls is enormous. Restrictions on women's rights could increase violence against women and increase mortality and morbidity rates. As more people believe that women should stay at home and as more women stay in the private sphere, the lives of millions, even billions, of women and girls are simply made worse. Yet beyond the harm caused by stagnation or rollbacks of women's status, these changes may pose another significant threat in the form of more political violence around the world. More specifically, a decline in women's status globally may foreshadow more civil conflict, terrorism, interstate war, and state repression. An overwhelming body of literature in political science finds that women's status is related to the occurrence of all these types of political violence.[3] This means that a global decline women's status could be followed by more frequent civil conflict, terrorism, interstate war, and/or repression. Thus, the goal of this book is to improve our understanding of whether and how different aspects of women's status are connected to these forms of political violence. More specifically, we explore how four aspects of women's status—women's inclusion, women's rights, harm to women, and beliefs about women's gender roles—affects civil conflict, terrorism, interstate conflict, and state repression.

Before we can accomplish this goal, however, we must overcome two problems that have made it difficult to probe these relationships in the past. First, much of the academic and policymaking literature suggests a relationship between *"gender inequality"* and conflict. Using the term gender (in)equality as a catchall phrase for different aspects of women's status, however, prevents researchers from developing specific theories about *how* women's status (not gender inequality) affects political violence. Moreover, it prevents researchers from accurately measuring concepts and therefore conducting analyses that adequately test their claims. Thus, the first step to exploring any relationships between women's status and political violence requires overcoming the problems of *concept stretching* and *measurement invalidity*.

We overcome these two problems by engaging in a process of *differentiation and delineation* of concepts and measures. We differentiate gender equality from women's status, and further distinguish four aspects of women's status: women's inclusion, women's rights, harm to women, and beliefs about women's roles. We then create measures of these four concepts that address common measurement problems and allow for a more adequate examination of the relationship between women's status and different forms of political violence. This process allows us to isolate conceptually and empirically the different aspects of women's status that past research suggests are linked to the occurrence of political violence. The differentiation and delineation of concepts and measures allows us to provide evidence that women's gender inclusion in politics, as well as more flexibility with regard to beliefs about women's gender roles in society, are associated with fewer terror attacks. Women's rights, especially when coupled with large numbers of women's organizations in a society, are associated with less state violence. Harm to women is correlated with a higher risk of civil conflict and inter-state war onset. Differentiating and delineating concepts and measurements allows us to clarify links that would remain obscure without this exercise.

The rest of this chapter more explicitly describes the problems of concept stretching and measurement invalidity and presents our solutions. We then describe the contributions of this book and conclude with an outline of the chapters.

The Problem

Quantitative scholarship on gender and international relations (IR) emerged in the 2000s with a call for testing the relationship between "gender (in)equality" and conflict onset using aggregated indicators.[4] Robert Keohane suggested that researchers could treat "gender equality" as an independent variable (1998, 197). Mary Caprioli, in particular, answered this call and published a series of articles (2000, 2003, 2005) using "gender equality" as an independent variable to understand its effect on different forms of conflict— the beginnings of the quantitative work on the feminist peace theory.[5] This work set the stage for several strands of research that have used quantitative methods to understand the link between "gender equality" and conflict management, processes, and outcomes (Cohen and Karim 2022), as well as the link between conflict and post-conflict "gender equality" (Webster, Chen, and Beardsley 2019; Webster et al. 2020). There is also a robust and growing quantitative scholarship to explain variation in the participation of women in rebellion, insurgency, and acts of terrorism, women in peacekeeping missions, women in politics, and women's rights, as well as on examining variation

4 POSITIONING WOMEN IN CONFLICT STUDIES

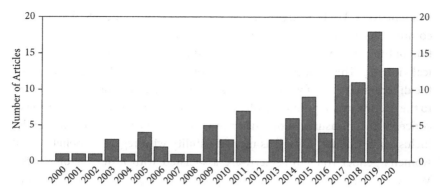

Figure 0.1 Number of Articles Using Quantitative Methods on Gender/Sex and Conflict

in wartime sexual violence, all of which have been bundled together in the larger literature on "gender and conflict."

Figure 0.1 displays the number of studies published per year that can be reasonably categorized as part of this growing literature.[6] It shows that this body of research is, in fact, growing. In the past 20 years, the number of conflict studies that incorporate concepts related to sex or gender in the study of peace and conflict has generally increased. While there was an average of 1.4 studies per year published for the first 5 years of this time period, the average over the last 5 years was nearly 10. Figure 0.2 indicates that men as well as women are contributing to this body of research, though the vast majority of these studies (nearly 80%) have at least one female author. Figure 0.3 shows where these studies have been published. Notably, more research on gender, women, and peace and conflict have been published in subfield specific journals, with only a handful of studies being published in discipline-wide journals.

Despite the proliferation of studies, there appears to be little consensus among these studies on what gender equality means, and often when the term is referenced, it is not defined. Some scholars define or refer to it as the lack of an equal power/status relationship between men and women, whereas others refer to it as the degree of discrimination against women. Some describe it in terms of policies, while others describe it in terms of social relationships. In other instances, studies do not use "gender equality" to describe their main concept of interest but instead use terms such as gender hierarchy, gender relations, gender ideology, women's empowerment, and women's

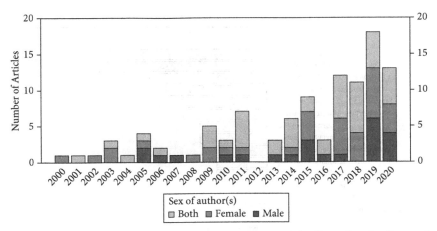

Figure 0.2 Number of Articles Using Quantitative Methods on Gender/Sex and Conflict by Sex of Author

rights. Sometimes these terms are used interchangeably. For example, Beath et al. (2013) use the terms gender equality and women's empowerment interchangeably in the text. Sometimes gender equality is a catchall phrase for these other terms, other times they mean the same thing, and sometimes they are distinguished from one another. In searching the literature for clear definitions of terms, we have found that authors almost always assume that readers know what "gender," "equality," and "gender equality," mean. In short, despite there being a proliferation in the study of "gender equality" in peace and conflict studies, there is no consensus on the definition of what gender equality means; there is also uncertainty about the boundaries of the concept; and in many instances, gender equality refers to women in the theory and analysis.

Furthermore, the way that quantitative scholars have used gender stands in contrast to how other scholars writing about gender and conflict used the concept of gender.[7] Some work (Sjoberg 2013, 2014) finds a co-constitutive relationship between gender and conflict, meaning they cannot be separated. This work treats gender as an analytical framework (see the discussion below on pp. 9–11). Gender is defined as a verb, and the purpose of a study is typically to examine how different phenomena are gendered. In this understanding, gender cannot be measured using one indicator.

Conflating sex and gender is problematic for a number of reasons. A lack of a clear consensus on the concept of gender, sex, and women leads to a

6 POSITIONING WOMEN IN CONFLICT STUDIES

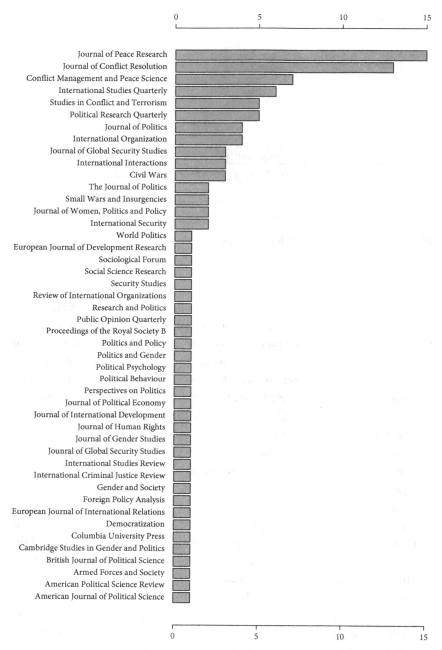

Figure 0.3 Placement of Articles Using Quantitative Methods on Gender/Sex and Conflict

masking of the power relationships that continue to exist when gender is used as a catchall phrase for women. Extensive critiques to this effect are offered by Arat (2015), Ellerby (2017), and Sjoberg, Kadera, and Thies (2018). Specifically, Sjoberg, Kadera, and Thies (2018: 852) argue that when gender means women, scholars miss out on studying gendered expectations, gendered behaviors, and behaviors among those who identify as different genders. Arat (2015) suggests that the conflation of sex and gender leads to gender equality being equated with liberal feminism, which places women's rights and inclusion at the heart of policy change. According to her, "the overall women's rights approach of the UN is still informed by the demands and expectations of liberal feminism, which seeks integrating women into male dominant domains and structures, without contesting the foundation and function of those structures" (Arat 2015, 675). Gender is used as a shortcut for women's inclusion and rights (Ellerby 2017). The consequence of this shortcut is that there can be no real change for women because they are still operating under the same oppressive structures (Ellerby 2017, 188–89). In short, both Arat (2015) and Ellerby (2017) argue that when gender equality is used as a technocratic term for including women without really discussing how gender shapes the experiences of both men and women within institutions, it becomes a way to acknowledge power without changing its source.

Building on this work, we also argue that a lack of a clear consensus on the concept of gender, sex, and women's status makes uncovering relationships between gender inequality/women's status and conflict a thorny problem. We contend that a conflation of gender with women prevents us from examining how women's status affects outcomes. When the term gender is used, it serves as a sort of mask (or as feminist scholars argue, a lens) that prevents the study of any one concept regarding women in isolation.[8] We believe that this masking leads to two fundamental problems that prevent us from learning more about whether and how women's status is connected to political violence. First, drawing on the rich body of literature on conceptualization in political science (Sartori 1970, 1984; Collier and Mahon 1993; Collier and Levitsky 1997; Gerring 2001; Goertz 2006), we argue that the current use of gender equality "stretches the concept" in a way that misrepresents its actual meaning. The use of women's status interchangeably with gender equality has occurred in political science and the policymaking world to increase "extension" or to increase the contexts in which "gender equality" can be applied (Collier and Mahon 1993; Sartori 1970, 1984). Many policymakers and

8   POSITIONING WOMEN IN CONFLICT STUDIES

scholars have used the concept of gender equality to mean women's status, thereby stretching of the concept of gender equality. Doing so obscures differences in the explanations that link different aspects of women's status to different forms of political violence. In other words, when policymakers and scholars say that gender equality reduces civil war, we do not know if they mean women's rights, women's inclusion in politics, or some other concept. Using the term "gender equality" as a catchall phrase makes it difficult to assess how these various conditions should, in theory, be related to conflict.

Second, policymakers and scholars have used various indicators and indices to measure "gender equality," most of which measure outcomes related to women's status and thus cannot be considered valid measures of gender equality. In many cases the indicators are not highly correlated with each other, which suggests they should not be treated as measures of the same concept, whether the relevant concept is gender equality or something else. Further, in cases where indicators are combined into a single scale (which is common practice for scales produced by intergovernmental organizations, IGOs), they are often combined in problematic ways that raise concerns about the validity of the resulting scale. These problems lead to measurement invalidity, or misalignment between the measure and the concept. If indicators are not clearly connected to the concepts they are supposed to measure, then it is not possible to say anything about the relationships between those concepts. Conclusions drawn from analyses using invalid measures may be inaccurate or misleading. The use of "gender equality" to refer to a range of conditions related to women's status thus also makes it difficult to assess which particular concepts are related to political violence and which are not.

The Solution

To overcome the challenges of concept stretching and measurement invalidity, we engage in a process of *differentiation* and *delineation*. We carefully differentiate women's status from gender equality, and we distinguish different aspects of women's status—women inclusion, women's rights, harm to women, and beliefs about women's gender roles—from one another. We delineate each concept by giving it an explicit definition, creating a measure for it, and describing the theoretical connections identified in the literature between the concept and the forms of political violence explored in this book.

masking of the power relationships that continue to exist when gender is used as a catchall phrase for women. Extensive critiques to this effect are offered by Arat (2015), Ellerby (2017), and Sjoberg, Kadera, and Thies (2018). Specifically, Sjoberg, Kadera, and Thies (2018: 852) argue that when gender means women, scholars miss out on studying gendered expectations, gendered behaviors, and behaviors among those who identify as different genders. Arat (2015) suggests that the conflation of sex and gender leads to gender equality being equated with liberal feminism, which places women's rights and inclusion at the heart of policy change. According to her, "the overall women's rights approach of the UN is still informed by the demands and expectations of liberal feminism, which seeks integrating women into male dominant domains and structures, without contesting the foundation and function of those structures" (Arat 2015, 675). Gender is used as a shortcut for women's inclusion and rights (Ellerby 2017). The consequence of this shortcut is that there can be no real change for women because they are still operating under the same oppressive structures (Ellerby 2017, 188–89). In short, both Arat (2015) and Ellerby (2017) argue that when gender equality is used as a technocratic term for including women without really discussing how gender shapes the experiences of both men and women within institutions, it becomes a way to acknowledge power without changing its source.

Building on this work, we also argue that a lack of a clear consensus on the concept of gender, sex, and women's status makes uncovering relationships between gender inequality/women's status and conflict a thorny problem. We contend that a conflation of gender with women prevents us from examining how women's status affects outcomes. When the term gender is used, it serves as a sort of mask (or as feminist scholars argue, a lens) that prevents the study of any one concept regarding women in isolation.[8] We believe that this masking leads to two fundamental problems that prevent us from learning more about whether and how women's status is connected to political violence. First, drawing on the rich body of literature on conceptualization in political science (Sartori 1970, 1984; Collier and Mahon 1993; Collier and Levitsky 1997; Gerring 2001; Goertz 2006), we argue that the current use of gender equality "stretches the concept" in a way that misrepresents its actual meaning. The use of women's status interchangeably with gender equality has occurred in political science and the policymaking world to increase "extension" or to increase the contexts in which "gender equality" can be applied (Collier and Mahon 1993; Sartori 1970, 1984). Many policymakers and scholars have used the concept of gender equality to mean women's status, thereby stretching of the concept of gender equality. Doing so obscures differences in the explanations that link different aspects of women's status to different forms of political violence. In other words, when policymakers and scholars say that gender equality reduces civil war, we do not know if they mean women's rights, women's inclusion in politics, or some other concept. Using the term "gender equality" as a catchall phrase makes it difficult to assess how these various conditions should, in theory, be related to conflict.

Second, policymakers and scholars have used various indicators and indices to measure "gender equality," most of which measure outcomes related to women's status and thus cannot be considered valid measures of gender equality. In many cases the indicators are not highly correlated with each other, which suggests they should not be treated as measures of the same concept, whether the relevant concept is gender equality or something else. Further, in cases where indicators are combined into a single scale (which is common practice for scales produced by intergovernmental organizations, IGOs), they are often combined in problematic ways that raise concerns about the validity of the resulting scale. These problems lead to measurement invalidity, or misalignment between the measure and the concept. If indicators are not clearly connected to the concepts they are supposed to measure, then it is not possible to say anything about the relationships between those concepts. Conclusions drawn from analyses using invalid measures may be inaccurate or misleading. The use of "gender equality" to refer to a range of conditions related to women's status thus also makes it difficult to assess which particular concepts are related to political violence and which are not.

The Solution

To overcome the challenges of concept stretching and measurement invalidity, we engage in a process of *differentiation* and *delineation*. We carefully differentiate women's status from gender equality, and we distinguish different aspects of women's status—women inclusion, women's rights, harm to women, and beliefs about women's gender roles—from one another. We delineate each concept by giving it an explicit definition, creating a measure for it, and describing the theoretical connections identified in the literature between the concept and the forms of political violence explored in this book.

Differentiation through Definition

To differentiate gender equality from women's status, we first define gender (in)equality, women's status, women's inclusion, women's rights, harm to women, and beliefs about women's gender roles. Gender as a concept was created to contest power hierarchies. It was established in the 1970s to challenge the essentialist and deterministic ideas about natural differences between men and women, as these were used to justify women's subordination (Ellerby 2017). The concept became an analytical tool for critical theorists to illustrate how masculine and feminine identities were socially constructed through practices that scripted appropriate behavior for men and women. Feminist scholars from the post-colonial tradition also emphasize the importance of studying power hierarchies among different femininities (Mohanty, Russo, and Torres 1991).

We identify four characteristics of gender (in)equality. First, gender is a *social construction*. When feminists use the word gender, they are not referring to the biological differences between males and females,[9] but to a set of culturally shaped and defined characteristics associated with masculinity and femininity (Tickner 1992, 7). Gender is first and foremost a social construct and secondly an expression of power (Sjoberg 2013, 47). It is an institutionalized entity or artifact in a social system invented or constructed by a particular culture or society that exists because people agree to behave as if it exists or to follow certain conventional rules (2013, 5). Gender is definable as stereotypes, behavioral norms, and expectations assigned to men and women. Societies, organizations, and individuals may produce and reproduce multiple masculinities and femininities. As such, genders are variable, discursive, and socially constructed (Sjoberg and Via 2010, 4).[10]

Second, the term "gender" implies a power hierarchy (Enloe 2014; Scott 1999; Pettman 1996; Sjoberg 2010; Sjoberg and Gentry 2007), as outlined comprehensively by Cohn (2013, 11). Gender is a social structure that shapes individuals' identities and lives; it is a way of categorizing, ordering, and symbolizing power, of hierarchically structuring relationships among different categories of people and different human activities symbolically associated with masculinity or femininity. Gender not only applies to male and female persons, it "constitutes a central organizing discourse in all societies we know of, "a set of ways of thinking, images, categories, and beliefs, which not only shape how we experience, understand, and represent ourselves as men and women, but which also provide a familiar set of metaphors, dichotomies, and values which structure ways of thinking about other aspects of the world"

(11, emphasis original). Both women and men tend to assign a more positive value to masculine characteristics. Manliness is typically prized whereas femininity is undesirable. As such, to feminize something or someone is to directly subordinate that person, political entity, or idea because attributes and entities perceived as feminine are lower on the social hierarchy than those perceived as neutral or masculine (Sjoberg 2006, 34).[11]

Third, gender is relational, which means that privileging who and what is masculinized is inextricable from devaluing who and what is feminized (Sjoberg and Gentry 2011, 7). Scott (1999, 49) suggests that the fixed binary (i.e. male/female) legitimatizes a set of unequal social *relationships*. Through the use of language, symbols, and culture, individuals see the world in these binary oppositions to one another. She states that Western understandings of gender are based on a set of culturally determined binary distinctions such as public versus private, objective versus subjective, self versus other, reason versus emotion, autonomy versus relatedness, and culture versus nature. The first of each of these pairs of characteristics is typically associated with masculinity and the second with femininity. Thus, definitions of masculinity and femininity are relational and depend on each other for their meaning; in other words, what it means to be a "real man" is to not to display undesirable, "womanly" qualities such as weakness and irrationality.

Fourth, and last, the fluidity of gender refers to variation in the characteristics associated with different identities, whereas rigidness refers to fixed identities. There are two ways in which gender may be a dynamic or fluid concept. Gender-based expectations for human behavior are not constant across time and place. The content of gender categories changes over time, place, culture, religion, and host of other factors (Sjoberg and Via 2010, 4). Gender interacts with other factors to produce social and political relations while being produced by them (Sjoberg 2013, 6). Thus, gender is shaped by society and can change as society changes. Additionally, fluidity refers to people's ability to transition in and out of different gender identities. In contrast, rigidity refers to when men are expected to conform to strictly masculine identities and women to strictly feminine identities. Gender identities for Butler (2004) are performances. Individuals perform gender in relation to their surroundings, meaning that these performances can change constantly. Conforming to gender roles based on assigned sex is a societal expectation. When this expectation is not met, this deviance is punished. Butler (2004) defines gender as the mechanisms through which "woman" and "man" and "masculine" and "feminine" become legitimate conceptual categories and whereby institutions of gender organize social behavior through practices that include rewarding conformity and punishing digressions. Punishment comes in the form of infantilizing, ignoring, trivializing, or even actively casting scorn upon what is thought to be feminine (Enloe 2004, 4–5). Thus, in short, fluidity can refer to an individual's ability to engage in or perform multiple or different gender identities without punishment, whereas rigidness refers to norms that dictate fixed gender roles, expectations of conformity, and sanctioning deviations from prescribed roles.

The valuing of certain characteristics over others is what constitutes the hierarchy or inequality. Fraser et al. (2007, 26) argue that the "status hierarchy" is key to understanding gender (in)equalities, which are the institutionalized patterns of cultural value that privilege men and masculinity and devalue women and feminine. Adding inequality to gender suggests that a particular gender identity is valued less than others. If gender inequality means the privileging of masculine characteristics over feminine ones, or the practices that sustain hegemonic masculinity, *gender equality* means equality in the value of the different traits that define masculinity and femininity.

To get to a state of *gender equality*, feminist scholars argue that we must analyze the way binary oppositions operate in difference contexts, rather than accepting them as fixed, and seek to displace their hierarchical construction. When these differences between women and men are no longer assumed to be natural or fixed, we can examine how relationships of gender inequality are constructed and sustained in various arenas of public and private life. In committing itself to gender as a category of analysis, contemporary feminism also commits itself to gender equality as a social goal.

Gender equality, as defined here, is different than the concept of women's status. We define women's status as having two different characteristics. First, the term "women" indicates that the concept refers to people who biologically identify as girls or women. We use the term "identify" because scholars have argued that there is some degree of social construction of sexual organs. For example, Kinsella and Sjoberg (2019) give the example of an agenetic (XY chromosome) male with an "inadequate penis" or "one that physicians believe will be incapable of its function," who is then made female. There are also humans born without sexual organs or who are intersex who are assigned a sex at birth. Thus, this definition encapsulates anyone who accepts their body parts as female.

The second characteristic is the importance or value assigned to a person in relation to other people within society. "Women's status" refers to the value society typically assigns to people identified as women relative to the value it typically assigns to people not identified as women. This is consistent with the way status as it relates to social groups is defined in sociology (Berger, Ridgeway, and Zelditch 2002). It is also consistent with literature on the role of status in IR theory, which describes status as a collective belief about a person, group, or state's ranking on valued attributes (Renshon 2017, 33). Status thus refers to the position of a person or group in a hierarchy relative to others and individual and collective perceptions of that position in that hierarchy.[12] Thus, status is based on social relations among people and groups, and those with higher status are perceived as possessing valuable qualities that those with less status lack.

Concepts that share at least one characteristic with women's status constitute aspects of women's status. While there are many aspects of women's status that we could study, we opt to examine variation in different types of status. Those who are esteemed, or who have high status, are more likely to be included in public life and have formally recognized rights; they are less likely to experience harm and more likely to be perceived as being capable of accomplishing any goal or task. These aspects of status capture some important obstacles that often confront women, including the public/private divide, formal status discrepancies in law and policy, structural violence, and belief systems that limit women to certain social roles. Thus, in this manuscript, we explore these four aspects of women's status: women's inclusion, women's rights, harm to women, and beliefs about women's gender roles.[13]

To be transparent, we go into more detail about the choice to focus on these four concepts, as we chose the aspects of women's status based on our experiences. Our initial conceptual framework relied on liberal feminist concepts related to representation, participation, and protection (Ellerby 2017). International organizations such as the UN, whose women, peace, and security agenda is driven by a liberal feminist conception of equality, are interested mainly in these concepts, and we wanted to interrogate their meaning. As we broadened our focus, we started to consider the concepts of women's participation and empowerment. However, fieldwork by one of us demonstrated that women's participation and women's empowerment often happen in private spaces. Because the liberal feminist concept we wish to capture is focused on public spaces, we chose to adopt the concept of "women's inclusion" instead.

The concept of women's rights has been widely used in the literature. While a narrow view of the concept includes only laws, some literature on women's rights and fieldwork have demonstrated the importance of also including policies in our understanding of women's rights. Work in the field in Zambia and Ghana demonstrated that norms trickle down from policy as much as they do from the law. For example, such policy frameworks as a National Action Plan on UN Security Council Resolution 1325 signal the importance of gender mainstreaming to the security forces, who do not make changes unless there is policy guidance from above. In line with Tripp (2015), and Htun and Weldon (2018), we thus expand our understanding of women's rights to include policies, to capture how women are affected by institutions.

We also began with a focus on concepts we termed "women's risk" and "women's vulnerability." However, we eventually realized that while these two terms captured a structural element measuring the propensity for harm, it was important for us to make sure that our concept captured both actual harm and violence against women as well as the risk of or vulnerability to harm. Firsthand experience with survivors of sexual violence in Liberia clearly demonstrated the importance of capturing actual harm as well as structural harm. Additionally, personally witnessing the 2014 Ebola epidemic in Liberia and its gendered effects, such as higher rates of maternal mortality, led to the conclusion that the structural element of harm to women was equally important to our research questions.

For information about our final concept (beliefs about women's gender roles), we drew on one of the discipline's most established methods for gathering data: public opinion surveys. While public opinion surveys, like any data source, are prone to potential problems, they get closer to personal experiences than the other sources we use: people form their opinions based on lived experiences. Moreover, fieldwork has shown us the importance of beliefs about women's gender roles in the policymaking world. For example, fieldwork with the security forces in Zambia, Ghana, Bangladesh, and Liberia demonstrates that the views of men and women about women's gender roles largely dictate what women are and are not able to do. Individual and societal discrimination is largely based on ideas about the appropriate roles of men and women. People's personal beliefs largely dictate their behavior towards women. In sum, the four concepts developed in this book originated from a mix of the literature and field experience.

Table 0.1 highlights all six concepts mentioned here and demonstrates that while they are different, they also share some characteristics.[14] Women's status, women's inclusion, women's rights, harm to women, and beliefs about women's gender roles all share the characteristic of "pertaining to those that biologically identify as girls or women." The table also shows that beliefs

14   POSITIONING WOMEN IN CONFLICT STUDIES

Table 0.1 Characteristics of Concepts

Concept	Characteristic 1	Characteristic 2	Characteristic 3	Characteristic 4
Gender Inequality	social construction of masculine/ feminine identities	hierarchy that subordinates certain identities	identities that are relational	fluidity/ rigidity of identities
Women's Status	pertinent to those that biologically identify as girls or women	a person's standing or importance in relation to other people within a society		
Women's Inclusion	pertinent to those that biologically identify as girls or women	visibility/ presence	public space	
Women's Rights	pertinent to those that biologically identify as girls or women	(supra) governmental legal or policy codification	a freedom to act in certain ways or freedom from undesirable actions or states	
Harm to Women	pertinent to those that biologically identify as girls or women	individual, physical, or bodily violence	production and reinforcement (constitutive) of structures that subordinate	increased risk of morbidity and/or mortality
Beliefs about Women's Gender Roles	pertinent to those that biologically identify as girls or women	perceptions	relational identities for men and women	rigidity/ fluidity of identities

about women's gender roles are related to gender inequality, as they share two characteristics. Generally, however, the table shows that these concepts are different from one another. As such, they should be measured separately and theorized about separately.

Delineation through Measurement

It is important to not only differentiate concepts by defining their characteristics, but also to develop measures that are clearly linked to those concepts and can serve as useful representations for analysis. The first step in this process is accomplished through explicit conceptualization: clear definitions are necessary to evaluate whether an indicator is a good representation of the relevant concept. The next step is to identify and collect one or more indicators that correspond to instantiations of the concept, and that can distinguish between different values or levels (high or low) of the underlying concept, or between the different categories that make up the concept. Indicators may then be used individually or combined into scales, which requires making decisions about how to combine them.

As we have already discussed, in much of the literature on gender and conflict the term "gender equality" is not defined in much detail or perhaps at all, which makes it hard to assess whether the outcomes used to measure that concept actually represent instances or different degrees of gender equality. Rather, conceptualization is often implicit, and the process begins with the operationalization of "gender equality" as an outcome related to women, such as fertility rates or the rate of women's participation in the labor force. Conceptual stretching thus leads to the empirical conflation of gender equality with outcomes related to women's status. This disconnect between concept and indicator makes it difficult to draw clear conclusions from the relationship between indicators of the concept and indicators of conflict and political violence. An indicator may be correlated with conflict, for example, but if the underlying construct it measures is unclear it is also unclear why the correlation exists.

Our approach to measuring women's status begins with definitions of key concepts, as already discussed. In this book we explicitly define the concepts of women's inclusion, women's rights, harm to women, and beliefs about women's gender roles. These definitions inform our choice of indicators for each concept. We create a measure of women's inclusion using indicators that correspond to women's presence (or absence) in specific parts of public life, including government, the formal economy, and education. Our measure of women's rights is derived from indicators of formal legal recognition that women have the same rights as men, as well as formal rules intended to protect women from discrimination and harm. To measure harm to women, we combine indicators of women's health outcomes, their health outcomes relative to men (where appropriate), access to health-related resources, and exposure to physical violence. Our measure of beliefs about women's gender roles combines survey items that ask respondents whether men and women are suitable for similar social roles and are deserving of equal treatment.

16 POSITIONING WOMEN IN CONFLICT STUDIES

Because we clearly define each concept, it is relatively straightforward to evaluate whether these outcomes can be reasonably considered instantiations of the concept in question.

In some cases, our measures are created from commonly used indicators in the research. Though we argue these indicators are not valid measures of gender equality, they may still be useful as indicators of women's status. However, common practice is to treat these as measures of the same underlying concept, and to assess the relationship between the concept and the outcome of interest (e.g. conflict) by seeing whether each individual indicator is correlated with the outcome. This is difficult to justify, as commonly used indicators are often not highly correlated with one another. Even if the underlying concept is well defined this practice can lead to confusion, as it is difficult to interpret results when some indicators of a concept are related to the occurrence of conflict, for example, while others are not.

A related problem occurs when groups of indicators are combined into aggregate scales to measure "gender equality." Aggregation usually involves applying a pre-specified formula that gives equal weight (or importance) to each indicator, that does not adequately account for the relationships between the indicators, and that assumes the resulting scale corresponds perfectly to the underlying concept, meaning it contains no measurement error. This introduces several potential problems. Combining indicators into a single scale implicitly assumes they measure the same concept. Since commonly used indicators are in some cases not highly correlated, this assumption is sometimes difficult to justify. Weighting each indicator equally requires making the (likely unrealistic) assumption that every indicator is equally informative about the (single) underlying concept. Assuming that a scale created from several indicators contains no measurement error also requires a leap of faith. Even in the case of instruments that measure the physical properties of tangible objects, random measurement error is a possibility.[15] When measuring the abstract properties of abstract entities like societies or countries, the possibility of measurement error should, arguably, be a large concern. All of these potential problems affect the validity of the scale itself or the validity of comparisons or associations using the scale. As with single indicators, then, aggregate scales can suffer from validity problems that make the results of an analysis difficult to interpret and possibly produce misleading conclusions.

In contrast to these approaches, we ensure delineation in measurement in two ways. First, instead of treating every indicator as a measure of the same concept, we use our conceptualization of four distinct aspects of women's status to inform the separation of indicators into different groups that correspond to each of these aspects. Second, we combine each set of indicators using models that account for the correlations between them. In this way, the models help to evaluate and justify the assumption that the indicators we use are in fact related to a single, underlying concept. This also addresses the problem of assigning equal (and arbitrary) weights to the input variables, as variables that are highly correlated with the others in the model will be assigned more weight. Finally, the models also produce an estimate of measurement error that can be used when making comparisons (between countries or over time) or examining the association between the scale and indicators of conflict and political violence.

Delineation through Specific Theory

Once the concepts are clearly defined and measurements are derived, it is easier to identify and trace the theoretical connections between each concept and different forms of conflict, and to evaluate the empirical connections between them. In this manuscript, we are specifically interested in exploring how women's inclusion, women's rights, harm to women, and beliefs about women's gender roles affect civil conflict, terrorism, interstate war, and state repression. Differentiating these concepts makes it possible to assess these connections more coherently.

First, differentiating women's inclusion from other concepts allows us to clarify how the inclusion of women into public spaces, especially in politics, affects the decision making of governments. It also highlights some commonalities between explanations for different forms of violence. There is research to suggest that different types of women hold different views than dominant men, and when there is more diversity, governments make different decisions with respect to the use of violence (Goldstein 2001; McDermott 2015; Eichenberg 2016; Regan and Paskeviciute 2003; Barnhart et al. 2020; Barnhart and Trager 2023; Brooks and Valentino 2011; Saiya, Zaihra, and Fidler 2017; Best, Shair-Rosenfield, and Wood 2019; Huber 2019; Melander 2005b). Thus, women's inclusion could create conditions that lead to more peaceful decision-making. At the same time, groups who oppose the state, whether foreign governments or domestic dissident groups, might interpret more women in public (political) spaces to mean the state is more conciliatory or weaker (Shair-Rosenfield and Wood 2017; Powell and Mukazhanova-Powell 2019; Schwartz and Blair 2020; Schramm and Stark 2020). These perceptional stereotypes about women in public spaces might make these groups more or less violent toward the government. Women's inclusion is also central to the argument that barriers to women's meaningful participation may inhibit meaningful action, and the related argument that women sometimes have to perform in masculine ways to maintain their position (Thomas and Adams 2010; Koch and Fulton 2011). Both of these dynamics may hinder the supposed pacifying effect that women's inclusion has on political conflict.

Second, differentiating women's rights from other concepts allows us to develop the argument that the adoption of women's rights by states could signal adherence to the rules of the "liberal order." Similar to the adoption of liberal domestic institutions more generally, by formally recognizing women's rights, states might signal their openness to claim-making by different groups. Separating women's rights from similar concepts also allows us to explore the role of women's advocacy groups, thus nuancing previous research contributions by Htun and Weldon (2010, 2012, 2018), Tripp (2015), Ferree and Tripp (2006). Drawing on previous work, we theorize that women's advocacy groups that push for women's rights also serve as monitors or "watchdogs" of state behavior. Advocacy organizations that focus on women's rights might also contribute to broader societal efforts to prevent state violence. This means that where there are more women's rights in combination with women's advocacy groups, there may be less state violence.

Third, by differentiating harm to women from other concepts we are able to link together arguments posed by Hudson et al. (2009), Hudson, Bowen, and Nielsen (2020), and Caprioli (2000, 2003, 2005) about the effect of structural and physical violence against women on normative constraints on violence at the societal level. When states devalue women's lives, people develop a tolerance for the social and psychological costs of violent conflict. Witnessing violence against family members (mostly women) within the household has a similar effect. Conceptual delineation also clarifies two other potential connections between harm to women and conflict. Harm to women may lead to high levels of morbidity and mortality and create shortages of women. Armed groups may then exploit these actual or perceived shortages for recruitment (Hudson and Den Boer 2002, 2004; Hudson and Matfess 2017; Donnelly 2019). Harm to women also prevents women from fully participating in political mobilization and social movements. With fewer women involved, non-violent movements and peace movements become less successful, and violence becomes more of an option for reordering the status quo.

Finally, by differentiating beliefs about women's gender roles from other concepts we develop two arguments that connect rigid beliefs to conflict and political violence. First, where societies are characterized by more rigid beliefs about women's social roles, this indicates a willingness to use preemptive violence to maintain the status quo. Second, there may be larger pools of recruits for potentially violent groups when more people believe strongly in maintaining traditional social roles for women.

Broadly, differentiation and delineation allow us to identify at least twelve different explanations for how women's inclusion, women's rights, harm to women, and beliefs about women's gender roles are related to different forms of political violence. We are better able to clarify which concepts are related to others and *how* they might be related. The results from our analysis reveal that women's political inclusion and beliefs about women's gender roles are negatively related to terrorist attacks; women's rights are negatively related to state repression; and harm to women is associated with a higher probability of civil conflict onset and the initiation of violent interstate conflict. Thus, some aspects of women's status are related to some types of political violence, but these relationships are hardly uniform. Without undergoing the process of differentiation and delineation, we might continue to believe that "gender equality" leads to less violent conflict globally. Because we separate these concepts, we are able to identify the aspects of women's status for which backsliding poses the largest risk of political violence.

Our approach is not without flaws. Differentiating gender (in)equality from women's status means that we limit our focus to two particular groups (people who identify biologically as women and people who do not) and ignore differences within these groups. Women (and not women) are by no means a monolithic group, and we acknowledge that there is tremendous variation within this group, including socio-economic, racial/ethnic, regional, and cultural variation. However, we opt to center our analysis on the category of women as a group because relative to most men, most women have lower status.[16] This provides a foundation from which a larger and richer research agenda can be built that focuses on how the oppression of different types of women affect political violence. To use the United States as an example, examining the status of Native American women, African American women, Latina women, or Latinx women might tell us something different

20 POSITIONING WOMEN IN CONFLICT STUDIES

about political violence in the US than examining the status of women within the US in general. What we provide in this book is a starting point from which this sort of analysis can proceed. By carefully differentiating and delineating concepts such as "harm to Latina/x women," from "harm to women," we might uncover that the theories from Chapter 5 are more or less applicable to Latina/x women. That may also point us to the need for new theories for how "harm to Latina/x women" affects political violence. In short, using the process outlined in this book not only helps to develop, clarify, and identify commonalities between theories about women's status, it can also be used to the same effect where theories about the status of different types of women (or groups) as well.

Furthermore, while we do not engage in intersectional analysis, the process outlined in this book is conducive to intersectional analysis.[17] In particular, by creating classical subtypes or diminished subtypes, we can see how adding or removing an essential characteristic of a concept shapes the theories that leverage that concept and whether and how the implications change. We use the concept of "harm to women" to illustrate this point. From Chapter 5, we learn that harm to women means an increased risk of morbidity and/or mortality through the production and reinforcement of structures that subordinate and/or through individual physical or bodily violence of those that identify as girls or women. If we add a fifth characteristic, "pertaining to people who identify as Latina/x women," what happens? This requires us to understand how structural violence against Latina/x women affects political outcomes. We must refine our theory from Chapter 5 to consider how structural violence is carried out against this particular group relative to women in general. We know that in the United States state violence is more likely to target members of this group (compared to women in general)—e.g. higher levels of detention (Becerra et al. 2022; Escobar 2016; Lopez and Pasko 2021). The state's use of violence against this group could legitimize the use of violence against countries in Latin America (e.g. US public opinion about strikes in Mexico (Slattery 2023)). This latter theory is different from the theories presented in Chapter 5 but demonstrates how the intersection of women and Latinx work together to produce political violence. We strongly advocate for this kind of theorization moving forward.

In addition to the limitations of our conceptual approach, there are also limitations to our approach to measurement that we discuss in Chapter 2 and the conclusion. Nevertheless, we engage in a reflexive process by being transparent about our choices about data collection and describing them in detail. First, we acknowledge that our position vis-à-vis those who are being studied—women—is about as distant as one can be from the lives of the individuals the data represent and the research assistants/researchers who collected the data. Our "composite indicators," which are "made up of separate systems of counts and ratios merged together," are far removed from the underlying lived experiences they record and are thus susceptible to some general critiques of indicators, such as those made by Merry (2016, 15), which we take up in the subsequent chapters. Yet, we argue that there is merit in discussing new and alternative ways to develop indicators related to women. We acknowledge that our concepts and measures are derived from our own individual expertise, but we have tried to be transparent about the decisions we make and the processes that we use. We engage in a discussion about the use of these measures versus alternative ones and thus partake in a dialogue about the conditions under which certain concepts, measures, and indicators can and should be used.

Contribution

Our book makes several contributions to the fields of IR and comparative politics. First and foremost, our book joins the voluminous literature on gender and conflict, but makes a significant contribution by parsing out more specific concepts as well as the theoretical connections between women's inclusion, women's rights, harm to women, and beliefs about women's gender roles and different forms of political violence. The various connections we identify help to highlight similarities between theories that connect the different concepts to conflict and political violence. Our analysis and findings also provide a clear research agenda for examining more closely how women's inclusion, women's rights, harm to women, and beliefs about women's gender roles are related to political violence. The concluding chapter highlights this research agenda and some opportunities for more refined analysis.

Second, we overcome the related problems of conceptual stretching and measurement invalidity by providing explicit conceptual definitions of gender equality and different aspects of women's status and adopting a measurement approach that addresses common problems. Given that we are writing to a broad audience that includes students, scholars of these fields, and policymakers, this manuscript lays out step by step the process for separating gender equality from women's status and women's status from inclusion, women's rights, harm to women, and beliefs about women's gender roles. For many, the steps we take to make this point may appear tedious. Yet, we believe that a slow dismantling and reassembly of concepts and measurement schemes is necessary to provide a broader audience a sound understanding of the importance of clearly defining and demarcating concepts, and of carefully matching concepts to measures. This is particularly the case for scholars who use quantitative methods and who rely on proxy measures. Scholars have provided similar dismantling and reassembly for concepts such as democracy (Collier and Levitsky 1997; Munck and Verkuilen 2002; Coppedge et al. 2011), which ultimately led to the creation of better ways to conceptualize and measure the concept, such as the Varieties of Democracy Project.[18] There is no reason that women's inclusion, women's rights, harm to women, and beliefs about women's gender roles should not be subject to the same scrutiny. It also provides a step-by-step guide for others who wish to partake in this type of exercise for other contested or conflated concepts. Additionally, by using the framework of concept stretching, we can apply important advancements developed in comparative politics (e.g. Sartori 1984; Gerring 1999; Collier and Levitsky 2009) to IR.

Third, we advance research on the topic by detailing common problems related to the measurement of women's status and develop and make available four *new* measures: women's inclusion, rights, harm to women, and beliefs about women's gender roles. We advocate for the use of measurement models similar to ours, which are becoming more common in some areas of political science, to address the problems we identify. We use these models to develop measures of our concepts that offer several advantages over previous efforts. We then use these measures to examine the relationships between women's status and different forms of political violence. Our effort thus provides new measures that scholars and policymakers can use to assess the causes as well as consequences of women's inclusion, women's rights, harm to women, and beliefs about women's gender roles.

Fourth, our book engages with feminist literature on gender and conflict by demonstrating how the differentiating and isolation of concepts can actually be useful for theorizing about gender. By studying women's inclusion, women's rights, harm to women, and beliefs about women's gender roles separately, we can analyze more clearly the role of gender in conflict and political violence. For example, by looking at women's rights in isolation, we are able to pinpoint the important role of women's advocacy organizations in reducing state repression. Additionally, the null results with respect to women's inclusion require a further examination of the power hierarchies that exist in public spaces and that constitute barriers for women in those spaces.

Moreover, while our null results may not come as a surprise to some scholars, they are important for re-evaluating existing theories, refining them, and developing scope conditions. The null results in the book require us to consider why there may not be a relationship among women's inclusion, women's rights, harm to women, and beliefs about women's gender roles and some forms of political violence. That women's rights do not help reduce all forms of political violence indicates that women's rights may not signal a state's adoption of liberal values and invites us to investigate why this might the be the case. Maybe the tie between women's rights and other liberal values are not as strong as previously thought. Delineating and examining each of our concepts, and its relationship to political violence, in isolation, leads to results that force us to refine and rethink larger theories.

Importantly, our manuscript is helpful for policymakers looking to prevent political violence globally and for those who seek to improve women's inclusion, women's rights, harm to women, and beliefs about women's gender roles. In the concluding chapter, we derive specific policy recommendations based on the findings of the book. Consistent with some critiques of the prominence of liberal feminism in global governance (Arat 2015; Ellerby 2017), we advocate for moving beyond a narrow focus on women's inclusion in public spaces. Of all the concepts we examine in the book, the evidence for a connection between inclusion and political violence is the weakest. This stands in contrast to some of the policy recommendations that have grown out of UN Security Council Resolution 1325, which focus heavily on women's inclusion. This is not to say that women's inclusion should not be a policy goal, only that women's inclusion alone cannot be seen as a cure for conflict and political violence. Efforts at inclusion should be accompanied by efforts to make sure that women are empowered in public spaces as well as included, so that their participation can be meaningful instead of purely symbolic. Additionally, given our findings regarding state violence, we recommend funding women's advocacy groups with fewer restrictions or conditions for aid. Clearly the preferences of international donors and advocacy groups must align, but donors should let groups set their priorities to reflect the needs and concerns of locals rather than those of donors. A third recommendation is that policy efforts should focus on changing beliefs about women's gender roles, in addition to changing outcomes. This entails efforts to change public opinion so that beliefs about women's gender roles are more flexible. A final recommendation is to address with whatever means available structural and physical violence against women. This should not be a hard sell. Improving access to family planning and maternal healthcare, addressing health disparities between men and women, and ending impunity for violence against women has obvious and immediate benefits to women. Further, of the concepts we examine, our results concerning harm to women provide the strongest evidence of a link between women's status and large-scale political violence. This suggests that policies to reduce or prevent harm are beneficial to society as well.

Finally, if there is currently widespread backsliding or decline in women's status, separating out and measuring each concept allows us to determine which specific aspects of women's status are most affected by this trend. In this way, our measures can be used not only to conduct analysis on the relationship between women's status and political violence, but also to better understand a global recession in women's status.

Outline of the Book

Our book is organized into two parts. In the first part, covered by Chapters 1 and 2, we go into detail concerning the problems of concept stretching (Chapter 1) and measurement invalidity (Chapter 2). We explain how the first problem leads to the second and how a disconnect between concepts and indicators in turn creates a disconnect between the logic that motivates a hypothesis and the empirical test of that hypothesis. These chapters also discuss our solutions of differentiation and delineation and how our approaches to conceptualization and measurement solve the problems we identify in these chapters. In both chapters, we make a pivot from studying gender (in)equality to studying women's status globally and its relationship to political violence.

The second part of the book shifts to deriving our specific concepts and measures, and explaining how women's inclusion, women's rights, harm to women, and beliefs about women's gender roles are connected to the occurrence of civil conflict, terrorism, interstate war, and state repression. Each of these centers on a different aspect of women's status: Chapter 3 focuses on women's inclusion, Chapter 4 on women's rights, Chapter 5 on harm to women, and Chapter 6 on beliefs about women's gender roles. Each chapter starts by enumerating and defining the essential characteristics of the concept and then explaining our measurement strategy for each concept. We then spend the bulk of these chapters exploring the ways in which each concept is related to different forms of political violence. Each chapter concludes with the results of an analysis that speak to this relationship. The concluding chapter of the book sums up our findings and contextualizes them. We also highlight the limitations of the book, present policy recommendations, and outline an important research agenda for scholars going forward.

Notes: characteristics are not listed in any particular order—their order here does not matter. In Chapters 3–6, we go into detail about deriving the characteristics of women's inclusion, women's rights, harm to women, and beliefs about women's gender roles.

PART I
FROM "GENDER (IN)EQUALITY" TO THE STATUS OF WOMEN

1
Solving the Concept Stretching Problem

Introduction

The unanimous passage of UN Security Council Resolution 1325 in 2000 marked a watershed moment at the UN and in the world. The resolution signified that for the first time, the UN would be mandated to make women in peace and conflict an active part of their agenda. The resolution outlined four pillars: participation, protection, prevention, and relief and recovery. Since 2000, the UN has created the "women, peace and security (WPS) agenda" by passing nine additional resolutions: 1820 (2009), 1888 (2009), 1889 (2010), 1960 (2011), 2106 (2013), 2122 (2013), 2242 (2015), 2467 (2019), and 2493 (2019). A cursory glance at these resolutions suggests that their primary focus is on the protection pillar, with six of the resolutions focusing specifically on wartime sexual violence. The participation pillar is the focus of three resolutions, and the prevention pillar is the focus of one resolution. According to the UN, the WPS agenda guides work to "promote gender equality and strengthen women's participation, protection and rights across the conflict cycle, from conflict prevention through post-conflict reconstruction" (PeaceWomen 2014).

The words "gender equality" appear numerous times throughout the resolutions, often linked to peace. Indeed, the implied assumption of this agenda is that only by furthering the WPS agenda can governments achieve sustainable peace. Secretary General António Guterres championed this idea in his campaign to become secretary general (Donner and Gupta 2020). On February 8, 2020, he stated that "although by now we clearly understand the benefits—indeed the imperative—of inclusion and gender equality for achieving peace and sustainable development, our actions fall short" (United Nations Secretary General 2020). In another statement from 2019, he said, "gender equality is a key instrument of peace and security. To promote human rights for all, as gender equality is a central instrument for human rights. To ensure development for all, as gender equality is a fundamental tool for development" (United Nations Secretary General 2019). These statements and

Positioning Women in Conflict Studies. Sabrina Karim Daniel W. Hill Jr., Oxford University Press.
© Oxford University Press 2024. DOI: 10.1093/9780197757970.003.0002

30 FROM "GENDER (IN)EQUALITY" TO THE STATUS OF WOMEN

the agenda demonstrate that the link between "gender equality" and peace is an established assumption among elite decisions makers in international organizations.[1]

Yet, the WPS agenda is not necessarily an agenda about gender equality. Rather it is an agenda to improve *women's status* in the world. By women's status, we mean the everyday conditions and societal positions of those who identify biologically as women.[2] An agenda for improving women's status focuses on protection from harm and poor living conditions and on ensuring women's participation in public life. It is an agenda that seeks to increase *women's inclusion* in traditionally masculine spaces such as politics and the security sector. It is an agenda that seeks to increase *women's rights* through the creation of legal frameworks to protect women's interests and mitigate *harm to women* that results from physical violence as well as structural conditions that detract from women's health and well-being. And, it is perhaps an agenda to change *beliefs about women's gender roles*, albeit this is never explicitly stated in the resolutions. Based on the texts of the various resolutions passed in connection with WPS, the potential link between gender equality and peace that the secretary general describes is better described as a potential link between women's status and peace. In short, the WPS agenda is an agenda about women as its name specifies, and not necessarily an agenda about gender equality.

The distinction between gender equality and women's status matters because their conflation undermines a close examination of the concepts and mechanisms that tie women's status in society to political violence. Specifically, conflating the two creates theoretical, methodological, and measurement problems for scholars studying women, gender, peace, and conflict. It leads to concept stretching whereby gender means everything from women's rights to sexual violence. Indeed, the use of gender instead of sex masks the theories that link gender equality to peace, and the theories that link women's status—including women's inclusion, women's rights, harm to women, and beliefs about women's gender roles—to peace and conflict.

This chapter and the next identify and discuss these problems. We argue that only until these concepts are used and measured correctly can we develop novel theories, and only then can we draw meaningful and accurate conclusions about interlinkages between the status of women in a society and the level of political violence in that society.

We begin by using concept stretching as an analytical framework for understanding the conflation between sex and gender. We then show that this stretching leads to conceptual and theoretical problems. We show the extent of the problem in academia and in the policymaking world before turning to a set of solutions to address the concept stretching problem.

Is "Gender Equality" Conceptually Stretched?

Concept stretching is the distortion that occurs when a concept does not fit cases to which it is applied (Sartori 1970, 1984). In the context of this project, concept stretching can occur when other measures are used interchangeably with gender equality such as women's empowerment, women's rights, etc. Our goal is to differentiate gender (in)equality from women's inclusion, women's rights, harm to women, and beliefs about women's gender roles, with which it has been confounded. In doing so, we provide coherent characteristics and ensure that the conceptualization of gender (in)equality, women's inclusion, women's rights, harm to women, and beliefs about women's gender roles has theoretical and field utility (Gerring 1999).[3] Differentiation is done through defining and adding attributes to the concept (Sartori 1984). These attributes not only provide the defining characteristics of the concept, but also enable us to distinguish it from other concepts, as these criteria provide boundaries for the concept. However, these attributes must stay true to the core, essential meaning of the concept in order to be coherent (Gerring 1999). Assigning attributes should ensure better theory (theoretical utility) and should not harm other, related concepts (field utility). The number of defining characteristics should also be parsimonious (Gerring 1999, 371). In order to choose such criteria, Sartori (1984, 15–85) suggests collecting a representative set of definitions, extracting their characteristics, and constructing a matrix that organizes these characteristics meaningfully. To ensure field utility, he suggests that this exercise should be conducted with neighboring concepts as well. These are the steps that we follow. We limit the number of defining characteristics to two-four to ensure parsimony and to follow the examples in the literature.

From the Introduction, recall that our definition of gender (in)equality includes four characteristics. First, the concept of gender includes *socially constructed masculine and feminine roles*. Second, gender is *relational* as identities are defined against one another (Sjoberg 2013, 106). Third, the fixedness of gender ranges from *fluid to rigid* in both societal expectations about conformity and individuals' adherence to gender roles. Fourth, when

32 FROM "GENDER (IN)EQUALITY" TO THE STATUS OF WOMEN

the word inequality is added (or not added, in the case of some feminist scholars),[4] it implies *hierarchies of power* or *(re)-productions of power that subordinate certain identities*. These hierarchies privilege and normalize the masculine over the feminine, through cultural productions and re-productions. The term *gender (in)equality* refers to the value of the last two attributes of gender: the fluidity/rigidity of those identities, and the extent to which (re)productions of power subordinate (feminine) identities. Gender equality means there is no hierarchy among, or subordination of, certain gender identities and that people are not expected to adopt prescribed gender roles, i.e. identities are fluid. Gender inequality describes a situation where identities are rigid, and one or more identities are treated as subordinate. For people to receive equal treatment regardless of their gender identity, it must be the case that society values femininity and masculinity equally and that people are not expected to adopt a particular identity based on their assigned sex.

Using this definition, the concept of gender equality is "stretched" when the label is used to describe phenomena that do not fit these criteria. This is bound to occur when gender equality is used as an umbrella term for women's issues and/or when the term is used interchangeably with other concepts related to women. These other concepts may be related to gender equality, or they may be different concepts altogether. To prevent concept stretching, we must understand the relationships among different concepts related to women and/or gender. We use the analytical tools of kind hierarchies with classical subtypes and part-whole hierarchies with diminished subtypes to evaluate the relationship between gender equality and related concepts so that we can identify instances of concept stretching.

Classical Subtypes

Kind hierarchies with classical subtypes imply a certain kind of relationship between different concepts (Collier and Levitsky 2009). Each subordinate concept has the attributes of the superordinate concept and additional attributes that differentiate it (271). The more defining attributes the concept has, the further "down the ladder" it is from the "root" concept. As the number of attributes increases relative to the root concept, the new concept (subtype) gains intension, meaning the number of attributes that determine membership in the category increase, but loses extension as it will necessarily apply to fewer cases (Sartori 1970, 1984; Collier and Mahon 1993). Moving up the ladder or removing attributes results in more general categories or concepts with increased extension. The root concept would be considered a special case of these more general categories. For example, note that gender in its most basic form includes attributes 1 and 2 in Box 1.1. We can then add characteristics to develop classical subtypes of gender. Adding "fluidity of identities" and "equal valuation of identities" makes gender become gender equality. This means that in a kind hierarchy framework gender (in)equality could be considered a classical subtype of gender.

If a concept under examination has all the attributes of gender equality plus some other attributes, the concept would be considered a subtype of gender equality. The concept would have the dimensions of gender equality already identified: (1) social construction of masculine/feminine identities, (2) identities that are relational, whether against one another or to their environment; (3) fluidity/rigidity of identities; (4) a hierarchy that subordinates certain identities. Additionally, it would have other dimensions that distinguish it from gender equality. Box 1.1 illustrates how other concepts might become subtypes of gender (in)equality. Such a concept would need attributes 1–4 *plus* 5, or 6, etc. The characteristics of x and/or y distinguish the concept from gender (in)equality, but they retain all the attributes of the root concept so we would still consider them a type of gender equality.

Box 1.1 Classical Subtypes of Gender (In)equality

1) social construction of masculine/feminine identities +
2) identities that are relational, whether against one another or to their environment +
3) fluidity/rigidity of identities +
4) a hierarchy that subordinates certain identities +
5) x +
6) y + . . .

> **Box 1.2 Classical Subtypes of Gender (In)equality: Patriarchy**
>
> 1) social construction of masculine/feminine identities +
> 2) identities that are relational, whether against one another or to their environment +
> 3) fluidity/rigidity of identities +
> 4) a hierarchy that subordinates certain identities +
> 5) institutionalized regime

One possible example of a classical subtype of gender inequality is patriarchy (Box 1.2).[5] One definition of patriarchy is a system in which men rule societies (Walby 1989). Thus, it is a special case of gender inequality differentiated by the fact that inequality is institutionalized within a regime or within the political system. Patriarchy refers to socially constructed and relationally defined masculine/feminine identities (1 and 2) that make these identities rigid and subordinate feminine identities (3 and 4) and that are institutionalized in the political system (5). As such, it loses some extension relative to gender inequality. For example, there can be gender inequality in groups, but this does not necessarily mean the groups are patriarchal, unless that gender inequality is institutionalized so that men control group decision-making. A closely related example of a classical subtype of gender may be "gender regime," which includes dimensions 1–4 in Box 1.1 plus the fifth dimension of the state's policies (Mohanty, Russo, and Torres 1991).

Another classical subtype of gender inequality, as shown in Box 1.3, is misogyny. Manne (2018, 33–34) defines misogyny as "a property of social systems or environment as a whole, in which women will tend to face hostility of various kinds because they are women in a man's world, who are held to be failing to live up to patriarchal standards." Thus, the definition incorporates all the dimensions of gender inequality because it refers to the rigid nature of gender identities (3) in relation to others (2) that are socially constructed (1) and a hierarchy that subordinates femininity (4). However, it adds the attribute of punishment for those who are subordinate, whether or not they transgress norms about gender roles. Because gender inequality does not

> **Box 1.3 Classical Subtypes of Gender (In)equality: Misogyny**
>
> 1) social construction of masculine/feminine identities +
> 2) identities that are relational, whether against one another or to their environment +
> 3) fluidity/rigidity of identities +
> 4) a hierarchy that subordinates certain identities +
> 5) punishment

imply that all individuals who are subordinate face punishment, gender inequality does not necessarily entail misogyny.

Diminished Subtypes

An alternative way of thinking about the relationship between concepts is to use a "part-whole" hierarchy that is arranged so that superordinate categories have more attributes than subordinate categories. In this framework the removal of attributes or dimensions from the original (root) concept results in "diminished" subtypes. In a kind hierarchy such a concept would be referred to as a more general (superordinate) category, but in a part-whole framework the category defined by the absence of attributes is treated as the subordinate category, so that a "special case" means a case is missing something relative to the original and can be thought of as a partial instance of the original concept. Differentiation then entails identifying the attributes that are missing from the root concept. This can help identify concepts that could be characterized as "partial gender equality"—some concepts related to women's conditions, for example, may have some elements of gender equality, but not others.

There are several possible examples of diminished subtypes of gender (in)equality that we can highlight. In Box 1.4 the concept of *social inequality* could be a diminished subtype of gender inequality because it holds attributes 2, 3, and 4, but not 1. The basis of the hierarchy or power asymmetries between different identities is not specified in this definition. These asymmetries are not necessarily based on masculine and feminine roles. Rather, there exist

36 FROM "GENDER (IN)EQUALITY" TO THE STATUS OF WOMEN

Box 1.4 Diminished Subtypes of Gender (In)equality: Social Inequality

1)
2) identities that are relational, whether against one another or to their environment +
3) fluidity/rigidity of identities +
4) a hierarchy that subordinates certain identities

Box 1.5 Diminished Subtypes of Gender (In)equality: Gender Hierarchy

1) social construction of masculine/feminine identities +
2) identities that are relational, whether against one another or to their environment +
3)
4) a hierarchy that subordinates certain identities

---

additional hierarchies based on other sets of relational, fluid, or rigid social categories that reproduce power and subordinate some groups.

Similarly, Box 1.5 shows that *gender hierarchy* could be a diminished subtype of gender inequality because it is missing the dimension of "rigid identities." When there is a gender hierarchy, individuals may still be able to move in and out of different identities, and the identity that is privileged may shift depending on the context. For example, while warrior masculinity (brave, courageous, aggressive masculinity) is often understood as the ideal form of masculinity, in some societies, metrosexual masculinity (a masculinity defined by being well-dressed and groomed) may be at least as privileged, or even more privileged. Thus, masculine identities are fluid, but there is still a hierarchy of gender identities. Hierarchy means a set of relations that classifies some units or items as superior, thereby differentiating one or some as dominant and the rest as subordinate (Sjoberg 2013, 85). Gender hierarchy thus shares with gender equality both of the characteristics that define "gender" and one but not both of the characteristics that define "inequality" as applied to gender.

SOLVING THE CONCEPT STRETCHING PROBLEM   37

Using these two analytical tools—classical subtypes and diminished subtypes—we can identify the relationship between gender equality and other concepts, allowing us to uncover when concept stretching has occurred. We compare gender equality to women's status to illustrate concept stretching.

Women's status is concerned with "sex" rather than gender. As we know, sex does not refer to the social roles associated with biological distinctions, but rather to the biological and genotypical characteristics that make "boys" boys and "girls" girls. Often, people think of genitals in making this distinction: girls/women have vaginas, while men/boys have penises. However, some people are born without either male or female genitalia and some are born with both. Thus, a better way to conceive of sex is to think of chromosomes. Women/girls have two X chromosomes, while men/boys have one X and one Y chromosome. Yet even this chromosomal distinction is contested.[6] Further still, using any biological marker to define sex labels as "men" and "women" overlooks people who do not identify with those labels despite their chromosomal (or other biological) makeup. As such, we cast a broad net with respect to what it means to be a woman and define the first characteristic as pertaining to those who biologically identify as girls or women. The second characteristic defines status as the relative position of a person (woman) in society. Status means holding a collective belief about a person, group, or state's ranking on valued attributes (Renshon 2017, 33). The concept is relative as it requires us to identify a person's position in relation to another. The relative nature of women's status implies a comparison to another type of person or group, which remains unspecified. The comparison may be with men, with other women, or with other individuals or groups. This characteristic is close to the gender equality attribute, "identities that are relational, whether against one another or to their environment," but the overall concept remains different because it is tied to sex, not gender identities.

Box 1.6 provides the two characteristics that make up women's status. What stands out is that women's status is not related to gender (in)equality, nor is it directly related to patriarchy, misogyny, social inequality, or gender hierarchy. They do not share any characteristics as Table 0.1 showed in the

---

Box 1.6 Women's Status

1) pertaining to those that biologically identify as girls or women +
2) a person's standing or importance in relation to other people within a society

38 FROM "GENDER (IN)EQUALITY" TO THE STATUS OF WOMEN

previous chapter. Rather, women's status is a very different concept from gender equality and the concepts that are "family" to gender equality. This renders any interchangeable use of gender (in)equality and women (status)— such as the examples from the Introduction—problematic precisely because they are different concepts. We highlight these problems in the next section.

Problems with Stretching the Concept of Gender (In)equality

Stretching the concept of gender inequality leads to significant problems with theory development. Concept stretching happens when scholars, policymakers, and practitioners use gender inequality to mean women's status or vice versa. Concept stretching is a problem for theory development and testing. Without a common conceptual understanding of gender equality, the term has been used as an umbrella category that lumps together several concepts that are more usefully thought of as being distinct or as subtypes. This leads to inaccurate theories, and it leads to limited understanding about what aspect of the concept explains the proposed theory.

Missing Theory

Using terms interchangeably obfuscates different theoretical mechanisms through which related concepts might affect outcomes of interest. Indeed, treating distinct concepts as synonymous with gender (in)equality overshadows different theories through which change may happen. There are likely to be multiple theories that explain a certain phenomenon. Concept stretching may result in one term being used in connection with all these theories when, in reality, there are potentially several concepts and theories at work. Furthermore, if we treat indicators of concepts that are distinct from gender equality as measures of that concept, we do not gain a clearer understanding of whether gender equality, or alternative concepts like women's rights and women's inclusion, might lead to peace.

There are multiple theories that explain why "gender equal" societies are more peaceful (Caprioli 2000; Caprioli and Boyer 2001; Melander 2005a; Hudson 2012). One theory posits that societies in which individuals commit higher levels of micro-level violence (in the household) are more prone to be violent at the macro level (Hudson and Den Boer 2002; Hudson, Bowen, and Nielsen 2020; Hudson 2012). A second theory posits that when women hold positions of power, they can influence matters of war and peace within a state and that women's leadership results in more peaceful policies. The assumption is that dominant male "warrior" gender roles lead to a higher likelihood of war, while feminine roles promote peace (Melander 2005a). These two theories indicate that the independent variable is not "gender equality" broadly, but for the former, harm to women, and for the latter, women's inclusion in politics. Using the term gender (in)equality to refer to the explanatory concept thus masks the "true" theory at play. In short, if gender (in)equality is used as a catchall phrase or umbrella term to describe other concepts, then we lose theoretical specificity.

We highlight three other examples in the literature. First, Caprioli (2003) examines the relationships between gender equality and peace, but uses the percentage of women in the labor force and fertility rate, measures which correspond more closely to the concepts women's inclusion and harm to women. An increase in the number or proportion of women in the formal labor force is consistent with the principles of liberal feminism with its emphasis on women's participation in public spaces. However, this measure does not necessarily indicate changes in any of the characteristics of gender (in)equality. The same is true of decreases in the fertility rate, which is best treated as a measure of the indirect harm done to women by structural conditions in society. Developing an argument about the link between women's inclusion, harm to women, and conflict would allow for analysis that uses more accurate operationalization of the relevant concepts. In short, Caprioli (2003) and others have found evidence that the number or proportion of women in the formal labor force (women's inclusion) and fertility rate (harm to women) are related to peace and conflict, not necessarily that gender equality is related to peace and conflict. The link is not necessarily between gender equality and non-violence, but rather harm to women and societal violence, and the inclusion of women in politics and non-violence in society. Here, the use of "gender" masks the ability to theorize separately about the different ways that the status of women—women's inclusion and/or indirect harm to women—affect outcomes.

To give another example, consider a study by Saiya, Zaihra, and Fidler (2017) that examines terror attacks using a cross-national, quantitative analysis. Their main claim is that restricting women's political, economic, and social rights increases terror attacks that target US citizens abroad. They define women's social rights to include "the rights to equal inheritance, marriage equality, property ownership, traveling abroad, obtaining education, and

40 FROM "GENDER (IN)EQUALITY" TO THE STATUS OF WOMEN

participating in the community," as well as "freedom from certain practices like female genital mutilation, forced sterilization, domestic violence, and sexual harassment" (424). According to the authors one reason this constellation of conditions could be related to violent attacks:

> concerns the place of women in the home . . . if women are treated in a manner that is fair and nonviolent, it instills in children the importance of dialogue, discussion, and reasoning as legitimate means of resolving conflict . . . if the perspectives of women are silenced as a result of cultural tradition, the marketplace of ideas will be stifled. If women are more averse to resorting to terrorism, societies that regulate women also limit important potential voices of moderation at the societal level. (424–25)

In this study there are at least three distinct concepts at play that are potentially relevant to predicting political violence. The first is "women's rights" in the sense of formally recognized legal rights (to own property, travel outside of national borders, and so on). The second is women's inclusion in public spaces, including opportunities for education and participation in the community more broadly. The third concept is violence against women in the household. There are also at least two distinct theories invoked. One is related to violence against women specifically: violent norms that govern interactions in the household permeate society and result in recourse to violence in political disputes. The other is that women are, perhaps "naturally" averse to using violence, and if they are excluded from public discussions, they cannot exert their peaceful influence on debates related to contentious political issues. Yet, the theories are lumped together and tested as a bundle.

As these examples show, theories provided in the literature can be separated into distinct theories, but only when the correct concept is used. We believe that disentangling and differentiating these concepts and theories is important because they have different observable implications. If different concepts are bundled together, we cannot identify the observable implications (or theory) for any one concept. Further, the only way to examine whether the parsing out of theories matters is to use different indicators that accurately measure the concepts. Using an indicator that combines concepts does not allow us to determine whether all or only some of the concepts are related to violence, which in turn does not allow inferences about which theories are at work.

Finally, when we do not engage in the process that Collier and Levitsky (2009) suggest—differentiating related concepts by identifying attributes that are missing—it makes it more difficult to understand whether the concept or parts of the concept are related to the outcome of interest. For example, there is a lot of evidence that *social inequality* is important for peace (Cederman, Gleditsch, and Buhaug 2013). Based on Box 1.4, the dimensions of "identities that are relational, whether against one another or to their environment," "a hierarchy that subordinates certain identities," and "fluidity/rigidity of identities" are important for peace. It may be the case that "social construction of masculine/feminine identities" *is not* important for peace. Or, if we find that gender hierarchy leads to violence, then we know that "social construction of masculine/feminine identities," "identities that are relational, whether against one another or to their environment," and "reproductions of power that subordinate," contribute to violence, then the rigidity of gender roles may not be a precondition for violence. While all four characteristics must be present for a case to "count" as an instance of gender (in)equality, only some of those characteristics might impact outcomes such as peace. Without understanding which dimensions do or do not contribute to peace, we are unable to develop more specific theories about the effects of gender (in)equality.

The addition of attributes also helps us to see relationships between concepts and outcomes. For example, much of the international relations theory on status,[7] does not include the attribute of "pertaining to those that biologically identify as girls or women," and thus has analyzed the role of status in international relations without a gendered angle. Thus, we might also "see more theory" by adding attributes to existing concepts.

Concept Stretching in the Literature

Just how common is the problem of concept stretching? Figure 1.1 shows the quantitative scholarship using gender and/or sex in defining concepts since 2000. Gender is much more common than sex, but these studies rarely mean gender. Rather, they almost always conceptualize and measure the status of women in society. As such, scholars use different proxies for "gender equality" because no agreed upon definitions or measure exist. The use of different proxies has led to a proliferation of fragmented empirical research that uses different indicators to measure the same concept. The consequence,

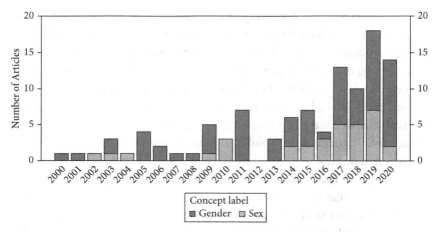

Figure 1.1 Number of Articles Using Quantitative Methods on Gender and/or Sex

as Sjoberg, Kadera, and Thies (2018) warned, is that results across different studies are not directly comparable, and are potentially erroneous.

Policymakers, too, have not consistently engaged in concept stretching. Ellerby (2017) devoted a book to showing how "gender equality [has] come to be a 'catch all' for any policy meant to address discrimination against and exclusion of women" (2). She argues that the term has been co-opted by international organizations and policymakers to further the goals of liberal feminism, which is distinct from the original agenda of the feminists in the 1970s.

Different international organizations have defined gender equality in different ways. Table 1.1 describes these definitions. Even across agencies within the UN, the definition and understanding of gender equality varies. UN Women defines it as a situation where people's "rights, responsibilities and opportunities" are not being determined by sex, and the "interests, needs and priorities of both women and men are taken into consideration" and "given equal weight." UNICEF defines it broadly as a circumstance in which "women and men, girls and boys have equal conditions, treatment and opportunities." The UNDP describes it as the removal of "legal, social and economic barriers" to the empowerment of girls and women. Differences in the way gender equality is defined for the purposes of policy will of course lead to different policy prescriptions for how to achieve it.

What is similar across the UN agencies and most of the IOs, however, is that gender equality is molded into the framework of human rights. The UN agencies adopt the position that gender equality is a fundamental human right. What then, is the difference between women's rights and gender equality? What is the difference between women's empowerment and gender equality? The definitions adopted by IOs do not provide us with much of an answer. The inability to answer these questions suggests that gender equality as a term has been "fixed," "shrunk," "stretched," and "bended" to meet the needs of policymakers (Ellerby 2017). As is demonstrated from the examples in Table 1.1 but also in the academic literature, the term has been used to describe everything from women's rights to women's inclusion and representation, concepts which fall under the umbrella of liberal feminism (Arat 2015). If there is no unified understanding of "gender equality" and the different concepts are conflated, then how does one improve gender equality across the world? Ellerby (2017) and Arat (2015) provide a warning. The consequence of this shortcut (what we call concept stretching) is that there will be no real change for women because they are still operating under the same oppressive structures (Ellerby 2017, 188–89). As they argue, when gender equality is used as a technocratic term for including women without really discussing how gender shapes the experiences of both men and women within institutions, it becomes a way to acknowledge power without changing its source.

It is important to highlight that scholars in feminist studies of conflict can also engage in concept stretching. By focusing on gender as an all-encompassing concept because of the argument that gender and the status of women are co-constitutive, such scholarship might overlook how the status of women in society, including women's inclusion, women's rights, harm to women, and beliefs about women's gender roles, affect outcomes individually. That is, a focus on hierarchies, identities, social construction, and fluidity may take away from understanding how specifically those who biologically identify as girls or women affect outcomes related to peace and conflict. Put a different way: gender undeniably shapes women's status, but by using gender to broadly explain outcomes, we might miss the unique and specific way that women's rights, women's inclusion, harm to women, or beliefs about women's gender roles individually affect different outcomes.

The goal of some feminist work is to explain how gender is constructed, performed, and maintained and how it can be deconstructed in the international system (Tickner 1992, 24).[8] This work critiqued "traditional

44 FROM "GENDER (IN)EQUALITY" TO THE STATUS OF WOMEN

Table 1.1 Gender Equality Definitions among International Organizations

Source	Definition
International Rescue Committee, Implementation guide: Preventing violence against women and girls: Engaging men through accountable practice.	"When rights, responsibilities and opportunities will not depend on whether individuals are born male or female" (International Rescue Committee 2014, 13)
DCAF, OSCE/ODIHR, UN Women "Security Sector Governance, Security Sector Reform and Gender," 2019	"the rights, responsibilities and opportunities of individuals will not depend on whether they are born male or female. Equality does not mean 'the same as'—promotion of gender equality does not mean that women and men will become the same. Equality between women and men has both a quantitative and a qualitative aspect. The quantitative aspect refers to the desire to achieve equitable representation of women—increasing balance and parity—while the qualitative aspect refers to achieving equitable influence on establishing development priorities and outcomes for women and men. Equality involves ensuring that the perceptions, interests, needs and priorities of women and men (which can be very different because of the differing roles and responsibilities of women and men) will be given equal weight in planning and decision-making" (Myrttinen 2019, 11).
	"Gender equality can also be understood as 'the absence of discrimination on the basis of a person's sex in opportunities, the allocation of resources or benefits, or in access to services'" (Myrttinen 2019, 11).
UNICEF, "Gender Equality: Glossary of Terms and Concepts."	"The concept that women and men, girls and boys have equal conditions, treatment and opportunities for realizing their full potential, human rights and dignity, and for contributing to (and benefitting from) economic, social, cultural and political development. Gender equality is, therefore, the equal valuing by society of the similarities and the differences of men and women, and the roles they play. It is based on women and men being full partners in the home, community and society. Equality does not mean that women and men will become the same but that women's and men's rights, responsibilities and opportunities will not depend on whether they are born male or female."
	"Gender equity may involve the use of temporary special measures to compensate for historical or systemic bias or discrimination. It refers to differential treatment that is fair and positively addresses a bias or disadvantage that is due to gender roles or norms or differences between the sexes. Equity ensures that women and men and girls and boys have an equal chance, not only at the starting point, but also when reaching the finishing line. It is about the fair and just treatment of both sexes that takes into account the different needs of the men and women, cultural barriers and (past) discrimination of the specific group."

SOLVING THE CONCEPT STRETCHING PROBLEM   45

Table 1.1 *Continued*

Source	Definition
	"Gender equality implies that the interests, needs and priorities of both women and men and girls and boys are taken into consideration, recognizing the diversity of different groups and that all human beings are free to develop their personal abilities and make choices without the limitations set by stereotypes and prejudices about gender roles. Gender equality is a matter of human rights and is considered a precondition for, and indicator of, sustainable people-centred development" (UNICEF 2017, 3).
UNDP Gender Equality Strategy 2018	" universal respect for human rights and human dignity in which every woman and girl enjoys full gender equality and all legal, social and economic barriers to their empowerment have been removed" (UNDP 2018, 3).
UN Women: The United Nations Entity for Gender Equality and the Empowerment of Women - Office of the Secretary—General's Envoy on Youth.	"refers to the equal rights, responsibilities and opportunities of women and men and girls and boys. Equality does not mean that women and men will become the same but that women's and men's rights, responsibilities and opportunities will not depend on whether they are born male or female. Gender equality implies that the interests, needs and priorities of both women and men are taken into consideration, recognizing the diversity of different groups of women and men. Gender equality is not a women's issue but should concern and fully engage men as well as women. Equality between women and men is seen both as a human rights issue and as a precondition for, and indicator of, sustainable people-centered development." (UN Women 2013)
Gender and Health, World Health Organization, 2023	"Gender refers to the characteristics of women, men, girls and boys that are socially constructed. This includes norms, behaviours and roles associated with being a woman, man, girl or boy, as well as relationships with each other. As a social construct, gender varies from society to society and can change over time."
	"Gender is hierarchical and produces inequalities that intersect with other social and economic inequalities. Gender-based discrimination intersects with other factors of discrimination, such as ethnicity, socioeconomic status, disability, age, geographic location, gender identity and sexual orientation, among others. This is referred to as intersectionality." (World Health Organization 2023)
"Women's Rights." Human Rights Watch.	"Human Rights Watch is working toward the realization of women's empowerment and gender equality—protecting the rights and improving the lives of women and girls on the ground." (Muscati 2014)
"Global Issues: Gender Equality and Women's Empowerment," Peace Corps	"Gender equality means that men and women have equal power and equal opportunities for financial independence, education, and personal development" ("Global Issues: Gender Equality and Women's Empowerment." n.d.).

Continued

46 FROM "GENDER (IN)EQUALITY" TO THE STATUS OF WOMEN

Table 1.1 *Continued*

Source	Definition
Frequently Asked Questions about Gender Equality." United Nations Population Fund, 2005	"Gender equity is the process of being fair to women and men. To ensure fairness, strategies and measures must often be available to compensate for women's historical and social disadvantages that prevent women and men from otherwise operating on a level playing field. Equity leads to equality. Gender equality requires equal enjoyment by women and men of socially-valued goods, opportunities, resources and rewards." (United Nations Population Fund 2005)
"Gender Equality." European Institute for Gender Equality, 2023	"Gender equality implies that the interests, needs and priorities of both women and men are taken into consideration, thereby recognising the diversity of different groups of women and men. Gender equality is not a women's issue but should concern and fully engage men as well as women. Equality between women and men is seen both as a human rights issue and as a precondition for, and indicator of, sustainable people-centred development" (European Institute for Gender Equality 2023).

international relations" for being myopic in nature, focusing too much on the state, particularly great power politics, and ignoring the gendered social histories and relationships that help construct the global order.[9] To make the case, gender is used as an analytical framework to understand social phenomena. In using gender as an all-encompassing framework, however, it is possible to miss out on understanding important variation that is occurring within the view of the lens. That is, the part of the spectrum perceptible to the tint of the lens prevents us from seeing phenomena of a certain hue. We provide two examples here of how the use of gender as the sole analytical framework can sometimes obscure important questions and theories.

One explanation for how gender shapes violence focuses on masculine identities, including militarized masculinity (Cohn 1987; Tickner 1992). Men dominate national security arenas and shape discourse that perpetuates the use of violence (Cohn 1987). For example, presidents must be patriotic, and when we think of a patriot we think of a man, often a soldier who defends his homeland and especially the women and children of the nation from dangerous outsiders. He is the ultimate hero of the nation. But for heroes to continue to exist, for masculinity to maintain its status in society, the nation must be under constant threat. Thus, security is the utmost priority of the state because it maintains masculinity and prioritizes it over femininity. Here, militarized masculinity is a socially constructed identity, created through social practices. An analysis of the status of women in relation to militarized masculinity, however, is less of the focus. Rather, women's status in a given society is assumed to be a part of the practices that create and maintain militarization. But this assumption makes invisible the ways in which this might happen. For example, when women are included in spaces where militarized masculinity is dominant, what happens? As women's rights are adopted in the spaces where militarized masculinity dominates, what happens? We cannot answer these questions nor learn exactly which practices shape variation in militarized masculinity in a society without divorcing the concept of women's inclusion and women's rights from militarized masculinity. In other words, separating out and looking at the individual effects of women's inclusion and women's rights better allows us to see how *gender* is constructed.

The literature also explores how women's caregiving and relationships with men sustain patriarchal systems that perpetuate violence (Enloe 2014). This is the subject of Enloe's *Bananas, Beaches, and Bases*, in which she shows how personal relationships between men and women sustain international politics. In particular, Enloe (2014) shows how states and their leaders rely on men to behave in a masculine way to sustain order. As Enloe argues, governments need diplomats and spies to conduct foreign policy, and they need male soldiers to fight wars, but women cannot inhabit these positions. This is because states and their leaders also need wives who are willing to provide their diplomat and soldier husbands with unpaid services so those men can better perform their prescribed roles. In the case of diplomats, forming relationships with other wives helps develop trusting relationships between diplomat husbands. More fundamentally, for the National Security Advisor in 1961 to engage in debates about the Bay of Pigs invasion, he needed his wife to manage the household for him. He relied on her unpaid labor so that he could maintain his status as the breadwinner at home and as a protector of the country. In short, women have their place and men have theirs, and this gender order or conformity enables the sustenance of the international political order (Enloe 1983, 5). Here, while we get a better picture of the role women play in sustaining hierarchies, we once again lack an understanding of what happens when there are major shifts in society related to women's status. What happens when more women are included in political spaces? What happens when harm to women leads to a decline in female bodies to sustain these hierarchies? What happens as there are global shifts in the way that women are viewed such that it becomes inappropriate to for "women to be stay at home wives and mothers"? Once again, these questions are not necessarily always asked under an all-inclusive paradigm of gender. By separating out women's inclusion, harm to women, and beliefs about women's gender roles, we get a clearer picture about how shifts in these concepts affect the creation and maintenance of the gender order.

The Solution: A Move to Differentiating Gender Equality from Women's Status

The solution is simply *differentiation* and *delineation*. Scholars, policymakers, and practitioners should divorce the concept of gender (in)equality from women's status. Moreover, they should differentiate among different aspects of women's status. This means clearly defining the boundaries of individual concepts and linking those concepts to the theory and the outcome of interest. On one hand, this is not a novel suggestion; many scholars have argued about the problems associated with conflating gender and sex (Sjoberg, Kadera, and Thies 2016; Kinsella and Sjoberg 2019). On the other hand, our move to differentiate is not equivalent to a theory of gender that demonstrates the co-constitutive nature of gender, sex, and political violence (Sjoberg 2013, 2014). While gender inevitably conditions all social phenomena, we believe that there is some merit in exploring each individual concept separately because only then can we gain a better understanding for *how* gender is co-constitutive with other concepts—women's inclusion, women's rights, harm to women, beliefs about women's gender roles, civil war onset, inter-state war onset, state repression, human rights, and terrorism. Our move, rather, is to differentiate gender from women's status and women's status from women's inclusion, women's rights, harm to women, and beliefs about women's gender roles. This enables us to focus on the effect that each concept has on the phenomenon of interest (political violence). We believe that this move leads to identifying novel theory building and testing.

Differentiating women's status from gender equality centers the theorization on bodies rather than structures. In this case, the focus is on women and their status in society, and how different facets of women's status affect political violence. We specifically explore the facets of women's status that have previously been theorized about in the quantitative literature on political violence. This includes women's inclusion, women's rights, and harm to women.[10] We include a fourth concept—beliefs about women's gender roles—as we believe that perceptions about women's status are as important as actual indicators of status.

Status means looking at where women are allowed to be present and where they are not. Higher status would mean that women are omnipresent in society, but especially present in the political (and economic) realm. As such, we explore the impact of women's inclusion on political violence. Status also means exploring the degree to which women are protected by laws and policies. When women have no rights, they have little status in society because they are not considered equal citizens. As such, we incorporate a chapter on women's rights. Women's status also entails looking at their societal well-being. As such, we look at the degree to which women are harmed in society. Finally, the way in which women are viewed in society is also related to their status. If people believe that women have equal status, then this is an important indicator of their actual status. Thus, we also explore beliefs about women's gender roles as a concept in this book. Together, these concepts capture women's status in society, but by differentiating them from women's status as an overarching concept, we can see how each concept affects political violence differently.

In order to accurately differentiate concepts and the individual theories that link the concept to different political violence outcomes, we apply the steps taken in this chapter to differentiate concepts through the assignment of attributes (Sartori 1984; Gerring 1999; Collier and Levitsky 2009). In subsequent chapters, we provide the attributes for women's inclusion, women's rights, harm to women, and beliefs about women's gender roles. The exercise demonstrates that the concepts do not share more than one core attribute.[11] Moreover, as later chapters demonstrate, we find that not only are the concepts theoretically different, measures of each are not highly correlated with one another. The differentiation thus suggests that they are different concepts all together and therefore require separate theorizing for how they affect levels and types of political violence. As such, we provide theories that directly pertain to each concept. Chapters 3–6 show how each concept affects civil conflict, inter-state war, state repression, and terrorism. In separating out these concepts, we see that not all facets of women's status affect political violence in the same way.

Conclusion

This chapter started by highlighting how an entire policy agenda—the women, peace, and security agenda—has couched the need for improvements of women's status as a conflict prevention tool in terms of gender equality. The goal of this chapter was to show how this type of concept stretching—using gender as a catchall phrase for many different concepts—can be limiting and even harmful to this agenda. In particular, it leads to missing theory, and as we shall see in the next chapter, measurement invalidity. When we use gender as an overarching concept to mean women, we miss out on the different ways in which women's inclusion, women's rights, harm to women, and beliefs about women's gender roles affect political violence. We are unable to see whether and how women's inclusion affects terrorism specifically or how harm to women affects civil conflict onset. These connections are obscured by the fog of conceptual ambiguity. Importantly, this is a conflation that policymakers and scholars make regardless of epistemology.

Our solution—a pivot from gender inequality to women's status via differentiation and delineation—enables better scholarship and policymaking. Differentiating and defining concepts allows for the development of more and better theories, which can be tested in a more accurate way. On the policy front, differentiating gender from women's inclusion, women's rights, harm to women, and beliefs about women's gender roles enables more targeted and accurate policy recommendations.

2

Solving the Measurement Invalidity Problem

Introduction

In the past several decades, measurement and quantitative analysis have become ubiquitous in social science research. IOs including the UN have fully embraced the use of indicators. They have gathered data and developed scales to measure various political, economic, and social conditions. These are used to assess change over time at the global level and in particular countries and to compare conditions across countries. Most of these indicators are concerned with "development" and other concepts related to economic growth. Perhaps the best known of these scales is the Human Development Index (HDI), created in 1990 by the UN as an alternative measure of "development" that is based on an explicit conceptualization that considers more than aggregate levels of wealth (Sen 2001). Like every indicator, the HDI is not perfect and has been subjected to numerous critiques (some of which are mentioned later in this chapter). However, it does show that while no indicator is a perfect representation of what it measures, some are more useful than others. It is difficult to argue that a development scale that includes outcomes related to health and education alongside wealth is no better than one that includes wealth alone.

Like the UN, the World Bank has come to rely heavily on indicators. As an organization whose explicit mission is to promote economic development, many of the measures the World Bank produces are intended to assess whether government policies are effectively promoting economic growth. Beginning in 2004, the World Bank's Doing Business project created a series of indicators to rank countries according to how "business friendly" their legal systems are, meaning how favorable the legal environment is toward those operating a private firm. Countries were ranked based on data collected from questionnaires distributed to legal and business professionals in each country. In 2021 the World Bank announced that it would discontinue

Positioning Women in Conflict Studies. Sabrina Karim and Daniel W. Hill, Jr., Oxford University Press.
© Oxford University Press 2024. DOI: 10.1093/9780197757970.003.0003

the Doing Business project after bank staff were accused of manipulating data to improve the scores of certain countries, including China, Saudi Arabia, and the UAE. The bank published an internal report corroborating these allegations. The report also found "multiple cases where national governments have attempted to manipulate . . . scores by exerting pressure" on survey respondents. It also criticized the project for a lack of transparency about the underlying data and for selling consulting services to countries who were interested in improving their scores (Shalal 2023). The project has since been replaced by the very similar Business Ready (B-READY) project.[1]

In the case of the HDI, we see a scale that is grounded in a well-developed concept and that is created from indicators that have a clear connection to the concept. In the case of the World Bank's legal scales, we see a set of indices that have a less coherent conceptual motivation, are created using an opaque process with ample opportunity and motive for intentional manipulation, and in some cases seem to measure something different than what their creators claim they measure. The comparison serves to illustrate our central claims in this chapter: measurement validity is important for sound research. If indicators and scales are to be useful, they must be grounded in well-defined concepts, created in a transparent way so that others may scrutinize them, and in the case of scales, aggregated using well-justified methods.

In Chapter 1 we made the pivot from gender equality to women's status to overcome concept stretching. In this chapter, we identify existing problems with the measurement of concepts related to gender equality and women's status and offer solutions for them. Our chief concern is measurement validity or the problem of indicators not accurately measuring the concept. We then outline our approach and explain how it addresses these problems. We are in favor of creating scales from several indicators, as no single indicator adequately captures our concepts of interest. However, the creation of scales involves several steps that all have potential pitfalls. Our approach, which is to use formal measurement models to combine multiple indicators into scales, avoids these pitfalls. We point to several promising projects in political science that use this approach and explain how our indicators build on these efforts and add to them. Our goal is for the measures we use in this chapter to be more like the HDI and less like the Doing Business indicators.

We begin the chapter with a discussion about the merits of quantification and go on to identify problems associated with measurement. In the last part of the chapter, we present our solutions to these measurement problems.

Is Quantification Useful at All? Identifying the Benefits of Quantitative Measurement

The World Bank example calls into question the use of indicators to represent social phenomena in general. As such, it is worth reflecting on the use of formal measurement in conducting analyses and drawing conclusions about the social world. Merry (2011) provides a comprehensive critique of quantification,[2] or the use of numeric or categorical scales to represent social phenomena. She has four main concerns. She argues that quantitative indicators oversimplify complex concepts, producing knowledge that is partial, distorted, and misleading. The process of creating indicators is a social and political one, which means that the indicators are never objective. Moreover, quantification marginalizes substantive discussion about the phenomenon of interest, creating a space where debates are focused on technical issues that are of secondary importance. Finally, Merry is concerned with the creation of an "audit culture" in which indicators are used to assess state behavior and practices.

It is true that indicators are intended to be relatively simple representations of complex concepts. Representing a concept with an indicator for the purpose of analysis can be useful *as long as researchers are aware of the limitations of indicators*. Much of the concern that numbers do not adequately reflect the complexities of the real world is rooted in questions about the validity of particular indicators. These are legitimate questions. Drawing valid inferences depends on having valid measures of theoretical concepts in the first place.

Constructing quantitative indicators certainly does not eliminate the use of human judgment in research. However, it does not necessarily obfuscate the judgment involved in drawing conclusions from facts, provided that researchers are honest and transparent about the way they construct and use indicators. Human judgment, with all of its potential errors, is always involved in the process of creating measures, as well as the process of using those measures to draw (tentative) conclusions about the world. This does not pose a problem as long as the underlying concept to be measured is clearly defined and the rules for translating concepts into indicators are clear and principled (Schedler 2012). These are necessary conditions for creating valid and reliable (i.e. reproducible) measures.

Quantification is not intended to obstruct further substantive debate about the nature of gender equality, women's status, political violence, or other social phenomena, or debate about how to effectively promote their realization. The act of creating an indicator does not have to prevent further debate about the substantive content of a concept (this book is proof of that!). Every good indicator starts with a clear operational definition of a well-defined concept, meaning (at minimum) rules for identifying extensions of the concept as explained in Chapter 1. If the concept and its operational definition are clear, then it is possible to debate whether the indicator is a good measure, i.e. whether the operational definition closely matches the conceptual definition. It is also possible to debate the content (intension) of the concept itself, but since concepts are theoretical constructs there is never a "correct" or "true" definition. In these debates the questions are whether one has adopted the appropriate concept to measure given one's goals, and whether the operationalization adequately reflects the concept.

Finally, though critics of indicators admit that they can be used to demonstrate shortcomings in government performance (Merry 2011; Rosga and Satterthwaite 2009), they worry that using indicators to assess performance has the effect of turning the indicator itself into the goal. This means states may devote resources to improving their scores on indicators rather than actually improving their behavior, policies, and the conditions for people living in those countries. When this happens, the indicator ceases to be a usefully accurate representation of the phenomenon it is supposed to measure. While this is a serious problem for developing indicators that allow one to examine state practices, this phenomenon is likely to occur in *any* situation where a person or organization is aware that they are being assessed with an indicator rather than directly monitored, even if the indicator is not quantitative.[3] We would suggest that, rather than the abandonment of indicators and attempts to monitor states more generally, strategic behavior necessitates cautious use of indicators, as well as more creative and carefully constructed measures (Conrad, Haglund, and Moore 2013, 2014; Conrad, Hill, and Moore 2018).

Further, the development of sound indicators can contribute to important substantive discussions about the nature of women's status and how to effectively promote its realization. The use of indicators that measure state violence, for example, has allowed scholars to examine questions such as whether increased economic openness is associated with violent repression (Apodaca 2000; Hafner-Burton 2005; Richards, Gelleny, and Sacko 2001) and whether economic sanctions have detrimental effects on human rights conditions (Clay 2018; Liou, Murdie, and Peksen 2020; Peksen 2009; Wood 2008). These are not esoteric questions; they are substantive questions that have important implications for policy and advocacy and that are best answered through careful empirical analysis.

In short, we believe that these critiques of quantitative indicators point to the need for *better indicators for the purpose at hand* rather than the futility of the entire measurement enterprise. Specifically, researchers need to use multiple data sources and indicators, address the problem of missing data, use transparent procedures so that their indicators can be closely evaluated by others, consider potential sources of measurement error, and critically examine their indicators before drawing firm conclusions.

Indicators always simplify reality, but simplifying reality is necessary for any analysis. In our view, there are good reasons to use indicators to study social phenomena. Indicators are useful mainly because they allow for statistical analysis, which has relatively clear (though hotly contested) rules for drawing conclusions from evidence, and provides a way to explicitly express uncertainty about conclusions. We believe the principal advantage of quantitative analysis is its ability to systematically (and with the current state of technology, quickly) analyze large amounts of information. However, this advantage can be entirely undercut without careful attention to concepts and measures. The disconnect between "gender equality" and the indicators we discuss in this book illustrates this pitfall and points to the importance of distinguishing between sex, women, and gender, and of paying more attention to conceptualization and measurement.

Concerns about Measurement Validity

Connecting Concepts and Indicators

Measurement validity refers to whether an indicator captures all of the relevant aspects of the concept, so that there is a good match between the intension of the concept and instances identified as falling within its extension (Adcock and Collier 2001). This requires a clearly defined concept and an operational definition that clearly connects the relevant aspects of the concept to the features of the cases under examination. The most serious problem with many existing measurement efforts is that they are missing at least one of these requirements.

It is common to use several different indicators to measure "gender equality" in a single study.[4] Using several alternative indicators is not necessarily a problem, but the indicators must have some clear connection to the concept of interest. Additionally, different indicators of the same concept should have some (statistical) relationship to each other. In the case of "gender equality" there is often an acknowledgment that an indicator in fact measures another concept such as women's rights or women's empowerment even though the term "gender equality" is used in the theoretical argument, perhaps interchangeably with the others. Specifying the relevant concept and how it corresponds to the chosen indicator is crucial to ensuring measurement validity. In these cases, multiple indicators muddle measurement efforts since they may have no clear connection to the concept of interest or any obvious connection to each other. At some point the disconnect between concept and indicator becomes large enough that it may be more useful to theorize about concepts related to women's conditions and use available measures that accurately capture those concepts.

Indeed, an overview of the literature that measures "gender equality" shows enormous variation in preferred indicators. Figure 2.1 shows the indicators used in the quantitative literature to measure "gender (in)equality."[5] The figure shows that the most commonly used indicators (excluding sexual violence in conflict)[6] are education outcomes (which usually means the ratio of male to female school enrollment at either the primary or secondary level), female participation in the labor force relative to men, the number of women in the legislature (as a percentage or proportion) and the closely-related CIRI political rights scale, and fertility rates—we refer to these as the "usual suspects." Some of these concepts have a tenuous conceptual connection to gender equality and are only weakly associated with each other.

Additionally, IOs tend to use similar indicators as measures of "gender equality." For example, the UN's Gender Inequality Index (GII) includes several measures that capture women's status, not gender equality. It measures inequality in three domains: reproductive health, empowerment, and economic status. Reproductive health is measured using maternal mortality ratios and adolescent fertility rates, empowerment is measured as the share of parliamentary seats held by each sex and completion rates for secondary and higher education for each sex, and economic status is measured by labor market participation rates for men and women fifteen years of age and older. It is clear from these examples that while there are a handful of indicators that are used more commonly than others, there is no clear consensus on which indicators are the most useful for measuring "gender equality."

One reason some of these indicators are so frequently used is that they have reasonable cross-national and temporal coverage. It has only

SOLVING THE MEASUREMENT INVALIDITY PROBLEM 57

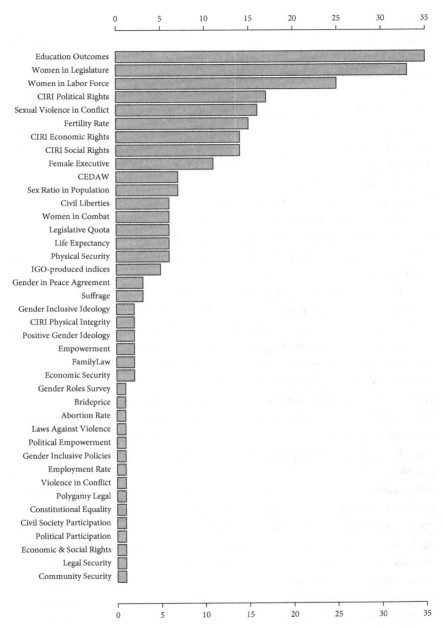

Figure 2.1 Indicators used in Quantitative Scholarship on Gender and Conflict

recently become common practice for governments and IOs to collect sex-disaggregated data about outcomes related to health, education, etc. Going farther than a few years into the past requires compiling data from the historical record, something many scholars have done (and are doing), but which takes significant time and resources. This often forces researchers into a tradeoff between valid measurement and sample size—they must choose between a more theoretically appropriate indicator and one that produces a sample large enough to provide reasonably precise estimates, such as fertility rate, for which there are data starting from 1960 that cover nearly 200 countries. Researchers may be more inclined to use fertility rate to measure "gender equality" because there are simply more data, which makes it easier to conduct statistical analysis. But if the theory they propose does not feature the aggregate fertility rate as a concept, and if there is no clear connection between the relevant concept and the fertility rate, it is not clear what we learn from such an analysis.

While many studies use several separate indicators of outcomes related to women's health, education, and so on, it is also common to combine several indicators into a scale. Aggregating multiple indicators into a single scale is useful because no single measurable condition can adequately capture a concept like "gender equality." There are potentially many different outcomes that are relevant to the concept. Instead of comparing all of the relevant conditions across cases simultaneously, an index combines them into a single score that provides some (partial) information about all of the relevant conditions. While a composite index or scale is appealing in principle, there are potential pitfalls that accompany such an approach. Creating a scale requires several decisions, including which variables to include as components, how to combine them numerically (aggregation), and how much weight to give to each component.[7] There are several prominent IGO-created scales that measure "gender equality," each of them approaching these decisions in slightly different ways, as discussed in more detail later in this chapter. For now, our main concern is that the indicators used to create these scales suffer from the same problems mentioned earlier: there is little effort to connect the indicators to the concept of gender equality and little consideration of whether the indicators have any meaningful relationship with each other.[8] Whether one uses a single indicator or a scale that combines several indicators, the validity of the measure will be in question if there is no clear conceptual definition or if there is no account of how the indicator is related to the concept.

Lack of Agreement between Indicators

It is also concerning that some of the indicators most commonly used to measure "gender equality" (individually or in combination with each other) are not highly correlated with one another. The idea that a measure of a concept should be correlated with measures of other concepts that are similar or related (in expectation) is known as "convergent validity," and it is a basic and ubiquitous criterion used in psychology (e.g. Westen and Rosenthal 2003). If a measure does not track closely with measures of similar concepts, and certainly if it does not track closely with measures of *the same* concept, the validity of the measure is questionable.

Some of the most commonly used measures of "gender equality" in conflict research do not appear to track together very closely (Forsberg and Olsson 2018; Hill and Inglett 2016; Regan and Paskeviciute 2003). Figure 2.2 displays correlations for four of these most commonly used measures: fertility rate, the percentage of parliamentary representatives who are women, the percentage of the labor force made up of women, and the ratio of female to male enrollment in secondary school. Correlation coefficients (ρ) are shown for each year, and so are based on cross-national associations.[9] The plot shows, for example, whether the countries that tend to have many women in the labor force relative to the average country also tend to have a lower than average fertility rate, and also whether the association between these two outcomes has changed across time. For all pairs of indicators except fertility rate and school enrollment, the correlation coefficients are not particularly strong in any year. Fertility rates and the secondary enrollment ratio are the most strongly correlated; the correlation between these two indicators ranges from −0.74 to −0.52 and has trended slightly closer to 0 over time. Fertility rate and female legislative representation are the next most strongly correlated pair, with a modestly sized coefficient of about −0.4 in the early 1960s. This association has weakened noticeably over time, likely reflecting increasing descriptive representation for women in the legislatures of developing countries. The proportion of the labor force that is female is the most weakly correlated with the others. The correlations between this variable and women in parliament are positive but also very modest (about 0.3) over time. The correlation between fertility rate and the proportion of the labor force that is female is close to 0 for the entire period. The association between the enrollment ratio and the proportion of the labor force that is female moves back and forth between positive and negative but is actually negative for

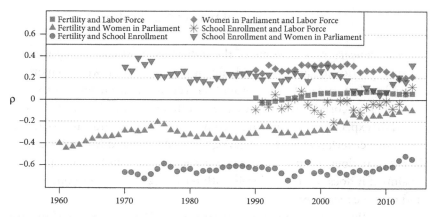

Figure 2.2 Yearly Correlation Coefficients for "Usual Suspect" Indicators

most years. The weak and sometimes unexpectedly signed coefficients across pairs of indicators suggest that they may tap into separate concepts and that it may not be good practice to use them as substitutes for one another.[10]

Apart from these variables, scholars often use ordinal scales from the CIRI human rights data project to measure "gender equality" (Cingranelli, Richards, and Clay 2014). The CIRI data have three scales that measure women's economic, social, and political rights. Higher numbers mean that outcomes are closer to the standards set by relevant international human rights law. Many of these studies are focused on compliance with international law, and CIRI's scales are intended to measure consistency between state practice/law and the international legal standards codified in the UN's Convention on the Elimination of All Forms of Discrimination Against Women (CEDAW). Like the "usual suspects" that frequently appear as independent variables in analysis, the CIRI scales have relatively good cross-national and temporal coverage.

Though the scales measure a broad set of practices and laws, in some cases they are strongly related to the outcomes variables most often employed by IR scholars, as shown in Figure 2.3, which depicts the distributions of "usual suspect" variables at each value of the relevant CIRI scale. The political rights scale in particular sharply separates countries with few women in the legislature from those with a relatively large number of female legislators. Also, the median of the fertility rate distribution changes noticeably across values of the social rights scale, and at the highest category of the scale the distribution is relatively concentrated at a value of 1. Similarly, though the median does

SOLVING THE MEASUREMENT INVALIDITY PROBLEM 61

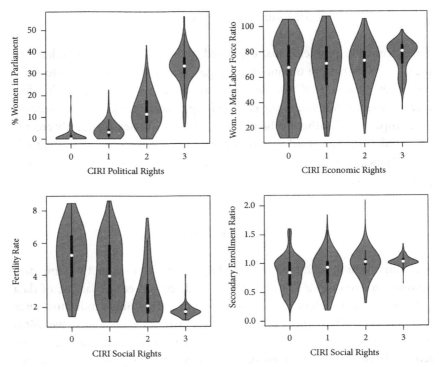

Figure 2.3 Violin Plots for "Usual Suspects" for Each Value of the Relevant CIRI Scale

not appear to change substantially, the values of the secondary enrollment ratio become concentrated around 1 (parity) at the highest value of the social rights scale. Although these three indices surely measure more than these outcomes, analyzing them alongside the outcome variables is likely to produce similar results and lead to similar conclusions.

This analysis suggests that, in addition to being difficult to justify conceptually, common measurement practices suffer from a lack of convergent validity. They are likely to produce disparate results, which makes it difficult for findings to accumulate in a meaningful fashion. The measures discussed here should not be used as substitutable measures of the same concept. They are perhaps driven by some common phenomenon, which is a claim to which the models we present later in this chapter can speak. But continued use of these indicators is likely produce the "mixed'" findings that appear in many bodies of research, even if existing data are updated to include a longer period of time.

Problems with Aggregate Scales

Apart from the problems just discussed, there are three others related to measurement that are unique to aggregate scales, most of which (to date) have been created by IGOs. Two of the problems we discuss directly affect measurement validity: missing data and aggregation methods with undesirable properties. Another problem is that aggregate scales are usually created and used with no consideration of measurement error, which potentially affects conclusions drawn from the scale. We briefly explore each of these problems here.

Missing Data

One complication with the creation of aggregate scales is that missing data become an even more acute problem. As discussed earlier, a lack of data is a non-trivial problem if one wishes to use only a single indicator, since there are only a handful (e.g. fertility rates) with extensive coverage. Most procedures used to combine several component variables into a single scale require information about all of the components to produce a value for the scale. That is, using standard approaches, it is not possible to assign a "score" for observations (e.g. countries) that are missing information for one or more of the components. The more indicators one wishes to include in a scale, the more likely it is that any particular observation will be assigned a missing value. This tradeoff is reflected in the sparse coverage of several of the sex parity indices produced by IGOs and INGOs (International Non-Governmental Organizations), which typically cover around a hundred countries for a few years. The UN Gender Development Index (GDI), the oldest of theses indices, covers the years 1995–2010 in five-year increments and has been available annually since then. On the other end of the spectrum, the OECD's Social Institutions and Gender Index (SIGI) has been calculated for the years 2014 and 2019 (using different variables and methodologies, so scores for the two years are incomparable).

The problem with this approach is that it only uses part of the available information for each country—the information that is also available for other countries. This potentially affects a scale's content validity since it means that indicators relevant to the concept are omitted. It is possible for the relative positions (rankings) of different countries on a scale to change with the addition of more information, meaning conclusions drawn from the scale may change.

Aggregation Methods

A second problem with many existing scales is related to aggregation, or the way that the different input indicators are combined to calculate a single value for the scale. For the most part, the scales created by IGOs were conceived primarily as measures of aggregate welfare and developed in the tradition of welfare economics, which significantly impacted the approach taken to aggregation. Aggregation formulas are usually selected because they satisfy properties that development and welfare economists have deemed desirable in measures of aggregate welfare.[11] In some circumstances it may be justifiable to impose certain mathematical properties on a scale. But in some cases, aggregation schemes are adopted without good justification and produce undesirable consequences.

The formulas used for some "gender equality" scales suffer from several problems. First, they are often so complex that the nature of the relationship between inputs and the scale is nearly opaque. This makes it difficult to determine how a change in an input variable will affect the scale. Second, they sometimes result in relationships between input variables and the scale that make little conceptual sense. Third, they are usually selected with little to no examination of the relationships between the input variables. Finally, they typically give equal weight to the inputs without much justification.

Three prominent examples will serve to illustrate the first two points. First, since 2010 the UN's HDI/GDI uses the geometric (rather than arithmetic mean) to combine indicators, as the arithmetic mean (or simple average) treats the indicators as perfect substitutes. This means that a country could compensate for a decrease on one dimension by an equivalent increase on another dimension. Using the geometric mean creates a multiplicative relationship between the components, so that the effect of each input on the index depends on the values of the other inputs (though their marginal contributions, or weights, are all the same). Anand (2018) points out some odd features that result from this formula that affect the validity of the scale.[12] These features of the index do not appear

64 FROM "GENDER (IN)EQUALITY" TO THE STATUS OF WOMEN

to be deliberate, but instead are unfortunate, initially unnoticed, but logical consequences of the formula chosen to aggregate the indicators. Because the aggregation formula obscures the relationship between the components and the index, these features had to be uncovered by using derivative calculus to determine the marginal impact of each input on the scale (Anand 2018, 3–8).

As a second example consider the GII, which was intended to address shortcomings of the GDI and is calculated using an even more complicated formula.[13] The creators of GII wanted a measure that could account for correlations between indicators, so that the index would be more responsive to cases where one sex is favored on all of the components. Unfortunately, the formula for the GII also obscures some undesirable properties of the scale.[14] As with the GDI, these properties were unintended and had to be discovered through a careful analysis of the mathematical properties of GII. The scale ends up penalizing countries with higher than minimal, but still relatively low, levels of mortality and fertility, which appears to heavily affect conclusions drawn from the scale. Gaye et al. (2010, 20) suggest that reproductive health indicators are the most influential in determining which countries receive the poorest scores: "Regional patterns reveal that reproductive health is the largest contributor to 'gender inequality' around the world." Though the scale's bias toward wealthier countries is partly due to the inclusion of maternal mortality and adolescent fertility as components, both of which are likely to be worse in less developed countries for reasons unrelated to gender equality (Permanyer 2013, 6–13), this bias is also a result of the way the components are aggregated.

As a final example, we examine the OECD's SIGI, which measures "discrimination against women in social institutions" and "captures the underlying drivers of gender inequality."[15] The SIGI is supposed to capture four dimensions of discrimination/inequality: discrimination in family, restricted physical integrity, restricted access to productive and financial resources, and restricted civil liberties. The variables used to calculate SIGI are all bounded by 0 and 1, and higher values indicate greater inequality between women and men. The OECD uses a non-linear transformation to combine indicators into sub-indices, and then uses the same formula to combine the sub-indices into the final SIGI score.

The justification for this is the same as for the HDI/GDI's use of the geometric mean: the marginal contribution of each variable to each sub-index, and of each sub-index to the final SIGI index, depends on the value of the others, so that "increases in one indicator can only partially compensate for decreases in others."[16] Effectively, each component has a weaker effect on the score if the other components have relatively high values (indicating high inequality). If one inequality component increases by some fixed amount, the effects of others on the scale diminish so that a country cannot get back to its previous, lower index value if another component decreases by exactly that amount. While this seems reasonable on its face, it means that overall inequality, as measured by SIGI, increases more quickly as one component increases if the other two are at low values, so that countries are penalized more for increases in one component if they are doing relatively well on the others.

As mentioned earlier, another problem with the indices just discussed is that they impose certain characteristics on the scale without much, if any, examination of the component indicators and the relationships between them. The intentionally imposed properties of these scales, such as diminishing marginal impact or varying rates of substitution, are not justified by empirical evidence. Rather, they are adopted for "theoretical" reasons that are not always clear and that have little or nothing to do with the observed relationships between the input variables.

With respect to aggregation, the last problem we discuss has to do with the weights given to the indicators in a scale. Here "weight" refers to each component variable's relative contribution to the index. Changes in variables with more weight will result in larger changes in the index value than equivalent changes in variables with less weight. Most existing scales weight each component equally, as with the GDI, the GII, and SIGI. This approach has clear normative appeal. It treats all the variables as equally influential in the scale, which avoids arguments about whether any particular input is more consequential for "gender equality" than others. For example, the OECD states that each component of SIGI receives equal weight because "each sub-index/indicator/variable of discriminatory social institutions has equal value," and "no sub-index/indicator/variable is more important than another in terms of deprivation experienced by women."[17] However, whether each variable is as normatively important as the others is a separate question from whether they are equally informative about the underlying concept. The assignment of equal weights assumes that all components are equally informative, which may not be the case. Differences of the same degree in "gender equality" between countries, or over time, may result in larger differences on some component indicators than others. There is no reason to rule out this possibility by assumption. The ratio of female to male participation in the labor force, for example, has been criticized as being an inappropriate measure of both women's status and gender equality (Arat 2015; Ellerby 2017). It may be the case that differences between participation in the formal labor force are less informative about differences in women's status than, for example, differences in the division of household labor. Assigning different weights to these different components is not necessarily an endorsement of one as "more important" than the other. It could instead be an acknowledgement that there is a tighter link between concept and indicator for some of the components included in the scale.

The alternative to assuming equal weights for all indicators is, of course, to assign different weights to different components. As noted, weights are often given a normative interpretation, which is probably why this is the less common choice. Even if there is a reason offered for assigning more weight to a particular component, it will be difficult to assign specific weights in a way that is not arbitrary to some degree.[18] However, while the common approach of assigning equal weights may be more "neutral," it is not obvious why it should be the default approach. To quote Hawken and Munck (2013, 824), "This weighting choice seems to be largely a default option used less out of reasoned analysis than a sense that agnosticism regarding all possible weighting schemes somehow constitutes a justification for assigning equal weights to indicators and conceptual dimensions." The scores assigned to each country, and more importantly their relative positions on the scale, will obviously be sensitive to the choice of weights. Both approaches risk giving indicators weights that cannot be justified by the relationships in the data and degrading the validity of the resulting scale.

Measurement Error

The final problem related to measurement invalidity we discuss, and perhaps the most under-examined, is measurement error. In most analyses, individual measures or composite scales are assumed to contain no random measurement error. This assumes that an indicator discriminates perfectly between countries with different levels of "gender equality," meaning that two countries with different scores have different levels of "gender equality" with probability one. Given the numerous difficulties with measuring abstract concepts and the conceptual complexity of concepts like gender equality and women's status, the assumption of no measurement error is a strong one. While random measurement error does not affect the validity of an indicator, it has significant implications for the accuracy of any conclusions drawn from it, including descriptive and correlational/causal inferences.

In the case of single indicators that are intended to be proxy measures, the assumption of no error is clearly not true. Since proxy measures are indirect, changes in these indicators potentially reflect many things other than changes in the underlying concept. For example, school enrollment ratios may change for reasons unrelated to changes in "gender equality" or women's status. Existing composite scales implicitly assume no error by producing a single score for each country rather than a potential range of scores. This is troubling in light of the recognized problems with the various formulas used to create these scales. Given the dependence of scale values on the formula used for aggregation, the scale's sensitivity to these choices should be evaluated. Conclusions about which countries have relatively low/high values may change drastically when using different aggregation methods on the same set of data. In such cases the index may be of questionable value.

A frequent purpose of cross-national measures is to make explicit, descriptive comparisons between countries. Scholars have heavily criticized this practice (Liebowitz and Zwingel 2014), and this discussion raises cause for concern about using existing measures for this purpose. Overstating the precision of an indicator by failing to account for random measurement error runs the risk of concluding erroneously that conditions for women in Country A are certainly better than in Country B. Such indicators may be used for policy decisions about, e.g. aid allocation, where countries are "means-tested" before receiving aid or, conversely, punished with reductions in aid for failing to meet a certain level of equality. In this context the potential cost of creating a rank ordering using an indicator that assumes no measurement error is large.

There are also significant risks in ignoring measurement error in causal/correlational analysis. Researchers may wish to use an index in a regression model, e.g. to determine whether the index is associated with a lower risk of political violence. If the analysis ignores measurement error, it is likely that results will be inaccurate and misleading.[19]

The Solution: Four New Measures

In this section we describe our approach to measurement and explain how we address the problems discussed in the previous section. Our approach is to pivot from measuring gender equality to measuring different aspects of women's status, because current indicators (Figure 2.1) tend to better capture women's status rather than gender (in)equality as pointed out earlier in this chapter and in Chapter 1. Our goal is to make use of these data to create valid measures of concepts. Using Bayesian measurement models, which address many of the concerns mentioned here, we can use these indicators to create four scales related to women's status: women's inclusion, women's rights, harm to women, and beliefs about women's gender roles. In doing so, we build on the work of other scholars who have created scales to measure hard to measure concepts; we also highlight these contributions here.

The Advantages of Measurement Models

Bayesian measurement models provide a way of addressing most of the problems discussed earlier. The one problem they cannot solve is ensuring a good match between concept and indicator. How close an indicator matches a concept is a theoretical question that cannot be directly evaluated using any empirical model. Ensuring a good match between concept and indicator requires careful attention to conceptualization before indicators are selected and aggregated.[20] Measurement models can, however, address many of the issues that affect the validity of a scale after a concept is defined and input variables are selected.

First, the models we use are based on the idea that there should be agreement among indicators of the same concept. The models can be used to infer whether indicators all correlate with a single, underlying concept. Second, they address the problem of missing data. As we explain later, because the models are Bayesian, they allow for the inclusion of indicators that are missing values for some observations. Third, measurement models provide a flexible approach to aggregation. The standard approach is to use a predetermined formula that treats a concept such as "harm to women" as a function of women's health outcomes, education ratios, etc. The approach we adopt, in contrast, treats the observed indicators as functions of the underlying concept. This fits more comfortably with the way people tend to think about proxy indicators like fertility rates, i.e. a high fertility rate is caused by the features of a country or society that we are interested in measuring. Additionally, with these models we can estimate the relationships between the concept and input variables, which are usefully summarized by parameters that have a relatively straightforward interpretation. These relationships are much easier to infer than they are in the formulas discussed earlier. The parameters for each variable also effectively indicate how much weight it receives in the resulting scale. Weights may differ across inputs and are determined by the degree to which an indicator covaries with the other indicators in the model, keeping with the principle that indicators of the same concept should be correlated. This means that some of the features of the aggregation formula are determined by the observed relationships in the data, rather than by a priori reasoning.[21] Fourth, Bayesian models produce an estimate of measurement error in addition to an estimate of the underlying concept. This error can be incorporated into descriptive or correlational analysis to ensure more cautious conclusions that do not overstate the precision of the scale. Bayesian measurement models thus provide a way of explicitly incorporating into our indicators the uncertainty inherent in the measurement of abstract concepts.

Measurement Models for Women's Inclusion, Women's Rights, Harm to Women, and Beliefs about Women's Gender Roles

We use Bayesian measurement models to aggregate indicators into measures of women's inclusion, women's rights, harm to women, and beliefs about women's gender roles. These models have gained popularity in political science in recent years. For example, this approach has been used to measure facets of another key concept in political science: regime type. The Varieties of Democracy (V-Dem) project, another enormous effort, has produced hundreds of indicators that measure different features of domestic political institutions (Coppedge et al. 2017). Much of V-Dem's data comes from survey responses that are collected from thousands of respondents with country- or region-specific expertise. Respondents provide Likert scale ratings to questions about conditions in particular countries for a period of time that ranges from as far back as 1900 to the present day. The data contain many indicators related to the status of women, particularly as it relates to political participation, and women's gender roles in society. V-Dem uses measurement models similar to ours to produce many of their scales, though the aggregation process sometimes involves several steps.[22] We add to V-Dem's efforts by creating indicators of some concepts that are not measured by any of V-Dem's scales.

Other scholars have used the approach to create cross-national measures of many concepts of interest in comparative and international politics, including democracy (Armstrong 2011; Pemstein, Meserve, and Melton 2010; Treier and Jackman 2008), judicial independence (Linzer and Staton 2012), human rights violations (Clay et al. 2018; Fariss 2014; Schnakenberg and Fariss 2014), party ideology (Hooghe et al. 2010), and numerous features of domestic political systems (Coppedge et al. 2022). This is a promising development since, as explained earlier, measurement models offer a relatively flexible and empirically justified approach to aggregation. We build on this work by using a similar approach and incorporating some of these other scales into our measures.

Like the V-Dem project, to aggregate indicators we use formal measurement models which we describe in detail later. Measurement models, which include models familiar to most political scientists such as factor analysis, have gained widespread acceptance in the social sciences, and psychology in particular. However, in efforts to produce measures of "gender equality" their application has been less common than the application of the aggregation formulas favored by economists. Measurement models have several advantages over that approach.

The Bayesian measurement models we use are similar to factor analysis in that they use observed indicators to determine whether there is a common "factor," or latent variable, that can explain some of the covariance between the indicators.[23] As already explained, these models fit comfortably with the way researchers often think about the indicators used to measure these concepts in that they treat them as imperfect measures of the underlying construct. Unlike traditional factor analysis, our models do not treat each indicator as a continuous variable. For most of our models we use Bayesian mixed factor analysis,[24] which integrates factor analysis with item response theory (IRT) models and can accommodate continuous, binary, and ordinal indicators (Quinn 2004).[25] The models can be used to determine whether the indicators are meaningfully related to an underlying latent variable and to produce latent variable estimates that serve as a measure of the concept of interest. They use relatively relaxed assumptions about the relationships between concept and indicators and produce estimates of these relationships that are relatively easy to interpret.

We incorporate some commonly used indicators (from Figure 2.1), which of course are not perfect, but neither are they entirely uninformative about women's status. We also incorporate novel datasets, including indicators from the WomanStats scales that measure violence against women and from the World Values Survey (WVS) measuring beliefs about women's gender roles. This collection of novel data on important conditions related to women's status is promising. With respect to both WomanStats and the WVS, the main advantages of our models are their ability to (1) evaluate the relationship between the scales and the concept they measure, and (2) produce measures of harm to women and beliefs about women's gender roles with estimates of measurement error.

There are simply not many reliable sources for different forms of sexual and gender-based violence. This dearth of data led to the creation of WomanStats (Caprioli et al. 2009), a multidisciplinary project devoted to collecting cross-national data on a number of conditions related to women's status, including women's physical security.[26] This ambitious effort has produced a large amount of both quantitative data and qualitative contextual information that cover a range of issues and, notably, go well beyond the usual focus on the conditions emphasized by liberal feminism, namely women's participation in politics and the formal economy. As discussed earlier, frequent use of those indicators has been driven partly by a lack of data on other conditions that are, in many cases, more relevant to the research question, so this is a welcome development. For researchers conducting quantitative analysis, WomanStat's most important contribution to date is data on several forms of violence against women, including some aggregate indices. We build on the WomanStats project by using several of their indicators to develop our measure of harm to women. This allows us to utilize the information contained in the scales as well as the advantageous features of our models.

Another promising measurement effort that we build from concerns beliefs about women. Inglehart and Norris (2003) present an argument that links industrialization to changes in beliefs about women's gender roles in society via a gradual, two-phase process that begins with industrialization and eventually leads to changes in people's beliefs and acceptance of women in positions of leadership and other non-traditional roles. To examine this argument the authors construct a scale from the WVS that measures respondents' attitudinal support for women's gender roles in society. They use five Likert scale items from the WVS to develop an aggregate, cross-national scale that covers

72 FROM "GENDER (IN)EQUALITY" TO THE STATUS OF WOMEN

fifty countries. Rather than creating an aggregate scale by averaging WVS items, we use a measurement model to construct a scale.

Using these indicators and other data (e.g. from Figure 2.1), we create four latent variable scales for the concepts: women's inclusion, women's rights, harm to women, and beliefs about women's gender roles.[27] Figure 2.4 shows the global mean for each scale, with uncertainty, over time.[28] We can see that there are steady improvements in women's inclusion, women's rights, and beliefs about women over time (higher values indicate improvements) as well as a reduction of harm to women over time (higher values indicate more harm). There is a notable jump in women's rights in the 1990s, which likely corresponds to the 1995 Beijing Conference's calls for more women's rights. Interestingly, this jump coincided with a slight decline in beliefs about women's

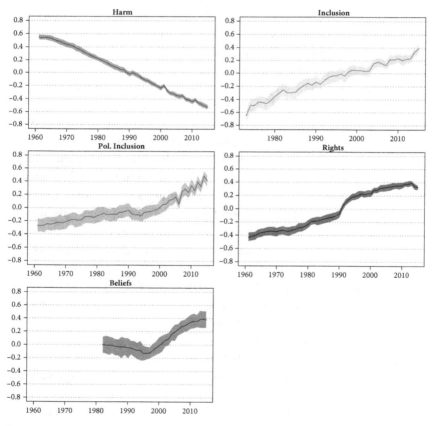

Figure 2.4 Latent Variables over Time

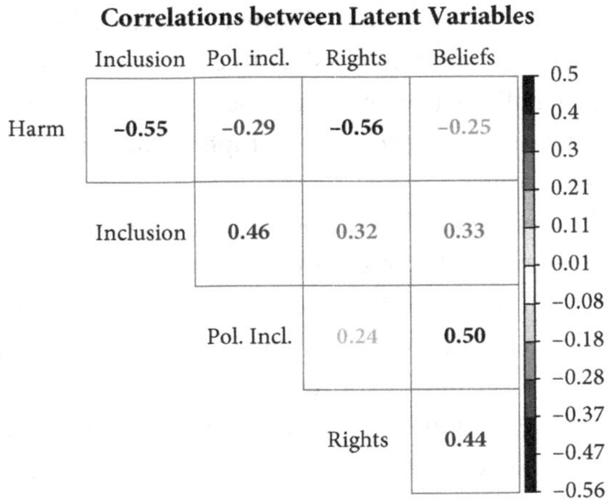

Correlations between Latent Variables

	Inclusion	Pol. incl.	Rights	Beliefs	
Harm	-0.55	-0.29	-0.56	-0.25	0.5 / 0.4 / 0.3
Inclusion		0.46	0.32	0.33	0.21 / 0.11 / 0.01
Pol. Incl.			0.24	0.50	-0.08 / -0.18 / -0.28
Rights				0.44	-0.37 / -0.47 / -0.56

Figure 2.5 Correlations between Latent Variables

gender roles, perhaps a sign of backlash from the adoption of new laws about women. Figure 2.5 shows the correlations between the scales: darker shades indicate stronger correlations and lighter shades indicate weaker correlations. The weaker the correlation, the stronger the evidence that the scales are measuring distinct concepts. Overall, the strongest correlations are around 0.55 (in absolute value), while the weakest are around 0.2, indicating that the concepts are largely distinct from one another. These correlations are informative about potential relationships between the concepts. For example, beliefs about women's gender roles is more strongly correlated with women's rights than is women's political inclusion. This suggests that women's political inclusion may not be necessary for improvements in women's rights, but may positively influence beliefs about women's gender roles.

Using these scales provides many benefits. As discussed earlier, missing data is a common problem in cross-national studies of "gender equality" that has prevented the creation of many aggregate scales with good cross-national and temporal coverage. One general advantage of Bayesian models is that they allow for missing values in the dependent variable (see Jackman 2000). Dependent variables are assigned a (prior) probability distribution, and when missing values are encountered during estimation the model will use a random draw from this distribution. This gives Bayesian measurement models a tremendous advantage over traditional factor analysis, since we can estimate a model even if the observed indicators have many missing values, and also estimate the latent variable for observations that are missing data for the observed indicators. Using the traditional approach, the models depicted here would in some cases not be possible to estimate, or they could only be estimated using a small fraction of the available cases. Bayesian models allow us to create scales that have extensive geographic and temporal coverage relative to traditional models.

As already discussed, another attractive feature of these models is that they provide a way to quantify measurement error. One prominent critique of attempts to quantify conditions related to women and human rights is that quantification gives a false appearance of objectivity and certainty (Goldstein 1986; Liebowitz and Zwingel 2014; Merry 2011; Rosga and Satterthwaite 2009). Only by taking seriously the issue of measurement error can we ensure that numeric scales do not create the impression of certainty where none exists. The models we use do just that. Bayesian models produce a distribution of latent variable values for each case rather than a single value. The mean of each posterior distribution is our estimate for that observation, and we can use the standard deviation or quantiles of the posterior (e.g. the fifth and ninety-fifth percentiles) to express our uncertainty about the estimate. This allows us to account for measurement error by sampling from the posterior distributions of the latent variables. The resulting scale will therefore not give the impression of being more precise than it really is.

To illustrate how this uncertainty can be incorporated into inferences drawn from the scales, we present some of the latent variable estimates from our model for beliefs about women's gender roles. As we discuss in detail in Chapter 6, our beliefs variable can be thought of as measuring the flexibility of (aggregate, country-level) beliefs about women's gender roles. Figure 2.6 shows the posterior distributions of the latent variable for Norway, Australia, and Ethiopia for the year 2014. We created the figure by taking a large number of random draws from the posterior distributions for these country-years, using the estimated means and standard deviations.

In Figure 2.6, the mean value for Norway is higher than the mean for Australia, which is higher than the mean for Ethiopia. However, because we can produce a distribution of scores for each country instead of a single value, we do not have to interpret this ordering to suggest that beliefs are definitely more flexible in Norway than they are in Australia, and so on. We can instead calculate the probability that the latent variable value for Norway is higher than for Australia by taking the proportion of random draws for Norway that are larger than the random draws for Australia, which is 0.94. The probability that beliefs are more positive in Australia than they are in Ethiopia is

SOLVING THE MEASUREMENT INVALIDITY PROBLEM   75

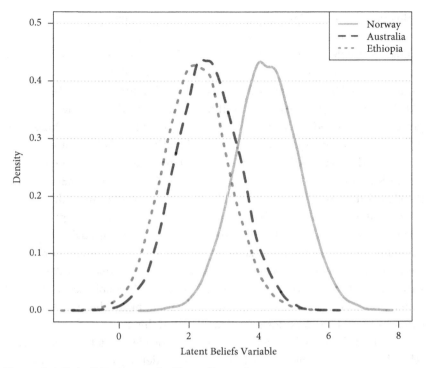

Figure 2.6 Beliefs Estimates for Three Countries

just 0.62, reflecting the larger amount of overlap between those distributions. Thus, Figure 2.6 shows the advantages of incorporating measurement error into the actual measure because we are able to see and incorporate the possible distribution of beliefs in each country rather than a single estimate.

Just as we can use the uncertainty in the latent variable estimates to make descriptive inferences, we can incorporate it into regression models, as we do in the following chapters. This is accomplished through an iterative process: draw one set of values from the posteriors for all country-years, use them as an independent variable in a regression model, store the regression estimates, and repeat. By doing this many times and pooling the resulting regression estimates, we can incorporate the uncertainty in the latent variable estimates into the regression estimates.

The measures created through this process constitute the main independent variables used in this manuscript. Our analysis in subsequent chapters uses regression models to examine how our measures of women's inclusion, women's rights, harm to women, and beliefs about women's gender roles are related to our outcome variables. We include four dependent variables in our analysis: civil conflict/war, terror attacks, interstate war, and state repression. For data on intrastate conflict we use indicators from the UCDP/PRIO armed conflict data (Themnér and Wallensteen 2014). Our measure of external conflict comes from the Correlates of War project's Militarized Interstate Dispute (MID) data (Palmer et al. 2020). For information on terror attacks we use the Global Terrorism Database or GTD (LaFree and Dugan 2007). As indicators of state violence, we use the Political Terror Scale or PTS (Gibney et al. 2019) and the Cingranelli-Richards (CIRI) Physical Integrity Rights Index (Cingranelli, Richards, and Clay 2014). Higher values on these variables mean less state repression. We opt for these dependent variables because they are the most commonly used in the quantitative literature presented in Chapter 1. As such, we go into much more detail about our independent variables in subsequent chapters than our dependent variables.[29] The measures of political violence are well established and do not suffer from conceptual stretching and measurement invalidity to the same extent as the concepts explored in Chapter 1 and this chapter.

In each of the next four chapters, we begin by clearly defining a concept related to women's status, which allows us to identify observed indicators that are connected in a straightforward fashion to the concept in question. The models we use to aggregate indicators are able to address many of the concerns about validity that arise once concepts are clearly defined and indicators chosen: they ensure that indicators all correlate with an underlying construct, they make it relatively simple to evaluate the relationship between concept and indicators, they aggregate input variables in a way that can be justified by the relationships in the data, they account for missing data, and they produce scales that admit some measurement error.

Conclusion

The measurement of social phenomena has become ubiquitous. It is commonplace in social science research and in policy analyses conducted by national governments, IGOs, and NGOs. Organizations, including private businesses and universities, are perpetually developing "key performance indicators" to assess whether they are meeting their goals. This practice is likely to continue. Though there are certainly reasons to be skeptical of indicators, the trend toward developing them is not necessarily cause for alarm. In our view, the most compelling critiques of indicators are ultimately rooted in concerns about measurement validity, not concerns about the act of measurement per se. We agree with Merry (2011, 2016) that indicators are simplifications and that they are never entirely objective. They are thus potentially, but not necessarily, misleading. This points to the need for indicators that are developed transparently, which allows others to evaluate the judgements required to make indicators, and to reproduce them.

This chapter has outlined several concerns about existing measures of "gender equality" that are related to measurement validity. Most fundamentally, the concept is often not clearly defined, which makes it difficult or impossible to assess the connection between the concept and the indicators used to measure it. As we demonstrated in Chapter 1, gender equality has been conceptually stretched. The lack of conceptual clarity is apparent from the plethora of indicators used in existing research, which in many cases are not strongly related to one another. Additionally, common methods of aggregating indicators suffer from a number of problems, as discussed above.

Chapter 1 differentiated the concepts of gender equality and women's status. As a subsequent step, we differentiate these indicators from being measures of gender equality to being measures of different aspects of women's status. The remainder of this book is devoted to delineating four different concepts related to women's status—women's inclusion (Chapter 3), women's rights (Chapter 4), harm to women (Chapter 5), and beliefs about women's gender roles (Chapter 6)—and examining how they may be connected to civil conflict, interstate war, state repression, and terrorism.

PART II
THE STATUS OF WOMEN AND POLITICAL VIOLENCE

3

Women's Inclusion and Political Violence

In October 2017, Jacinda Ardern became prime minister of New Zealand, the third female head of state in the country that was the first in the world to give women the franchise, in 1893 (Barnes 2020). Because the beginning of her term coincided with Donald Trump's presidency in the United States, she was often deemed the "anti-Trump" in news media (though it would also be accurate to call Trump the anti-Ardern) (*BBC News* 2020). More generally, Ardern stood out from other heads of states in many ways. She was the first democratically elected head of state to take maternity leave, and she brought her child to the floor of the 2018 UN General Assembly meeting, the first head of state to do so. She was one of the only heads of states to nearly eradicate Covid-19 in the summer of 2020. Her approach to crisis relied on empathy, not strength, as she publicly cried and hugged victims of the 2019 Christ Church mosque terrorist attacks. Her actions were clearly feminine, as were many of her policies—from banning semi-automatic weapons to making feminine sanitary products free. At the same time, she received death threats, she has been harassed online, and her leadership did not change public opinions about women's roles in New Zealand society.[1] Her ascent is an example of how women's inclusion in the political sphere can lead to different approaches to politics and conflict resolution.

Yet, Ardern's approach to politics does not necessarily generalize to other female leaders. Female leaders and politicians, such as Indira Gandhi, Golda Meir, and Margaret Thatcher, to name a few, are known for their hawkish attitudes toward conflict resolution: Indira Gandhi engaged in a war with Pakistan; Golda Meir oversaw the Yom Kippur war in the Golan Heights; and Margaret Thatcher started the Falklands War. These examples raise the question of whether women's inclusion in politics affects political violence at the societal level. More broadly, does women's inclusion in politics and society lead to a reduction of different forms of political violence? If so, how?

To answer these questions, this chapter begins by carefully conceptualizing women's (political) inclusion and provides a new measure of it. The bulk of the chapter is then devoted to theorizing about how women's inclusion is linked to

Positioning Women in Conflict Studies. Sabrina Karim and Daniel W. Hill, Jr., Oxford University Press.
© Oxford University Press 2024. DOI: 10.1093/9780197757970.003.0004

82 THE STATUS OF WOMEN AND POLITICAL VIOLENCE

political violence. The last part of the chapter tests these hypotheses. We find that women's political inclusion is correlated with a decrease in terrorist activity, but more broadly, we find little to no evidence of a link between women's inclusion broadly and political violence. This does not mean that women's inclusion should stall or reverse. Rather, it means interrogating the larger structures that accompany women's inclusion to understand how the gendering of women's inclusion affects political violence.

Conceptualizing Women's Inclusion

Women's inclusion is concerned with "sex" rather than gender. As we know, sex does not refer to the social roles associated with biological distinctions, but rather to the biological and genotypical characteristics that make "boys" boys and "girls" girls as specified in Chapter 1. Women's inclusion thus captures the degree to which women's actual physical bodies are present in the public sphere. By public sphere, we mean politics, the formal economy, commerce, law, security, and medicine, environments traditionally dominated by men. Historically, women have been relegated to private spaces such as the household and have not been included in public activities such as education, voting, or running for office. Thus, this concept aims to capture women's presence and "visibility" in the public sphere.

Scholars often focus on "parity" between women and men, meaning that the number of women is equal to the number of men. This underscores that women's inclusion is typically conceived in relative rather than absolute terms. Gauging the extent of inclusion requires accounting for the number of women *and men* that occupy a particular public space. The inclusion of women into the public sphere may in some cases be zero sum in that an increase in the number of women could detract from men's inclusion. For example, there may be a finite number of seats available for parliament, so that women's inclusion means the number of seats occupied by men decreases. Research has, for instance, found that women push out mediocre men from parliament (Besley, Persson, and Rickne 2017).

Since inclusion is about counting women and men's bodies it can be defined most simply as the proportion or percentage of people in some public space who are women. Much work emphasizes that particular thresholds for women's inclusion may be consequential. The focus on "parity," for example, suggests the normative goal of having women account for 50% of the inhabitants of some public space. One goal of research on women's inclusion is to establish whether there is a threshold for inclusion beyond which meaningful political changes occur. When women reach somewhere between 15% (Kanter 1977) and 30% (Thomas 1994) of elected politicians in politics, there may be increased attention to women's interests (Phillips 1995; Broughton and Palmieri 1999; Bratton 2005, 97). Some have suggested the percentage of women may need to reach 30% or more for them to be able to overcome the masculine social norms that often exist in legislatures (Kanter 1977; Dahlerup 2006; Beckwith and Cowell-Meyers 2007). This "critical mass" gives them enough influence over decision-making to change outcomes in their favor. Dahlerup (2018) suggests that substantive changes occur when the ratio is close to parity, somewhere between 40% and 60% (Dahlerup 2017, 31–32). Relatedly, female monopoly occurs when women comprise 90% or more of the public space (31–32).

Exclusion, of course, is the opposite of inclusion. It refers to the lower end of the "proportion who are women" continuum, in which there is a relatively small number of women in public spaces, or no women at all. Exclusion is historically thought to have been "natural, as societies perceived women as lacking competence in the arena of the politics and the economy" (Dahlerup 2017, 14–15). This exclusion from public spaces was an inherent part of the social contract. Men were entitled to dominance over women's bodies and labor in exchange for protecting them from physical threats, and all male citizens—historically white men with property—could participate in public spaces, but women were relegated to private spaces (Pettman 1996). Men who were not citizens were also given power over women's bodies as a way to give some power to a "lower class" of men who were denied political power (7). In this way, "the body politic" was established as an exclusively male space. Through the work of male political theorists, then, the public/political role of the individual citizen took on masculine characteristics, and manhood was associated with ruling (8).

In sum, women's inclusion has three characteristics. These are summarized in Box 3.1. Measurement of the concept occurs in terms of ratios of women's bodies relative to men's bodies, or women's bodies relative to total bodies, in environments that are considered "public."

If researchers want to narrow the concept down to inclusion in a particular public space, then additional characteristics can be added to limit the definition to a subset of public spaces. Women's inclusion in politics, or women's inclusion in the formal workforce would necessitate adding a sub-characteristic to "public space" that defines the public space (or spaces) of interest. This concept would then become a classical subtype of women's inclusion.

84 THE STATUS OF WOMEN AND POLITICAL VIOLENCE

Box 3.1 Characteristics of Women's Inclusion

---

1) pertinent to those that biologically identify as girls or women
2) visibility/presence
3) public space *(in politics)*

Measuring Women's Inclusion

As we discuss in Chapter 2, to create our scales we use Bayesian measurement models, which have several advantages relative to alternatives. Since the concept "women's inclusion in public spaces" encompasses multiple public spaces, measuring it adequately requires multiple indicators that will have to be aggregated in some way. Aggregating indicators into a scale with formulas like those discussed in Chapter 2 involves imposing strict assumptions about the relationship between the components and the scale that may not be empirically justified. In contrast, our approach uses the observed relationships between the components to determine if they can be safely treated as indicators of the same concept, and to determine the strength of the relationship between the scale and each component. This approach is also able to handle components with missing values and produce an estimate of measurement error for each observation.

To measure women's inclusion, we draw on a number of variables from several data sources, which are shown in Table 3.1.[2] The model combines indicators that capture women's inclusion in the formal economy, different branches of the national government, and education from primary school to university. These variables all capture *outcomes* that relate to women's inclusion, visibility, and participation in public life.[3] As we have both continuous and binary variables, we use mixed factor analysis, where "mixed" means we can include continuous, binary, and ordinal variables (Quinn 2004). In this chapter (and appendix) we provide some more details about the models and explain how to interpret them. Because the models for each concept are similar, in later chapters we provide less exposition of the measurement models, covering only what is different from previous models.

Our main goal is to estimate the posterior distributions for the latent variable so that we can use the means and credible intervals to draw inferences

Table 3.1 Indicators for Inclusion Model

Source	Variable
International Labor Organization	Labor force ratio
	Wage and salaried worker ratio
V Dem	Female head of government
	Female share of parliamentary seats
	Female head of high/constitutional court
UNESCO	Bachelor's degree ratio
	Expected schooling ratio
	Female share of graduates in engineering
	Female share of graduates in science
	Out of school ratio
	Primary education enrollment ratio
	Upper secondary education completion ratio
World Bank Gender Statistics	Family and domestic worker ratio
	Female share of graduates in social science, business, and law
	Female share of professional and technical workers
World Bank WBL	Female share of justices on high court
	Female share of ministerial positions
	Proportion of firms with female ownership

about cross-national and temporal differences in women's inclusion. We are also interested in the estimates of β (and α for binary variables) since they indicate how strongly related each indicator is to the latent variable. Because they characterize the strength of the relationship between a component and the latent variable, the β parameters effectively indicate the relative weights the model assigns to the observed indicators. If an indicator bears only a weak relationship to the latent variable this suggests it is not very informative about the underlying concept. Variation in the latent variable will be weakly related or unrelated to variation in the observed indicator, so the indicator will not contribute much to our scale.

The item parameter estimates for the inclusion model are shown in Figure 3.1. The estimates are shown as dots, and the 95% credible intervals (the Bayesian equivalent of a confidence interval) are shown as horizontal lines.[4] The estimates suggest that the indicators generally tap into a single, common latent variable—what we call women's inclusion.

86 THE STATUS OF WOMEN AND POLITICAL VIOLENCE

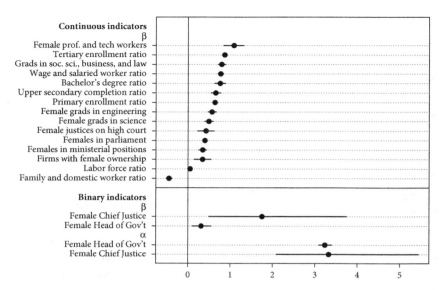

Figure 3.1 Estimates from Measurement Model Women's Inclusion Model

The credible intervals for nearly all of the β parameters exclude 0. The exception is the proportion of women in the labor force, whose estimate has credible intervals that overlap slightly with 0.[5] In addition, the estimates are all sensible in that components that should correlate positively with women's inclusion in public spaces, which includes all but one indicator, have positive estimates for β. The one item that should correlate negatively with inclusion (the ratio of female to male family/domestic workers) has a negative estimate. The variables that contribute most to the latent variable are those that measure higher-level educational outcomes, including tertiary enrollment and bachelor's degree completion, and outcomes related to the nature of women's participation in the formal economy.[6]

To make the interpretation of these estimates more intuitive, Figures 3.2 and 3.3 show the relationships between the inclusion variable and four of the observed indicators. Figure 3.2 shows how two continuous indicators, the proportion of legislative seats held by females, and the tertiary enrollment ratio, are related to the inclusion variable. Because each continuous variable is standardized in the measurement model, the y axis shows standardized values (z scores, or number of standard deviations from the mean) for the observed variables. The β estimates for these variables can be interpreted the same way as standardized coefficients in a linear regression. For example,

WOMEN'S INCLUSION AND POLITICAL VIOLENCE   87

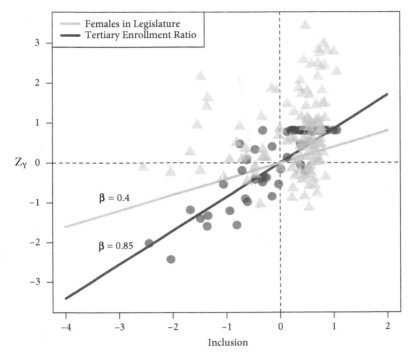

Figure 3.2 The Relationships between Women's Inclusion and Two Continuous Indicators

the estimate for the enrollment ratio is 0.85, which means that the enrollment ratio increases by 1 standard deviation, the latent variable increases by 0.85 standard deviations. The estimate of 0.4 for the proportion of legislators who are female indicates this variable has a weaker relationship with inclusion in public spaces. The observed values for each indicator (for a single year) are also shown in the figure to illustrate that, for the indicator with the larger β estimate, the latent variable tracks more closely with the indicator.

Figure 3.3 depicts the relationship between women's inclusion and the two binary indicators in the model. This figure shows "item characteristic curves," which are commonly used in IRT models and shows the probability that the binary variable equals 1 changes as the latent variable changes. An indicator with a larger β (discrimination) is better at separating observations that have higher values on the latent variable. This is shown by the steepness of the curve for a female head of high court relative to the curve for a female head of state. The probability of the former changes much more quickly than for the latter as the inclusion variable increases, and so provides more

88 THE STATUS OF WOMEN AND POLITICAL VIOLENCE

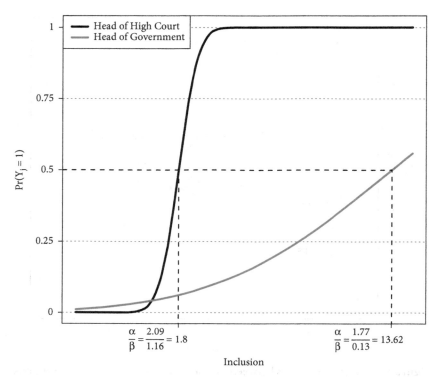

Figure 3.3 The Relationships between Women's Inclusion and Two Binary Indicators

information about the latent variable. Calculating $\frac{\alpha}{\beta}$ for each indicator gives the value of the latent variable at which the probability that $Y=1$ is 0.5, or the "difficulty" for the indicator. The difficulty for a female head of the high court is lower than for a female head of state, meaning a female head of state is only likely at very high values of the latent variable. In fact, a female head of state is unlikely until the inclusion variable reaches almost 14, which does not occur in practice. The largest observed value for the inclusion variable is about 2. Thus, the difficulty of 1.8 for female head of high court combined with a relatively large discrimination parameter indicates that this variable sharply separates cases with very high values of inclusion from those with high, moderate, or low values of inclusion.

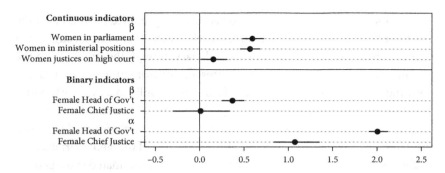

Figure 3.4 Estimates from Women's Political Inclusion Model

Measuring Women's Inclusion in Politics

In addition to the model just outlined, we estimate a model in which the observed indicators are limited to those that measure women's inclusion in positions of political leadership: whether the head of government is a woman, whether the chief justice is a woman, the share of chief justices who are women, the share of parliamentarians who are female, and the share of ministers who are female. The resulting latent variable will thus measure women's inclusion in political leadership rather than in public life more broadly, which is a more appropriate concept for some of the theoretical arguments discussed later in this chapter. Estimates from this model are shown in Figure 3.4.

Interestingly, the estimates for these variables are slightly different in this model than in the more general inclusion model. Most noticeably, the β estimates for the variables that measure women's inclusion in the judiciary are smaller than in the previous model, which means they are not as strongly related to the latent variable, so the latent variable estimates are not strongly affected by variation in these variables. While the estimate for the proportion of women on the high court and female chief justice are both positive, the estimate for female chief justice is negligible. The fact that it is very close to 0 and has wide credible intervals suggests that this indicator is uncorrelated with the latent variable. For our purposes, this means the variable effectively receives no weight and so will have no impact on the latent variable estimates, except perhaps to increase the uncertainty around the estimates. In contrast to women in the judiciary, the estimates for female head of government, the share of parliamentary seats, and ministerial positions are larger than they were in the previous model. This means that the presence of women in the executive branch and legislature correlate with each other more strongly than either of them do with women in the judiciary, though the results from the first inclusion model suggest that the presence of women in the judiciary is meaningfully related to the presence of women in public spaces more broadly. Additionally, although female head of government is more strongly related to the political inclusion scale than to the more general inclusion scale, in both cases it is an unlikely outcome at any observed value of the latent variable.

The estimates thus suggest that women's inclusion as estimated in the general model is related most strongly to inclusion in education (particularly higher education), in areas of the workforce traditionally occupied by men (though not their general presence in the labor force), and in judicial, and to a lesser degree, legislative, positions in the government. In contrast, the political inclusion scale is most strongly related to women's inclusion in legislative and ministerial positions in government, but not in the judicial branch. A female head of government is only modestly related to the political inclusion scale. This is because its rarity (3% of cases) makes it unlikely even at the highest value of the latent variable. The two scales are only modestly correlated at 0.46, suggesting that women's inclusion in educational and professional areas is distinct from, and not strongly related to, inclusion in higher positions in government.

Women's Inclusion and Political Violence

There are numerous arguments that link women's inclusion to different manifestations of political violence. These arguments can be usefully grouped into two types. The first group of arguments has to do with the idea that women as individuals or as a group tend to behave in certain ways or have particular preferences that differ in systematic ways from men. Some of these assume that women are simply more disposed than men to settle conflicts peacefully. As we discuss later, arguments of this type may rightly or wrongly attribute this disposition to biological factors or to the process of socialization. While there are simpler and more complex variants of this line of reasoning, they all rely on the assumption that women are typically less willing than men to use force to settle political (and group- or individual-level) disputes. Simpler arguments suggest that once one makes assumptions about women, it is a foregone conclusion that, if women are the ones making the decision to resort to violence, violent outcomes are less likely. More complex arguments look at the conditions under which women can effectively exert a pacific influence. Moreover, other arguments suggest that women do not directly affect decisions to use force through their supposed pacific tendencies, but instead contribute to a host of conditions that make the use of force less likely. We summarize these three strands of literature noting that they all rely in one way or another on women's actual preferences or contributions.

A second group of arguments focuses on the how perceived stereotypes about women who are included in public spaces affects actions by actors. These are theories based more on strategy rather than on structural factors (Cohen and Karim 2022). They draw attention to common gender stereotypes that affect people's behavior and the decisions they make. They draw connections between political violence and the inclusion of women in public spaces by pointing out the different ways these stereotypes might affect how women behave as well as the behavior of others toward women. Our discussion ultimately leads us to expect that any observed relationship between women's inclusion and political violence should be tenuous at best.

Women Are More Disposed toward Peace or Create the Conditions for Peace

Women are More Disposed toward Peace

Many arguments about women's inclusion rely on the assumption that men and women have different understandings about the appropriate use of violence—with women favoring violence less frequently, or in a smaller range of circumstances, than men. One school of thought posits that differences in attitudes toward violence can be explained by biological differences between men and women. These explanations rely on the notion that women are inherently peaceful and embody feminine traits such as caring and nurturing, whereas men are inherently violent and embody masculine traits such as aggression, and so tend toward a "natural" role as protector. Caprioli (2000) calls this line of argument "biological determinism," in which physiological differences between men and women determine the social roles they play. Melander's (2005a) definition of what he terms the "essentialist theory" is similar: women have certain fixed qualities because of their reproductive role, the most relevant one being an aversion to violence.

In contrast, and in addition, to arguments that posit physiological sources of divergent dispositions toward violence, some have suggested that women are

92 THE STATUS OF WOMEN AND POLITICAL VIOLENCE

socialized to hold preferences about the use of force that differ systematically from men's. From birth, women are *expected to be* more polite, less aggressive, more caring and more conciliatory than men (Gilligan 1982; Eisenstein 1983; Goldstein 2001). These traits are then externally reinforced throughout women's lives—people respond more positively to women who act in stereotypically feminine ways and negatively toward women who do not. As such, women may be socialized to choose more peaceful ways of resolving conflicts, whereas men are socialized to be more assertive and aggressive.

Scholars have explored this claim that differences in physiology and socialization are related to differences in aggressive and violent behavior. Goldstein (2001) explores whether sex differences in anatomy (genetics, testosterone, size and strength, brains and cognition, and female sex hormones), group dynamics (male bonding, working in hierarchies, in-group/out-group psychology, and childhood sex segregation) explain why men are more prone to war. He concludes that there are sex-specific differences in testosterone levels, size and strength, brains and cognition, and female sex hormones. According to his evidence, men have higher levels of testosterone; they have greater average size and strength; they are more likely to engage in rough and tumble play and be aggressive in play; and they have spatial skills. Concerning socialization, he finds that men are more accepting of competitive hierarchies. Additionally, boys are more likely to segregate in play during childhood, which reinforces their group identity from an early stage. He concludes that, together, these patterns of socialization make men more prone to violence. The last point about sex segregation during childhood is important because Goldstein (249) suggests that it sets the foundation for war by making men more prone to favor violence as a way to resolve conflict.

McDermott (2015, 767–70) focuses more on physiological sources of sex-specific behavior and lists a number of behavioral differences between men and women that may be related to reproductive biology: "men possess a psychology that privileges group behavior; whereas women on the other hand tend to prefer dyadic interactions of deep emotional engagement, likely because such practices helped with establishing bonds with children, potentiating children's cognitive and emotional development, and with mothers and sisters who helped with child care." McDermott also suggests that females will not want to engage in physical battles because this can compromise their ability to have or raise children. Moreover, some experimental work has also shown that men and those with high levels of testosterone are overconfident about winning wars (Johnson et al. 2006; McDermott et al. 2007; McIntyre et al. 2007; Sell, Tooby, and Cosmides 2009). For example, McDermott et al. (2007) finds that high-testosterone subjects are much more likely to engage in unprovoked attacks against their opponents than their lower-testosterone counterparts. This result was driven by the fact that males, who have sometimes much higher levels of testosterone, attacked more than females did.

Sex-specific beliefs about international conflict are noticeable in a number of public opinion studies, which are designed to determine whether there are discernible differences between men and women rather than determine *why* differences may exist. As such, these studies generally shy away from biological determinism or essentialism. Early studies using data from the United States found a sex gap concerning uses of force in international politics. Conover (1988) finds that women were less likely to approve of conventional war, nuclear war, and defense spending. Conover and Sapiro (1993) find that women were much less supportive of the 1990–1991 Gulf War. These results are consistent with more recent work. Eichenberg and Stoll (2012) find that women were less supportive of defense spending on average, but that the over-time variation in support for defense spending among men and women was very similar. Eichenberg (2016) analyzes sex-specific differences in US public attitudes toward the use of military force in twenty-four cases from 1982 to 2013, including the wars in Afghanistan and Iraq and the crisis in Syria. He consistently finds that women are less supportive of using force, with this result holding across time and intervention scale. In his book, Eichenberg (2019) found that women are consistently less supportive of the acceptability of war, particularly in the United States and Europe. Brooks and Valentino (2011) use a survey experiment to find that the sex gap is strongly dependent on the specific context of the war, with men supporting conventional wars and women supporting humanitarian interventions. Notably, all these studies use data exclusively from the United States. Early public opinion studies in the Middle East, in contrast, *did not* find evidence of a gap between men and women (Tessler and Warriner 1997; Tessler, Nachtwey, and Grant 1999). However, Barnhart et al. (2020) conducted a meta-analysis of survey experiments across ten previous studies (using data mostly from the United States, but also the UK and Japan) and original survey experiments in Egypt, Israel, Turkey, and the United States, and they find that women are less approving of the use of force vis-à-vis a peaceful alternative by anywhere from 4% to 30%.[7]

There are two important things to note about these studies. First, women and men do not have preferences such that any randomly chosen woman will view violence less favorably than any randomly chosen man. Rather, men and women's preferences follow overlapping distributions such that men, on average, view the use of force more favorably than women. However, some men are more pacifistic than some women. Public opinion studies suggest that it is *likely* that a randomly chosen woman will view violence less favorably than a randomly chosen man, but she may not be much more likely.

To illustrate the probabilistic nature of this claim, Figure 3.5 represents a stylized example of the distributions of women and men's preferences (assumed to be normally distributed). The more overlap there is between the two distributions, the more alignment there is between the preferences of men and women. In the real world these distributions may have large variances based on context. There may also be large variation in the personality traits of people who identify as men, women, or another gender identity.[8] In Figures 3.5a and 3.5b, there is some subset of women who are more positively disposed toward violence than some subset of men. Note also that Figure 3.5a models a higher degree of overlap between the distributions than Figure 3.5b. For the two distributions shown in Figure 3.5a, the probability that a man views the use of force more favorably than a woman is about 0.55, or a 55% chance. In Figure 3.5b it is about a 75% chance. Public opinion studies suggest that, depending on the time and place, either of these pictures could be a reasonably accurate representation of women's and men's actual preferences. For example, during times of national security crises, Figure 3.5a may be more likely. Though men have a consistently more favorable view of the use of force

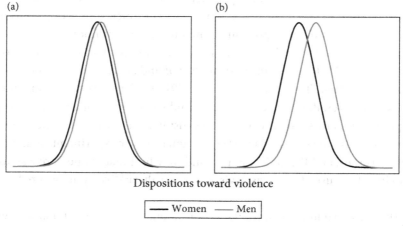

Figure 3.5 Women's and Men's (Hypothetical) Dispositions toward Violence

in foreign policy, the size of this difference varies from year to year, country to country, region to region, and even moment to moment. Since the physiological differences between men and women that are thought to be related to preferences about violence do not necessarily vary over time and space, some of the differences in attitudes toward force must be due to socialization and context. In fact, recent research suggests that this difference may not exist between women and men who express support for equality between women and men (Wood and Ramirez 2018).

The second important thing to note is that these studies use averages for women and men, but beliefs about the appropriateness of using force to settle political disputes likely varies a great deal across women (and men) due to a variety of factors. If men and women have systematically different beliefs about the use of force because they tend to be treated and socialized differently, it is worth considering variation in the experiences of women who belong to different social groups. A more complex study could thus incorporate other identities. The differences in existing studies likely reflect sex gaps in public opinion regarding war between women and men in socially dominant groups. It would be useful to examine whether such a difference exists among men and women in minority groups, or between women in socially dominant and women in minority groups. Nincic and Nincic (2002), for example, argue that in the United States women and Black people, and especially Black women, are likely to feel that their interests are not well represented in the political system and are thus less willing to support the state in pursuit of its goals—especially when the costs of these goals are high, as in times of war. Nincic and Nincic find that Black women are consistently less supportive of military action than White men, White women, and Black men. Importantly, their argument does not suggest that women are inherently more peaceful— in fact it implies that if Black women felt that the US government's policies actually worked to their benefit, they would be more supportive of military action.

Closely related to the claim that women are more peaceful than men is the idea that women approach negotiations in ways that are more likely to lead to mutually agreeable outcomes. Kolb and Coolidge (1988) posit that women have a distinct approach to negotiation that includes a relational view of others and an emphasis on communication, interaction, and dialogue. The importance of meaningful dialogue to women means they are more willing to consider the other side's interests and be flexible in negotiations. Such an approach may make conflictual outcomes less likely in group-level political disputes. Boyer et al. (2009) present evidence from an individual-level study that uses foreign policy simulations to assess whether men and women tend to negotiate in meaningfully different ways. Their results suggest that groups composed entirely of women are more collaborative, less conflictual, and less reciprocal (transactional) in negotiations with other groups than mixed-sex groups or groups composed entirely of men. Shair-Rosenfield and Wood (2019) also emphasize differences between women's and men's approaches to negotiation processes in their study of civil conflict termination. They argue that women have a more consensual approach that lends itself more readily to compromises. The results of their analysis suggest that, for countries experiencing civil conflict, women's presence in the legislature is positively related to the probability that the conflict ends with a negotiated settlement.

If women favor peace more strongly than men, or approach potentially conflictual interactions in a more conciliatory way than men, one may conclude that women's inclusion in such interactions will make a peaceful outcome more likely. However, women's inclusion in public spaces does not automatically lead to an ability to affect the occurrence of political violence. More complex arguments provide an account of how and under what conditions women's ostensibly "peaceful" dispositions influence political decisions.

Women's Inclusion Affects Political Decisions

There are two ways that politicians (regardless of sex) may engage in peaceful behavior based on women's inclusion in public spaces. First, the (female) selectorate theory begins with the premise that women will necessarily be a part of the minimum winning coalition as the selectorate expands (Bueno de Mesquita et al. 2004). Adding a large pool of voters who are more responsive to the costs of conflict is likely to change the calculus of political leaders as they contemplate the use of force (Tomz and Weeks 2013). Assuming women view the use of force less favorably, political leaders are less likely to resort to violence as more women enter the selectorate.

When women participate in leadership selection, they change the leader's incentives, forcing them to become more responsive to issues they perceive are important to women. That is, politicians, both male and female, pay attention to the preferences of women as they enter the selectorate. Barnhart et al. (2020) and Barnhart and Trager (2023) suggest that women's first public inclusion into the political sphere—enfranchisement—leads politicians to shift away from bellicose policies as they seek to gain women's votes. They argue this occurs precisely because of women's typically more anti-war preferences. As new voters (women) are more prone to non-violence, politicians will be more likely to respond to these policy concerns and vote against inter-state war. More broadly, when a large proportion of women in a society are involved in the political process, even at the local level, women's influence (and perceived preferences) can act as a strong constraint on government behavior (Regan and Paskeviciute 2003, 292). This argument thus posits that when women join the selectorate, whether that entails extension of the franchise to women or their inclusion in elite groups who hold sway, politicians (both male and female) will favor more pacific policies to gain the support of their new constituents. The effect of women's inclusion on peace is specific to groups that hold political capital. Note this does not require women to be political leaders themselves, but only a part of the public sphere.

Second, some political leaders may be more in tune with the preferences of female voters than others. Female politicians may be more likely to represent women's preferences because they are women themselves. In contrast to the female selectorate theory, female representatives may vote to enact policies they believe women prefer, not because they wish to secure votes, but because they are motivated to represent the interests of a social group with which they identify based on a shared identity. The idea that women in the legislature and other government positions are more inclined than men to represent the (non-violent) preferences of women relies on the concept of substantive representation (Pitkin 1967). Substantive representation refers to a relationship between the represented (women) and representative (female elected officials) in which the representatives are responsive to the interests of those they represent. This implies that the preferences of the represented and the actions of the representative will converge (Pitkin 1967). Despite there being enormous heterogeneity in the category of women as a political group (Reingold 2003, 2008; Hooks 1982), female representatives might have a higher likelihood of "hitting the target" in terms of acting for women (Phillips 1995, 53–55).[9] Legislation created by women may thus represent the policy preferences of women and groups who claim to represent women's interests, such as women's movements and feminist organizations.

With respect to female legislators, there is some evidence that substantive representation occurs and affects the occurrence of violence. For example, Haglund, and Richards (2018) show that countries with higher

98 THE STATUS OF WOMEN AND POLITICAL VIOLENCE

female legislative representation rates are more likely to adopt and enforce laws preventing violence against women in post-conflict environments, precisely because they are representing women's interests. Shea and Christian (2017) find that countries with greater proportions of female legislators are more likely to participate in humanitarian military interventions, particularly when humanitarian crises disproportionately affect the lives and security of women and children. This is because women are more likely care about the vulnerability of women and children in humanitarian crisis situations (Brooks and Valentino 2011). In addition to following public opinion, if there is a political movement that women support, female legislators might vote on behalf of the women in the movement (Weldon 2011). In sum, female legislators may substantively represent women and their perceived interests. If female constituents or women in general hold pacifistic views or engage in politics for peace, female legislators will be more likely to make decisions that reflect these views.

Women Create the Conditions for Peace

There are also a number of explanations for how women's inclusion affects political violence that do not rely on the assumption that women have a stronger preference than men for peaceful dispute resolution. That is, women as a group are not assumed to have preferences that are (even on average) more pacifistic than those of men. In some cases, the arguments discussed here posit that women have systematically different experiences from men and that these differences are relevant to conflict, but not because women are simply more averse to conflict. Women do not produce peace by pressing for peaceful outcomes or influencing decision-makers to do the same. Instead, women's inclusion in public spaces creates political and social conditions that give the government or society more capacity to achieve peaceful outcomes, or that make potentially violent disputes less likely to arise in the first place.

Several arguments in this group of explanations emphasize the importance of diversity in experiences. Some variants of this argument focus on diversity in general rather than on differences between the life experiences of women and men. The idea is that diversity in personnel generates innovative approaches to problem solving (Kirton 2003; Østergaard, Timmermans, and Kristinsson 2011; Parrotta, Pozzoli, and Pytlikova 2014; Bogers, Foss, and Lyngsie 2018). Groups of people with different experiences bring different ideas to decision-making. Diversity also creates more conflict within groups, which can be conducive to better group performance and morale (Jehn, Northcraft, and Neale 1999). When women are not included in decision making, Saiya, Zaihra, and Fidler (2017) argue, this "quash[es] the free marketplace of ideas," silencing the perspectives of women and leaving out of the discussion their ideas about problem solving and conflict resolution. In short, diversity yields more deliberation and policy options, which leads to groups making better-informed decisions, and presumably better-informed decisions lead, on average, to peaceful conflict resolution.

Notably, the idea that diversity is conducive to peace suggests that women and men *making decisions together* leads to better group decision-making that avoids recourse to violence. In contrast, the idea that women are more opposed to violence than men suggests that *women alone* produce peace by providing a counterweight to men's aggressive tendencies. According to the latter, a group consisting entirely of women is ideal for peace. The former implies that something closer to parity is ideal, since a group of only women would have a less diverse set of experiences than a group composed of equal numbers of women and men. This argument also suggests that group diversity along many dimensions, for example class or ethnicity, can play a role in changing group decision-making processes. If diversity is better, then diversity within and beyond the category of women (and men) is also better.

One variant of the diversity-in-experiences argument suggests that the inclusion of women in particular (rather than the inclusion of people with distinct life experiences generally) is conducive to peace because of the policies women tend to implement. Many women, particularly women who have low socio-economic status, belong to racial or ethnic minorities, or identify as gay or transgender, have life experiences that are very different from the typical politician who, in many countries, is an upper class, cisgender male belonging to the dominant racial or ethnic group. That women commonly lack access to education, adequate healthcare, positions of political power, and life opportunities in general is a basic fact that motivates much social science research, not to mention advocacy and policy. Thus, women may be more likely than men to implement policies that benefit disadvantaged groups, in part because women tend to be a disadvantaged social group. Along these lines, Best, Shair-Rosenfield, and Wood (2019) argue that women hold policy preferences that align more closely, on average, with common grievances among rebel groups, such as promoting public education and health. They find that women's inclusion makes conflicts more likely to end with a negotiated settlement. Shair-Rosenfield and Wood (2017) argue more generally that women, possibly due to their shared life experiences, are more likely than men to prioritize redistribution and social welfare spending. Their analysis suggests that in post-conflict societies the inclusion of women in the public sphere reduces the chances of conflict recurrence, possibly because women are more likely to address inequalities that often provide motivation and support for rebel groups in mobilizing against the state (Cederman, Gleditsch, and Buhaug 2013).

Finally, some have called attention to a link between the inclusion of women and society's capacity to address conflict and prevent violence. "Social capacity" refers to the "distribution of skills, power, and resources in a society" (Forsberg and Olsson 2021). When women are excluded from public life, roughly half of the population is denied the opportunity to participate in education, the formal labor force, and political decision-making. The exclusion of women (or any other large group of people) creates a situation where "development" in the broadest sense is stunted, since a large segment of the population has little freedom of choice and thus little ability to engage with society in a meaningful way. Gizelis (2009, 2011) argues that women's exclusion leads to low levels of domestic (social) capacity and social capital, where the latter is defined as "resources embedded in social structures that can be mobilized towards a purposive collective action" (2011, 524). She argues that post-conflict peace-building efforts will be more successful where societies are more inclusive of women, because resources can be more effectively deployed to organizations (including women's groups) to facilitate connections between otherwise isolated social actors. More generally, if women (and other groups) have a clear stake in the peace-building process, they will be more willing to participate in it, and efforts to build and maintain peace are more likely to be successful where they can get more "buy in" from the local population.

How Variation in Women's Preferences and Experiences Shape Political Violence: Hypotheses

This discussion suggests several distinct ways in which women's inclusion can matter for political violence. Women may be involved in decisions that lead directly to conflict or peace, in which case they may advocate for peaceful solutions or influence group decision-making in ways that make peaceful resolution more likely. They may also affect these decisions indirectly, if their peaceful dispositions are aggregated through political institutions to affect decision makers who may or may not be women. It is also possible that the inclusion of women affects conflict even more indirectly, by producing policies that diminish societal grievances that could lead to anti-state mobilization, or by increasing social capacity and reducing intergroup conflict generally, including conflict involving the government. Next, we elaborate on how each of these explanations applies to different forms of political violence.

If women simply have more peaceful dispositions than men, then women who are included in decision-making spaces will be more likely, on average, to pursue policies that de-escalate a crisis. In the language of bargaining models, this means that women will tend to view the costs of war as large relative to the value of the issue under dispute, and therefore more likely to make concessions that avoid war. Barnhart et al. (2020) present two formal models, one in which they assume that the costs of war relative to the "prize" increase with women's inclusion, and another in which the value of mutual cooperation is assumed to increase with women's inclusion. Increasing the costs of war for one side (or both) results in a larger bargaining range, meaning a larger set of mutually acceptable agreements that avoid war and makes that side more willing to make concessions that satisfy the other side. Arguments that rely on women being more peaceful than men suggest that when women are involved in foreign policy decisions or are a large enough part of the selectorate to affect the costs of war for political leaders, then international conflicts are less likely to occur.

Another possibility, already suggested, is that when women take part in negotiations where the use of force is a possibility, the two sides will find it easier to identify an agreement that satisfies them both. This is implied by the variant of the diversity-in-experiences argument that claims women's inclusion leads to better group decision-making. If this is the case, then including women may increase the likelihood of a peaceful outcome without increasing the perceived costs of war. Instead, states may find it easier or more efficient to locate the range of peaceful agreements that avoid war, or to identify potentials for issue-linkages and side payments that lead to successful negotiations. This produces a similar conclusion: the more women there are in these decision-making roles, the less likely it is that the government will initiate conflict. From these suggestions, we might formulate the following hypothesis:

H3.1a: The probability of interstate conflict initiation decreases as women's inclusion in public spaces generally, and political spaces specifically, increases.

Similar to the propositions outlined earlier concerning interstate war, women's inclusion may decrease the likelihood of civil conflict or war by virtue of women's lower tolerance for the costs of war. In interactions with domestic opposition groups, including groups who have mobilized for armed conflict, women in government positions may be more likely to make concessions that avoid war. In cases where women do not occupy leadership positions but still comprise a large and politically influential group, they may press political leaders to concede to avoid conflict, for example, suggests that when more women are involved in frontline non-violent protest activity, the group is more effective at gaining concessions (Chenoweth and Marks 2022; Chenoweth 2021). The inclusion of women in political spaces may also lead to more sincere and deliberative negotiations between the government and opposition groups and so make it easier to find mutually acceptable solutions that lead groups to demobilize. All of this suggests that women's inclusion may cause governments to take a less belligerent stance toward dissidents and rebels during potentially conflictual interactions.

Huber (2019) focuses on terror attacks specifically and develops a variant of the "female selectorate" argument that points to a slightly different mechanism. She argues that the cost to dissident groups for attacking civilian targets increases with women's inclusion, so that such attacks are less likely to occur. This is because women are more strongly opposed than men to violence against civilian targets. As women become more politically influential, dissident groups who target civilians suffer larger losses in public support, which harms their ability to achieve their political goals. This is similar to arguments summarized earlier, but rather than focusing solely on how women's preferences might constrain the government it considers a more complex interaction that involves governments and dissident groups competing for public support:

The argument that women more strongly prefer policies geared toward redistribution and social welfare also has implications for civil conflict and terrorism. If women favor policies that benefit potentially aggrieved groups, then potentially conflictual interactions involving the government may be less likely to occur. This requires neither that women view conflict as costlier nor that they are more skilled at negotiating peaceful solutions. Rather, fewer situations arise in which opposition groups consider resorting to force, but presumably the probability of conflict in such a situation remains unchanged. The effect is nevertheless that conflict is less likely to occur. Along these lines, Harris and Milton (2016) argue that where women have greater influence in government, the government is less likely to adopt repressive policies and practices that could serve as motivation for terror attacks.

Arguments that invoke the concept of social capacity work in a similar way. Women's inclusion may capture an aspect of domestic capacity that is distinct from wealth and economic modernization (Gizelis 2009, 2011). If so, its effects on peace do not necessarily occur during interactions between the government and opposition groups. Instead, women's inclusion leads to (or possibly reflects) denser networks among social and political actors, which in turn lead to more cooperative relationships between groups and reduced opportunities for conflict.

These arguments suggest that women's inclusion makes civil conflict less likely because the government will be more willing to respond with policy concessions to demands from domestic groups and more capable of productively negotiating with groups who make demands. Further, there will be fewer groups who have a reason to mobilize for violence. Similarly, the government will be more likely to make concessions or adopt other negotiation tactics that make terror attacks more likely, and dissident groups will view terror tactics as counterproductive and will have fewer reasons to seriously consider turning to violent tactics in the first place. This leads to two more hypotheses:

H3.2a: The probability of civil conflict decreases as women's inclusion in public spaces generally, and political spaces specifically, increases.

H3.3a: The frequency of dissident terror attacks decreases as women's inclusion in public spaces generally, and political spaces specifically, increases.

Research on women's inclusion and state violence is relatively sparse but relies on similar made above. Melander (2005b) argues that if women have an aversion to violence then women in positions of political power are more likely than men to take active measures to prevent and stop violent abuses of human rights. State violence is often conceived as a response to a perceived threat to a leader's tenure (Davenport 2007; Ritter 2014), but can also be viewed as the result of principal–agent problems between political

104 THE STATUS OF WOMEN AND POLITICAL VIOLENCE

leaders and security forces (Butler, Gluch, and Mitchell 2007; Conrad and Moore 2010; Haschke 2017). This means women's inclusion may reduce state violence because the government is less likely to respond to perceived domestic threats with force, or because the government is more likely to devote resources to monitoring and punishing security forces who commit acts of abuse, or both. Though Melander (2005b) focuses on women as decision makers, it is possible to apply the female selectorate argument to state violence. That is, even if they do not occupy positions in the government, women as members of the public may put political pressure on leaders that results in less state violence.

The argument that women prefer and implement policies that produce fewer grievances suggests another possibility. If state violence is a response to challenges to the government, or results from the anticipation of such challenges (Nordås and Davenport 2013; Danneman and Ritter 2014; Ritter and Conrad 2016), then a less aggrieved population should reduce incentives for state violence. Similar to the argument about civil conflict, this suggests that women's inclusion may negatively impact state violence by making disputes between the government and opposition groups less likely to occur or by decreasing the anticipation of their occurrence. Such disputes may result in civil conflict, but they often result in violence on a smaller scale, including abuses that target opposition groups and their supporters.

H3.4a: State violence decreases as women's inclusion in public spaces generally, and political spaces specifically, increases.

Perceptional Stereotypes of Women

A different class of arguments examines perceptional stereotypes about women and how they might affect political violence. This approach does not assume that women differ from men in their dispositions toward violence, their approaches to decision-making, or in the policies they prefer. Rather, women are *perceived* to be different, and this perception can be consequential for actors' behavior. Perceptions of women in politics tend to be driven by gender stereotypes that portray women as more peaceful (Koch and Fulton 2011; Best, Shair-Rosenfield, and Wood 2019). These stereotypical perceptions can affect the strategic behavior of women themselves and their opponents. While some have suggested that such stereotypes work toward peace, most arguments along these lines predict that women's inclusion makes conflict *more* likely, for two reasons. First, female politicians are well aware of gender stereotypes and may try to counter them by behaving more assertively and aggressively, including in disputes with international and domestic opponents. Second, adversaries and opponents may be more combative toward women based on the stereotype of women as peaceful and conciliatory. The combined effect of women behaving aggressively to establish their credibility and opponents perceiving them as weak makes violent conflict more likely (Caprioli and Boyer 2001). We begin by explaining how stereotypes about the peaceful nature of women could lead to peace and then move to how they might induce conflict.

Stereotypes may cause people to view women as more trustworthy and more credible bargaining partners. Groups in domestic conflict may perceive agreements between belligerents as more likely to be implemented because they are more trusting of women, thus lending more credibility to the government's commitment to peace. Shair-Rosenfield and Wood (2017) argue that women positively influence public perceptions of governance quality and elite credibility, thereby increasing the chances that rebel groups will find a negotiated settlement credible. Moreover, armed groups may expect that women's inclusion in politics will be more likely to result in policies that are social welfare enhancing and less punitive toward former opponents of the government. The inclusion of women in security organizations in post-conflict countries can also be used to build trust with the public, due to gender stereotypes (Karim 2019). As a result, the terms of an agreement may hold because rivals and/or rebels trust the women responsible for enforcing the agreement. This provides further reason to believe that H3.1a, H3.2a, and H3.3a are correct.

Other arguments, however, lead to the opposite conclusion, namely that gender stereotypes affect behavior in such a way that women's inclusion makes conflict more likely. Women in leadership positions are sometimes viewed as ineffective on matters of security unless they exhibit qualities typically associated with masculinity. This causes them to behave in a more masculine (i.e. aggressive) fashion in order to establish their credibility.[10] The pressures to behave in a more masculine way for strategic reasons are likely stronger for female executive leaders rather than for female legislators (Thomas and Adams 2010). Koch and Fulton (2011, 4) argue that the executive office is more of a masculine space than the legislative branch. They posit that "because male and female politicians are stereotyped as holding different character traits, ideologies, and issue competencies, women may confront credibility challenges in masculinized leadership positions, such as executive office." Women often face the contradiction of needing to prove their multifaceted or masculine attributes to obtain and retain executive leadership positions.[11] As summed up by Koch and Fulton: "when it comes to masculinized leadership positions, like executive office, this challenge to gain credibility may lead women to present themselves as more masculine, in an attempt to combat the stereotype" (4).

Concerning international conflict, because they feel pressured to perform masculinity, female leaders may engage in behavior that makes conflict more likely in order to signal their security credentials. Powell and Mukazhanova-Powell (2019) argue that because female executives are judged more harshly on foreign policy, they will be pressured to make fewer concessions in bargaining. The implication is that female leaders tend to discount the costs of war, resulting in a smaller bargaining range and a greater chance of conflict (2019). Similarly, some have suggested that women leaders may incur higher "inconsistency costs" for backing down from a conflict due to stereotypes. Schwartz and Blair (2020) suggest that when women back down during a confrontation, domestic audiences are more likely to view their behavior as a result of individual characteristics rather than external factors. The reverse is true for male leaders who back down. This means women pay a higher political price for backing down from a threat than men, which leads to the unnecessary escalation of disputes to armed conflict. Additionally, Schramm and Stark (2020) find that among countries with more institutional constraints on the executive, female leaders are more likely to initiate conflicts, presumably to demonstrate their resolve (and therein their masculinity).

Besides creating pressure to demonstrate competence to their supporters by behaving in masculine ways, gender stereotypes can also affect the behavior of women in leadership positions because adversaries view female leaders through the lens of gender stereotypes. Gender stereotypes that portray women as less willing to use force might invite challenges from foreign governments, who expect they will be able to extract large concession from female leaders. Indeed, this is what Dube and Harish (2020) propose in their study of European queens, who may have been perceived as easy targets of attack by virtue of being women. This perception could have resulted in them participating in more wars by encouraging aggressive behavior by other monarchs. Using the first-born male and sister as instruments, Dube and Harish find that polities ruled by queens were 27% more likely to participate in interstate conflicts compared to polities ruled by kings, thereby showing that societies ruled by queens experienced more inter-state war.

Similarly, Powell, and Mukazhanova-Powell (2019) suggest that male leaders, in particular, do not want to back down or lose a conflict to a female leader, since female leaders are perceived as especially weak. This means that male leaders may increase their resolve when they face a female adversary; they tend to view the costs of war as smaller (or the value of the prize as larger) when bargaining with female leaders. Post and Sen (2020) find that when female leaders threaten and/or initiate a dispute, leaders in the other state are more likely to discount the threat as a bluff and reciprocate hostile action. Thus, female leaders may not behave more aggressively in order to demonstrate to a domestic audience that they are up to the task of leading; rather, the biased perception of their opponents alone can make disputes more likely to escalate to conflict (2020).

The logic of bargaining models suggests other ways that opponents' perceptions of women can increase the likelihood of conflict (see for example, Reiter and Wolford 2021). Opponents may perceive women as easy targets because they expect women to be more sensitive to the costs of war (women are less willing to fight) or because they overestimate their chances of winning conflicts against a female leader (women are less capable of fighting). Either perception, if wrong (on average), can result in a kind of information problem. If opponents view women as less willing to fight, the perceived range of mutually acceptable agreements will expand to include those that are more favorable to the opponent, and opponents will be incentivized to make larger demands. The other possibility, that opponents view women as less capable of fighting in the event of a conflict, has a similar effect: the bargaining range shifts in favor of the opponent, which also leads to larger demands. This means that an opponent who holds either or both perceptions is more likely to threaten force to change the status quo and to demand larger concessions. If their perceptions turn out to be wrong, these demands make conflict more likely.[12]

Though arguments about the effects of gender stereotypes on political violence tend to focus on international conflict, similar dynamics to those just described are possible in the context of disputes with domestic opponents. If women are perceived as systematically less credible on matters of security, there is no reason to expect that these perceptions only affect their behavior, and the behavior of those with which they interact, in disputes with foreign governments. Women will feel no less of a need to demonstrate a willingness to use force, or "competence," in intrastate disputes. Domestic audiences are

108 THE STATUS OF WOMEN AND POLITICAL VIOLENCE

likely to evaluate men and women differently in their interactions with dissident or rebel groups. Additionally, domestic opponents may perceive women leaders, or governments with a relatively large number of women, as more willing to make concessions than male-dominated governments. This could lead to more belligerent behavior by groups who have mobilized to pressure the government. In short, gender stereotypes may affect any political interaction where violent conflict is a possibility.

In addition to using bargaining models to analyze civil conflict (Walter 1997, 2009; Salehyan 2007; Thyne 2012), conflict researches have begun using them to analyze terror attacks by dissidents, which can be usefully understood as the result of coercive bargaining between governments and dissident groups (Kydd and Walter 2006). This suggests that the logic outlined here applies to these forms of violence. If female leaders, or governments with a non-trivial number of women, are under pressure to exhibit "toughness" in interactions with domestic groups, they will be less willing to accommodate demands and more likely to use a forceful approach that could result in human rights abuses and armed conflict and could provoke a violent response from dissident groups. It is also possible that domestic opponents will assume that governments that include women tend to have a larger perceived cost for conflict and will therefore make larger demands that are likely to result in conflict. This reasoning would also apply to governments whose selectorate includes a large number of women, as dissident or rebel groups might infer a high cost of conflict from the composition of the selectorate.

Arguments about perceptions of women thus have implications for civil conflict, state violence, and dissident violence, in addition to international conflict. This reasoning suggests the opposite of H1.1a, H1.2a, H3.3a, and H3.4a. Rather than women's inclusion decreasing the occurrence of these forms of political violence, we should expect inclusion to have a null or even a positive effect on the onset of interstate war, intrastate war, terrorism, and state violence. Thus, we offer the following hypotheses as well:

H3.1b: The probability of interstate conflict initiation increases as women's inclusion in public spaces generally, and political spaces specifically, increases.

H3.2b: The probability of civil conflict increases as women's inclusion in public spaces generally, and political spaces specifically, increases.

H3.3b: The frequency of dissident terror attacks increases as women's inclusion in public spaces generally, and political spaces specifically, increases.

H3.4b: State violence increases as women's inclusion in public spaces generally, and political spaces specifically, increases.

Does Women's Inclusion Affect Levels of Political Violence? Testing the Hypotheses

We now move to testing the aforementioned hypotheses using the scale that we developed at the beginning of the chapter. We examine and summarize the statistical results concerning women's inclusion and political violence and discuss their implications. Figure 3.6 displays the coefficient estimates for the women's inclusion and women's political inclusion variables from regression models using each of the measures of political violence discussed in Chapter 2.[13] It shows coefficient estimates from models that exclude the control variables (but include random effects for country and, in the case of conflict and war onset, a time counter) as well as estimates from models with all of the control variables included.[14]

Our analysis as summarized in Figure 3.6 provides little quantitative support for the claim that women's inclusion in public spaces, and in political spaces in particular, has a statistical effect on peace and conflict outcomes. Recall that one set of explanations predicts more peaceful outcomes as women's (political) inclusion increases, while the other predicts more conflictual outcomes as inclusion increases. We find little evidence that is consistent with either prediction. In most cases (23 out of 28 models) the coefficients for inclusion and political inclusion are statistically insignificant. In the case of conflict onset, women's inclusion is negative and statistically significant, but only in the absence of control variables. For only two outcomes are the estimates significant while including control variables: terror attacks decrease as women's political inclusion increases,[15] and state violence *increases* as women's inclusion in public spaces increases.[16] Thus, we find more support for H3.3a (inclusion decreases terror attacks) and H3.4b (inclusion increases state violence) than any other hypothesis in this chapter, though we note that the evidence in favor of H3.4b is not entirely consistent with any of the theories we discuss here, as we explain later.

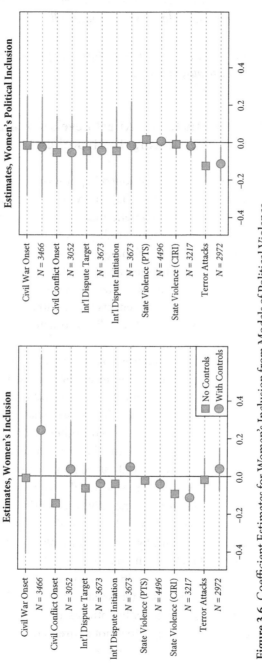

Figure 3.6 Coefficient Estimates for Women's Inclusion from Models of Political Violence

Before discussing the results for terror attacks and state violence, we address the null findings that characterize most of our models. There are several possible explanations for these findings. First, several arguments that expect women's inclusion to be conducive to peace also assume that women are systematically different from men in their support for the use of force and violence in politics. One possibility is that the microfoundational assumption underpinning these arguments is simply incorrect. There may in fact be significant overlap in women and men's dispositions toward the use of force. That is, the normal distributions shown in Figure 3.5 may be indistinguishable, so that in most contexts a randomly selected woman would be just as likely as a randomly selected man to express support for uses of force. As discussed, a number of studies find evidence of differences between men and women's attitudes toward the use of violence in political disputes (Barnhart et al. 2020; Barnhart and Treger 2023), but these studies also suggest that men and women's individual preferences are contingent and so cannot be assumed to be constant across time and place. It may be that in the places most prone to conflict, the dispositions of men and women are more likely to be indistinguishable. Contexts which are prone to widespread violence might theoretically produce socialized preferences within an entire population that are systematically different from those within peaceful contexts. Though some public opinion studies have been conducted in places where violent conflict is at least occasionally a fact of life, subjects are typically responding to questions about hypothetical foreign policy scenarios. As research on conflict recurrence and interstate "rivalry" has demonstrated, actual violent conflicts tend to take place within/between a limited and familiar set of countries. In a setting where the risk of actual conflict is perpetually heightened, there may be no difference between the way women and men view the use of force. Indeed, there is evidence that support for the use of violence is conditioned by features of the underlying dispute itself, such as its length and salience to the public (Ben-Shitrit, Elad-Strenger, and Hirsch-Hoefler, 2017).[17]

Second, concerning the diversity in experiences mechanism specifically, it is possible that women's inclusion is not strongly correlated with actual diversity in people's life experiences. Recall that the argument concerning this mechanism is that a more diverse set of people leads, on average, to more creative and varied approaches to conflict resolution, which in turn makes attempts at resolution more successful. Applied to women as an undifferentiated mass, this argument overlooks that fact that "women" is a broad category that includes a range of societal groups (classes, ethnicities, castes, etc.)

112 THE STATUS OF WOMEN AND POLITICAL VIOLENCE

who may or may not be represented even as more women are included in public spaces. Indeed, many women who have leadership positions in politics have (male) family members who have histories of serving in politics as well.[18] Many female heads of state, for example, are women from family dynasties. Thus, there just may not be diversity at the elite, decision-making level. Given that inequities between women exist in every country,[19] there is likely more homogeneity in the groups of women who gain access to power and influence than this argument assumes. As such, simply including more women may or may not lead to much variation in conflict resolution strategies.

Third, the idea that women's dispositions toward conflict or negotiation style makes peace more likely relies (perhaps implicitly) on the assumption that women have reached parity with men in their physical presence as well as their influence. If reaching some numeric threshold is necessary to make a difference, it may be that this threshold is rarely met, perhaps because presence only translates into influence at a ratio that is higher than parity. It is possible that the null results for H3.1a, H3.1b, H3.1c, and H3.1d, and the lack of support for the sex specific preferences and diversity in experiences theories are due to an insufficient number of women in public spaces, particularly in leadership positions. Authors that posit a "critical mass" usually place the threshold for women in decision-making roles at 33% or 50%, numbers not reached in the vast majority of societies.[20] Notably, research suggests that under majority rule decision-making something close to parity (50%) is required for equal participation (Karpowitz, Mendelberg, and Shaker 2012). As such, women may simply not have enough power to implement policy changes that are more pacific. Additionally, even when there is a "critical mass," women may not be able to meaningfully change policies because of the hierarchies based on gender and race that exist in many public spaces (Hawkesworth 2003). As mentioned by Arat (2015), just because women are visible in public spaces does not mean they wield power in those spaces.[21] The inclusion of women may set them up for failure or lead to a "glass cliff" (Dahlerup 2017, 109).[22] Institutions may lack "women's machinery" or special units charged with promoting women's status, including offices, commissions, agencies, ministries, committees, secretaries, or advisors for the status of women (Stetson, Mazur, and Mcbride 1995; Chappell 2002). Without structural changes to the environment in which women are included, it becomes more challenging for women to have a impact on policies.

WOMEN'S INCLUSION AND POLITICAL VIOLENCE   113

A fourth possibility is suggested by the mechanisms behind the hypothesis that women's inclusion will make conflict more likely, which are not mutually exclusive. The logic of this hypothesis suggests that even if there are systematic differences between men and women regarding their support for violence, the inclusion of women in public spaces may not translate into peaceful outcomes in the aggregate. Women (and men) in politics or the security sector are likely to have preferences that differ systematically from those of the general public. As discussed in this chapter, there are good reasons to expect, and evidence to support the claim, that women in public spaces face pressure to perform masculinity in the interest of professional success. This raises the possibility of a sorting mechanism that would obviate the effect of peaceful preferences among women, since women from the more belligerent end of the distribution would be more likely to end up in positions of political power. That is, the "right" women may lack access to power for a variety of institutional and structural reasons.

Further, organizational culture can shape how men and women behave, regardless of their initial, underlying attitudes about the use of force (Rabe-Hemp 2009; Hawkesworth 2003). A masculinized environment or culture in the workspace can put pressure on women to demonstrate that they belong, and as a result they often behave in a "masculine" way in order to fit in. As such, once women begin to adopt the prevalent norms of the organization, they may be just as inclined as men to advocate for the use of violence in political disputes. This could also negate the effect of women's preferences, even if they are more peaceful on average. Yet another possible mechanism along these lines is that people are more likely to behave belligerently toward women, which could also cause women to behave aggressively even if they are typically inclined toward peaceful dispute settlement. In sum, less peaceful women may be overrepresented in public spaces, women may become less peaceful in response to organizational/institutional norms, or women may be more frequent targets of aggressive behavior and respond in kind. Any of these could result in women in public spaces behaving more aggressively than the average woman in the larger population, whether or not women in the larger population tend to be more peaceful than men.

All these possibilities raise doubts about the tendency of policies that promote women's inclusion *in isolation* to reduce societal conflict. Rather, the analysis suggests that, if women's inclusion can facilitate peace, it must be accompanied by structural reforms that promote *gender equality as defined in this book's* Introduction. This will ensure that gender stereotypes do not guide decisions; that structures enable women to make a difference in policy outcomes; and that those with "truly diverse" preferences and experiences have access to power.

Notably, we found no evidence that perceptional stereotypes have *any* influence on interstate conflict, despite the fact that this argument has gained the most traction in research on the topic. Arguments about stereotypes suggest that people perceive women to be weak and easily coerced and that this perception causes people to behave more aggressively toward women in political disputes, causing some female leaders to reciprocate aggression in order to demonstrate strength and counter the perception of weakness (Post and Sen 2020; Powell and Mukazhanova-Powell 2019; Schramm and Stark 2020; Schwartz and Blair 2020). Our analysis suggests that countries with high levels of women's political inclusion are no more likely to be targeted in fatal interstate disputes, nor are they more likely to initiate disputes in order to communicate strength. However, in this context it may be necessary to examine multiple stages of an interaction, as governments with female leadership may behave aggressively only once a dispute is initiated (Post and Sen 2020). There is also some evidence that states with male leaders in particular, rather than all states (on average), behave more aggressively toward states with female leadership (Dube and Harish 2020), though we would add that the typical state is characterized by predominately male political leadership.

In contrast to a lack of results for women's inclusion in public spaces generally, we do find that women's *political* inclusion has a negative and significant coefficient in the model of terror attacks. In the other models the estimates for this variable are insignificant and close to 0, though they generally have the sign one would expect to observe based on the first set of hypotheses, which associate women's inclusion with peace. The result for political inclusion indicates that countries in which more women are included in political spaces tend to have fewer domestic terror attacks. One potential explanation for this finding is that women's inclusion leads dissident groups to expect a loss of legitimacy if they adopt terror tactics (Huber 2019). The fact that terror attacks are negatively related to political inclusion, but not inclusion in public spaces generally, suggests that the composition of the government affects this expectation more strongly than the composition of the selectorate (the coefficient for women's inclusion in all public spaces is actually positive).

Interestingly, women's political inclusion is negatively related to terror attacks, but not intrastate conflict. This is consistent with explanations that view inclusion as something that decreases opportunities for conflict rather than as something that keeps conflictual interactions from escalating to large-scale, organized violence. The argument that inclusion produces policies that enhance social welfare, as well as social capacity arguments, posit this kind of relationship between inclusion and violence. Armed conflict requires a relatively large group of people to mobilize against the state. The onset of conflict indicates the presence of a large group with intense grievances and a high capacity for collective action. It is possible that women's political inclusion makes it less likely that this mobilization threshold is crossed (because of enhanced social capacity and/or policies that produce fewer or less intense grievances), but that once it is crossed political inclusion has no effect on the onset of conflict. This could explain why political inclusion is negatively associated with terror attacks, which typically involve relatively few participants and low levels of violence, but not armed conflict between the state and rebel groups.

More difficult to explain is the positive relationship between women's inclusion and state violence. It is tempting to attribute this finding to gender stereotypes that generate pressure on women to "act tough" toward domestic groups that challenge the state and its policies. However, this result only holds for *women's inclusion in public spaces* generally. We find no evidence that *political* inclusion affects state violence. The stereotype argument is about how perceptions of women affect the behavior of women as political decision makers, and so cannot explain why general inclusion would put more pressure on the state to behave aggressively toward dissidents than political inclusion.[23]

One potential explanation for this puzzling result draws on research by Berry (2018), who finds that men may attempt to reassert control through violence as women's inclusion in public spaces increases. Berry focuses on post-conflict societies where women's roles have changed as a result of conflict, but the proximate cause of violence is inclusion, which of course can increase in the absence of conflict. This points to one reason we might observe increases in repression with more women's inclusion: male leaders may engage in more repression when they see dramatic change in sex composition in spaces that were previously dominated by men.[24] Research on repression and "youth bulges" provides some evidence that demographic changes are related to state violence (Nordås and Davenport 2013; Davenport and Appel 2022). The idea is that the anticipation of dissent is due to a relatively large number of young people/women, which leads to preemptive repression. While changes in sex composition should not lead a government to expect more dissent, it may cause men to perceive that their societal status is threatened, which may cause them to view any dissent they observe as more threatening. We explore this possibility more in the book's Conclusion.

Indeed, we suspect that (typically) male-dominated governments may view acts of dissent and resistance as more threatening as women's inclusion increases. This heightened perception of threat is driven by fear of the loss of status, privilege, and power. As women's presence in public spaces grows, so does the general perception (among men) that men are "losing out." As women are given more opportunities and start to achieve as much or more than men in school and in professional life, and are less likely to perform unpaid domestic work, including childcare, men may begin to feel that opportunities for success and recognition are being unfairly taken away from them (Mutz 2018, Clark, Khoban, and Zucker 2022). Feelings of loss and even humiliation may lead to aggressive behavior, which at the individual level may manifest as violence against women. Among those who are in government or otherwise have some control over the machinery of the state, these feelings may lead to aggression and violence toward groups who are (perceived to be) challenging their authority. Such violence may target dissidents and also non-dominant social groups who are viewed as threatening to social order. This could explain why women's political inclusion does not have a positive relationship with state violence; women have no reason to feel threatened by their own inclusion, so women who occupy positions of political power have no reason to respond more aggressively to challenges to their authority.

Moreover, as women are integrated into public spaces, they feel more comfortable engaging in contentious politics (e.g. Afghan women likely felt more comfortable protesting in the streets when the Taliban did not ban them from public spaces.). This means that protest activities have the potential to grow as more people join them, increasing opportunities for the state to repress such groups. In line with this argument, as more women participate in public spaces, women become key actors in social movements. Social movements with more women's participation are more successful (Chenoweth and Marks 2022). Some states could use pre-emptive repression as a strategy to prevent social movements from growing as they see women's participation in the public sphere grow.

Conclusion

Will more "Jacinda Arderns" reduce global political violence? The answer from this chapter is not necessarily. Our analysis provides no reason to expect that policies in more inclusive societies will be any different from the policies of Indira Gandhi, Golda Meir, or Margaret Thatcher. Based on evidence from this chapter, any dampening effect that women's inclusion has on political violence is limited at best. Our sole finding to support the claim that inclusion leads to peace is that women's political inclusion is associated with fewer terror attacks.

The behavior of female leaders such as Indira Gandhi, Golda Meir, and Margaret Thatcher may not be anomalous. That is, many women may simply not be more peaceful than men, particularly in places that are prone to conflict for other, underlying reasons. The political career of Indira Gandhi is illustrative, as it was characterized by a number of violent episodes. In addition to adopting a hawkish foreign policy, Gandhi became one of the more repressive rulers of India (Prakash 2019). Her tenure ended with her assassination, which itself was a response to the Indian military's assault on Sikh militants inside the Golden Temple in Punjab. Since independence, the Indian government has been involved in a relatively large number of international conflicts, as well as domestic conflicts with various insurgent groups, which have resulted primarily, though not entirely, from its hostile relationship with Pakistan. Given this history and context, perhaps it should not be surprising that female leadership did not cause a sudden shift toward more peaceful politics. It is possible that attitudes toward violence are strongly conditioned by its occurrence and duration (Ben-Shitrit, Elad-Strenger, and Hirsch-Hoefler, 2017), as well as with the underlying conditions that tend to precede conflict, so that in conflict-prone countries there is no discernible gap between the attitudes of men and women.

Moreover, few women accompanied Indira Gandhi, Golda Meir, and Margaret Thatcher in their roles as political leaders. They were surrounded by men and situated in masculine institutions. Lacking a "critical mass" of women, and lacking institutional structures that could translate their physical presence into decisive influence, they did not have the support to pursue policies more conducive to peace.

Finally, it is possible that Indira Gandhi, Golda Meir, and Margaret Thatcher were not the "right" women for the job. They mostly came from political dynasties and/or were all privileged in certain respects. Indira Gandhi came from a political dynasty. Golda Meir spent a large part of her life in the United States, of which she was a naturalized citizen. Margaret Thatcher was an Oxford-educated, White woman. Thus, they represented the views of particular groups of women. Perhaps their dispositions were atypically aggressive compared to other women, meaning their preferences may have fallen to the right side of the distribution in Figure 3.5. Or perhaps, because their experiences reflected those of women in dominant social groups, they were not so different from those around them as to lead to more innovative approaches to conflict resolution.

At the same time, perhaps female politicians could implement policies that prevent terrorist attacks. It is possible that Jacinda Ardern's socio-economic policies addressed grievances held by different groups such that resorting to violence was not necessary. She might have implemented policies that addressed or prevented some of the grievances that can become motives for political violence, including those that create a more equitable distribution of resources. Yet, the presence of more women in public spaces could be threatening to men. Jacinda Ardern eventually left her political career citing threats to her life (McClure 2023). Those who feel threatened could engage in violent protest, with the state cracking down. In New Zealand, the police cracked down on violent protest over Covid-19 policies, which included anti-woman rhetoric.[25]

Despite our ambiguous findings, conclude with a strong warning about this chapter. While we do not find overwhelming evidence that violence decreases as women's inclusion increases, we wish to strongly emphasize that this is not a good reason to view women's inclusion as a less desirable goal. Whether or not women's inclusion makes politics more peaceful, or increases economic productivity, or trade volume, or produces some other measurable aggregate gain, is a separate question from whether it is normatively desirable. Moreover, the same question is rarely asked of men. Does the inclusion of men in politics lead to peace, increase economic productivity or trade volume, or produce some other measurable aggregate gain? Our null results from this chapter indicate that it does not. The inclusion of men does not lead to a pacifying effect on state behavior. Yet, we rarely question whether men should be in positions of power or feel the need to justify their inclusion by demonstrating that it leads to desirable societal outcomes. By implicitly arguing that women must serve some purpose in exchange for their inclusion, we risk aiding in the same discrimination that prevents their inclusion in the first place. Women's inclusion must be accompanied by structural and institutional change with respect to gender equality if it is to have any discernible impact on political violence. We highlight some suggestions along these lines in the Conclusion.

4

Women's Rights and Political Violence

Introduction

During her confirmation hearing to become secretary of state, Hillary Clinton told the US Senate Foreign Relations Committee in no uncertain terms, "I want to pledge to you that as secretary of state I view [women's] issues as central to our foreign policy, not as adjunct or auxiliary or in any way lesser than all of the other issues that we have to confront" (Zenko 2015). This statement was based on the understanding that women's rights are integral to peaceful states and stability. Hillary Clinton's tenure as secretary of state reflected her rhetoric. She made women's rights the central focus of foreign policy. This included a four-year plan for the State Department and USAID related to women and girls, the adoption of the US National Action Plan for UN Security Council Resolution 1325, the creation of the position of US Ambassador-at-Large for Global Women's Issues, and the issuance of "Policy Guideline Advancing Gender Equality and Promoting the Status of Women and Girls," among many other initiatives and policies. Yet, at the same time that she implemented these policies and initiatives, she was also one of the more hawkish members of the cabinet. She actively lobbied for President Obama to intervene in Libya in 2011, and she pressed for the United States to funnel arms to rebel groups in Syria's civil war. Thus, on one hand, she championed women's rights and inclusion abroad, but on the other hand, she also advocated for the use of force to achieve policy goals.

The United States was not the only country in the 2000s and 2010s to adopt a women-centered foreign policy. In 2015, Sweden's foreign minister Margot Wallström announced that the government would be adopting a "feminist foreign policy" (Government Offices of Sweden 2014). This meant promoting gender equality and human rights nationally and internationally. In responding to the frequently asked question of exactly what a feminist foreign policy entails, Wallström has referred to a feminist toolbox, which consists of three Rs: Representation, Rights, and Reallocation (Aggestam and Bergman-Rosamond 2016). Yet while Sweden promoted

Positioning Women in Conflict Studies. Sabrina Karim and Daniel W. Hill, Jr., Oxford University Press.
© Oxford University Press 2024. DOI: 10.1093/9780197757970.003.0005

women's rights abroad, it continued to export arms abroad as well, including some to the ongoing conflict in Yemen (Sundström and Elgström 2020; Vucetic 2018). This led to a public debate in Sweden about whether arms sales and feminism can co-exist. In 2022, the Swedish government officially abandoned their feminist foreign policy, with Foreign Minister Tobias Billström stating that, "gender equality is a fundamental value in Sweden and also for this government, but we're not going to continue with a feminist foreign policy because the label obscures the fact the Swedish foreign policy must be based on Swedish values and Swedish interests" (Walfridsson 2022, 1). The promotion of women rights via Sweden's foreign policy was short lived.

These examples suggest that policymakers value women's rights on normative grounds but also view them as something that can be used instrumentally to promote peace and political stability. This view begs the questions of whether and how women's rights are related to political violence at the societal level. To answer these questions, this chapter begins by carefully conceptualizing women's rights and provides a new measure of that concept. The bulk of the chapter is then devoted to theorizing about how women's rights are linked to political violence. The last part of the chapter examines available evidence to determine if there is a clear connection between women's rights and various forms of political violence. We find that there is a link between women's rights and lower levels of state violence, and that this relationship grows stronger as there are more women's rights organizations in a country. We conclude the chapter with some reflections about the implications of this finding.

Conceptualizing Women's Rights

The concept of women's rights is firmly situated in the "rights" literature that focuses on law and legal philosophy. Rights are entitlements to perform certain actions and also obligations to refrain from actions that interfere with the rights of others. Holding a right means that one is free in one or more of a variety of senses. Having a right often entails a *freedom to* act in certain ways or freedom from undesirable actions or states (Wenar 2020). As such, a person's rights amounts to an obligation on the part of others to treat them in a certain way. Rights determine what is or is not permissible, and they structure governments, the content of laws, and shape morality (Wenar

2020). Moreover, there is often a connotation of individualism embedded in the rights framework (Dahlerup 2017, 9). Individual rights are sometimes in contention with a collective goal. For example, the right for individuals to own property runs contrary to communal practices of land ownership that are meant to benefit the collective over the individual.

After World War II, the world embraced "human rights," as a concept, with the UN adopting the Universal Declaration of Human Rights (UDHR) in 1948 (UN General Assembly 1948). The UDHR lists thirty "rights and freedoms" that cover a wide range of issues including equality under the law, non-discrimination, civil and political rights, the right to work, as well as rights to basic necessities, healthcare, and education. The declaration is an ambitious document but was never given the status of a treaty, so signatories do not assume any formal obligation to implement its provisions. It took nearly twenty years for UN delegates to draft binding treaties containing provisions that corresponded to the rights and freedoms outlined in the UDHR and that were acceptable to a majority of member states. In 1966 the General Assembly adopted the International Covenant on Economic, Social, and Cultural Rights (CESCR) and the International Covenant on Civil and Political Rights (CCPR), both of which received the requisite number of ratifications to enter into force into 1976. Together with the UDHR, these documents are sometimes referred to as the "international bill of human rights."

These three documents collectively form the foundation of modern international human rights law, and yet they make scant mention of issues related to women. The preamble to the UDHR declares that member states have "faith in the equal rights of men and women," but the only other mention of women is in the first clause of Article 16, which says that men and women have the right to marry and have a family. All three texts include broad provisions declaring that the rights and freedoms they outline are to be applied equally to all individuals, regardless of their "race, colour, sex, language, religion, political or other opinion, national or social origin, property, birth or other status." The CCPR requires states to prohibit legal discrimination on the basis of these same individual characteristics and bans the execution of pregnant women. The CESCR is the most specific of the three regarding equality between men and women. It contains a provision in Article 7 whose sole purpose is to explicitly acknowledge that women and men have equal economic, social, and cultural rights as defined by the convention: "Fair wages and equal remuneration for work of equal value without distinction of any

WOMEN'S RIGHTS AND POLITICAL VIOLENCE   123

kind, in particular women being guaranteed conditions of work not inferior to those enjoyed by men, with equal pay for equal work."

It was not until the 1970s that women's rights became central to the UN treaty regime. The decade of the woman from 1976 to 1985, as well as the four UN World Women's Conferences between 1975 and 1995 held in Mexico City (1975), Copenhagen (1980), Nairobi (1985), and Beijing (1995), established the link between women and rights. These conferences sought to use the human rights framework to advocate for the rights of women (Friedman 1995). The goal was to get the international community to understand women's rights as integral to human rights.

The efforts of women's groups all around the world led to several international achievements related to the advancement of the women's rights agenda. In 1979, the UN General Assembly adopted the Convention on the Elimination of All Forms of Discrimination Against Women (CEDAW), which articulates (in Articles 1 and 2) a set of norms that prohibit all forms of discrimination, against all groups of women, in all spheres of life. It has since been ratified by 188 UN member states, which means it has been nearly unanimously adopted.[1] CEDAW is known as the women's rights treaty because it identifies a comprehensive list of women's interests in equality across a wide range of areas, including political rights, education, employment, economics, foreign policy, health, rural life, and marriage and family life (Baldez 2011, 2014). Tripp (2019, 40) defines women's rights as the legislation and constitutional changes that are fought for and supported by women's organizations. Taking a (legal) positivist view, the codified rules that exist in domestic and international law are what constitute "rights."

The decision to convene the Fourth United Nations Conference on Women (FWCW) was taken after a meeting of the Commission on the Status of Women in 1990 concluded that little progress had been made in advancing the status of women across the world since the end of the United Nations Decade for Women (1976–1985) and since the adoption of CEDAW by the General Assembly. The conference, held in Beijing, led to the "Beijing Declaration," an affirmation of the human rights of women, including rights to education, health, and freedom from violence, and the exercise of citizenship in all its manifestations. The Platform for Action outlines action for the human rights of women in twelve interrelated critical areas, from the right to education to freedom from poverty and violence. The success of CEDAW and the Beijing Declaration rests on decades of women's organizing both informally and at the UN level (Bunch and Fried 1996).

124   THE STATUS OF WOMEN AND POLITICAL VIOLENCE

This history of the term "women's rights" shows us that the origins of the concept are largely international and legal. As such, the term entered political science literature largely through IR scholarship. The most commonly used dataset to measure women's rights in IR is the CIRI Human Rights Data Project: the scholars who created it rely largely on CEDAW to define women's rights (Cingranelli, Richards, and Clay 2014).[2] The text of CEDAW at various points speaks of women's rights in the "political, social, economic, and cultural fields." Accordingly, CIRI's definition of women's rights entails rights to legal protection and equal treatment in the political, economic, and social spheres, and the dataset has separate measures of each (401–403).

Based on academic and policy research on women's rights, the concept is defined in a way that captures policies and laws in which women's entitlements or freedoms are enshrined. They are codified commitments to addressing the needs of women. Realizing them typically involves changes to domestic or international law or policy documents. These policies are aimed at giving women more choice and freedom in their lives (Bunch 1990; Kerr 1993). Box 4.1 captures the dimensions of women's rights. (Supra)governmental legal or policy codification refers to the laws, regulations, and policies that governments or international actors adopt. These laws are about women's *freedom to act* in certain ways or freedom from undesirable actions or states. Importantly, the concept does not capture the actual condition of women on the ground, but rather the legal and policy frameworks available for their protection. Measures of women's rights should thus capture the legal structures in place to protect women, whether domestic or international. Relevant international law includes key treaties and resolutions such as CEDAW and UNSCR 1325 National Action Plans.

To create classical subtypes under the root concept of women's rights, we could add qualifiers, such as the commonly used labels "political," "economic,"

Box 4.1 Characteristics of Women's Rights

1) pertinent to those that biologically identify as girls or women
2) (supra)governmental legal or policy codification
3) a *freedom to* act in certain ways or freedom from undesirable actions or states

WOMEN'S RIGHTS AND POLITICAL VIOLENCE   125

or "social." This aligns with the way women's rights are discussed in the text of CEDAW, and the way they are disaggregated in the CIRI Human Rights Data Project, which has resulted in women's rights being disaggregated this way in many analyses in IR research (Cingranelli and Richards 2010, 401, 424).

Recent scholarship on women's rights demonstrates that the concept of women's rights can be usefully disaggregated along two other dimensions. Htun and Weldon (2018) suggest that "women's rights" is a subcategory of gender justice and sex equality. Women's rights are legitimate claims for greater parity in the well-being, life chances, and opportunities of women and men. Advancing women's rights requires changes in many spheres of life such as politics, the family, the market, and civil society, and requires reimagining our communities and nations as more inclusive and egalitarian.[3] Htun and Weldon reconceptualize women's rights by distinguishing between policies that change prevailing patterns of social organization and those that do not. Social organization is defined along two dimensions: (1) a class-status dimension that pertains to state-market relationships, questions of socio-economic redistribution, and the social and legal positions of some subset of women defined by status, and (2) a doctrinal/non-doctrinal dimension pertaining to the religious doctrine, cultural traditions, or sacred discourse of major social groups. Laws and policies are then classified according to whether they challenge the status quo as it relates to women's class or status and also according to whether they challenge prevailing religious, cultural, or discursive practices. Thus, we can define several more classical subtypes of women's rights: class-based women's rights (e.g. laws/polices about maternal leave, public funding for abortion), status-based women's rights (e.g. laws/policies about violence against women, family law), non-doctrinal women's rights (e.g. laws/policies about quotas, public funding, or childcare), and doctrinal women's rights (e.g. laws/policies about abortion) (9).

Importantly, the concept of women's rights does not include the degree to which legal rules are implemented or enforced. If implementation or enforcement of women's rights is considered, this amounts to adding a fourth dimension and thus the creation of another classical subtype. The concept "enforcement of women's rights" includes an additional dimension that captures the extent of implementation of the policy and/or legal means and processes that exist to address and redress violations of the right in question. Htun and Weldon (2018), for example, measure women's rights in terms of government laws and policies in different domains including violence against women, family law, equality in the workplace, family leave, childcare,

126　THE STATUS OF WOMEN AND POLITICAL VIOLENCE

the legality of abortion, and reproductive rights in general. They do not code the implementation of these laws, nor their enforcement, but focus strictly on policy adoption. This approach makes it possible to examine the relationship between legal/policy adoption and actual conditions on the ground since it does not combine them into a single concept.

Measuring Women's Rights

We develop a latent measure of women's rights, meaning *institutionalized* legal protection for women. For this measurement model we use indicators that cover a wide range of legal protections, including those designed to promote women's inclusion in the "public sphere" (e.g. suffrage, property rights), laws designed to protect women from harm (e.g. legislation that criminalizes various forms of domestic violence), legislation related to basic citizenship rights (e.g. getting a passport), and protection in the workplace (e.g. laws related to equal pay and maternity leave benefits). Most of these indicators are taken from the World Bank and V-Dem; all are listed in Table 4.1.

As with the women's inclusion model, the variables for the women's rights model are all continuous or binary, so we use the same Bayesian mixed factor analysis model as in Chapter 3.[4] Item parameter estimates from the rights model are shown in Figure 4.1. The figure shows that the items generally correlate with the latent variable as expected. All of the V-Dem variables are positively related to the latent variable and none of the credible intervals contain 0. The β_j parameters for the V-Dem items generally suggest a strong relationship between these indicators and the latent rights variable.[5]

The β parameters for the binary items are generally positive as we would expect, which indicates that the probability the item equals 1 increases, in some cases sharply, as women's rights increase. The credible intervals for 5 of the 62 items contain 0.[6] β estimates are negative for two items: whether there is a clause in the constitution related to non-discrimination based on sex, and whether women are required to obey their husbands by law. It is intuitive that the estimate for the latter is negative: as legal protection for women's rights increases these laws are less likely to exist.[7] It is less intuitive that the estimate for constitutional provisions is negative, but this could indicate that such provisions are seen as unnecessary in countries where many legislative provisions already exist to protect women's rights.

WOMEN'S RIGHTS AND POLITICAL VIOLENCE   127

Table 4.1 Indicators for Rights Model

Source	Variable
World Bank	Equal Pay
	No Discrimination in Hiring
	No Child Marriage
	Domestic Violence Legislation
	Marital Rape Criminalized
	Sexual Harassment Legislation
	Equal Property Rights in Marriage
	Married Women Must Obey Husband
	Married Women Can Have ID
	Non-discrimination in Constitution
	Unmarried Woman Can Have Passport
	Married Woman Can Have Passport
	Unmarried Woman Can Leave Country
	Married Woman Can Leave Country
	Married Woman Can Leave Home
	Married Woman Can Have a Job
	Married Woman Can Sign Contract
	Married Woman Can Register Business
	Married Woman Can Open Bank Account
	Married Woman Can Choose Where to Live
	Unmarried Woman Can Give Children Citizenship
	Married Woman Can Give Children Citizenship
	Unmarried Woman Can Be Head of Household
	Married Woman Can Be Head of Household
	Married Woman Can Give Citizenship to Husband
	Married Couples Share Responsibility for Expenses
	Unmarried Women Have Property Rights
	Sons and Daughters Have Equal Inheritance Rights
	Female and Male Spouses Have Equal Inheritance Rights
	Women's Testimony Treated Equally
	No Dismissal of Pregnant Workers
	Mothers Get Same Position after Leave
	Employers Must Give Nursing Breaks
	Women Can Work Night Hours
	Women Can Have Same Jobs as Men
	Unmarried Women Can Get ID

Continued

Table 4.1 *Continued*

Source	Variable
	Valuation of Unpaid Work
	Women Can Work Hazardous Jobs
	Women Can Have Jobs Deemed Immoral
	Women Can Have Jobs Deemed Arduous
	Domestic Violence Legislation Covers Physical Violence
	Domestic Violence Legislation Covers Sexual Violence
	Domestic Violence Legislation Covers Emotional Violence
	Domestic Violence Legislation Covers Economic Violence
	Domestic Violence Legislation Protects Unmarried
	Special Court for Domestic Violence
	Sexual Harassment Criminalized
	Sexual Harassment Legislation Covers Workplace
	Sexual Harassment in Workplace Criminalized
	Sexual Harassment Legislation Covers School
	Sexual Harassment Legislation Covers Public Places
	Women Can Have Same Occupations as Men
	Women Can Do Same Job-Related Tasks as Men
	Domestic Violence Criminalized
	Domestic Violence Legislation Protects Family
	Domestic Violence Legislation Protects Former Spouses
	Protection Orders for Domestic Violence
	Protection Orders Remove Perpetrator from House
	Protection Orders Prohibit Contact with Victim
	Sexual Harassment Civil Penalties
	Sexual Harassment Civil Penalties Cover Workplace
	Child Marriage Criminalized
V-Dem	Women's Suffrage
	Women's Property Rights
	Women's Access to Justice

Women's Rights and Political Violence

We describe four potential theories that link women's rights to political violence. First, a formal legal framework for protecting women's rights indicates acceptance of liberal norms more generally, including the non-violent settlement of international political disputes. Second, a formal legal framework for protecting women's rights signals that the state may be open to concessions to different groups. Third, women's rights provide opportunities for women's advocacy groups to serve as watchdogs of state behavior. Fourth, mobilization around women's rights creates pre-existing mobilization networks for women's groups and civil society groups more generally to pressure the state to settle conflicts peacefully.

Women's Rights as Signaling Liberalism

The end of World War II ushered in a new world order; this so-called liberal world order (Ikenberry 2011) is based on a set of enshrined rights, which are generally understood as commitments to republican representative democracy and classic liberal economic rights such as free markets and open trade (Doyle 2005). Ikenberrry (2009) highlights open markets, international institutions, cooperative security, democratic community, progressive change, and collective problem solving as liberal norms. These liberal norms or rights are considered to be desirable qualities among states in the postwar international order (Ikenberry 2012; Simmons 2009). States that adopt them are rewarded by the international community, and those that do not are often punished (Boyce 2013; Hafner-Burton 2008; Hendrix and Wong 2013; Lebovic and Voeten 2009; Simmons 2009). To signal compliance to the international world order, states might adopt international treaties or domestic policies promoting different rights, particularly human [women's] rights.

For much of history, legal codes have worked against women's interests. Hudson, Bowen, and Nielsen (2020, 88) and Hudson et al. (2012: 28) make this case forcefully with respect to the arena of family law. They argue that those who had more physical power were the ones who shaped laws in society. This meant that men created legal systems, including over "family law." Men created laws with respect to adultery as a crime for women but not for men; with the legality of female infanticide, male-on-female domestic violence, and marital rape; with polygyny legal but polyandry proscribed; with divorce easy for men and almost impossible for women. This 'family law' has only been mitigated in certain regions in the last 200 years with women's rights. Indeed, Inglehart and Norris (2003) note that while women's inclusion increased dramatically with economic modernization in the nineteenth and early twentieth centuries, the issue of women's rights did not receive widespread attention until the late twentieth century. Htun and Weldon's (2018)

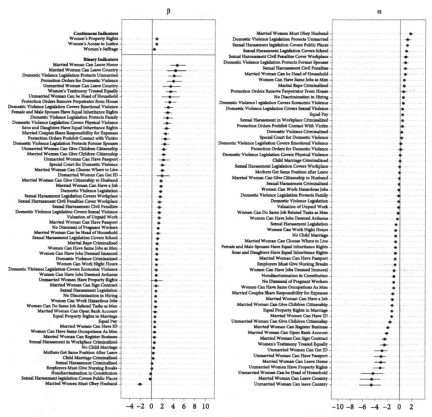

Figure 4.1 Estimates from Measurement Model for Women's Rights

analysis shows that domestic legal frameworks to promote women's rights only started to emerge in the twentieth century, which is consistent with the (brief) account of the development of human rights law presented earlier.

As the international human rights regime gained influence, it began to include women's rights as a part of its domain of concerns. Women's rights entered the international scene through the adoption by the UN General Assembly of CEDAW in 1979. The legal commitments in CEDAW were reinforced during the 1995 Fourth World Conference on Women in Beijing, during which then First Lady Hillary Clinton famously declared, "If there is one message that echoes forth from this conference, it is that human rights are women's rights . . . . And women's rights are human rights" (Clinton 1995). In 2000, the UN Security Council passed Resolution 1325, which institutionalized the WPS agenda at the international level. Thus, with these prominent international instruments, women's rights became an important liberal norm.

Though many states started to adopt women's rights laws domestically and commit to treaties such as CEDAW in the past few decades, Htun and Weldon (2018) argue that there is still substantial variation in both the adoption of laws that protect women's rights and the enforcement of those laws. Implementation and enforcement of women's rights makes adoption of women's rights a more credible signal that a state has sincerely adopted liberal norms, as it forces states to incur costs that demonstrate their commitment. Htun and Weldon (2018, 13) suggest that there are significant costs associated with legal reforms, innovations to criminal and civil justice procedures, changes to procedural rules, public awareness campaigns, and greater monitoring and accountability of officials.

Studies of the effectiveness of formal protection for rights posit several domestic conditions related to the enforcement of such protections. Haglund and Richards (2018) find that, where strong laws are adopted and the judiciary is relatively independent, the enforcement of laws related to gender-based violence in post-conflict environments improves. Strong domestic legal standards are important for enforcement and implementation, which require the provision of formal justice mechanisms, the monitoring of informal justice mechanisms, and the availability of justice services (Ní Aoláin, Haynes, and Cahn 2011, 79). This is consistent with research on human rights protections more generally. Keith, Tate, and Poe (2009) find evidence that the codification of rights protections into constitutional provisions is positively associated with respect for civil and political rights. Consistent with these findings, our indicators suggest that women's rights are positively correlated with women's (political) inclusion and more fluid beliefs about women's gender roles and negatively correlated with harm to women (see Figure 2.5). This suggests that, although there is certainly variation in the degree to which laws are enforced, there is typically more respect for rights where some formal legal framework exists than where none exists, irrespective of other conditions.

In the arena of international law, too, states are generally more likely to assume formal legal obligation when they intend to comply (Chayes and Chayes 1993; Downs, Rocke, and Barsoom 1996; Von Stein 2005). However, states only comply with treaties that require significant policy changes when there exists some mechanism to monitor and punish violations (Downs, Rocke, and Barsoom 1996). Since enforcement is not always a given, states may adopt human rights treaties and laws even when they do not necessarily intend to enforce or implement those rights and laws domestically (Powell and Staton 2009; Simmons 2009). Hathaway (2007) finds that states with

132 THE STATUS OF WOMEN AND POLITICAL VIOLENCE

less democratic institutions will be no less likely to commit to human rights treaties if they have poor human rights records, because there is little prospect that the treaties will be enforced. Hafner-Burton and Tsutsui (2007) find that very abusive states frequently ratify human rights treaties and that their human rights records are no better even long after ratification. Hafner-Burton, Tsutsui, and Meyer (2008) argue that states with poor human rights records tend to sign and ratify human rights treaties at rates similar to those of states with positive records because they provide a way to signal legitimating commitments to world norms at a low cost.

Thus, states may adopt human rights treaties or laws, but not enforce them. However, there are good reasons to believe that the formal adoption of women's rights makes it more likely that conditions for women will improve. With respect to CEDAW, several studies have found that ratification improves respect for women's rights (Simmons 2009; Hill 2010; Lupu 2013; Cole 2013; Englehart and Miller 2014). Simmons's study finds that treaty ratification generally improves human rights practices, but for some treaties conditions only improve in semi-democratic or "anocratic" regimes, and not in consolidated democracies or autocracies (Simmons 2009). However, with respect to CEDAW, ratification is associated with positive outcomes for women regardless of regime type. Thus, ratification of CEDAW seems to be a more sincere signal than ratification of other treaties.

In much the same way that adoption of formal protections for human rights in general has served as a way for countries to signal their commitment to the liberal world order, state adoption of domestic and international law to protect women's rights specifically signals commitment to the prevailing order. The gradual incorporation of women's rights into the stated values of the international community following the adoption of CEDAW and subsequent efforts by the UN means that women's rights now belong on the list of values such as free trade and representative government that are shared by liberal states. Just as many states in the twentieth century have institutionalized different aspects of the liberal world order, they have also (to varying degrees) institutionalized women's rights. When states adopt and implement laws related to women's rights it sends a signal to others that they are willing to accept the prevalent norms of the international community. It demonstrates states' recognition that women's rights exist and places them in a category of countries that are moving toward other international norms such as democratic governance and respect for human rights more broadly. Put another way, the adoption of women's rights signals that a state is trying to be a particular "type" of state: one that adheres to widely recognized norms that many states in the international community deem respectable. In fact, some states may be more likely to adopt women's rights as a signal of liberalism because they are a less threatening signal than actual adoption of democratizing reforms (Bush et al. 2023). Countries that are transitioning toward democracy may not want to fully engage in electoral reforms, but they want acknowledgement and aid from the international community. As such they adopt women's rights—still a liberal norm that signals commitment to a democratic world order but one that is perceived as a less costly option than reforms that would make their political system more competitive and loss of power for the incumbent regime more likely (2023).

States that are firmly embedded in the liberal world order have generally maintained peaceful relations for some time now, as the numerous studies on the "democratic peace" suggest. The reasoning behind the democratic peace is partly about the way political institutions can help states clearly communicate their intentions (Fearon 1994; Schultz 1998, 1999). But a related line of reasoning posits that the spread of democracy entails the emergence of shared norms about the use of force in politics "upon which . . . an edifice of international law and organization can be built" (O'Neal and Russet 1997, 269). As these norms become more widespread and institutionalized, conflict becomes less common due to the "emergence of a Kantian subsystem of states, within which the unprovoked use of force is illegitimate" (O'Neal and Russett 2015, 81). Given the (relatively recent) inclusion of women's rights as another shared value among adherents to the liberal order, the adoption of laws and policies to protect women's rights indicates that a state is more deeply embedded in the community of states that rejects the use of force to settle political disputes.

This all means that the adoption of formal protections for women's rights may be related to political violence. States and non-state groups that adopt women's rights often do so to signal that they are committed to liberal norms, including the rule of law and non-violent settlement of disputes. As such, we expect states that have adopted more extensive legal frameworks to protect women's rights to be less likely to initiate inter-state conflicts. These states signal to the international community that they are willing to be "good players" at the international level. This leads to the following hypotheses:

H4.1: The probability of interstate conflict initiation increases as states adopt more women's rights measures .

Women Rights as Signaling State Openness to Claim Making

In addition to signaling liberalism, when states adopt women's rights, they may signal a willingness to make concessions. As scholars have noted, it is costly for governments to enshrine rights to women (though, perhaps not as costly as other democratic reforms (Bush et al. 2023)). The necessary changes are costly because states are largely built by men and have historically excluded women: women have not historically been considered citizens. This is primarily because providing women with rights means that (elite) men (of certain races/ethnicities) lose their monopoly over power and resources (Pateman 1988). For example, providing women with property rights means that men no longer have exclusive access to this resource to divide among themselves according to their rules. Allowing women to work mean that men have less access to unpaid labor for their and more competition in the workforce. Despite the collective grievances that women have faced histori- cally, with very few exceptions,[8] women have rarely used violence to achieve political ends. Instead, states have made concessions to women after non- violent political activism, in the form of women's movements (Htun and Weldon 2018). This means that some states are more receptive to making concessions based on non-violent movements than others. States that have responded by instituting women's rights signal to the domestic constituents that they are open to making concessions to different groups. They also signal that non-violent movements can achieve political goals (Chenoweth and Stephan 2011). As a result, groups that want to make claims may learn that claim making via peaceful channels can be successful, and groups may use non-violent means to achieve other political goals that are costly to the state.

Non-state groups sometimes signal their commitment to norms of coop- eration and peace by advocating for women's rights within their own political organization. They signal these commitments to both the international com- munity and the state government. Asal et al. (2013) examine the tactics used by ethnicity-based political organizations in the Middle East. They find that organizations with a statement in their official platform (a policy) that specif- ically advocates for inclusion of women are less likely to pursue their object- ives using violent means and more likely to pursue them through protests and demonstrations. This suggests that such groups are signaling to the in- ternational community and to the state that they have adopted liberal dem- ocratic values, such as inclusivity, cooperation, and non-violence. Along the same lines, scholars have argued that rebel groups are motivated to comply with the principles of humanitarian and human rights law because they seek recognition of their legitimacy from the international community (Jo 2015). When these rebel groups signal these values, it signifies that they are looking to resolve conflicts in a peaceful manner.

When states and rebel groups adopt women's rights, they thus signal a willingness to make concessions. This allows for the peaceful resolution of conflict between the state and groups that want to make claims against the state.

H4.2: The probability of civil conflict onset decreases as states adopt more women's rights measures.

H4.3: The frequency of dissident terror attacks decreases as states adopt more women's rights measures.

Increasing the Number of Watchdogs

As states adopt more laws and policies to protect women's rights, they invite more attention and public scrutiny as to whether they are implementing and enforcing them, and also whether they are respecting human rights more broadly. When states formally recognize rights, interested parties have a clear reason to monitor progress in the protection of those rights. Some of this monitoring is done by IOs and their member states, particularly where international law is concerned. However, the bulk of the groups who monitor compliance with domestic and even international law are domestic NGOs. Once these "watchdogs"—be they civil society organizations or international actors—are monitoring the state more closely, they are more likely to expose any rights abuses that are perpetrated by the state.

Domestically, the enacting of protections for women's rights necessitates and generates the creation of advocacy organizations that push for women's rights and that hold states accountable for failing to implement and enforce the laws (Htun and Weldon 2018). Women's rights are impossible to achieve without robust women's organizing. A variety of groups may organize to push for formal protections for women's rights, including groups connected to political parties, grassroots organizations, women's research institutes, women's development organizations, and various other voluntary organizations (Katzenstein 1989). Research suggests that domestic mobilization by women's rights activists is responsible for the widespread adoption of those rights: legislation, policies, and treaties related to women's rights are often adopted and implemented as a result of efforts by advocacy groups (Htun and Weldon 2012). Joachim (2003) highlights how women's advocacy organizations are successful in influencing state interests with respect to violence. These groups not only ensure the adoption of relevant laws and policies, but they also monitor progress. In doing so, they provide a watchful eye on state behavior without which improvement is unlikely. Indeed, the more civil society groups there are to "watch" the state, the more successful they are at restraining state's behavior (Meernik et al. 2012).

Further, the adoption of women's rights creates new opportunities for women's groups to pressure the state through "naming and shaming"—the publicizing of violations of international or domestic law. Research suggests that this tactic often works to mitigate some forms of human rights abuses, though its effectiveness is conditional on the presence of NGOs, pressure by external actors, and regime type (Hafner-Burton 2008; Murdie and Davis 2012; Hendrix and Wong 2013; DeMeritt and Conrad 2019).

The adoption of women's rights (and other human rights) also draws the attention of foreign governments and international organizations, who may become more vigilant in monitoring the status of women's rights. Importantly, pressure from domestic and international actors can reinforce one another. There is evidence that foreign investment and multilateral aid is negatively affected by poor human rights practices and the publicizing of abuses—naming and shaming—by NGOs as well as by IOs (Richards, Gelleny, and Sacko 2001; Lebovic and Voeten 2009; Barry, Clay, and Flynn 2013). Moreover, a state's participation in the liberal world order via a rite of passage—the adoption of women's rights (and other human rights)—may come with additional benefits such as trade ties and alliances. With more watchful eyes and more policy entanglements, the government is less likely to engage in conflicts as this may undermine the benefits it receives from being a rule-following member of the (liberal) international community.

As women's advocacy organizations mobilize to facilitate the implementation and enforcement of women's rights, they will also scrutinize the state's behavior more broadly. This means they will be attuned to other abuses of human rights, particularly those that involve physical violence. The more laws related to women's rights states adopt, the more such groups will proliferate and the more closely they will monitor the state's behavior. Thus, states who adopt women's rights will be more vulnerable to naming and shaming. In this way, watchdog groups motivated by a concern for women's rights can help deter state violence. As such, we expect the following:

H4.4: State violence decreases as states adopt more women' rights measures. The strength of the relationship between state violence and women's rights increases as the number of women's rights advocacy groups increases.

Women's Rights Advocacy Transitioning to Non-Violent Advocacy

After women's rights are adopted, the role of women's rights organizations could extend beyond that of a watchdog. Civil society groups that grow out of advocacy campaigns for women's rights can also be easily mobilized for pro-peace movements. That is, the opportunity structures necessary for mobilizing large, non-violent movements are already in place in societies where women's groups have been active in the past. Pro-peace groups may learn from and co-opt the structures and strategies of feminist groups, creating "social movement spillover" (Meyer and Whittier 1994).

In particular, Htun and Weldon (2018) argue that large, autonomous feminist movements are often responsible for the adoption of what they call "status related" women's rights (rights related to violence against women) and "doctrinal policies" (family law). Violence against women is rarely raised as an issue, much less a policy priority, without pressure from women's groups (Weldon 2002). Thus, the existence of laws related to violence against women and family law indicate that there are likely pre-existing organizations that could be mobilized against violence in general.

Women's rights organizations could pressure the government to change their behavior on a whole host of issues, including non-violence. Hafner-Burton and Tsutsui (2005) propose a "paradox of empty promises" whereby governments that ratify human rights treaties as "window dressing"—meaning they don't intend to enforce them—find themselves facing the emergence of civil society groups who pressure them to follow their legal commitments. That is, "as nation-states make formal legal commitments to symbolize human rights compliance even while they are in violation, this process of 'empty' institutional commitment to a weak regime paradoxically empowers non-state advocates with the tools to pressure governments toward compliance" (1378). Similarly, Risse, Ropp, and Sikkink's (1999) "spiral model" explains how governments often acknowledge international human rights norms as a tactical concession and, by doing so, unwittingly contribute to domestic and international mobilization that pressures them to change their behavior. The inadvertent product of adopting human (women's) rights treaties is thus the strengthening of civil society. Similarly, the unintended result of adopting laws protecting women's rights, even without the intention to enforce them, is the creation of civil society groups, or women's groups, that can be mobilized for non-violence in the future.

Thus, states with expansive legal frameworks for women's rights tend to be home to women's organizations which can be mobilized for non-violence. For example, feminist groups have been prominent in anti-war movements in the United States, including those in response to the Vietnam War and the 2003 invasion of Iraq. In Liberia, women's organizations collaborated to form the Women of Liberia Mass Movement for Peace in 2003 to end the civil war. Women's rights protests in Iran turned into protests against government repression more broadly after the killing of Mahsa (Zhina) Amini in 2022 by the Morality Police (Afary and Anderson 2023). The Iranian government eventually abolished the Morality Police to appease some of the protester's demands. These examples demonstrate how the promotion of women's rights by women's advocacy groups is linked to non-violence more generally, and movements for women's rights can turn into movements against international and civil wars. As such, we expect that the adoption of women's rights and the existence of women's advocacy organizations (which typically undergirds the adoption of women's rights), there will be less interstate and intrastate conflict. As such, for H4.1 and H4.2, we hypothesize that the effect of women's rights will be stronger as the number of women's rights advocacy groups in the country increases.

Do Women's Rights Affect Levels of Political Violence? Testing the Hypotheses

We now move to testing the aforementioned hypotheses using the scale that we developed at the beginning of the chapter. In addition to the variables discussed in the Appendix to Chapter 2, we also add an indicator of the number of women's international non-governmental organizations (INGOs) with which people living in a country claim membership (Hughes et al. 2017). This indicator serves as a proxy for women's advocacy groups which, as mentioned earlier, are often responsible for the adoption of women's rights in the first place.[9] For these models we interact this variable with our measure of women's rights. This will allow us to examine whether women's rights are more strongly associated with peace where such groups are more numerous and thus better able to mobilize and pressure the state.

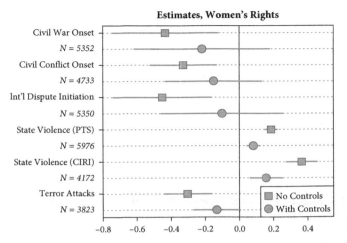

Figure 4.2 Coefficient Estimates for Women's Rights from Models of Political Violence

To ease interpretation, we begin by examining coefficients from models that exclude the interaction between women's rights and women's NGOs. These are shown in Figure 4.2, which displays estimates from models with and without control variables. Recall that the models without controls include random effects for country. The models of civil conflict and civil war onset also include time counters that indicate the number of "peace years." As in Chapter 3, the estimates are shown as dots and the horizontal lines show a 90% confidence interval around each estimate. These coefficients indicate the strength/direction of the relationship between women's rights and different measures of political violence *independent of the number of women's NGOs*. In all cases the coefficients have the expected sign, indicating that women's rights are negatively, or inversely, related to political violence. However, only for the models of state violence are the estimates statistically significant once the control variables are included. Higher values on the CIRI and PTS scales indicate fewer violent abuses of civil and political rights. The women's rights variable is positive and statistically significant in the CIRI and PTS models with and without control variables. These are coefficients from linear models and so indicate the expected change in each scale for a 1 unit increase in the women's rights score. Based on the models with control variables, a 1 unit increase in the women's rights scale corresponds to an increase of 0.16 in the CIRI scale and 0.08 in the PTS.

Further, the models of state violence are the only ones in which we find evidence that the relationship between women's rights and state violence is

140   THE STATUS OF WOMEN AND POLITICAL VIOLENCE

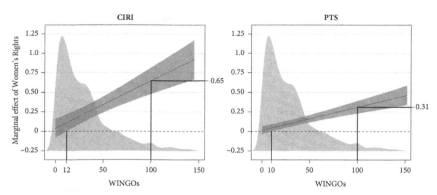

Figure 4.3 Marginal Effect of Women's Rights at Different Values of Women's INGOs (WINGOs)

conditioned by the presence of women's INGOs. Figure 4.3 plots the marginal effect of the women's rights variable, with 90% confidence intervals, across the range of the women's INGOs (WINGOs in the figure) count variable, using the approach outlined in Brambor, Clark, and Golder (2006). The solid line in the plot indicates the expected change in PTS or CIRI for a 1 unit change in women's rights, which is different at different values of the women's INGO variable. To determine the expected change for an increase in women's rights, pick a value (of women's INGOs) on the x-axis, then locate the corresponding y value for the solid line. When women's rights is equal to 100, for example the expected change is in CIRI for a 1 unit increase in women's rights is 0.65; for the PTS, it is 0.31. Where the lower bound of the confidence interval is above 0, the change is statistically significant. The lower bound is above 0 in the left plot when women's INGOs is 12, and in the right plot when women's INGOs is 10. Below these values the change is statistically indistinguishable from zero. As the women's INGO variable moves to its maximum the marginal effect increases to about 1 point on the CIRI scale, and to about 0.5 points on the PTS.

Our results suggest that the hypothesis that receives the most support is H4.3: more extensive formal protection for women's rights, especially when accompanied by women's advocacy organizations, is associated with less state violence. We can draw several conclusions. First, this finding is consistent with the well-known fact that that liberal democratic states are less likely to violently transgress human rights (e.g. Keith, Tate, and Poe 1999; Davenport 2007; Hill and Jones 2014), but is not subsumed by it as the negative correlation between women's rights and state violence holds when controlling for democracy. Nevertheless, it is possible that this relationship is explained by institutional features that are left out of our analysis. If countries that have adopted women's rights are likely to have adopted legal frameworks for rights protection more generally, this could bias our results. It is likely that the measure of democracy we use captures some variation in legal protections for civil and political rights more broadly, but even among states with similar levels of democracy there may be variation in legal protection for social groups who are at a relatively high risk for state violence, for example ethnic and religious minorities. It is plausible that governments who have adopted legal frameworks to protect such groups are also more likely to have adopted women's rights. This possibility is beyond the scope of our analysis but is worth exploring in future research.

Second, if our results indicate that women's rights have a constraining effect on state and government behavior, they also indicate that this effect depends on the presence of women's INGOs. That we find a strong conditional effect for women's rights suggests that this result has less to do with the fact that states adopt women's rights as a result of deeply embedded liberal values and more to do with the fact that when states formally adopt women's rights, they are subject to more scrutiny and pressure from domestic and international groups. That is, the results more strongly support the watchdog theory. A formal commitment to rights can facilitate mobilization, as it provides a framework for advocacy groups to shame the government by publicizing the fact that they are not meeting the benchmark they have set for themselves (Risse, Ropp, and Sikkink 1998; Simmons 2009; Murdie and Peksen 2015). Watchdog groups may then publicize evidence of other abusive practices, including state violence, and the government will be more susceptible to naming and shaming by domestic groups, the media, and international organizations for broader violations of human rights. As women's groups become more numerous, they may discourage abuse, as there is greater potential for domestic mobilization and demands for accountability in response to violence.

Third, although in some cases the adoption of liberal institutions may help us to predict how a state will interact with potential "adversaries"—including foreign governments and domestic opposition groups—this does not appear to be the case with women's rights. States do not necessarily signal, domestically or internationally, a commitment to liberal values when they adopt women's rights. Rather, states may adopt certain laws and treaties as window dressing. Indeed, despite the body of work that shows how CEDAW ratification improves respect for women's rights (Simmons 2009; Hill 2010; Lupu

2013; Cole 2013; Englehart and Miller 2014), at the end of the day, not all countries that ratify it adhere to peaceful norms. For example, Russia is a ratifier of CEDAW, but violates the treaty obligations,[10] and is a belligerent state. Indeed, the high number of countries that have ratified CEDAW—186 of 193 countries—suggests that it does not necessary serve as a signal for less belligerent state behavior. Thus, adoption of women's rights may not be an actual signal for any normative commitment.

A further explanation is that women's rights may regress when interstate conflicts are likely because a return to traditional order is necessary for war-making (Tickner 1992; Wegner 2021; Cohn and Enloe 2003). These scholars argue that militarization is a prerequisite for war, so states reverse women's rights in order to create and sustain a culture of nationalism. Sweden, for example, officially revoked their feminist foreign policy in 2022 while also increasing military spending and reintroducing civilian conscription in response to Russia's invasion of Ukraine. The point is not that Sweden should not be concerned about Russian aggression but that the government apparently views a feminist foreign policy as incapable of providing for basic self-defense.

The null results for interstate conflict are consistent with the literature on the relationship between democracy and interstate war. While it is well known that pairs of democracies are less likely to have a military conflict than non-democracies or countries with different regime types, the evidence regarding democracy and conflict initiation is less clear. Some studies find that democracies are less likely to initiate militarized disputes (e.g. Souva and Prins 2006), while others find no clear relationship (Ward, Siverson, and Cao 2007), and still others find that democracies may be more likely to initiate disputes depending on the regime type of the other country (Goldsmith et al. 2017). In short, there is clear evidence that intrastate conflict is relatively rare in democracies, and there is some evidence that democracies are less likely to initiate interstate conflicts, but the relationship is dependent on a number of contextual factors.

Moreover, the adoption of women's rights does not signal state acceptance of claim making by groups. The null results for civil and international conflict suggest that states who adopt women's rights are not necessarily less likely to experience civil conflicts or make concessions that would prevent terror attacks.[11] Indeed, in some cases women's rights are some of the first laws and policies to be reversed when conflict is viewed as a real possibility. Sometimes they are even the cause for mobilization. Traditional or right-wing groups are prone to politicize the adoption of women's rights and use it as a recruitment tool for their organizations. In some Latin American countries, and other places around the world, for example, the implementation of provisions, laws, and policies about gender and reproductive health have galvanized right-wing groups and mobilized countermovements (Corredor 2021; Korolczuk and Graff 2018). These examples show that when state governments make concessions to different groups of women in the form of rights (e.g. legalizing abortion or granting the right to vote), these actions could activate some groups to mobilize against these changes. This backlash by (conservative, right-wing) men overshadows any signal the state sends to other groups about its willingness to grant concessions.

Finally, it is notable that women's rights have no clear relationship with conflict even in the presence of NGOs mobilized around that issue. One explanation for this is that even if groups organized around the promotion of women's rights are likely to advocate for non-violence, this does not mean governments will be swayed by that advocacy. Women's groups may not easily be able to transition to non-violent advocacy and many groups may opt not to broaden their established goals; with minimal resources, they cannot easily expand their advocacy activities.

This may be especially true for advocacy campaigns against armed conflicts. Here the contrast between results for state violence and those for civil and interstate conflict are notable. State violence in many (perhaps most) cases targets members of disadvantaged social groups rather than dissidents who have mobilized to oppose the state (Haschke 2019; Beger and Hill Jr. 2019). Although the government and the public may perceive members of marginalized groups as threatening, it is unlikely that they will perceive them to be as threatening as an armed rebel group or a hostile foreign government. Thus it may be that governments and members of the public perceive pro-peace campaigns against intra- or interstate conflict as more threatening than those against state violence and so are more likely to actively oppose the former, which would explain why those campaigns are less effective.

Furthermore, groups that advocate for women's rights may sometimes be in favor of military intervention, especially when intervention is perceived as protecting the rights of women in other countries (Engle 2007). Indeed, the literature on public opinion discussed in the previous chapters finds that women are more likely than men to favor military intervention when the stated goals are humanitarian (Brooks and Valentino 2011). The US invasion of Afghanistan, for example, was framed as liberating the women of Afghanistan and giving them fundamental rights. In November 2001, US first lady Laura Bush proudly declared: "Because of our recent military gains in much of Afghanistan women are no longer imprisoned in their homes. They can listen to music and teach their daughters without fear of punishment. The fight against terrorism is also a fight for the rights and dignity of women" (Bush 2001). Similarly, much of the criticism over the United States' military withdrawal from Afghanistan in 2021 was couched in terms of concerns about women's rights (Scharff 2023; Filipovic 2021). And, Hillary Clinton included women's rights as a justification for intervention in Libya and other countries.[12] Like female leaders, there is likely significant variation among women's advocacy groups, especially when it comes to promoting women's rights internationally. This disagreement means that there may not be a united front when it comes to how women's rights advocacy affects inter- and intrastate conflicts. Some women's groups favor military intervention to promote women's rights while other vehemently oppose it. However, there is likely more consensus among women's groups against state repression, making women's mobilization more effective in preventing abuses by the state.

Conclusion

Secretary of State Hillary Clinton was a champion for women's rights globally, so much so that she advocated the use of violence to achieve that end. Her example demonstrates an inherent contradiction in how women's rights might be promoted globally and whether this promotion leads to peaceful outcomes. Indeed, our findings from this chapter highlight this tension.

While we find that states that have adopted women's rights tend to be less violent toward the civilian populations who live in their territorial jurisdiction, we find limited evidence that women's rights are associated with less conflictual behavior toward other states or between states and armed nonstate groups. These results are in line with research on democracy and the occurrence of inter- and intrastate conflict, which finds that this relationship is nuanced. Like democracy itself, women's rights have steadily become part of the "liberal world order." This has created the expectation that members of the liberal order (active or aspiring) will adopt international and domestic legal frameworks to protect women's rights, so that women's rights are viewed as a signal of liberal values and a willingness of states to make concessions more broadly. The findings in this chapter suggest that simply adopting laws and policies that are consistent with protecting women's rights is not a strong signal that a state is less prone to conflict. Rather, a deeper commitment is perhaps necessary, such as the actual implementation of women's rights, which sends a stronger signal of non-violence and willingness to make concessions to minority groups.

Having said that, we do find evidence of a connection between women's rights and state violence: states that adopt women's rights are less likely to commit violent abuses of civil and political rights. This relationship between women's rights and less state violence grows stronger as the number of women's advocacy organizations in the country grows. These results suggest the importance of watchdogs in the form of women's advocacy organizations for reducing state repression. Women's advocacy organizations play important roles in naming and shaming countries and bringing domestic and international spotlight onto the behavior of states. In short, women's advocacy and the promotion of women's rights *together* can prevent state repression. This means that Hillary Clinton's promotion of women's rights as a major pillar of US foreign policy during her tenure as secretary of state was not always contradictory to peaceful outcomes. What was perhaps missing, however, was more attention to and foreign aid directed at shoring up women's advocacy groups, because they are a key to generating this more peaceful outcome.[13]

It is worth emphasizing that women's rights alone provide no guarantee that states will refrain from violent human rights abuses, or even that they will respect the substance of laws and provisions for women's rights. As our opening chapter showed, women's rights are precarious just like any other set of rights. They can just as easily be taken away as given. As described in the Introduction, the global trend in recent years has been toward authoritarianism and away from liberalism (Mechkova, Luhrmann, and Lindberg 2017). This trend has been accompanied by signals as well: signals that governments are not pro-woman. As mentioned, Sweden quickly backtracked on its feminist foreign policy after a change in government. In the United States, the Supreme Court overturned a decades-old ruling that protected the right to an abortion. Russia has recently weakened its domestic violence laws to make it more difficult to impose a criminal penalty on perpetrators. Indonesia has criminalized sex outside of marriage. In Afghanistan, women are no longer able to go to school or work. This trend should serve as a reminder that there is no guarantee that any right will not be taken away in the future. As is the case with liberal democracy itself, states may "backslide" where women's rights are concerned. Research suggests that women's rights are related to, and may be a precondition for, the emergence of democracy (Wang et al. 2017), which suggests that the reverse is also true—erosion of women's rights may be a precursor to authoritarianism.

If backsliding on women's rights is a precursor to authoritarianism, then the watchdog role that women's advocacy organizations play becomes even more important for preventing not only state repression but also general democratic erosion. For this reason, we emphasize again that rather than legal frameworks alone, what appears to matter for both sustaining women's rights and for ensuring that states respect human rights in general and democracy more broadly is mobilization by civil society groups and advocacy organizations. In combination with strong laws, such groups can shine a spotlight on, and discourage, state violence and the possibility of a turn to authoritarianism. Thus, one path toward respect for basic civil and political rights is the strengthening of women's advocacy organizations globally.

5

Harm to Women and Political Violence

Introduction

The Mosuo women of China, who live near the Lake Lugu, close to the Tibetan border, have been living in a matriarchal society for thousands of years (Marsden 2018).[1] Lineage is traced through the women of the family, and property is handed down to women in the family. Women don't marry and children are raised by generations women of the same family. Mosuo men live with their mothers, and couples traditionally do not live together—the language has no word for "husband" or "father." Instead, women choose a partner by walking to their home at night. Everyone shares the family's belongings equally. Children take on the mother's surname. Mothers are the center of the society and women are responsible for all duties related to generating life and business whereas men are responsible for duties related to death and taking care of animals. Notably, the community has very little crime and has remained peaceful despite disruptions such as the Cultural Revolution of the 1960s.

The Mosuo community is not the only matriarchal community in the world.[2] The largest known matrilineal society, the Minangkabau, live in the highlands of West Sumatra. The indigenous Bribri of Costa Rica live in "clans," which are determined by their mother; only women are permitted to prepare the traditional cacao drink, used in sacred rituals, which gives them a certain spiritual superiority. The Umoja of northern Kenya grasslands are a society founded by women who were survivors of sexual and gender-based violence and ban men from living in the community. The Alapine Village in Alabama in the United States (or Womyn's Lands) is home to an all-female commune. The Akan in Ghana live in a matriclan in which identity, inheritance, wealth, and politics are all decided by women. And among the Khasi in India, mothers and mothers-in-law are the only people allowed to look after children, and children take on the mother's surname. What distinguishes these communities is that most women thrive in them, as their health outcomes are better and they suffer from less violence (Reynolds et al.

Positioning Women in Conflict Studies. Sabrina Karim and Daniel W. Hill, Jr., Oxford University Press.
© Oxford University Press 2024. DOI: 10.1093/9780197757970.003.0006

2020). Not only do women flourish, but the communities share a different set of values and norms that focus on non-violence. These matriarchal societies are egalitarian, economically balanced, and decisions are based on consensus and maternal values (Goettner-Abendroth 2012). In short, they appear to be more peaceful.

These examples draw attention to how the wellbeing of women in a given society is related to the occurrence of violence in that society. Matriarchal societies help ensure women's wellbeing, whereas patriarchal ones result in more harm to women. Despite almost all societies being patriarchal, we examine variation in harm to women and how harm to women affects levels of political violence. Specifically, this chapter addresses the question: how does harm to women in society affect the propensity for that society to engage in political violence?

To answer this question, the chapter begins by carefully conceptualizing harm to women and providing new measures of this concept. The bulk of the chapter is then devoted to theorizing about how harm to women is linked to political violence. The last part of the chapter tests the resulting hypotheses. We find that there is a link between harm to women and increased propensity for inter-state and intra-state conflict. We conclude the chapter with some reflections about the implications of this finding.

Conceptualizing Harm to Women

Harm to women as a concept is meant to capture the extent to which girls and women are hurt by individuals, groups, and/or the structural conditions that are created and perpetuated by state policies. The concept is defined in terms of outcomes related to women's experiences and the conditions in which they live, rather than the number of women relative to men in public spaces or the presence of policies or laws that protect women.

Harm usually refers to physical violence. Direct, physical violence obviously harms women. Individuals and/or groups cause physical harm to women in many different ways, including rape and other forms of sexual assault, domestic abuse, murder (femicide), and sex-selective abortions. Galtung (1969) provides a list of potential forms of physical harm that includes crushing, tearing, piercing, burning, poisoning, evaporation (nuclear explosion), denial of air, denial of water, denial of food, and denial of movement. Physical, direct, or personal violence thus manifests in applications of force that entail bodily injury or death or that restrict movement and access to basic necessities.

However, harm can be defined to extend beyond physical violence. Structural violence is also a form of harm. Galtung (1969, 168) used the term to refer to instances in which "human beings are being influenced so that their actual somatic and mental realizations are below their potential realizations." It is a condition whereby those on the margins of society have lower life expectancy because of an uneven allocation of resources (Tickner 1992, 13).[3] This definition enables an account of violence to include structural conditions that cause harm to women, in addition to physical violence. Structural violence manifests as inequality of power, resources, and life opportunities. Any condition that disproportionately hinders one or more identified social groups from developing their capabilities, dispositions, or potentiality counts as structural violence (Dilts 2012, 191–227). According to Galtung (1990), structural violence entails exploitation, but also the creation of a system in which individuals are unaware that they are being exploited. It also implies a nascent hierarchy in that there are oppressors and the oppressed. Structural violence is not necessarily visible, but leads to observable, inequitable outcomes. For example, taking away funds from healthcare has the effect of increasing maternal mortality. This example demonstrates that the outcomes of structural violence might be a result of policies (the reverse of women's rights), but the policies are upheld by culture and norms. The perpetrator is not limited to a single person or group, and physical harm may not be the goal of the policy. But systemic conditions created by groups that comprise the state can harm women and other groups by contributing to relatively high, and avoidable, morbidity or mortality.

Based on this discussion, we posit four dimensions that characterize harm to women. Box 5.1 highlights these dimensions. We note that unlike the other two concepts, harm to women is developed in the negative.

Box 5.1 Characteristics of Harm to Women

1) pertinent to those that identify as girls or women
2) inclusive of individual, physical, or bodily violence
3) constitutive of structures that subordinate [structural violence]
4) increased risk of morbidity and/or mortality

150　THE STATUS OF WOMEN AND POLITICAL VIOLENCE

The production and reinforcement of structures that subordinate is a necessary characteristic for the concept of harm to women, because the concept implies that violence occurs within, and as a result of, a social hierarchy. Without this dimension, any physical harm to women would be considered an extension of the concept. For instance, a woman injured by falling from a ladder is not an instance of harm to women. However, if social norms mandate that roof cleaning is the duty of women, some ladder-induced injuries would count as cases of harm to women because the existing social hierarchy relegates women to those dangerous roles. In this example, structural violence—the expectation that women engage in certain dangerous jobs—produces harm for women. The result of the norm that roof cleaning is for women increases women's risk of mortality. Similarly, the murder of a woman will not count as an instance of harm to women as defined here, unless the act of violence can be traced to an underlying social hierarchy that subordinates women. Certain societal norms may motivate the murder of women as an act of misogynistic violence. The feelings of shame and humiliation that precede acts of misogynistic violence often result from behavior that does not conform to social norms or to men's expectations: a husband earning less than a wife, or a woman turning down a marriage proposal. Another relevant set of norms is caste systems. Caste systems lead to a preference for sons over daughters (Mahalingam 2007), and this preference can lead to harmful outcomes for girls. Another example is narrow societal definitions of what it means to be a woman that are based on physical traits (as discussed in note 3). Where this understanding is entrenched and rigid it can become a motive in the murder of trans women. Thus, underlying structural conditions can lead to the targeted killing of women.

Measuring Harm to Women

Our measure of harm to women includes both direct forms of harm and indirect forms of harm. As measures of direct harm, we include the World Bank's Gender Stats project and the Woman Stats project, both of which are relatively recent data collection efforts. The proportion of women subjected to violence is an estimate created by the UN Statistics Division and is based on a number of surveys. Given its large range, this variable is treated as continuous in the measurement model. The Woman Stats rape prevalence scale is an ordinal scale coded 0 for countries/years where sources indicate that marital rape is rare or infrequent, 1 for cases where sources indicate that marital rape is not uncommon but by no means universal, and 2 for cases where sources indicate that marital rape is a significant problem (high prevalence). The marital rape scale is an ordinal coding of the officially reported rape prevalence per 100,000 people, with values coded as following. 0: 0, 1: 1–10, 2: 11–30, 3: 31–60, 4: >60. The Murder Scale is an ordinal scale coded 0 to 2. It is "designed to scale the sanction of or pressure for female murder in a given state, examining cultural/social practices that condone murder and/ or injuring of women. This includes murder as a result of accused witchcraft, elopement, suspicion of promiscuity, infidelity, rape, 'honor' killings, religious or ethnic practices, dowry deaths, acid attacks, etc."[4] It is coded 0 where there is no evidence of such practices., 1 where there is some evidence of such practices, and 2 where there is substantial evidence of such practices. These variables are shown in Table 5.1.

We also include structural violence and conditions that have a negative and disproportionate impact on the health and wellbeing of women. We include indicators related to reproductive health, the level of autonomy women have in their daily lives, and general health outcomes (like life expectancy and mortality rates) relative to men. The sources and indicators for this model are shown in Table 5.1.

To create a measure of harm to women we use a slightly different version of the models used in Chapters 3 and 4. This is because the three scales from Woman Stats are ordinal, which requires them to be treated differently than any of the variables in the models in previous chapters. This part of the model is similar to an ordered response regression (like ordered probit or logit), and is referred to as a "graded response" model in Item Response Theory.[5] The probability that any country-year falls into a particular category for one of the ordinal Woman Stats scales is modeled as a function of the latent variable and a discrimination parameter β, as well as threshold parameters, denoted τ, that separate the ordered categories. These parameters provide information about the values of the latent variable at which the ordered scale changes from one category to another and can be used in the same way as the α parameters for the binary variables in Chapters 3 and 4, as explained later in this chapter. The β parameters can still be interpreted as discrimination parameters, as they indicate how quickly the probability of moving from one category of the scale to the next changes as the latent variable changes.

Item parameter estimates from this model are shown in Figure 5.1. All of the indicators have the expected sign (the latent variable is positively related

152 THE STATUS OF WOMEN AND POLITICAL VIOLENCE

Table 5.1 Indicators for Harm Model

Source	Variable
Demographic and Health Surveys	Contraceptive prevalence
	Demand for family planning satisfied
	Family visit decisions made by wife
	Health decisions made by wife
	Unmet need for contraception
	Wife makes household purchase decisions
	Women decide what food to cook
	Women decide when to their visit family
	Women make daily purchase decisions
	Women make decisions about own health
	Women make major purchase decisions
United Nations	Infant mortality ratio
	Under 5 mortality ratio
UN Population Division	Adolescent fertility rate
	Fertility rate
	Life expectancy ratio
UNAIDS	Anti-retroviral drug access ratio
	HIV ratio
UNDP	Antenatal care visits
UNICEF	Births attended by skilled staff
	Prenatal care prevalence
World Bank Gender Stats	Child mortality ratio
	Proportion of women subjected to violence in past year
World Health Organization	Maternal mortality rate
	Stunted growth ratio
Woman Stats	Rape Scale (LRW Scale 4)
	Marital Rape Scale (LRW Scale 8)
	Murder Scale (Murder Scale 1)

to harmful outcomes and negatively related to beneficial outcomes), and none of the factor loadings have credible intervals that contain 0, though one of the discrimination parameters (for the Rape Scale) does,[6] and 20 of 27 continuous indicators have estimates larger (in absolute value) than 0.5, indicating moderate to strong correlations between these indicators and the latent variable. Item parameters for the continuous variables have the same interpretation as in previous chapters. For example, maternal mortality rate has an estimate of 0.84, indicating that it increases by 0.84 standard deviations for a 1 unit increase in the latent variable. Variables that compare women's and men's health outcomes, for example life expectancy, are measured as the ratio of women to men. So, the negative estimate for life expectancy indicates that as harm to women increases, the life expectancy of women relative to men decreases. Interestingly, the only variable that measures autonomy in daily life that has a positive β estimate is whether wives are primarily responsible for making household purchases.[7]

For the Woman Stats scales, the Murder and Marital Rape scales have positive and relatively large β estimates (about 0.7), indicating that movement from one category to the next is highly informative about the latent variable. As an example of how to interpret the item parameters for the ordinal scales, consider the Murder Scale, which ranges from 0 to 2 with higher values indicating that the murder of women is more prevalent. Its positive discrimination parameter ($\beta=0.72$) indicates a positive relationship between the latent variable and the ordinal scale in the sense that the probability of an observation moving from any category of the scale (except the highest) to the next (higher) category increases as the latent variable increases.[8] Regarding specific categories, we can infer from the positive estimate that the probability that an observation is in the *highest* category of the scale *increases* as the latent variable increases, and that the probability that an observation is in the *lowest* category of the scale *decreases* as the latent variable increases.[9]

In contrast to the Murder and Marital Rape scales, the estimate for the Rape Scale is positive but relatively small (about 0.2) and has 95% credible intervals that contain 0. Because of its weaker relationship to the latent variable, the different categories of the scale do not separate country-years that have lower or higher values of the latent variable as well as the other two scales, and it will not influence the harm to women scale as much as the other scales. We leave it in the model at the expense of increasing the error in the latent variable estimates in order to retain the information that it does contain.

Harm to Women and Political Violence

In this section, we discuss four separate explanations for how harm to women affects political violence. First, indirect harm indicates weak normative

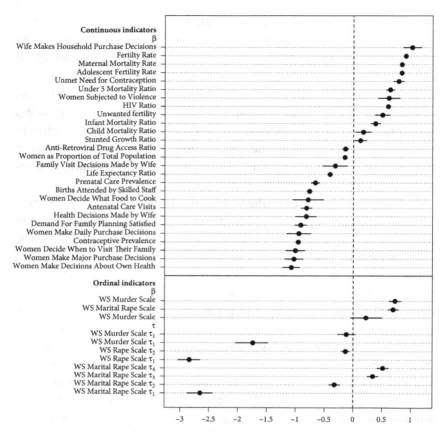

Figure 5.1 Estimates from Measurement Model for Harm to Women

constraints on the use of violence by states and non-state groups, meaning the cost for using violence in a society is low. This line of reasoning posits a connection between harm to women and the emergence and maintenance of structural inequality in which violence against "subordinate" out-groups is viewed as acceptable and even beneficial. Political violence can become an outgrowth of such inequality and the violence that supports them. Second, there is an argument that links harm to women to political violence through its effects on individuals rather than social structures. As individuals experience violence privately or perpetrate violence in the household, they become more prone to view violence as acceptable and to use it instrumentally. Third, harm to women can result in a population with more men than women. This shortage of women can contribute to recruitment efforts by armed groups and states (which are always armed). Fourth, and finally, harm to women prevents women from mobilizing politically, thereby decreasing the chances that non-violent politics work to resolve conflicts. Together these four theories point to a correlation between indirect and direct harm to women and interstate conflict, civil conflict, terrorism, and state violence. Next, we delve into each of them in more detail.

Harm to Women Weakens Normative Constraints on Violence

It is taken as axiomatic in most explanations for conflict that political entities, including states and non-state organizations, consider the costs (and benefits) of conflict when deciding whether to resort to violence. The costs for initiating violence include human, economic, and political costs. Importantly, it is not the absolute amount of destruction that matters to a decision maker, but rather their perception of the costs of using violence relative to the benefits. One reason an actor may have a high tolerance for costs is that they are more willing to accept civilian death and injury. Some actors are more willing than others to tolerate loss of human life, and states and groups who place low value on human life effectively have lower costs for starting conflict.

In places where some groups are systematically harmed by state policies and practices, the state is likely to perceive harm that results from conflict as more acceptable. That is, states that engage in structural violence are likely to discount the costs of violent political conflict. By definition, structural violence causes more harm to some groups than to others. The larger the proportion of the population that suffers from indirect harm, the more likely is the state to be agnostic about civilian wellbeing. Put another way, states that do not take care of certain groups indicate that they value human life less and are therefore less concerned about whether and how many civilians will die in the event of a violent conflict.

Structural violence against women serves as an indicator about how much value states place on human life. Caprioli (2005) argues that the inequalities between men and women present in every modern state meet Galtung's definition of structural violence. These inequalities reflect societal structures intended to subordinate women. Structural violence (indirect harm) against women may occur because state policies or practices contribute directly to the oppression of women. High levels of maternal mortality, lower access to healthcare for women, lack of access to birth control and reproductive care, taboos about menstruation, female genital cutting, and other harmful practices toward women indicate that the state and society place less value on women's lives. She argues that these conditions are maintained by societal norms that create a high tolerance for the use of violence, including violence in political disputes.[10] Structural inequality also relates to norms concerning violence in another way—it conditions a set of beliefs that can be used to justify inequality between social groups and to mobilize members of one group for conflict against other groups. For these reasons, Caprioli (2005) suggests that structural inequality and violence is related to inter- and intrastate conflict. In similar vein, Forsberg and Olsson (2021) refer to structural violence explanations as the "gender norms" explanation. In addition to poor performance on indicators of physical wellbeing, they argue that poor performance on social indicators such as educational outcomes suggests that society views the lives of men as inherently more valuable than the lives of women and that norms against violence may be relatively weak.[11]

States may also create structural conditions that contribute to direct, physical violence against women. In particular, failure to punish physical violence against women reinforces the idea that it is acceptable to harm women, and by extension reinforces the appropriateness of violent behavior in general. Hudson, Bowen, and Nielsen (2020, 111) suggest that "the relative rate of reinforcement is a significant predictor for the relative rate of aggressive behavior and the rate of reinforcement for violence against women is extremely high, resulting in overlearned violent acts that become automatic." They conclude that a low rate of punishment for violence against women will make individuals, groups, and states inhibited to use violence instrumentally (see also, Hudson et al. 2009, 25).

The devaluation of women's lives indicates a devaluation of all human life. Human life may then be considered expendable, a small price to pay for prevailing in a political conflict.[12] The state's treatment of women is thus an indicator of how much it values human life more broadly and how it perceives the cost of conflict relative to what it stands to gain through conflict. Violence against women helps groups of men establish social hierarchies in which they are the dominant group, and the treatment of women becomes a model for the treatment of other social groups, such as those based on ethnic identity.

A different version of the argument that harm to women leads to a willingness to use violence focuses on the roles of state violence and violence against women in creating and maintaining social hierarchies. In this argument, violence against women and state violence are not only related but are co-constitutive—each cannot occur without the other (Sjoberg 2013, 2014).

Here the focus is more on gender inequality, as the literature suggests that "the valuing of certain gender-based characteristics over others serves to cement axes of differentiation, discrimination, oppression, and violence" (8). As individuals, groups, and the state engage in harm to women, they perpetuate a cycle of harm within society.

To summarize, if leaders contribute to or simply do not care about harm to women, they are more likely to tolerate loss of life, and thus resort to violence when disputes arise. This means that harm to women is correlated with the likelihood of states initiating the use of violence in both the international and domestic context.

H5.1: The probability of interstate conflict initiation increases as harm to women increases.

H5.2: The probability of civil conflict onset increases as harm to women increases.

H5.3: State violence increases as harm to women increases.

An Evolutionary Perspective of Structural Violence

Studies by Hudson et al. (2009, 2012) and Hudson, Bowen, and Nielsen (2020) develop an argument about structural violence, but one that is grounded in evolutionary biology. They argue that the connection between harm to women and intergroup violence can be traced to a point in human history long before the development of modern states. They suggest that the *patrilineal/fraternal syndrome*, a term which refers to the subordination of women to ensure the survival of kinship groups, is the fundamental source of conflict in societies. They define the "first political order" as the customs and social structures that subordinate women to build up male-bonded kin networks. In this view, subordination of women through violence at the household level sustains kinship networks that are also violent. Hudson, Bowen, and Nielsen (2020) argue that physical coercion over women, patrilocal marriage, cousin marriage, son preference, low age of marriage, inequality in family law, bride price and dowry, polygyny, and no inheritance or property rights for women, serve to sustain violent kinship networks. This argument is based on a sweeping account of human history that begins

158 THE STATUS OF WOMEN AND POLITICAL VIOLENCE

before the Neolithic revolution, so we spend the next several paragraphs summarizing it.

Hudson et al. (2012) claim that, "the character of relations between men and women in society is the original template for all other relations within that society and between it and other societies."[13] This difference creates the basis for hierarchical social order. They argue that the first conflicts among humans fall along this line of distinction: girls and boys. Girls are cast as "out-groups" to boys, and boys having the socially dominant position in the community reinforces the hierarchy. This reinforcement can happen in benign ways such as teasing (e.g. "boys have cooties") or boys and girls playing separately on the playground. It can also take on a more aggressive form, for example boys reinforcing the subordinate role their sisters play in the household (e.g. expecting the girls to do certain chores and punishing them if they do not).

While men take a superior position to women in the social hierarchy, there is also a hierarchy among men. As human groups formed due to a need for increased protection against predators and other groups of humans, they tended to select stronger males as leaders in order to maximize protection against out-group males and minimize conflict between in-group males (Hudson et al. 2009, 14). Hudson et al. (2009) posit that this tendency created dominance hierarchies wherein a subgroup of superordinate (or "alpha") males dominates subordinate ("beta") males, and alpha males generally control (sexual) access to females. Alpha males use violence to sustain this social order, but alpha males provide protection to in-group women against out-group males. In exchange, women serve as partners to the men who protect them. "Beta" males or lower status males are the most likely to be threatened by a rise in women's status because they are most likely to lose their status as women compete for their positions. As such, they are more likely to use violence against women to maintain their status in the hierarchy (Hudson, Bowen, and Nielsen 2020, 38). Alpha males tolerate this violence by beta males because it keeps the social order intact.

Moving from intragroup to intergroup relations, violence between groups occurs because "dominant [alpha] males in coalition with male kin are able to adopt a parasitical lifestyle based on physical force: with very little effort, but with a willingness to harm, kill, and enslave others, they can be provided with every resource that natural selection predisposes them to desire: food, women, territory, resources, status, political power, pride" (Hudson et al. 2009, 16). As group identities developed, whether within clans or nations, they were closely associated with the identity of men as a group, because males typically had the prerogative to define group boundaries. Coercion of out-groups was often very attractive, as the dominant group could simply take what they wanted from other groups. In short, the ability and willingness to use violence to sustain hierarchy within kinship groups translated into violence with other kinship groups (nations) (Hudson, Bowen, and Nielsen 2020). While there has been a decline in kinship groups (clans, tribes, etc.) around the world, new forms of male-dominated kinship groups have emerged in the form of gangs, fraternities, and military units (36). Consequently, the patrilineal/fraternal syndrome lives on, but is stronger in societies where the practices mentioned here are still common.

We note that there is some opposition to the reliance on a biological evolutionary framework. For instance, Kinsella and Sjoberg (2019) argue that the use of a "feminist evolutionary analytic (FEA)" does not consider how the history and context of evolutionary theorizing facilitates the understanding that states and their institutions are neutral. The theory classifies heteronormative males and male sexualities as inherently aggressive, competitive, and violent.[14] Inherent in the assumption are female subordinates to male dominance (as well as the assumption that sexual relationships are heterosexual). In this way, FEA perpetuates the social hierarchies by articulating these binaries. The analysis, for example, ignores love and devotion by male partners.[15] Moreover, it focuses on reforming state institutions as the solution, which ignores the fact that the state is the site of violence. This means that a reduction of harm must be met with larger systemic changes (Kinsella and Sjoberg 2019).

Sustaining Social Hierarchy

We re-state the *patrilineal/fraternal syndrome* in the language of social hierarchy more broadly. Violence occurs due to deeply engrained norms that justify the existence of hierarchies and the use of violence to maintain them. Social hierarchy focuses mostly on habituation to violence, which effectively lowers the costs of using violence. It is also the case that a steep social hierarchy that greatly privileges one group creates a motive for violence by raising the stakes of social and political conflict. Privileged groups stand to lose much if the hierarchy is disrupted, and disadvantaged groups have much to gain by disrupting it. This is the case whether or not people are habituated to violence. This is one more reason to expect that structural violence increases the perceived value of conflict relative to the cost. It also suggests that individuals or groups who advocate for advancing the status of women or other traditionally marginalized groups may be viewed as particularly threatening. The ideology of Marxist-oriented groups, for example, typically challenges existing structural inequities, including those that subordinate women.

Depicting political opponents or activists as threatening to society itself has not been applied uniquely to left-wing political groups. Whatever the salient categories are, if the prevailing social order is defined by a steep structural inequality, then threats to the status of the dominant group can be portrayed as threats to the social order. Groups who pose such a threat are less likely to be viewed as opponents who can be reasoned with or with whom power can be shared.

To sum up, harm to women reflects the existence of a social hierarchy and attendant benefits for the dominant group, as well as normative acceptance of the hierarchy and the use of violence to maintain it. Groups at the top have clear self-interested reasons to defend the social order. Actual or perceived challenges to the status quo by members of subordinate groups are likely to be viewed by members of the dominant group as threats to their status or even their survival. Dominant groups are also likely to have normative reasons to defend their position. Their members are likely to have adopted a worldview that validates both their privileged position and the inferiority of groups toward the bottom of the hierarchy. In their view the prevailing social order is natural, which suggests that people who challenge it are trying to bring about something unnatural and should be stopped. While there are always material costs for conflict, there are smaller social and psychological costs to pay for harming members of groups who are viewed as inferior. Violence to suppress challenges to the dominant group's position and the larger social order is then easily justified. This provides a clear rationale for the use of force that applies equally to armed groups and groups using non-violent and even legal means to challenge the status quo.

This argument has implications for several kinds of political violence. Harm to women indicates the existence of structural inequalities that are created and maintained through violence. Where such inequities are more pronounced (as indicated by more extensive harm to women), dominant social groups, including political elites and their supporters, are more likely to use violence to advance their interests in interactions with international and domestic political opponents. Such societies are more likely to use violence to conquer new territory and assert dominance over other groups.[16] In countries where social orders have created (and are reinforced through) structural violence, and where physical harm to women is relatively common, states are also more likely to forcefully confront "internal" threats. Thus, this explanation provides additional support for H5.1, H5.2, and H5.3.

Early Exposure to Violence Normalizes Violence at the Individual Level

The theory just discussed is developed largely at the group or state level. There are also individual-level connections between harm to women and societal violence. One theory that discusses these connections focuses on the fact that violence is learned behavior, and individuals who have learned this behavior from an early age seek out like company. Individuals often learn to become violent from their families. If there is violence in the household (e.g. physical abuse, child abuse, domestic violence, intimate partner violence), those that experience this violence are more likely to become violent themselves and find acceptance among others who have similar experiences. Consequently, the more violence there is in households, the more violent interactions there may be in society more broadly. Moreover, individuals who perpetuate violence in the household find it much easier to perpetrate violence against strangers. Either way, early exposure to violence begets more violence. This individual theory can be aggregated up to the state level.

The first adults whom children observe regularly interacting are their parents/caregivers. When children witness violence at home, they are more likely to become violent themselves. Children who witness violence between their parents/caregivers are susceptible to adopting the aggressive behavior patterns they observe in their home.[17] Whitfield et al. (2003) find that boys who experienced domestic violence in their childhood home were more likely to become perpetrators later on. Such children are more likely to behave violently toward their peers and their partners in future relationships. Since patterns of violence in the household are often imitated, sons' imitation of their fathers' aggression toward their mothers may be the first step in perpetuating patterns of violence against women across generations (Hudson, Bowen, Nielsen 2020: 112). Hudson et al. (2009: 22) further state that children are inadvertently trained to be violent by family members through positive reinforcement of coercive behavior combined with little positive reinforcement for prosocial behavior, and these parenting practices are also handed down from one generation to the next. Societal violence is consequently a result of individuals who learn that violence is useful at home (Hudson, Bowen, Nielsen 2020; Hudson et al. 2019; Hudson et al. 2012).

If domestic violence is relatively normal in the household, then violent conflict resolution at the societal level, militarism, and war are more likely than they would be otherwise (Hudson et al. 2009). In cultures where violence against women persists, individuals (particularly male individuals) are committing continual, possibly daily, acts of aggression and violence. Societies in which a relatively large number of people have become used to using violence to resolve family conflicts and interpersonal disputes are more likely to be involved in large-scale violent conflicts compared to societies where individual level violence is less common. In short, violence is more likely at the group level because it is an acceptable way to resolve conflicts at the individual level.

Individuals who are violent toward their partners are more likely to be violent toward other members of society. If people (usually men) find it easy to commit violence against others (usually women) they know—their wives, girlfriends, or female family members—they will find it much easier to commit violence against strangers. In the words of John Stuart Mill, the tyrant at home becomes the tyrant in the state, and the tyrant at war with other nations, and "home is the training ground for 'bigger' games" (Hudson and Leidl 2015, 91). This is perhaps why perpetrators of terror attacks often have a history of domestic violence. The man who attacked a synagogue in Pittsburgh; the man who sent pipe bombs to Trump opponents, the man who murdered two Black people in Kentucky; the man who murdered people in an Orlando night club; the list goes on and on: these men had records of abusing women prior to perpetrating terror attacks.

Individuals who have been repeatedly exposed to violence in the household and have come to model that behavior themselves may also be more susceptible to joining violent groups. This is because they have learned to view violence as both instrumental and acceptable (Hudson, Bowen, Nielsen 2020). They may also be attracted to these groups because their experiences are similar to those of group members. Having experienced violence and associated trauma, they may feel less alienated and ashamed when they are surrounded by people who have similar experiences and shared beliefs.

In short, the extent of a person's exposure to violence at home is positively related to their use of violence in interpersonal interactions. The act of engaging in violence against a loved one can embolden individuals to engage in violence toward societal and political entities, a form of violence that is much less personal.

H5.4: The frequency of dissident terror attacks increases as harm to women increases.

This argument also has implications for intrastate conflict as such people may also be more prone to join insurgent/rebel groups more broadly. This provides another reason to expect support for H5.2.

Harm to Women Creates Shortages of Women

Another explanation we develop here connects harm to women to political violence through its effects on demographic changes. Harm to women results in higher female mortality and can create a shortage of women and a disproportionate number of boys and men, which can threaten the security of states and the people who live in their territorial jurisdictions. In particular, these shortages can create a problem for marriage markets in societies where the typical expectation is that a person will eventually enter into heterosexual marriage. Harm that leads to premature deaths among women results in fewer women who are available to marry men. Some have argued that the risk of political violence is heightened under such conditions.

Hudson, Bowen, and Nielsen (2020) suggest that sex imbalances caused by harm to women can disrupt marriage markets. There are many "missing women" in the world (Sen 1992). In fact, there are reports of 90 million missing girls in seven Asian countries (Hudson et al. 2012; Hudson and Den Boer 2002). Edlund et al. (2013) finds that between 1988 and 2004, a 0.01 increase in the sex ratio raised violent and property crime rates by some 3%, suggesting that the rise in excess males may account for up to one-seventh of the overall rise in crime in China. Son preference, sex selective abortions, and infanticide are some of the direct causes of the shortage of girls in the world. Girls may also die at a higher rate than boys as a result of indirect harm. One example is the privileging of boy's lives over girl's when it comes to healthcare and sanitation (Rovito et al. 2017; Sweetman and Medland 2017). Girls might be more likely to suffer from unhygienic conditions in societies where menstruation is taboo (Winkler 2019). Women may also be subject to harmful

164   THE STATUS OF WOMEN AND POLITICAL VIOLENCE

practices such as female genital cutting (Yount et al. 2020). In short, girls are subject to harm that can prevent their existence or lead to their early death.

A related reason for the "obstruction in marriage markets" is the high price of marriage and dowries (Hudson, Bowen, and Nielsen 2020). Marriage payments are a known concept in almost all societies, but are concentrated in some countries (Anderson 2007). They either take the form of dowries whereby the bride's family pays an agreed upon sum to the groom's side or bride price whereby the groom's family pays a sum to the bride's side (Anderson 2007), through direct payment, gifts, or even the expectation that the bride's family will pay for the costs of a wedding (Encyclopaedia Britannica 2014).[18] The prices for marriages and dowry can be as much as four to six times annual household income (Anderson 2007). To date, most studies about marriage payments have been carried out in South Asia, but some have been undertaken in other parts of the world, including the United States (Hughes 1978; Otto and Andersen 1967).[19] High dowry costs can lead to a preference for sons, which can result in selective abortions and fewer girls being born (Bhalotra, Chakravarty, and Gulesci 2020).

Practices such as these and other more direct forms of harm such as femicide, intimate partner abuse, and rape can affect women's morbidity rates in countries such that there are fewer women in society. This, in turn, subverts the social expectation of heterosexual marriage: fewer women in society means fewer women for men to marry. According to different scholars, this distortion has several implications, although much of the evidence is still contested. First, some scholars assume that unmarried men are more prone to negative influences than married men (Hudson and Den Boer 2002). Men who are left out of the "marriage market" are more likely to come from poorer, lower class families, more likely to be vagabonds, unemployed or underemployed, and have less social and political capital (Hudson and Den Boer 2002). Some case studies of violent conflict suggest that these kinds of men are more likely to join armed groups (Mueller 2000). Indeed, a number of studies have suggested that disproportionate numbers of young people among a country's population, or "youth bulges," and *male* youth bulges in particular, are linked to violence (Urdal 2004; Yair and Miodownik 2016; Moller 1968; Nordås and Davenport 2013)). Youth bulges harm social cohesion and facilitate social unrest, as the presence of relatively large numbers of unemployed, less "controllable" young men raise societal "volatility" (Boyden 2007, 265; Moller 1968). Hudson and Den Boer (2002, 15) conclude that "the sheer number of 'bare branches,' coupled with distinctive outcast subculture that binds them together and their lack of 'stake' in the existing social order predisposed them to organized banditry."

However, there is mixed evidence for the conclusion that single men are more prone to violence and that imbalanced sex ratios are associated with more societal violence.[20] Rather, what is more likely is that non-state actors capitalize on opportunities arising from harm to women. Instead of a shortage of supply, armed groups may use a demand side argument: some use marriage as a recruitment tool (Hudson and Matfess 2017). Donnelly (2019) outlines how armed groups provide marriage in a controlled manner when they are trying to foster internal cohesion, but do so with less oversight when they are trying to control a population. Marriage becomes a way for rebel groups to enhane their political project (Matfess 2024). The Revolutionary United Front (RUF) in Sierra Leone had elaborate codes of conduct for marriage and used it for recruitment (Marks 2014). Baines (2014) finds that in the Lord's Resistance Army in Uganda, forced marriage and the regulation of sexual relations reproduced a political project of imagining a "new Acholi" nation. Thus, rebel groups' awareness of the importance of marriage suggests that they recognize opportunities to fulfill the desires of "bare branches" when society cannot.

This discussion provides another rationale for H5.2 and H5.4: harm to women is correlated with civil conflict onset and terror attacks because it creates shortages of women, a phenomenon that armed groups can use to co-opt young men into violent groups.

Harm to Women as a Strategy to Prevent Women's Political Mobilization

There is a growing literature that suggests that when women become a part of political mobilization, movements are more successful (Chenoweth and Marks 2022). In particular, when it comes to non-violent protests, women's participation makes those movements successful because the non-violent nature of the political activism makes it safer for women to join. As a result, the movement is larger in scale and uses more diverse and creative tactics and strategies to motivate reform. Such movements also tend to be more re-strained in responses to repression and therefore more legitimate in the eyes of the public and international community (Chenoweth and Marks 2022). This means that governments have a reason to deter women's participation in claim-making if they want to preserve the status quo power hierarchy.

166   THE STATUS OF WOMEN AND POLITICAL VIOLENCE

Authoritarian regimes may be especially concerned with preventing women's participation in political mobilization because women's involvement in movements often transforms into calls for democratization (Chenoweth and Marks 2022). The case of Iran's Mahsa Amini protests provides a clear example of this expansion of claims. Protests erupted in Iran after the morality police arrested and beat to death a twenty-two-year-old woman, Mahsa Amini, for violating Iran's strict rules requiring women to cover their head with a hijab. The protests started after her funeral in the western city of Saqqez with women ripping off and burning their hijabs, but quickly spread to the rest of the country. The demands of the protesters grew from more freedom for women to calls for overthrowing the regime (Afary and Anderson 2023). The security forces brutally repressed the protests, killing over 500 and detaining over 20,000 people.[21] Authoritarian governments like Iran are thus hesitant to let women's movements grow because their involvement may the "canary in the coalmine" forecasting their downfall. Because of the threat posed by women's mobilization, such governments will support ways to demobilize women, including enabling or allowing harm to women.

Women's mobilization in non-violent social movements is key for conflict prevention and resolution in several ways. First, if high numbers of women are involved in social movements, then the political claims of different movements will be achieved without violence, thereby obviating the need for the use of violence. Second, the state may be less likely to repress women who are protesting because it might delegitimize the regime to physically attack women. It is likely inappropriate in some countries, for example, to hit (elderly, pregnant, elite) women who might be on the frontlines of a protest. This means that when all different kinds of women participate in political mobilization, the state may be less likely to use repression against them. Third, women may mobilize to bring peace when violence within or between countries is immanent or has started. Peace mobilization could be key for preventing and ending civil wars and interstate wars. If women lead these movements, they are likely to be more successful (Dayal and Christien 2020, Ta-Johnson, Keels and Bayram 2022). For example, one of the most famous instances of women's mobilization leading to the end of a war is the Women of Liberia Mass Action for Peace campaign, which used innovative tactics that drew on societal taboos such as threatening to bare their bodies in deliberate public nakedness (Prasch 2015), helped end the fourteen-year-long civil war in Liberia (Adjei 2021).

If women are key agents for political reform, then the *absence* of women's mobilization in social movements might mean that society experiences more violence. What creates the absence of women from political activism? States could pass policies and laws that prevent women from being politically active. They may refuse to pass laws that promote women's rights or overturn women's rights laws and policies because of fears that this empowerment will lead to larger political reforms. Regimes may also use violence to prevent women from being included in public spaces. Yet, while state policies might prevent women's mobilization, there are still many instances where women mobilize despite restrictions (e.g. Iran and Saudi Arabia).

A less obvious and perhaps more long-term strategy to demobilize women is to enable, allow, or turn a blind eye toward harm to women. This could mean not implementing women's rights laws or it could mean tolerating violence against women and other harms. Broadly, it means devaluing women's security and protection. If women are sick, disabled, unhealthy, and/or abused, they likely do not have the ability, energy, motivation, time, and/or space to become politically active. Women who experience violence daily (whether structural or perpetrated by partners or family members) face a host of adverse health challenges (Zlotnick, Johnson, and Kohn 2006; Loxton et al. 2017; Bacchus et al. 2018), which may make them reluctant or unable to engage in political activity. While there is some literature that suggests that exposure to violence improves political activism,[22] many women are faced with not only experiences of political or criminal violence, but intimate partner violence and/or structural violence. The compound nature of this violence is likely to prevent many women from participating in politics.

Moreover, states do not have to be explicit about this demobilization strategy. They can pass women's right's laws and reap the political benefits from doing so (Bjarnegård and Zetterberg 2022). At the same time, they have an incentive to not enforce the laws. States may allow harm to women to occur because it is a less costly way to deter women's mobilization. By not directly addressing women's harm, the state lets violence happen and deters women's mobilization and claim-making capacities but retains the veneer of progress. This is why perhaps a state can have violence against women laws but high rates of violence against women. Enloe (2014: 111) states that, "if women are kept in marginalized roles as domestic caregivers [through violence]—by men who are lovers or by fathers or husbands—then the chances of halting foreign-financed invasion, ending an unfair military-bases treaty, or holding accountable multinational corporate employer will be slim." In this sense, male elites "depend on domestic violence and the constraints it enforces on women's public activism as much as they do on alliances with

168   THE STATUS OF WOMEN AND POLITICAL VIOLENCE

men in the local elite" (111). The idea is that by keeping women in subordinate positions through structural and physical violence, women are unable to organize for change at a mass scale.

Because women's mobilization in social movements is important for preventing political violence, women's demobilization through (structural) violence (or harm to women) is likely to lead to more intra- and interstate war. Additionally, we expect that because women's participation can sometimes act as deterrence for repression, women's absence in protests and social movements more broadly might make repression more likely. Thus, this theory leads support for H5.1, H5.2, and H5.3.

Does Harm to Women Affect Levels of Political Violence? Testing the Hypotheses

We now move to testing the afore-mentioned hypotheses using the scales that we developed at the beginning of the chapter. Figure 5.2 displays coefficient estimates from regression models with and without the control variables discussed in Chapter 2. As a reminder, the models with no control variables include random effects for country, and the models of civil conflict and civil war onset also include time counters. The dependent variable for each model is listed on the vertical axis. Confidence intervals that do not cross the vertical line at 0 indicate a statistically significant effect ($\alpha = 0.10$).

The coefficients for harm to women are in the expected direction, with the exception of some of the models that use measures of state violence as the dependent variable (harm to women is negatively associated with state violence as measured by CIRI, though the relationship is not statistically significant). We find the most support for H5.1—that harm to women is associated with interstate conflict initiation—and for H5.2—that harm to women is associated with a higher probability of civil conflict onset. Only in these models is the coefficient for harm to women significant after including all control variables.[23]

In contrast, we find weaker evidence that harm to women is related to state violence and terror attacks: there are statistically significant relationships (as measured by the Political Terror Scale) when no control variables are included in the model, but neither are significant in fully specified models using these forms of violence as dependent variables.

The results indicate that the theories that receive the most support are those that view harm to women as reflections of norms that increase tolerance for violence generally. This includes the "violence begets violence" explanation

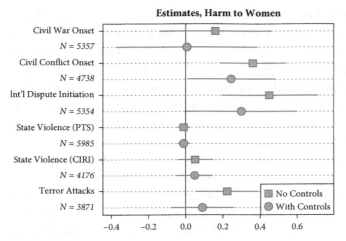

Figure 5.2 Coefficient Estimates for Harm to Women from Models of Political Violence

that focuses on the role of structural violence in facilitating political violence. States with higher levels of harm to women are more likely to become involved in international and internal conflicts because norms that justify interpersonal violence and help sustain social hierarchies make the use of force a more attractive option for settling conflicts with political opponents. The stakes of political conflict are likely to be higher, and the costs for using violence are likely to be lower, where such norms are prevalent.

It is reasonable to expect that lower normative barriers to violence would correlate with an increase in both violent interstate disputes and civil conflict. Those who live in a society in which violence against roughly half the population is routine and institutionalized will find it easier to justify (to themselves and others) the use of force against political opponents. This is the case whether their opponents are members of another ethnic or religious group, the political opposition, their own government, or a foreign government. By the same reasoning, a government that does not value the lives of their own citizens is likely to have a high tolerance for civilian casualties whether fighting takes place within the country or outside of it. They are thus likely to view acts of aggression against other governments, and the escalation of domestic political disputes into violence, as acceptable. This is to say that in a society characterized by pervasive harm, individuals will be more likely to view violence as acceptable, which facilitates the mobilization of groups of people for violence in both domestic and international politics.

170 THE STATUS OF WOMEN AND POLITICAL VIOLENCE

We also find some support for the shortage of women theory, as our measure of harm to women accounts for sex imbalances in the population. However, this specific indicator (sex imbalance) contributes only weakly to the latent variable ($\beta=-0.15$), which means that the relationship between harm to women and civil conflict mostly reflects a relatively high risk of conflict among countries with high levels of structural and physical violence against women rather than among countries with large male-to-female population imbalances.

We also note that the results lend support to the theory about strategic demobilization of women. If harm to women prevents women's non-violent mobilization (for peace), then inter- and intrastate war is more likely. States allow harm to women to occur because doing so prevents women from mobilization for political reforms, and thereby makes any movement for political reform less successful. Thus, not only do some states have a lower threshold for violence when they allow harm to women to occur, but some states may even find it strategic to allow harm to women to occur.

Additionally, we find that harm to women is related to the onset of civil conflict (i.e. conflict that results in more than 25 fatalities in a single year) but not the onset of civil war (which results in more than 1,000 fatalities in a single year). This suggests that harm to women may affect the onset of low-intensity conflict that eventually results in a civil war but does not affect the escalation of violence once it begins. Most civil wars during the time period we analyze began as low-intensity conflicts, which means that most of the civil war "onsets" in the data are actually ongoing conflicts that increased in intensity. In the data set we analyzed, 76% of the cases of civil war onset had an active conflict the prior year, and in about 93% of the cases of civil war incidence (which includes ongoing wars) had an ongoing conflict or war the previous year. Harm to women may thus increase the risk of conflict but not escalation to civil war. In other words, the norms and social structures related to harm to women may be related to the initiation of violence to resolve a political conflict but may also be unrelated to the dynamics that lead to the escalation of violence. Examining this more directly would require a different kind of statistical model, and we leave such an examination to future work.

While we find relatively weak evidence concerning the relationship between harm to women, state violence, and terror, it is important to bear in mind that there is a close relationship between civil conflict, dissident terror, and state violence. As discussed in Chapter 2, about 81% of the countries that experience at least one terror attack also experience at least one year of intrastate conflict or war. Additionally, state violence is almost certain to occur during civil conflicts: using either measure of state violence, only in about 1% or fewer cases of conflict are there no reported incidents of state violence. It may be that harm to women is indirectly related to these forms of violence through its relationship with civil conflict, which would explain why the coefficient estimate for harm to women would shrink when controlling for civil war. With respect to terror, harm to women may increase actors' general propensities to use violence to settle political disputes without affecting the decision of dissident groups to resort to terror tactics. It may be that terror attacks are less effective in places where violence is a common or even everyday occurrence, as these attacks are not the spectacles they are usually intended to be and thus lose some of their emotional impact. It may also be that in places where the state is less responsive to (roughly half) the population's basic needs, and cares less for their welfare, states are less responsive to attacks on the civilian population (see Li 2005, 283). In the same vein, harm to women may impact conflict without having an independent effect on state violence. States may be inclined to use force in disputes with domestic opponents but not necessarily more likely to target the civilian population with violent abuse, holding armed conflict constant.

Finally, the relationship between harm to women and civil conflict holds when controlling for the political exclusion of ethnic minorities. This is notable since the argument that structural violence is a cause of political violence conceives of all social hierarchies based on dominance and subordination as grounded in similar norms (Caprioli 2005). This suggests that (structural) violence against out-groups of every variety should generally go hand in hand. It is therefore conceivable that harm to women is correlated with the onset of civil conflict because it is more pervasive in places where ethnic minority groups face discrimination and exclusion, which is a common motive for armed rebellion (Cederman, Gledtisch, and Buhaug 2013). Our results indicate otherwise: harm to women taps into a component of social hierarchy that is related to conflict independent of ethnic political exclusion.

Conclusion

This chapter started out by listing the few societies where women can organize such that harm to women is mitigated: their practices, institutions, and cultures enable women to thrive, and suggest three observations that are relevant to conflict. First, they place a high value on all human life and do not view some groups as more deserving of harm than others, which makes violence more costly and less likely to be used except as a last resort. Second, these societies feature less structural inequities in which resources are distributed disproportionately to particular groups, reducing the incentive to challenge the status quo and also to use violence to defend it. The household is also organized differently—Mosuo men live, for example, with their mothers, and couples traditionally do not live together—which also likely reduces intimate partner abuse/domestic violence. Household practices of cooperation are therefore more likely to be transmitted from one generation to another rather than norms about the appropriateness of using violence. In these communities and more generally in communities with less harm to women, it is possible that peace begets peace. Third, women in these communities are more fully able to participate in political mobilization because they do not experience harm in the same way as women in more patriarchal societies do. Their political mobilization makes non-violent claim-making more successful, leading to a society that is more free of violence.

The results of this chapter support the idea that societies that harm to women tend to experience more interstate and civil conflict. What is necessary then to reduce the occurrence of violent conflict is to foster a norm globally that all human life has equal value. This means, among other things, convincing people to value women's lives. To accomplish this, we clearly have something to learn from matriarchal societies that have been valuing (female) life for generations.

6

Beliefs about Women's Gender Roles and Political Violence

Introduction

On May 23, 2014, John Doe[1] drove to the Alpha Phi sorority house near the University of California, Santa Barbara with the intention of murdering all the women inside. He banged on the door, but no one opened it. This did not deter him, however. By this point he was intent on violence and had, in fact, already stabbed and killed three people, including two of his roommates. After leaving the sorority house, he drove through the streets shooting and hitting people with his car before committing suicide. The terrorist attack left six dead and another fourteen injured.[2] In his autobiographical manifesto, the attacker discussed his deep resentment toward women and outlined his plans for "retribution," which targeted women who were "spoiled, heartless, wicked bitches" for rejecting him and "starving [him] of sex."[3]

This terrorist attack is not an isolated event. There are many instances of womanhaters committing terrorist attacks. The internet is full of people who hold deep-seated animosity toward women, and some of these people carry out deadly attacks. These *beliefs* about women are rampant on the internet in what is called the "manosphere," or websites and forums that advocate for either a return to more traditional gender norms or a world without women.[4] Radical anti-woman beliefs are pervasive on the internet because it is a medium through which men (and women) can privately and anonymously voice these beliefs and discuss them with other like-minded people. However, beliefs about traditional gender norms are not uncommon and are not confined to people who frequent the darker and more extreme corners of the internet.[5] One study in Germany found that nearly a third of young men believe that violence against women is acceptable (Hofmann et al. 2023). In the United States, in 2017, 30% of men agreed that men should strive to be "alpha males," and 20% of women agreed. This suggests that almost a third of men in the United States, and about a fifth of women, believe that men

Positioning Women in Conflict Studies. Sabrina Karim and Daniel W. Hill, Jr., Oxford University Press.
© Oxford University Press 2024. DOI: 10.1093/9780197757970.003.0007

should adhere to rigid gender norms that prescribe dominance and aggression.[6] Prominent politicians and political groups also hold similar beliefs. Republican New Hampshire State Senator Robert Fisher was identified as the creator of a Reddit manosphere forum. In that forum, Fisher claimed that women were of "sub-par intelligence" and that "rape isn't an absolute bad, because the rapist I think probably likes it a lot" (Bacarisse 2017). These disparaging sentiments are not a far cry from well-known comments Donald Trump made in a video.[7] that was widely distributed about one month before he was elected president of the United States. The Proud Boys, a US far-right armed group, have not hidden their disdain for women. In fact, the Proud Boys originated as a group devoted to reinforcing traditional gender roles (Dowless 2022).

These groups and individuals who hold anti-woman beliefs more generally sometimes perpetrate violence publicly. For instance, members of the Proud Boys were actively involved in the January 6 attack on the US Capitol, and as of December 31, 2021, eighty-three Proud Boys members and sympathizers have allegedly carried out ideologically motivated crimes in the United States (Jensen, Yates, and Kane 2022). President Donald Trump's outspoken support for violence has even put the United States on the radar of several political violence watchdogs and NGOs (Hill Jr. 2016).[8] These examples shed light on how beliefs about women's gender roles—especially beliefs that such roles should be rigid or that women should assume "traditional" roles—are associated with political violence. Specifically, in this chapter we explore how societies in which more people hold rigid views about women's gender roles are susceptible to terrorism, intrastate conflict, and state violence.

As in previous chapters, this chapter begins by carefully conceptualizing beliefs about women's gender roles and provides a new measure of the concept. We then theorize about how beliefs about women's gender roles is linked to political violence. The last part of the chapter tests these hypotheses. We find that there is a link between beliefs about women's gender roles and terrorism. We conclude the chapter with some reflections about the implications of this finding.

Conceptualizing Beliefs about Women's Gender Roles

Characteristic of beliefs about women's gender roles women *women or those individuals who biologically identify as girls or women* and *perceptions.*

"Perceptions about women," however, is too broad a concept. To this, we add two more attributes that pertain to gender: belief in the existence of relational identities/roles, and beliefs about the rigidity/fluidity of those identities. The first of these, belief in the existence of relational roles, is the strength of the belief that certain responsibilities, tasks, jobs, etc. are best suited for women, while others are best suited for men. These roles are conceived of as relational and depend on each other for their meaning: the roles that are not suited for women are instead suited for men, while men are viewed as not fit to fulfill the roles best suited to women. The second of these attributes, rigidity/fluidity, captures the strength of the belief that people should conform to the gender roles that correspond to their assigned sex. While the relational identities aspect refers to the belief that there is a "natural" division of labor between women and men, rigidity/fluidity refers to how strongly opposed or acceptant someone is of departures from traditional roles or identities. By adding these characteristics, we create a narrower concept, "beliefs about women's gender roles," which is a classical subtype of "perceptions about women."

The concept of beliefs about women's gender roles captures the aggregate perceptions of the appropriate and inappropriate gender identities for those who identify biologically as girls or women. Box 6.1 highlights the characteristics of the concept belief about women's gender roles.

There are, of course, many characteristics one could add to the concept to create various classical subtypes. Scholars of gender and politics are interested in intersectionality, meaning groups or individuals with multiple, overlapping social identities. An analysis of the concept along these lines would amount to creating classical subtypes. For example, beliefs about women's gender roles could become beliefs about *Black* women's gender roles. This distinction would be useful for examining how beliefs about

---

Box 6.1 Characteristics of Beliefs about Women's Gender Roles

1) pertinent to those that biologically identify as girls or women
2) informed by perceptions
3) predicated on relational identities for men and women
4) assumes some degree of rigidity/fluidity of identities

176 THE STATUS OF WOMEN AND POLITICAL VIOLENCE

women's gender roles are affected by identification with or membership in different racial and ethnic (or other) groups. Given that perceptions of gender roles have been strongly conditioned by the experiences of dominant social groups, such an analysis may be necessary for a complete understanding of the concept.

Measuring Beliefs about Women's Gender Roles

Existing Measures

While women's inclusion, women's rights, and harm to women are frequently invoked and measured in research on gender and political violence, beliefs about women's gender roles are not. In this section we discuss potential ways of measuring this concept. Beliefs or perceptions is a crucial concept in the vast political science literature on public opinion. Research in this tradition usually measures people's perceptions about certain issue areas through surveys, whether by phone, email, or in person. Public opinion is "a general measure of the directionality and strength of issue-specific views and sentiments held by a relevant group" (Glynn and Huge 2008; Erikson and Tedin 2015). Generally, public opinion guides public policies (Page and Shapiro 1983). When public opinion about an issue is generally favorable, political figures are more likely to favor that issue and support policies that promote it. That is, politicians often take cues from public opinion and policies that reflect shifts in the number of people who support (or oppose) a particular issue.

Prior research on beliefs about women's gender roles, which as we discuss later is prolific, gives us confidence that the concept can be measured cross-nationally using survey items. For example, one could gauge the extent of agreement with the following statement: "Women should always take care of children." Individual responses could then be aggregated to get a sense of the prevalence of this belief in a particular country. If a relatively large number of people agree with this statement, or with similar statements that suggest women should conform to their gender roles, it implies that gender identities are relatively rigid in that society. In such a scenario, societal norms limit the set of gender roles considered appropriate for women. In contrast, if individuals believe that it is appropriate for women to engage in traditionally masculine roles—e.g. combat roles in the military or positions of political leadership—this implies greater fluidity in gender roles, meaning people typically consider a wider set of (feminine and masculine) gender roles as appropriate for women.

There is a long history of measuring attitudes about women (and gender roles) in the psychology literature. Prominent scales include the Attitudes Toward Women Scale (ATWS) (Spence, Helmrich, and Stapp (1973), Sex Role Behavior Scale (Orlofsky 1981), Chastity Scale (Mahalingam 2007), Modern Sexism Scale (MSS) (Swim et al. 1995; Swim and Cohen 1997), and the Sexist Attitudes toward Women Scale (Benson and Vincent 1980).[9] Importantly, these scales have mostly been developed and tested among White populations in the United States, Canada, and Europe. As such, findings based on them may not generalize to other settings or populations (Hayes and Swim 2013). To our knowledge, the batteries of questions are not used in cross-national surveys and have generally not been tested across time in different contexts. Thus, there is room for the development of culturally sensitive scales that measure beliefs about women at the cross-national level.

Our Measure

Our goal is to create a cross-national, time series scale for beliefs about women's gender roles. To accomplish this, we use survey data that includes questions about women in the WVS.[10] As discussed in Chapter 2, our approach builds on Inglehart and Norris (2003), who use 5 survey items from the WVS to create a scale that measures attitudinal support for "gender equality." Having conducted a factor analysis using the individual level survey data to select these 5 indicators from a pool of candidate indicators, they found 5 items that tap into a common conceptual dimension: people's self-reported attitudes about whether women are as capable of men of being political leaders, whether women have less of a right to a job than men when jobs are scarce, whether university education is less important for girls than boys, whether women must have children to be fulfilled, and whether the respondent approves of a woman having a child but not wanting a relationship with a man. After identifying these items, they sum them into an additive 5 point scale at the individual level and then take the mean for each country across all respondents and multiply the result by 20, so that the final scale ranges in principle from 0 to 100. Their analysis includes 50 countries.

178   THE STATUS OF WOMEN AND POLITICAL VIOLENCE

We use the most recent data from WVS, which allows us to expand the number of countries and years used in the analysis. Our approach to measurement offers some clear advantages. Because the model automatically imputes values for years that are missing data (by drawing from the prior distribution in case of a missing value), we can estimate scores for years between the different waves of the WVS, which significantly increases the temporal coverage of the measure. It also avoids averaging across the survey items, which gives equal weight to each item and so ignores information the measurement model provides about the relationship between the construct and indicators.

To create our measure, we first identified eight items that measure people's beliefs about women's gender roles, shown in Table 6.1. We include four of the five indicators used by Inglehart and Norris: whether women make worse political leaders than men, whether jobs should be reserved for men when they are scarce, whether it is more important for men to be educated than women, and whether women must become mothers to feel fulfilled. We also include questions about whether it is acceptable for a married woman to have a higher-paying job than her husband, whether women make worse business executives than men, whether it is justifiable for a married man to beat his wife, and whether women having the same rights as men is an essential aspect of democracy.[11]

The model we use for beliefs about women departs from those used in the previous chapters.[12] To produce latent variable estimates at the country-year level, we must first aggregate the individual responses to the country-year level. To do this we create binary versions of each survey item that is not already binary. We code responses in the category that corresponds to the most flexible beliefs about women's gender roles as 1 and all other responses as 0. For example, we code a value of 1 for responses to the question of whether men make better political leaders than women if the respondent answered, "disagree strongly." For each country, we then sum the number of responses classified as 1s. The probability that a randomly selected individual from that country will give the answer coded as 1 is then modeled as a function of the latent variable. Alternatively, we can think of this as modeling the expected proportion of the respondents that will give the answer coded as 1 as a function of the latent variable. The model allows for temporal dependence in the latent variable, which means the values for country-years beyond the first time period (1981) will be correlated with the value for that country in the previous year. This will have the effect of smoothing out the time series for

BELIEFS ABOUT WOMEN'S GENDER ROLES & POLITICAL VIOLENCE   179

Table 6.1   World Values Survey Items for Beliefs Model

Item	Potential responses
Men make better political leaders than women	1–4 (1: Agree strongly; 4: disagree strongly)
Men have more right to a job than women when jobs are scarce	Agree, disagree
University is more important for boys than girls	1–4 (1: Agree strongly; 4: disagree strongly)
A woman has to have children to be fulfilled	Agree; disagree
It is a problem if women have more income than their husbands	1–4 (1: Agree strongly; 4: disagree strongly)
Men make better business executives than women	1–4 (1: Agree strongly; 4: disagree strongly)
Is it justifiable for a man to beat his wife?	1–10 (1: Never; 10: Always)
Is women having the same rights as men essential to democracy?	1–10 (1: Not essential; 10: Essential)

each country and reducing the uncertainty in the estimates, which is useful due to the gaps in temporal coverage between survey waves.

To aggregate these responses to the country-year level we use the binomial distribution with a logit link function, effectively making this an IRT model with a logit link.[13] As with the models that include binary indicators, the β parameters have the same interpretation as the discrimination parameters in an IRT model: positive values of β indicate that the probability of a "correct" response increases as X increases, and negative values indicate that the probability decreases with X. The α parameters are again similar to "difficulty" parameters in an item response model: α is proportional to the level of the latent trait at which a respondent is more likely than not to respond correctly, which can be calculated as $\frac{\alpha}{\beta}$.

Estimates for the item parameters are shown in Figure 6.1. The β_j parameters are all positive, meaning the survey items (recoded so that a positive response indicates more flexible beliefs) are all positively related to the latent trait. The items with the largest discrimination are the questions about women having children and whether men are more deserving of jobs. Estimates for the α_j and β_j parameters for the latter indicate that the typical respondent is likely to strongly disagree with the statement "women must have children to be fulfilled" once the latent variable is greater than 0.91,

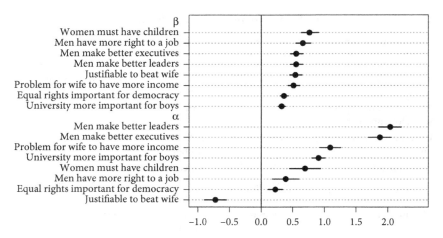

Figure 6.1 Estimates from Measurement Model for Beliefs about Women's Gender Roles

which is just below the eightieth percentile. Similarly, the typical respondent is likely to strongly disagree with the statement "men have more right to a job than women when jobs are scarce" when the latent variable is greater than 0.59, which is around the seventieth percentile. In other words, these items separate country-years that are in the top 20% and 30%, respectively, on the beliefs about women scale.[14]

Beliefs about Women's Gender Roles and Political Violence

"Beliefs about women's gender roles" as a concept means perceptions about women's identities relative to men's—whether membership in the categories "man" or "woman" defines appropriate behavior and how sharply membership differentiates appropriate behavior for people to whom membership in those categories is ascribed. Beliefs about women can be relatively rigid, with individuals expecting women's behavior to conform to traditional gender roles, or more flexible, meaning individuals are willing to accept more gender fluid roles for women. We posit that there are at least two theories that point to potential connections between beliefs about women's gender roles and the occurrence of political violence. One is the "uphold the status quo" theory, which suggests that rigid beliefs about women's gender roles is indicative of a society where the status quo is entrenched and where those in power have the most to lose.

BELIEFS ABOUT WOMEN'S GENDER ROLES & POLITICAL VIOLENCE   181

Violence is used to maintain the status quo. The second theory is the "gateway for recruitment" theory, which suggests that armed groups may appeal to potential recruits by exploiting (rigid) beliefs about women's gender roles.

Upholding the Status Quo

A person's beliefs about gender roles indicate how strongly (or not) they prefer sex conformity to gender. When preferences for conformity are salient in a society, individuals in that society do not believe it is appropriate for men to behave in a feminine way nor do they believe that it is appropriate for women to behave in a masculine way. Rigid views, or a strong preference for conformity, indicate a preference for the sustenance of gender inequalities— because the masculine is prized above the feminine, men who perform masculinity will always dominate (Tickner 1992). Because masculine men (usually defined by White, heterosexual men) hold the most privileged position in society (and globally), they have the most to lose if the status quo is disrupted and may be the most likely group to resist changes to existing social hierarchies and the norms that sustain them. They may find violence acceptable as a way to maintain the status quo and be more likely to support or participate in its use (Barnes, Brown, and Osterman 2012). In contrast, more flexible beliefs about women's gender roles indicate that individuals are not so beholden to traditional beliefs or committed to the status quo and perceive little benefit to maintaining social hierarchies. This makes them less willing to use or support the use of violence in response to challenges to the status quo.

Note that the "upholding of the status quo" argument is the "other side of the coin" in theories of inequality and violence, which suggest that "men rebel" when they are relatively deprived (Gurr 2015).[15] In the typical grievance-based account, group-level differences in status and power can motivate mobilization by individuals who experience *relative* deprivation, meaning individuals compare their situational status to what their situational status could be and perceive an inequality. Relative inequality has become a common explanation for the use of politically motivated violence by groups who have experienced discrimination and political exclusion, and who have relatively little wealth compared with other groups (Cederman, Gleditsch, and Buhaug 2013). Groups who sit atop the social hierarchy are overrepresented in politics and who have a disproportionate amount of wealth are typically given less attention in these accounts. In contrast, we suggest that those who want to preserve the status quo as it relates to social hierarchies— including gender role conformity and consequently male dominance—are likely to accept and condone the use of violence to achieve this goal. This is in line with how Walter (2023) explains grievance theories of civil war onset whereby the dominant, majority group feel threatened, that their power is slipping, and resort to violence to uphold the status quo. Similarly, we suggest that those who hold more rigid ideas about women's gender roles are more prone to accept and support the use of violence in response to perceived threats to social order.

A large body of research in social psychology supports the notion that some people have a deeply held preference for maintaining a social hierarchy in which some groups dominate others.[16] Social dominance theory starts from the position that all human societies are organized around social hierarchies based on age, sex or gender,[17] and "arbitrary set" groupings that are not based on "the human life cycle," i.e. on biological processes related to reproduction and aging (Pratto, Sidanius, and Levin 2006). Arbitrary set groupings include a large number of socially constructed categories, such as those based on class or income, as well as categories that political scientists would characterize as ethnic identities (Chandra 2006). Much of the research in this vein is focused on the concept of "social dominance orientation," which refers to individual approval and support for the broad notion (without reference to a particular group) that group-based hierarchies are a good and necessary part of society. Social dominance orientation has been linked to a number of negative and hostile attitudes and behaviors toward members of out-groups, including support for the use of force and violence to enforce anti-immigration policies, and is correlated at the country level with political instability and violence (Kunst et al. 2017). Thus, according to social dominance theory, those who are predisposed to value a hierarchy whereby individuals have specified roles in society are likely to want to keep the social order intact, including gender roles for men and women. Indeed, though social dominance orientation is correlated with both sexism and ethnic prejudice, it is correlated more strongly with the former than latter (Pratto, Sidanius, and Levin 2006, 283).[18] In short, beliefs about women's gender roles are relevant to more general beliefs about the desirability of a society where some groups dominate others. Where beliefs about women's gender roles are relatively strict, this suggests a predilection to view the subordination of women and other groups as a good thing that should be maintained by force if necessary.

BELIEFS ABOUT WOMEN'S GENDER ROLES & POLITICAL VIOLENCE   183

States can co-opt the idea of changing beliefs about gender roles as justification for initiating violence. Other states are categorized as threats because of their belief systems about women's gender roles. For example, in the United States during the Cold War, reinforcement of traditional gender roles was seen as a way of protecting society from the dangers of Soviet Communism, dangers which supposedly included the de-feminization of women through their roles in politics and the workforce (May 2008). In Latin America, too, Communism was viewed by the right as a threat to "traditional values." Anti-leftist propaganda emphasized that, by sending women to work, Communist governments would effectively destroy households and leave women as "stern, desexed repressors who have lost their feminine traits of compassion and are therefore willing to participate in the breakup of the family" (Power 2008, 940). These images appealed to, and were propagated by, women in right-wing activist circles no less than men (Power 2015).

Indeed, the "upholding the status quo" mechanism applies to men *and to women*, who may also hold rigid beliefs about women's gender roles. Women who believe strongly in traditional gender roles perceive benefits from the patriarchal structure of society in which men dominate. Women serve their traditional gender role in exchange for these benefits, which may include protection, social status, and material wealth. Many women favor this tradeoff and want to preserve feminine subordination. They perceive challenges to the status quo of traditional gender roles as a loss of their femininity (of what it means to be a woman) and a loss of the benefits of being "cared after." For this reason, conservative women often organize around preserving their traditional social roles.

The "upholding the status quo" theory is similar to the theory presented in Chapter 5 about tolerating low costs for violence. Both theories present normative arguments whereby values about cost to human life or values about importance of the status quo make violence more likely. However, they differ with respect to the relevant norm. Harm to women signals that a society places little value on human life. It does not necessarily signal that the regime should feel threatened about the future. In fact, harm to women is itself a way to maintain the status quo—to ensure that women remain in their social place. Rigid views about women's gender roles, on the other hand, signal high levels of conformity around traditional values. This conformity might shift in the future. Leaders have more to lose when more people conform. As such, pre-emptive violence is used to ensure that people remain conformed. Additionally, while harm to women and rigid beliefs about women's gender roles both make

184   THE STATUS OF WOMEN AND POLITICAL VIOLENCE

violence more likely, people do not have to have rigid views about women to accept harm to women. For example, women who want better reproductive care might also believe that a woman's primary role in society is to be a mother.

Beliefs about women's gender roles is an individual level attribute, but like any other individual attribute, it can be aggregated to the group or societal/ country level. People who hold rigid beliefs about women's gender roles are more likely to be willing to use force to maintain the status quo than people who hold flexible beliefs. At the group level, the more people in the group who are worried about perceived challenges to the status quo, the more likely they are to support and engage in violence to uphold it. If rigid views about women's gender roles are prevalent in a society or country, this suggests a broad tolerance for the status quo and a tendency to use violence to defend it. Because more rigid views are common in that society, challenges to the status quo will be perceived as threatening to a relatively large number of people.

The argument that countries in which people hold more rigid beliefs about women's gender roles are likely to place more value on the status quo has a general implication: governments in these countries are less likely to concede to or compromise with any group that is trying to change the status quo. State agents may target any person or group who is (perceived to be) a threat to the social order. This includes groups who are challenging the government's authority generally, but especially groups who are directly opposing the hierarchies that privilege certain groups over others, including those based on male dominance or the dominance of a particular ethnic or religious group. Rigid gender role beliefs may also increase the likelihood of state violence directed at marginalized groups who are not openly challenging the status quo but who are considered threatening because they are perceived as socially deviant. Thus, broadly speaking, the state may be more likely to target any group who is in favor of, or would benefit from, changing the status quo. This also means that domestic groups that have political demands are thus unlikely to gain concessions from the government. The state's intractability means that domestic political groups might resort to violence to gain concessions. This leads to the following hypotheses:

H6.1: When states have more rigid beliefs about women's gender roles, state violence will be more likely.

H6.2: When states have more rigid beliefs about women's gender roles, intrastate conflict will be more likely.

H6.3: When states have more rigid beliefs about women's gender roles, terrorism will be more likely.

It is also possible that states use the beliefs about women's gender roles in other countries to instrumentally portray them as threats: the portrayal, during the Cold War, of the dismantling by leftist groups of women's traditional roles as presenting a threat to the United States is an example of this. So, too is the current use of the same argument by Russia, Hungary, and Poland (Fodor 2021; Orlova 2018)[19] in portraying Western beliefs about women's gender roles in society as harmful to traditional values. This means that states with more rigid views about women's gender roles may be more likely to initiate interstate wars to prevent threatening gender ideologies from flowing into the country, which leads to the fourth hypothesis.

H6.4: When states have more rigid beliefs about women's gender roles, interstate conflict will be more likely.

Gateway for Recruitment into Armed Groups

Governments are not the only actors that may want to preserve a status quo characterized by social hierarchies that benefit particular groups. Shifts away from the status quo, even if only perceived, may result in mobilization by reactionary armed groups. Regardless of their specific ideology or political program, these groups may appeal to beliefs in traditional gender norms to attract recruits.

Ideology is generally acknowledged to play an important role in group mobilization, recruitment, and cohesion, but there are several ways of understanding its role in these processes. Theories of group organization that allow a role for ideology usually conceive of it in a broad way that allows any affinity to a social group to be characterized as "ideology" (Gates 2002; Weinstein 2005, 2006). Sanín and Wood (2014) consider an ideology to consist of identification with a group, their shared grievances and goals, and some understanding of how they might be addressed. Well-defined political ideologies play a role in recruitment and organization, but this usually happens once a group has established itself. Rather, when groups are starting to form, they must often rely on broader appeals to recruit members, largely because for any well-defined ideology the population of true believers is small (Leader Maynard 2019). Parkinson (2021) highlights that formal indoctrination may be less important for group cohesion than the socialization that occurs through everyday practices and reinforces general notions of group identity. Moreover, given that there are competing groups or a competitive market for recruitment, group ideology is not inflexible, and groups may change or adapt their ideologies and their policy goals to recruit more people (Tokdemir et al. 2021).

We argue that leaders and nascent groups can instrumentalize rigid gender belief systems for recruitment. These beliefs can constitute an "ideology" as defined here but are compatible with many different formal doctrines and political programs. Armed groups can use rigid gender beliefs as a recruitment tool by promising prospective members a world that conforms to such beliefs. There is reason to believe that those who hold rigid beliefs about women's gender roles may be more suspectable to recruitment. Individuals who hold patriarchal views are more likely to select into violent organizations. For instance, Bjarnegård et al. (2023) find that the military plays little role in socializing recruits into a militarized masculinity. In Thailand, those who already held patriarchal views opted to join the armed forces. If those with rigid beliefs about women's gender roles are more prone to join violent groups, this means that the more people in society that believe in traditional gender roles, the larger the pool from which (reactionary) dissident groups can recruit. In other words, nascent groups actively seek men (and women) who are unhappy about (actual, perceived, or anticipated) changes to the status quo, and this often takes the form of dissatisfaction with changes in men's status relative to women—a possibly widespread and tangible grievance (Blazak 2001). Groups engage these men (and women) in conversation about the possibility of a "return" to a world with strong, traditional gender norms, where (often, White, heterosexual) men are at the top. These conversations can lead gradually to radicalization, meaning a willingness to use violence to bring about the "return" of their idealized society. In this way, rigid beliefs about gender roles becomes a gateway for recruitment into armed groups.

The "manosphere" example from the beginning of the chapter provides a helpful way to understand this theory of recruitment. Before Donald Trump became US president in 2016, there was more stigma around holding White, nationalist beliefs (Crandall, Miller, and White 2018). People may have been less likely to voice racist beliefs prior to President Trump normalizing such language within the United States and globally (Giani and Méon

2021). Reactionary and right-wing activists also engaged in discussions about women's gender roles in society, and how the advancement of women was hurting men. Men experiencing a range of hardships—being unable to find romantic partners, not being admitted to a university, or losing their job and therefore their role as breadwinner—could relate to the belief espoused by these activists: that women were responsible. Activists in the manosphere regularly blame women for these hardships. Like the perpetrator of the attack discussed in the introduction to this chapter, they attribute the absence of a romantic relationship to women unfairly rejecting men. They also view women's advancement in society as a threat to their status, reasoning that a woman may end up "taking their spot" in school or the workforce. Depending on the group and/or activist, the suggested remedy is a return to traditional patriarchy or a world without women. Thus, men who experience these hardships may be more prone to engage with people who espouse similar views, whether online or in-person. And, the more men (and women) who believe in traditional patriarchy, the larger the group with which the messages will resonate. Once a person is drawn in, they become exposed to other ideologies that may normalize violence against specific social groups, such as White nationalism and other racist ideologies. This process is how the Proud Boys became a terrorist group;[20] their initial leader, Gavin McInnes, used hyper-masculinity to recruit followers (Kutner 2020).

The Proud Boys are only one example of reactionary groups that use people's rigid beliefs about gender roles as a gateway for recruitment. Reactionary groups in many countries, including state-based and state-sponsored groups, appeal to people's beliefs in traditional gender roles. These include a range of groups that profess extremist religious ideologies, such as the Islamic State (Speckhard and Ellenberg 2021), Hindu nationalist groups (Banerjee 2006), and extremist Christian groups (Sharpe 2000). Somewhat counterintuitively, espousing an extreme ideology can be advantageous for recruitment (Walter 2017). Theories of recruitment typically assume that individuals are motivated by a mixture of material and immaterial goals, and those who are attracted to a group primarily for ideological (immaterial) reasons tend to be more committed, effective, and disciplined than those who join for material gain (Gates 2002; Weinstein 2006). Further, in an environment where groups with similar ideologies are competing for recruits, staking out an extreme position allows a group to present its ideology as "purer" than its competitors (Walter 2017). Groups that include traditional gender roles as part of their ideology may be similarly incentivized to present themselves as the most committed defenders of male hierarchy.

In addition to religious extremists, right-wing groups (like the Proud Boys) are also likely to adopt traditional gender roles as part of their ideology. In many cases, right-wing groups that resort to terror attacks are involved first and foremost in conflict with a social group they deem to be subordinate, rather than a conflict with the state (Sprinzak 1995). To these groups, conflict with the state is of secondary importance and becomes necessary only if the state fails to support them or sides with the subordinate group. Right-wing terror is often directed toward ethnic or religious groups who right-wing militants believe are not deserving of equal socioeconomic or political status. Similarly, there are groups who believe that women should be, to varying degrees, marginalized and subordinated to men. Such groups are likely to sympathize with the view that women's advancement poses a threat to society. For these groups, their primary conflict is with those responsible for women's advancement and related social ills. This includes women who do not adhere to traditional gender roles, but also any person, group, or government who subscribes to egalitarian notions about gender roles. Since egalitarian beliefs are more likely to be associated with left-wing (and secularist) political groups than right-wing groups, opposition to them is more likely to animate right-wing (and religious) groups. In sum, reactionary groups may be motivated by beliefs about gender roles and appeal to traditional roles to recruit and strengthen their armed group. This provides another rationale for H6.2 and H6.3.

It is worth noting, however, that reactionary right-wing and religious extremist groups are not the only type of group that utilizes beliefs about women's gender roles for recruitment. Left-wing groups tend to adopt ideologies that include more fluid views about women's gender roles and may try to recruit or attract individuals by espousing these views. That is, leftist groups, often recruiting women, promise a world without traditional gender roles to men and women who join their ranks. This is perhaps why armed leftist groups are more likely to include women in an assortment of roles, including combat roles (Thomas and Bond 2015; Henshaw 2016; Wood and Thomas 2017; Darden, Henshaw, and Szekely 2019; Wood 2019). That both reactionary and leftist groups may use beliefs about gender roles as a gateway into armed organizations suggests more fine-grained versions of H6.3 and H6.4 that apply specifically to conflicts and terror attacks involving groups with religious extremist or right-wing ideologies.[21]

Do Beliefs about Women's Gender Roles Affect Levels of Political Violence? Testing the Hypotheses

Estimates from models using each measure of political violence as the dependent variable are shown in Figure 6.2. All of the estimates have the expected sign, meaning beliefs about women's gender roles are negatively related to each kind of state violence. However, once control variables are included, the coefficient for the latent variable is only significant in the model of terror attacks. This means we find the strongest support for the idea that political groups are more likely to resort to terrorism in societies in which rigid beliefs about gender roles are more prevalent. Or put another way, terror attacks are less likely in societies where beliefs about women's gender roles are more equitable.[22] We find weaker support for a link between rigid views about women's gender roles and state violence (the test statistics for the latent variable are just above the conventional cutoff for statistical significance without control variables and are just below it once control variables are added). We find weaker support still for a link between rigid views about women's gender roles and civil and interstate conflict.

Our results point to some support for the idea that rigid beliefs about gender roles are related to a willingness to defend the status quo with violence. There is only modest support for the negative correlation between state violence and the fluidity of beliefs about women's gender roles. This suggests

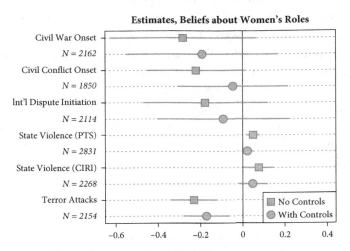

Figure 6.2 Coefficient Estimates for Beliefs about Women's Gender Roles from Models of Political Violence

that in countries where rigid beliefs are more common, the state may view dissidents and marginalized social groups, who are the most likely targets of state violence, as more threatening to the social and political order. They may be willing to use violence to defend the status quo.

Our result for terror attacks also provides support for this idea as applied to dissident violence—in some cases individuals or non-state groups may resort to violence in an effort to defend the status quo against perceived threats that the gender order will change in the future. It is possible that this result reflects backlash against governments or other state actors who are seen as contributing to the erosion of traditional roles. This result is consistent with the findings in Chapter 3 that show a *negative* relationship between women's political inclusion and terror attacks. As states become more egalitarian in their beliefs and in terms of political inclusion, terror attacks become less frequent. This means that both female politicians and their (and society's) beliefs about women's gender roles affect bargaining with political groups. The state may be willing to engage in reducing inequality, social policies, or make more concessions to groups as they are more flexible with respect to changes in the status quo and social hierarchy.

The relationship between beliefs about women's gender roles and terror attacks also suggests that rigid beliefs can be leveraged by violent political groups to attract recruits. We have already suggested that some religious and right-wing groups are the most likely to appeal to rigid beliefs as a recruitment strategy,[23] but our results indicate a negative relationship between the fluidity of beliefs and terror across all groups, not just those with particular ideologies. It is conceivable that there is a disconnect between a group's formal ideology and the degree to which it appeals to, or takes advantage of, beliefs about gender roles. That is, the typical group, regardless of their ideology, may find it easier to attract members and convince them of the usefulness of violence when aggregate beliefs about gender are more rigid. Investigating the variation in groups that might recruit based on beliefs about societal gender norms requires a more fine-grained examination. Some work has already started down this path (Kattelman and Burns 2022), but the role of beliefs about women in dissident violence requires more exploration.

We find little evidence of a relationship between beliefs about women and civil conflict. This is worth discussing given that normative arguments motivate the expectations that harm to women and beliefs about women's gender roles are related to political violence and that we find evidence of a relationship between harm and civil conflict in Chapter 5. While the estimates for our measure of beliefs in the models of civil conflict onset are negative, they are insignificant and smaller in magnitude than the estimates for harm to women reported in Chapter 5. What are the implications of these findings for the argument that subordination of women reflects permissive norms regarding the use of violence in political conflicts? First, it is worth noting that harm to women is not highly correlated with beliefs about women's gender roles,[24] suggesting that they are different concepts, and thus the lack of a correlation between civil conflict and beliefs about women's gender roles should not be surprising. Moreover, although the theories are similar, there are differences with respect to the normative implications of the argument. Harm to women is indicative of a high tolerance for cost whereas rigid beliefs about women's gender roles signals a commitment to the status quo. In the former, there are no future threats as the harm to women *is the way* to reinforce hierarchy. In the latter, people's beliefs can change and when there is full conformity, there is more to lose because people can only move away from this position. This justifies pre-emptive violence by the state (repression) or by non-state groups (terrorism). It does not necessarily mean that the pre-emptive violence translates into full-on conflict in society.

We also do not find evidence of a relationship between beliefs about women and interstate war. This might be because even though states with rigid beliefs about women's gender roles portray other states with more fluid beliefs about women's gender roles as threatening, this characterization may not be enough to push the state into actual war. There are many less costly actions that a state could take to prevent ideologies from entering the country such as blocking INGOs and development aid (Chaudhry 2022). As such, these actions are perhaps more likely than attacking the source country. Yet, the hypotheses would benefit from a dyadic test that explores whether interstate war is more likely between states with more rigid beliefs about women's roles and ones with more fluid beliefs about women's roles. We leave other scholars to conduct this analysis.

Conclusion

The Isla Vista attack mentioned at the beginning of this chapter is rarely cited as a terrorist attack in the media. But it was politically motivated, and the attacker professed to belong to (albeit poorly formed) anti-woman's groups—groups that have political beliefs about the appropriate roles for men and women. The link between beliefs and political violence in this example and the link made empirically in this chapter suggest that ideology about gender roles is an important factor for understanding political violence, especially terrorism. Whether state agents and decision makers (or armed groups) stand steadfast to the status quo in the face of threats, and/or nascent and violent political groups find recruits, (the changing) belief systems in a society serve as a sort of canary in the coal mine for understanding state behavior and for potential recruitment into armed groups.

We end the chapter by highlighting the importance of understanding beliefs about gender roles, not just women's gender roles. The chapter highlights how beliefs about *women's* gender roles affects political violence. However, not only are views about the appropriate role for women in society important, but also expectations about *men's* roles as well as views about *trans* people and other gender fluid identities. First, understanding how masculinity is understood is important and not always correlated with how people perceive women's roles. For example, it is possible that large majorities of people believe that women should be able to engage in a wider variety of masculine tasks (e.g. join the military, serve as politicians, etc.), while also believing that men should hold on to traditional roles (e.g. perform masculinity). Indeed, many in the manosphere opine about not being able to live up the standard set for men: they cannot live up to society's definition of masculinity (Ging 2019; Barnes and Karim 2024). Second, whereas much of the world is starting to hold more egalitarian views about women, there is less openness to gender fluid identities. Anti-trans beliefs, for example, is a clear indicator of groups and governments trying to maintain the status quo. Thus, future analysis of gendered belief systems should unpack differences in people's beliefs about the appropriate roles for all types of gender identities (Wirtz et al. 2020; Sjoberg 2012b). In doing so, we may find the specific beliefs that are more likely to be correlated with a propensity for political violence and do more to reduce the spread of or counter such beliefs.

7

Conclusion

If you are keeping up with the news these days, it often seems as if the world is entering into a period of decline for women's status. Headlines such as "This terrifying backslide on LGBTQ rights is a threat to women's rights too" (Jones 2022) or "U.S. ranks 43rd on gender parity index this year, sliding 16 slots from last year (Chuck 2023)" pop up in news feeds with distressing regularity. What do changes in women's status mean for political violence globally? Our book has attempted to explore this important question.

The primary objective of this book was to explore the connections between women's status and various forms of political violence. To do so, we departed from prior literature that tended to conflate gender and women, lack explicit definitions of key concepts, and use measures with little justification. Instead, we used a process of differentiation and delineation to separate gender from four concepts related to women's status—women's inclusion, women's rights, harm to women, and beliefs about women's gender roles—that the literature identifies as determinants of political violence. We define each concept explicitly and aggregate available indicators using measurement models that have several advantages over alternative methods. In this way, we avoided the problems of concept stretching and measurement invalidity. We also build on and develop theories that connect each concept to different forms of political violence and explore these connections empirically. What this process of differentiation and delineation reveals is that not all aspects of women's status affect political violence in the same way.

Table 7.1 summarizes the theories, hypotheses, and results from Chapters 3–6. We note that most of the hypotheses do not find support. These nulls results are important because the prior quantitative literature (Figure 0.1) found "positive" results for all the forms of political violence included in this book. In other words, much of the literature suggested that "gender equality" was something of a panacea that reduces the likelihood of interstate war, intrastate, war, terrorism, and state violence. However, our results paint a different picture. They suggest that not all aspects of women's status are associated with a reduced risk of every form of political violence.

Positioning Women in Conflict Studies. Sabrina Karim and Daniel W. Hill, Jr., Oxford University Press.
© Oxford University Press 2024. DOI: 10.1093/9780197757970.003.0008

Table 7.1 Summary of Results

Concept	Theory	Hypothesis	Result
Women's Inclusion	Women are more disposed toward peace or create the conditions for peace	H3.1a: The probability of interstate conflict initiation decreases as women's inclusion in public spaces generally, and political spaces specifically, increases.	No support
		H3.2a: The probability of civil conflict decreases as women's inclusion in public spaces generally, and political spaces specifically, increases.	No support
		H3.3a: The frequency of dissident terror attacks decreases as women's inclusion in public spaces generally, and political spaces specifically, increases.	Some support (women's political inclusion)
		H3.4a: State violence decreases as women's inclusion in public spaces generally, and political spaces specifically, increases.	No support
	Perceptional Stereotypes of Women	H3.1b: The probability of interstate conflict initiation increases as women's inclusion in public spaces generally, and political spaces specifically, increases.	No support
		H3.2b: The probability of civil conflict increases as women's inclusion in public spaces generally, and political spaces specifically, increases.	No support
		H3.3b: The frequency of dissident terror attacks increases as women's inclusion in public spaces generally, and political spaces specifically, increases.	No support
		H3.4b: State violence increases as women's inclusion in public spaces generally, and political spaces specifically, increases.	Some support(women's inclusion in public spaces)

CONCLUSION   195

Table 7.1 *Continued*

Concept	Theory	Hypothesis	Result
Women's Rights	Women's Rights as Signaling Liberalism	H4.1: When states adopt more women's rights measures, interstate war will be less likely.	No support
	Women Rights as Signaling State Openness to Claim-making	H4.2: When states adopt more women's rights measures, intrastate war will be less likely.	No support
		H4.3: When states adopt more women's rights measures, dissident terror attacks will be less likely.	No support
	Increasing the Number of Watchdogs	H4.4: As states adopt more extensive women's rights measures, state violence will decrease. The strength of the relationship between women's rights and state violence will increase with the number of women's rights advocacy groups.	Support
	Women's Rights Advocacy Transitioning to Non-violent Advocacy	H4.1, H4.2	No support
Harm to Women	Harm to Women Weakens Normative Constraints on Violence	H5.1: The probability of interstate conflict initiation increases as harm to women increases.	Support
		H5.2: The probability of intrastate war onset increases as harm to women increases.	Support
		H5.3: State violence increases as harm to women increases.	No Support
	Early Exposure to Violence Normalizes Violence at the Individual Level	H5.4: The frequency of terror attacks increases as harm to women increases.(Also H5.2)	Support for H5.2 but not H5.4
	Harm to Women Creates Shortages of Women	H5.2, H5.4	Support for H5.2, but not H5.4
	Harm to Women as a Strategy to Prevent Women's Political Mobilization	H5.1, H5.2, and H5.3	Support for H5.1 and H5.2

Continued

196 POSITIONING WOMEN IN CONFLICT STUDIES

Table 7.1 *Continued*

Concept	Theory	Hypothesis	Result
Beliefs about Women's Roles	Upholding the Status Quo	H6.1: When states have more rigid beliefs about women's gender roles, state violence will be more likely.	No support
		H6.2: When states have more rigid beliefs about women's gender roles, intrastate conflict will be more likely.	No support
		H6.3: When states have more rigid beliefs about women's gender roles, terrorism will be more likely.	Support
		H6.4: When states have more rigid beliefs about women's gender roles, interstate conflict will be more likely.	No Support
	Gateway for Recruitment into Armed Groups	H6.2, H6.3	Support for H6.3 but not H6.2

By differentiating gender equality and different aspects of women's status and using more valid measures that have a clearer connection to the relevant concept, we present a more nuanced picture and identify which aspects of women's status are associated with a lower risk for which forms of violence. This demonstrates the importance of differentiation and matching concepts to indicators. It allows us to separate conceptually and empirically some of the different potential paths between women's status and the risk of political violence, while avoiding the sweeping claim that increasing gender equality leads to a reduction in political violence.

Reviewing our results, it is important to bear in mind that they reflect *aggregate* relationships. We view our analysis as a starting point from which these relationships can be investigated further. Having sifted through the available country-level data, the next step forward is to conduct more fine-grained analyses that probe the potential mechanisms behind these relationships. Determining which specific aspects of women's status are reliably related to which forms of political violence is valuable, as we can organize our findings within different theoretical frameworks, which will be helpful for conducting more focused and refined analyses in the future. This could entail quantitative work that uses data at lower levels of aggregation (groups, individuals, smaller geographic areas, and shorter time periods, etc.) (as suggested by Cohen and Karim 2022) or qualitative work that provides a detailed account of the link between women's status and political violence in particular contexts. We return to this point later when discussing potential future areas of study.

Our analysis suggests women's political inclusion is associated with fewer terror attacks. One potential explanation for this pattern is that women's political inclusion creates a more diverse set of political leaders, who may implement policies that address existing grievances and/or may bargain in different ways with groups that use violence. Political groups prone to using violence may perceive female political leaders in a different way than they perceive male political leaders. However, this leaves unexamined variation among female politicians that may be relevant, which points to one opportunity for future research.

Our analysis also suggests that less rigid beliefs about women's roles is associated with fewer terror attacks. One explanation for this is that when more people in a given society hold more flexible views, violent political organizations have a smaller base from which to recruit. While our research finds that attacks tend to decrease regardless of the ideology of the political group, there are theoretical reasons to believe that right-wing/reactionary groups are more likely to use beliefs about women's (and men's) gender roles as a means of recruitment into their organizations. This is because these groups often advocate for traditional gender roles and rail against societal changes that foster more equity between men and women. They may prey on men who blame women for their misfortunes (e.g. attributing their inability to get a job to women making the job market more competitive) and use the specter of further movement toward equity to recruit members.

Concerning women's rights, we find that more extensive legal protection for women is negatively related to state violence and that this correlation is stronger as the number of women's advocacy groups in a country increases. While the analysis suggests that the negative relationship between women's rights and state violence becomes stronger with more advocacy groups, we do not distinguish among different types of women's advocacy groups. It is possible that certain types of advocacy groups are more effective at monitoring and pressuring the state than others. It is also possible that some women's advocacy groups will make no attempt to pressure the state, or will actively oppose such attempts, depending on the issue in question and the groups' respective goals. We hope this finding leads to more scholarly work

198 POSITIONING WOMEN IN CONFLICT STUDIES

that unpacks which groups engage in watchdog activity and which tactics are most successful in mitigating state violence and repression. This research would benefit from the creation of a more detailed cross-national, time series dataset on women's advocacy groups and from in-depth case analyses that trace the connections between women's rights, women's advocacy organizations, and state behavior.

We also find that in societies with greater harm to women, civil conflict is more likely, and the state is more likely to initiate violent disputes with other states. It is notable that of all of the concepts we examine, we find that only harm to women is associated with the initiation of violent inter/intra-state conflict.[1] The most prominent explanation for these connections is that harm to women weakens normative constraints on the use of violence in inter-group disputes. Weakening these constraints will affect the state's behavior toward other states, as well as its behavior toward non-state groups. This explanation calls attention to structural conditions that lower the perceived cost of using violence to resolve conflicts at the societal level. These include the nature of group relations within social hierarchies and habituation to violence at the individual level from an early age (e.g. due to intimate partner violence). These conditions are not mutually exclusive, and in fact existing arguments suggest that interpersonal violence against women and the (violent) subordination of women (and other groups) at the societal level go hand in hand. It is also likely that norms about using violence to maintain social hierarchies and norms about the acceptability of interpersonal violence track closely together and are both affected by exposure to physical violence and conditions of structural violence. The connection between these norms and patterns of behavior deserves closer examination. Our analysis cannot speak to this question as our harm to women scale combines indicators of structural and physical violence due to limitations in data on the prevalence of physical violence. We return to this point later.

A distinct explanation for the connection between harm to women and civil conflict is that rebel groups take advantage of a shortage of women—which may exist due to direct or structural violence—to recruit members by promising "brides" to those who join. This explanation applies only to civil conflict as it is about the recruitment strategies of rebel groups. Our analysis can speak to these different explanations to some degree. Our harm to women scale is not strongly related to sex imbalances in the population, which means that the indicators of structural and physical violence in our measurement model are not, for the most part, highly correlated with sex imbalances. In turn, the association we find between harm to women and civil conflict is largely the result of a correlation between conflict and structural/physical harm rather than conflict and sex imbalances. This suggests that rebel recruitment involving promises of sex or marriage may not be systematically related to conflict onset. That said, this is another theory that should be explored further.

Harm to women also demobilizes women from political activism. States that do not want to see political reforms have an incentive to keep women demobilized because women's participation in social movements makes those movements more likely to succeed (Chenoweth and Marks 2022). Our results suggest that harm to women could lead to more political violence because women are less likely to participate in non-violent peace movements and claim-making movements when they themselves experience daily violence. This is an important finding because it suggests that states may sometimes be strategically ambivalent about allowing harm to women to occur. By failing to enforce laws that protect women or doing little to curb everyday, structural violence against women, states potentially protect themselves from political reforms. This theory is different from the other theories on harm to women discussed in Chapter 5, which are more about structural conditions. Because this theory is strategic, we think that there are several steps in the causal chain that should be tested in future work. Scholars should look at the conditions under which harm to women demobilizes women; which movements are more successful when women participate; whether state governments regard women's mobilization as threatening and take actions to prevent it; and whether movements with fewer women in them turn violent.

The analysis yielded one unexpected finding that points to potential backlash that accompanies the advancement of women's status in society more generally. We find that women's inclusion is correlated with increases in state violence, but that women's *political* inclusion is *not* correlated with increased state repression. These divergent findings mean that state agents do not engage in more violence against civilians when women are in political leadership roles. Rather, states with (mostly) male leaders are repressing the population when there are more women in public spaces generally. In Chapter 3, we attribute this finding to male backlash, a mechanism also explored by Matfess, Kishi, and Berry (2022). We posit that (male) leaders may be more likely to engage in repression when there are dramatic changes in sex composition in public spaces. Visible changes in the number of women participating in public life may create a heightened sense of anxiety and concern among males, including political leaders, about loss of status. It could then be an observable condition that causes male leaders to perceive any challenge to their authority as more threatening. In other words, women's inclusion in society represents a visible change from the status quo—a status quo characterized by a social order (including gender roles) that leaders value and wish to protect.

The results from Chapter 6 also support the idea that backlash against changes in women's status may be related to political violence. In that chapter, we posited that rigid beliefs about women's gender roles and a corresponding desire to uphold the status quo (protect traditional roles) can lead to the use of political violence. Unlike women's inclusion, beliefs are not a visible phenomenon, so political violence may not be any more likely as beliefs change in women's favor (move away from traditional gender roles) because they may go largely unnoticed. Thus, backlash violence does not occur as beliefs become more flexible but rather when changes to the status quo would be perceived as more threatening—when beliefs become more rigid or when the majority of the population already hold rigid beliefs about women's gender roles. Thus, we posit that backlash is a response to visible improvements in women's status. This is perhaps also why women's rights do not necessarily trigger male backlash to the same degree. "Male backlash" might only occur when there are rapid, *visible* changes to the status quo.

At the same time, there are instances of backlash against the advancement of women's rights and policies (and policies related to gender more broadly). In Peru, for example, a new school curriculum on gender equality met with a hostile response. Through the "Con mis hijos no te metas" movement, many Peruvians pushed back against teaching "gender ideology" (Mayka 2023; Biroli 2019, 6). These anti-gender (counter-)movements are increasing in Latin America (Rousseau 2020). Thus, we believe that much more theorization and testing are required to understand when backlash occurs, whether it tends to be a response to visible changes rather than changes in laws, policies, or societal attitudes, and how it is connected to political violence perpetrated by the state or by non-state actors. It is likely that male backlash is not inevitable; rather, there are certain conditions under which it is more likely. A research agenda that aims to identify these conditions would be a valuable contribution.

In short, our analysis of the connection between different aspects of women's status and political violence helps to determine which claims receive

CONCLUSION   201

the strongest support, which in turn helps identify the most promising paths forward. Examining the implications of the explanations just outlined at lower levels of aggregation, and with an eye to further theoretical refinement, is one path forward, which we discuss further next.

Viewing the Results through a Gendered Lens

The exercise of clearly differentiating between gender and sex required us, to some extent, to peel back the "gender lens" when measuring women's status and examining its relationship to different forms of political violence. However, the process we undertook in this book also pushes us to interpret our results by thinking about the role of gender. Picking up the gender lens once again can help to contextualize our results. On one hand, feminist scholars would not necessarily be surprised by some of our null findings, because many have argued that there are a number of gendered factors to consider when determining whether women's status should be expected to reduce political violence. For example, scholars have frequently critiqued notions of women's rights that grew out of liberal feminism (Arat 2015; Berry and Lake 2021), which are concerned largely with women's inclusion in public spaces. That we find no clear association between women's inclusion and a lower risk of political violence, and less than overwhelming evidence concerning the role of women's rights in reducing violence, would thus not be surprising to these scholars.

The feminist critique of this conception of women's rights is that the goals of liberal feminism—greater access to education, political participation, and participation in the economy (Arat 2015, 676)—have become part of a neo-liberal agenda that privileges the individual (freedoms) over the collective. These kinds of rights and inclusion-focused frameworks could benefit women who belong to majority groups while harming women in minority groups. Kinsella and Sjoberg (2019, 15) argue that a framework focused on individual rights and women's inclusion implies the need for the liberal norm of protection (of women) under the law. However, only some women benefit from this protection (i.e. those in dominant social groups), while others suffer the consequences of the security state that such protections justify.[2] Feminist scholars have also critiqued the concept of women's inclusion on the grounds that analysis which groups "women" into a single, monolithic category is harmful. It makes invisible the power dynamics within that group

202 POSITIONING WOMEN IN CONFLICT STUDIES

(e.g. between women in different classes or ethnic groups) and can also be exclusionary because it creates boundaries for who can be considered to belong to the category "women" (e.g. are inter-sex people included in the concept of women's inclusion?) (Kinsella and Sjoberg 2019). Thus, these feminist critiques somewhat anticipate our null findings across many of the hypotheses related to women's inclusion and women's rights.

One the other hand, despite feminist critiques of our concepts and measurement, our "positive" results shed new light on the co-constitutive relationship of gender and violence in four ways. First, while feminist literature has theorized about male backlash,[3] our analysis demonstrates that the trigger for male backlash could be the visible presence of women in public spaces, more so than laws and policies about women and more so than changes in beliefs and attitudes that are perceived to be threatening to men. In other words, backlash is more likely in response to visible and tangible changes rather than abstract changes. This observation highlights the importance of understanding how gendered systems, and patriarchy more broadly, co-opt women who enter public spaces to make them less threatening to men and/ or how these systems punish women who are new to public roles. This co-optation and punishment happen through everyday practices, but our analysis shows that they can happen at the state level as well.

Second, our results show the importance of understanding the attitudes that both violent groups and citizens more broadly hold about women's roles. The process by which institutions are gendered involves the translation of individuals' belief systems into a set of institutional norms. Paying attention to gendered belief systems thus helps us understand how institutions are gendered and how they may come to facilitate violence. As already noted, beliefs vary quite a lot across individuals as well as over time. Variation in these beliefs can affect how (violent) groups, governments, and citizens interact with each other. A gendered analysis of systems and processes can help us understand how these beliefs are formed and how they can be changed. Our analysis shows that more fluid belief systems regarding women's gender roles are associated with fewer terror attacks. Of course, the process of terrorism itself shapes gendered views, perhaps crystalizing views about the need for securitization and more rigid gender norms in some parts of the population. The endogenous relationship between beliefs and terrorism interpreted through our findings mean that changes in beliefs about women's gender roles are particularly important when there is little actual violence. Convincing a majority of the population to adopt more flexible beliefs about

CONCLUSION 203

women's gender roles can be a buffer against state attempts to promote a securitized state, while also reducing the potential pool of recruits for groups who might consider violence in the future.

Third, while much recent feminist scholarship critiques a framework of rights and inclusion based on liberal feminism, our analysis suggests that in countries with more formal protections for women's rights there tends to be less state violence. It also suggests that, in addition to pushing states toward adopting women's rights, advocacy groups may be more effective watchdogs where women's rights are more extensive. That is, despite the possible negative consequences of rights-based frameworks, there is an advantage in that the advocacy around women's rights helps to create a vibrant civil society.[4] Of course, women's rights groups vary a great deal in terms of their goals, which are sometimes at odds with each other. They also vary a great deal in terms of their power and influence, and the hierarchy among them (Strolovitch 2006; Carpenter 2007; Martín de Almagro Iniesta 2005). Scholars have critiqued women's advocacy groups by pointing out that, among other issues, their agendas can be co-opted and that hierarchies among women and advocacy groups impede the effectiveness of advocacy in changing policy.[5] Yet, the contention and conflict among these groups may be useful for demonstrating how opposing views can be reconciled in non-violent ways. Our findings concerning state violence and women's rights may suggest not only that women's groups, together as a collective, are effective watchdogs for state behavior, but also that women's rights itself may create productive conflict among women's groups, conflict that serves as an example for how political disputes can be resolved in non-violent ways.

Fourth and finally, patriarchal systems create harm to women, and those same systems tend to be accompanied by more frequent political violence. Structural violence is thus associated with both harm to women and violence among groups within society. Normative constraints on violence in society become frail as general disregard for women's wellbeing becomes more pervasive. While perhaps not a novel theoretical development, this is one of the core arguments we draw on for our analysis in Chapter 5, which shows that there is consistent empirical support for these claims. What might be missed in the feminist literature, however, is how states might be strategic about harming women. State inaction in protecting women against physical and structural violence, and sometimes intentional policies that lead to more harm, enable the status quo power hierarchy. Strategic enabling of harm to women perpetuates gender inequality, a societal condition that

204 POSITIONING WOMEN IN CONFLICT STUDIES

restricts women from mobilizing for peace and other societal and political reforms.

Overall, our exploration of individual concepts provides more pathways through which political violence, gender, and women's status are all interrelated. We strongly believe that each of these pathways warrants further gendered analysis.

Limitations to the Quantitative Analysis

There are at least two important limitations to the quantitative analysis conducted in this manuscript: a lack of causal identification and missingness in the data. First, our analysis does not use a strategy for causal identification beyond a standard regression framework that addresses bias through statistical controls. We did take precautions to ensure our analysis was not affected by two clear threats to inference: biased estimates of the relationship between women's status and political violence due to the omission of unmeasured country-level characteristics; and biased statistical inferences due to failure to account for measurement error in our latent variables. If our inferences are faulty, it is not for either of these reasons. Of course, we include controls for country characteristics that are likely related to women's status and political violence. We also lag our independent variables to guard against the possibility that the relationships we find reflect the impact of violence on women's status, rather than the reverse. Our models of civil conflict and war also address the possibility that women's status may improve after conflicts end (Webster, Chen, and Beardsley 2019; Webster et al. 2020), by controlling for the number of years that have passed since the last conflict or war ended. However, we do not have a strategy for leveraging or mimicking exogenous variation in women's status, and for this reason we do not claim to have estimated causal effects. It is possible that our results are affected by endogeneity. In fact, to some degree we expect that violence and women's status are co-constitutive, meaning they condition each other.

While this is certainly a limitation of our analysis, it is not one that interferes with our principal goals: one of which is to parse the different concepts of interest and develop useful measures of each; another is to see whether each concept is associated with different forms of political violence. For the second goal, we are interested in determining which explanations receive the most support once we address common issues related to conceptualization and measurement. As already discussed, by determining which claims are most consistent with the evidence, we can get a sense for the kinds of analyses that are likely to be most useful going forward, for example which concepts are worth exploring further, and at what level(s) of analysis. We stress again that our results reflect *aggregate* relationships. Specifically, relationships in annual, country-level data. Causal identification at the country-year level is a difficult (maybe impossible) proposition. It is likely that we will have to get down to the group or micro-level, or conduct qualitative case studies, to find compelling evidence of causality between women's status and political violence. In this sense, we believe most analyses using annual country-level data must be treated as somewhat exploratory even when using statistical controls. Further, causal inference is a common goal, but is not the purpose of all statistical models. The measurement models we use in Chapters 3–6 provide one example of another potential purpose. Another is prediction, as in using women's status to predict future instances of political violence, which does not require a causal model. While we do not pursue prediction as a goal in this book, we are sure that such an effort would be especially welcomed in policy circles.

Another limitation of our analysis is that for some of the indicators we use in our measurement models, especially indicators of physical violence against women, there are many missing values. Our models are able to account for missing data, but this results in more measurement error in the latent variable. In one sense this is desirable, as the scale should contain more error when there is less information. One of the appealing attributes of our measurement approach is that it does not misrepresent the precision with which we can measure concepts like women's status. But if there is too much measurement error then a scale is of limited use, even for descriptive purposes, since we cannot say with any confidence that women's status in a particular country is different than in any other. The measures we develop in the book are precise enough to be useful but are still limited by the indicators they incorporate and thus the specificity of concepts that they can capture. This is most clearly the case with our scale that measures harm to women. To create this scale, we incorporate numerous indicators of structural violence against women but are able to include only four measures of physical violence.[6] Available data on physical violence are too sparse to create a useful measure of the concept "harm to women from physical violence." Having a measure of harm to women that does not make this distinction is useful for some purposes. It allowed us to conduct an analysis that provides stronger

206 POSITIONING WOMEN IN CONFLICT STUDIES

support for the claim that societal harm to women is associated with large-scale violent conflict. However, examining structural violence and physical violence separately would be enormously helpful. We could then get a better understanding of the connections between these types of harm, as well as a clearer picture of the relationship between harm to women and political violence, and between harm to women and norms concerning violent conflict. This will only be possible as more and better data on physical violence become available. Projects like Woman Stats are especially valuable for this reason.

Policy Recommendations

Despite the limitations of our data and analysis, our results point to several policy recommendations. First, our findings on women's inclusion indicate that public policies aimed at including more women in public spaces, such as quotas, do not go far enough. These policies must be accompanied by other reforms that create equitable spaces for women to thrive. Men already benefit from gendered spaces—for example, many men's bathrooms do not have diaper changing stations.[7] The underlying assumption is that men should not have to change diapers, and that this is the duty of the mother, thus relieving men of this "work." Moreover, public transit routes and timetables are often designed to accommodate the typical workday. This accommodates male workers at the expense of women because inequitable distributions of domestic labor in the home force women to seek employment in the informal economy at higher rates than men (Bonnet, Vanek, and Chen 2019). The result is a public transit system which disproportionately taxes women's time and labor through less direct routes and less accommodating timetables. Thus, enacting policies to create more equitable spaces should not be perceived as creating a burden, but rather as a way to create non-biases, equitable public spaces (as many public spaces are already oriented toward accommodating men).

Equitable policies for women to thrive include, first and foremost, ensuring that women are not discriminated against or harassed in the workplace (whether these are private offices, government officers, or any work site), with adequate accountability and whistleblower policies in place. There should be no pay gap between men and women (United Nations 2022), and women (as well as men) should be entitled to paid sick leave, parental leave, medical leave, and elderly care leave, among other types of leave. Quality childcare should also be subsidized. Public policies to ensure that women can thrive in public places should include protecting women from street harassment and violence. Finally, women should not be perceived as less competent than men in political, economic, or security tasks. There should be policies to reduce explicit and implicit biases.

Second, our findings on women's rights indicate that policies that promote women's rights should be accompanied by funding and resources to create a vibrant civil society, and particularly to strengthen women's advocacy groups. While there is international aid to promote women's rights globally, only a small proportion of it goes to women's advocacy organizations (Brechenmacher and Salgame 2022). Scholars have also written about the challenges faced by grassroots NGOs and organizations when trying to attract international funding (Autesserre 2014, 2021). Sometimes international priorities drive the activities of local NGOs: this led, for example, to a disproportionate number of women's groups working on sexual and gender-based violence in the Democratic Republic of the Congo (Lake 2018). When donors' agendas take priority over those of domestic NGOs, this can work against the needs and concerns of the people who are supposedly benefiting from aid. Given these challenges, donors should come up with better strategies for funding civil society organizations, such as "no strings attached" funding whereby groups have complete autonomy in how the funds are used or simplifying the bureaucratic loopholes through which organizations have to jump in order to receive funding. Indeed, Autesserre (2021, chap. 6) makes these same recommendations and suggests that the key to doing no harm is to listen to those on the ground about their needs. To sum up, we suggest that advocacy for women's rights should focus more on funding women's organizations on the ground to assist them in accomplishing the goals they have chosen themselves and should be accompanied by a reduction in bureaucratic barriers for local groups seeking funding.

Third, our findings about harm to women point to the importance of focusing on women's morbidity globally and the structural (and actual) violence that causes harm to women. The statistics on women's vulnerabilities depicts a desperate situation, as women around the world continue to suffer from large amounts of violence—whether avoidable death due to inadequate maternal healthcare or intimate partner violence. The data seem to show that women are often disproportionately affected by disease as well as natural disasters and climate change (Halton 2018).[8] This means that policies need to better ensure that women's lives are valued. States might start by focusing on women's health needs. For example, some countries, such as Spain, have started to take a gendered approach to the workplace by creating menstrual leave (Masih 2023). In 2020, New Zealand announced that schools across the country would provide free tampons and pads, and Scotland followed suit in 2021. These policies help ensure that women's reproductive needs are met and thus decrease harm to women.

Polices that reduce harm to women, however, are not enough according to our research. Because state policy often enables harm to women and because states may fear women's mobilizing and thus take a passive stance on preventing harm to women, it is also important to support political reforms that allow women to freely mobilize and to make resources available for women's mobilization and social movements.

Our chapter on beliefs about women's gender roles suggests that it is important to not only focus on policies that change structural outcomes, but also to advocate for policies that promote less rigid beliefs about women's (and men's and non-binary people's) gender roles. Scholars have found that it is much more difficult to change belief systems than behavioral outcomes (Paluck 2009; Paluck and Green 2009). However, research on norm and belief changes in social psychology has developed frameworks to explore how changes might occur, such as contact theory and information provision and updating, among other theories.[9] Moreover, international organizations such as Equimundo have developed interventions to promote healthy masculinities globally.[10] Policymakers should draw on existing academic literature and programmatic intervention as a starting point for developing programming and policymaking with the goal of promoting more flexible beliefs about women's gender roles, and they should devote more policy resources to this goal.

Finally, it is worth noting that none of the null findings should be interpreted as a reason to *not* promote women's inclusion, women's rights, reduction of harm to women, or change in beliefs about women's roles. Clearly, there is a moral imperative to continue championing policies to promote less rigid women's inclusion and women's rights, to reduce harm to women, and to promote beliefs about gender roles. Improving women's status should be viewed as inherently valuable, not instrumentally valuable. Additionally, women's inclusion, women's rights, harm to women, and beliefs about women's roles should be treated as the tip of the iceberg when it comes to recognizing and examining the interconnectedness of women's status, gender, and political violence. Policymaking should treat our null findings as

CONCLUSION 209

an invitation to continue funding research on this interconnectedness, as we have only scratched the surface here.

Future Areas of Study

Because our goal was differentiation and delineation of concepts, we did not closely examine the relationship between them, nor the conditions that lead to improvement or backsliding of the concepts. The analysis we did conduct suggests that the different aspects of women's status are for the most part not highly correlated, but that the correlations vary from pair to pair.

The chapters in this book point to many promising avenues for further research: here we outline two suggestions. First, as discussed earlier, we advocate moving away from the country as the unit of analysis and focusing on data (quantitative or qualitative) at lower levels of aggregation. For each hypothesis that receives some support in our analysis, there is a potential explanation that has (perhaps several) observable implications at lower levels of analysis. This points to many potential paths to a more complete understanding of the connection between women's status and political violence. Our second suggestion is that quantitative scholars bring gender into their theorization. We will now briefly explore a few ways they might do so.

Less Aggregated Data

Much of the existing quantitative work on women's status and political violence, including in this book, uses data collected at the level of the country-year. While analyzing annual, country level data can be useful, it has clear limitations. Given the large amount of country-year data that is publicly available, this kind of analysis allows us to see whether the relationships we examine generalize across countries and over reasonably long time periods. However, it also means that we are subjecting each hypothesis to a very coarse test. Arguably, at such a high level of aggregation it will be more difficult to find a meaningful relationship between women's status and political violence. The theories we draw on typically begin with individuals or groups rather than countries. Country-year data obscures outcomes at lower levels and hides sub-national variation more generally. An analysis that looks for general patterns across countries and time also does not account for scope conditions that may affect the applicability of different explanations. One of our recommendations therefore echoes the calls by Cohen and Karim (2022) to focus on theorizing and conducting (quantitative) analysis at the individual and group level.[11]

With this recommendation in mind, we can use the findings in this book as a starting point. Sorting the claims that receive support into different theoretical frameworks will be helpful for future efforts at empirical analysis and the development of theory. Some explanations that connect women's conditions to political violence can be categorized as structural and some as strategic, as Cohen and Karim (2022) suggest. Strategic theories focus on, and require exploring, individual or group-level decision-making, whereas structural theories focus on norms and institutions. Categorizing the theories in this way allows for a clearer understanding of the micro-foundations of each theory and also what is required for a more refined empirical analysis. If an explanation for one of our findings is more strategic than structural, for example, this may suggest that further analysis would benefit from examining more closely interactions between relevant actors, as well as their apparent goals or motivations and the tactics they use to achieve them. Structural explanations on the other hand may suggest that further investigation of sub-national, macro-level political and social conditions and political violence will be useful. Though the two types of explanation suggest a focus on different features of the environment and the actors involved, it is almost certain that analysis at lower levels of aggregation than the country-year will be productive regardless of whether the explanation is strategic or structural.

Consider the explanation for our finding concerning women's political inclusion and terrorism: political inclusion could change the nature of bargaining between the state and potentially violent groups. This is a strategic explanation that involves a complex interaction between the state, its political leaders, and various non-state groups, in which the preferences of the leaders and groups involved must be accounted for. Some female politicians may be more likely to make concessions to the political demands of particular groups. To use the example of two US legislators who have attracted much media attention, it is likely that Representative Alexandria Ocasio-Cortez's sponsorship of environmental legislation will appease groups very different from those appeased by Representative Lauren Boebert's advocacy of gun ownership rights. Examining this mechanism more closely requires more fine-grained information about interactions between state and non-state actors, including the specific political goals of non-state groups and the policy preferences of political leaders.

In contrast, the relationship between beliefs about women's gender roles and terror attacks may be explained by the fact that more rigid beliefs make it easier for violent groups to attract recruits. This suggests more of a focus on structural conditions, but further empirical analysis would still benefit from less aggregated data. While larger structural conditions are theorized to drive recruitment, examining disaggregated data on non-state groups, their political goals, and their recruitment tactics would be useful.[12] Further, as noted earlier, beliefs about gender roles are certain to vary across people and groups within societies. How such beliefs are distributed, for example whether they are polarized (bimodal) or not, may be relevant to group recruitment. Future studies could examine which groups use gender frames as a recruitment tool into their political (and possibly violent) organization, and how the nature of societal-level beliefs affects the behavior of such organizations.

Our finding with respect to women's rights is consistent with previous work that suggests women's advocacy groups are often responsible for the adoption of formal protection for women's rights and can serve as effective watchdogs for state behavior (Htun and Weldon 2018). This explanation proposes a strategic interaction between state actors and advocacy groups who are demanding change. As we have already discussed, more detailed data on advocacy groups, including their goals and the nature of their interactions with the state, would be helpful for examining this relationship more closely.

Explanations that link harm to women to political violence tend to focus on structural features. As we have noted, the most plausible interpretation of our results provides more support for arguments that suggest harm is related to political violence due to the underlying societal norms it reflects. More disaggregation is necessary to unpack the conditions under which each explanation holds. Structural conditions vary geographically within a country and thus some areas may be more prone to violence than others.

Yet other potential explanations are more strategic—that harm creates shortages of women, which allows rebel groups to recruit young men by offering them access to women, or that states allow harm to women to prevent their political mobilization. These theories can be studied using disaggregated data as well. Within countries that experience conflict, rebel recruitment as well as the occurrence and intensity of combat vary a lot across specific locations. Sex ratios in areas from which rebels draw support, and perhaps in areas that they occupy, should be more relevant to conflict

212 POSITIONING WOMEN IN CONFLICT STUDIES

outcomes than aggregate ratios.[13] Further, not all groups may resort to this recruitment tactic even if it is available, depending on their ideology or political goals.[14] It may also be that this kind of recruitment is endogenous to features of the conflict itself, in which case it could affect rebel group behavior during conflict but not conflict onset. Future work should further unpack the mechanism underlying this theory. Additionally, exploring how harm to women affects women's mobilization and state response requires moving to the individual or group as the unit of analysis—exploring whether and which forms of harm to women demobilizes women and testing whether social movements with more women are more successful and perceived as more threatening to state agents.

Our tentative explanation for the positive relationship between women's inclusion and state violence combines strategic and structural elements— women's inclusion in public spaces (a structural condition) causes political leaders to perceive challenges as more threatening (interactions are more likely to lead to state violence). This account also has observable implications at lower levels of analysis. For example, we might expect that the state's response to more organized forms of dissent, such as protests, will be harsher when women are more visible in public spaces. It may also be the case that the state is more likely to aggressively police minority groups it views as threatening when women are more visible in public spaces. This puzzling finding thus presents another opportunity for further analysis and theoretical development.

In short, every potential explanation for the relationships that we find between women's status and political violence has implications that can be tested at lower levels of spatial/temporal aggregation than the country-year. There are thus a number of opportunities for further analysis and theoretical development.

Bringing Gender Equality Back into the Fold

We conclude the book by returning to the concept of gender. Going forward, a research agenda on women's status should incorporate gender when possible, without stretching the concept or using invalid measures. *Gender equality* means equality in the value of the different traits that define masculinity, femininity, and androgyny. Research on gender equality should address, at minimum, how to enhance the value and prioritization of femininities, reproductive and unskilled work, non-violence, and a host of other

CONCLUSION 213

feminine values and practices. Sjoberg and Gentry (2011, 4–5) state that gender equality is about changing institutions such that the standards that define what it means to be a man or woman do not dictate either participation or how such participation is received.

Taking these suggestions into consideration, a quantitative research agenda on gender equality and political violence is possible. However, it means asking different, many of which have already been asked and researched. We pose a few of them here:

- Does society privilege the "soldier" over the "caregiving" man? More broadly, what type of man does a society privilege? How does the privileging of a particular type affect attitudes toward, or the occurrence of, political violence?
- Do soldiers or combatants, whether in the state security forces or insurgent groups, carry more prestige in society, organizations, and other groups? In the aftermath of war, are combatants and veterans given more privileges and consideration than civilians?
- To what extent do those who wield militarized power make decisions for the country? Does society prefer to have such leaders? What are the qualities that society values and privileges in political leaders?
- Do leaders and the public assume that security refers to militarized, national security as opposed to human security?[15] If so, how does that affect their attitude towards political violence?
- Are more resources devoted to militarism and militarization (e.g. the security forces, arms purchase, etc.) than social welfare? Why? What causes changes in priorities? What explains variation in preferences for military spending over social welfare?
- What are the primary characteristics of the hegemonic form of masculinity in society? Does hegemonic masculinity have any militarized elements?
- To what extent do men perceive a recent loss of masculine status? To what extent do leaders perceive the state has recently lost masculine status? Do perceptions of lost masculinity translate to a greater willingness to engage in political violence?
- Do women predominantly take on feminine roles and do men predominantly take on masculine roles? How rigid are individuals' beliefs that men should be masculine and women feminine? How do these beliefs affect dispositions towards, or the occurrence of, political violence?

- Is a woman's status in society related to her ability to fulfill feminine roles (e.g. supporting soldiers) during war? Is a man's status in society related to his ability to fulfill masculine roles (e.g. fighting) during a war?
- To what degree are people aware of biases and stereotypes about gender roles? How can awareness of each be increased? Does heightened awareness make peaceful conflict resolution more likely?
- Are women punished for behaving in a masculine way? Are men punished for behaving in a feminine way? Do societies that are more punitive toward gender deviance experience more political violence?
- Why are heteronormative frames more ubiquitous in some societies than in others? Under what conditions do political groups mobilize around defense of the heteronormative status quo?
- Has there been a recent shift in aggregate expectations for what it means to be a man or a woman? Do these shifts indicate changes in normative beliefs about the use of violence in politics?

These are just a small subset of possible avenues for empirically assessing gender inequality. Most of these concepts could be operationalized through survey questions as they are related to people's perceptions and beliefs. Researchers could then see whether these indicators correlate with violence, conflict, and war at the individual, organizational, or state level. While such an approach allows for an examination of the relationship between gender inequality and violence, it is bound to be at best a partial and indirect examination. There is a range of potential methods for measuring the concepts, from surveys and experiments to ethnographic memoirs. We stress that there is no single indicator or index that can be used to measure or even proxy for gender inequality. Nevertheless, we believe that there is merit in adopting a gendered lens to study political violence. Research at this frontier should therefore build upon the robust foundation already established by the contributions of Wibben (2010), Sjoberg (2010, 2012a, 2014). While we provide some thoughts in this section for how to do this research, there is a vast literature to draw upon to continue this work.

Conclusion

If the world is indeed entering into a period that marks a general decline in the societal status of women, this does not bode well. On the one hand, the measures of women's status we develop in this book suggest that, for the time period covered, the general trend in women's status was a positive one. On the other hand, our results suggest that, for some aspects of women's status, backsliding is typically accompanied by a higher risk of terrorism, inter- and intrastate conflict, and state repression, and some recent political developments certainly give the impression that some backsliding is occurring. However, it is important to keep in mind that our results also suggest the reverse: for some aspects of women's status, improvement is typically accompanied by a lower risk of political violence, meaning that improvement in women's status may represent one way of promoting more peaceful societies. Thus, these results suggest a forceful case can be made that policymakers and other concerned political actors should place more emphasis on reducing harm to women, creating more extensive protections for women's rights (accompanied by women's advocacy organizations), and promoting more flexible beliefs about women's roles in society. If women's status globally is indeed declining, there should be a sense of urgency about correcting this trend.

It is also important to keep in mind that our analysis suggests that the relationship between women's status and political violence is a qualified one. We find that women's status is related to violent conflict, but we do not find that improvements in every aspect of women's status are associated with a lower risk of political violence. For those aspects that are, further examination is necessary to get a full understanding of how they are connected to different forms of political violence. That is to say, we have evidence that there is a connection, but the complete nature of the connection is subject to uncertainty. What we can say for certain is that, as harm to women increases, to use one example, there are necessarily some women for whom the consequences are immediate and dire. The outcome is a bad one, whether it has a measurable association with the risk of political violence or not. Our analysis suggests that it does, which provides a reason to advocate for policies that decrease harm to women, and in some cases probably makes government officials more inclined to listen. But we wish to stress that the best reason to advocate for and implement policies that improve (or prevent declines in) women's status is that this will improve the daily lives of women.

In closing, we have a long way to go to improve women's status globally. More research and improved policymaking on women's status globally would be extremely valuable not only for understanding how we might create more societies characterized by less violence, but also for understanding how to improve the quality of people's lived experiences more generally.

Appendix

Appendix to Chapter 2: Data and Models for Subsequent Chapters

Here, we discuss the data for the dependent variables and the modeling strategy for our regression analysis.

Dependent Variables

Civil Conflict and War

For data on intrastate conflict we use two indicators from the UCDP/PRIO armed conflict data (Themner and Wallensteen 2014). The first is a measure of civil conflict, defined as armed conflict involving the government and a non-state actor that results in at least 25 battle-related deaths in a calendar year. The second is a measure of civil war, meaning an armed conflict that leads to at least 1,000 battle-related deaths during a calendar year. The incidence of civil conflict, not to mention civil war, is rare. The data for our latent variable models from Chapter 4 begin in 1960 (at the earliest). Since 1960 about 14% of cases in the data (or 1,473 country-years) experienced a civil conflict as defined by UCDP, while only about 4% (447) experienced a civil war. Figure A2.1 shows the average incidence of conflict by country. The figure makes it apparent that a relatively small number of countries experienced frequent conflict during this time: though the majority of countries experienced at least one conflict year, the top 18 countries (from Myanmar down to Somalia) account for over half of all conflict years.

The models using internal conflict or war as the dependent variable are logistic regression models of conflict and war *onset*. This means the analysis excludes ongoing conflicts; once a conflict begins the country drops out of the analysis until the beginning of a new "peace spell." Civil conflicts tend to last multiple years, and including ongoing conflicts would conflate the onset of a conflict with the continuation of conflict, which would in turn conflate the effects of the independent variables on these two distinct outcomes. These models include time counters that measure the number of peace years, i.e. years that have passed since the last conflict ended or since the beginning of the observation window, as is common practice when analyzing panel data with a binary response variable (Beck, Katz, and Tucker 1998; Carter and Signorino 2010).

As control variables in the civil conflict and war models we include the natural logarithms of GDP and population size from the World Bank, which effectively controls for GDP per capita. GDP per capita has become a standard control variable in models of civil conflict and is usually understood as a proxy for state capacity (Fearon and Laitin 2003). GDP per capita is also commonly used as a measure of economic development, which is thought to be causally related to societal attitudes about women and the inclusion of women in traditionally male, public spaces (Inglehart and Norris 2003). We also

218 APPENDIX

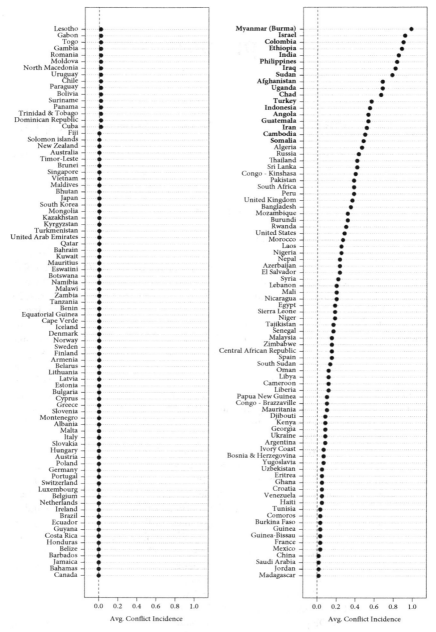

Figure A2.1 Average Incidence of Conflict for Every Countries in the Data

include a measure of democracy. Past research has found that democracy is related to civil conflict in a non-linear fashion: countries with political institutions that are neither fully democratic nor fully autocratic are at the highest risk for conflict (Hegre et al 2001; Jones and Lupu 2018). It is also not difficult to imagine that women's inclusion is correlated with democracy, as excluding women from politics necessarily limits political participation, which is one aspect of "polyarchy" as defined by Dahl (1971). As a measure of democracy, we use the electoral democracy (or polyarchy) index from the V-Dem data (Coppedge et al. 2021; Pemstein et al. 2021). This indicator is created from a number of components that are themselves estimated using measurement models that combine expert survey responses (Pemstein et al. 2010). The electoral democracy index combines indicators of freedom of association, free and fair elections, freedom of expression, whether the executive and legislators are chosen through elections, and the extent of suffrage. The index is an average of the weighted average of the components and their product. As an additional control variable we include a measure of the size of largest politically excluded ethnic group from the Ethnic Power Relations data (Vogt et al. 2015). Ethnic exclusion is strongly related to intrastate conflict (Cederman, Gleditsch, and Buhaug 2013; Buhaug, Cederman, and Gleditsch 2014) and, given that patriarchal societies tend to treat out-groups poorly and have less inclusive political systems (Hudson et al. 2009, 15–19), it is plausible that women's inclusion (and the rest of our concepts) are related to ethnic political exclusion. In these models the control variables, as well as the latent variables, are lagged by one year.

Interstate conflict

Our measure of external conflict comes from the MID data (Palmer et al. 2020). An international war is typically defined as a conflict between two sovereign states that results in at least 1,000 battle-related fatalities. Because there have been very few international wars during in the post-World War II period, most studies of interstate conflict analyze MIDs, as these include international conflicts short of war. For our analyses we focus on disputes that result in at least some actual violence, and so include MIDs where there was at least one fatality, which includes interstate wars. The MID data identifies an "initiator" and a "target" state in each recorded dispute. Though more common than interstate war, fatal MID initiation is still very rare; there are 230 cases where a country initiated at least one fatal MID in the course of the calendar year since 1960, which amounts to about 2.7% of country-years during the period under examination (beginning in 1960). The maximum number of MIDs initiated by a state in a single year is 4 (the United States in 1964). The majority of countries are involved in no fatal MIDs at all. The average number of fatal MIDs initiated per year for each country in the data is shown in Figure A2.2. Only three countries average more than one every 5 years: Pakistan, Iran, and Uganda. The United States and India average just under 1 fatal MID every 5 years.

For each dispute, the MID data distinguish between an initiator and a target state, with the initiator being the state who took the first recorded hostile action. Using the MID data, we estimate logistic regression models in which the dependent variable is the initiation of an MID that results in at least one fatality. This serves as a measure of aggression in foreign policy disputes. For our women's inclusion scales, we also estimate models in which the dependent variable is whether the country in question was the target in a dispute. This is to assess the relationship between being the targeted state in an MID and women's

220 APPENDIX

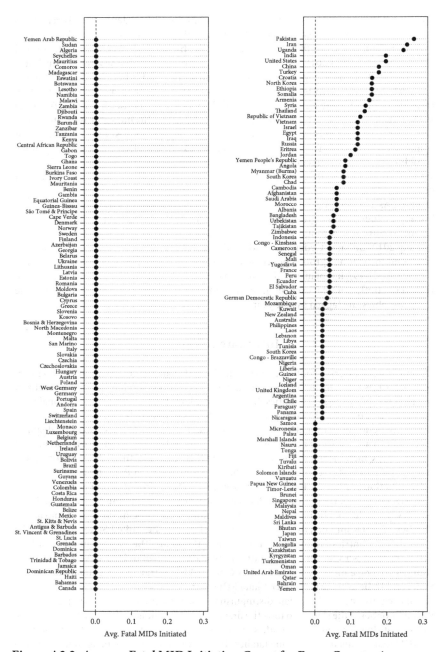

Figure A2.2 Average Fatal MID Initiation Count for Every Country in the Data

political inclusion, to see whether states behave more belligerently toward countries with women in positions of political leadership.

In all of the models that use either MID initiation or being targeted in an MID as the response variable, we use a standard set of control variables from studies that examine "monadic" dispute initiation (Lai and Slater 2006; Souva and Prins 2006). One is the electoral democracy index from V-Dem. As discussed earlier, electoral democracy is almost certainly related to women's inclusion, and developed democracies in particular are less likely to initiate conflicts with other countries (Souva and Prins 2006). We also include the natural log of GDP and trade as a percentage of GDP. These are both standard controls in the literature, and the amount of attention given to the relationship between economic outcomes and women's inclusion suggests they may be related to women's inclusion, as well. As additional controls we include the Correlates of War's (COW) Composite Indicator of National Capabilities, or CINC score, and the number of contiguous or neighboring states. The CINC score is still the default measure of military capacity used in quantitative studies of international conflict; it measures a country's global share of actual and potential military power, as a combination of total population, urban population, iron and steel production, energy consumption, military personnel, and military expenditure. While there is no particular reason to expect that the CINC score or the number of neighboring states is correlated with the status of women, they are probably the most commonly included variables in models of international conflict, and here we choose to follow established practices. The independent variables in these models are also lagged by one year.

State Violence

As indicators of state violence, we use the Political Terror Scale or PTS (Gibney et al. 2019) and the CIRI Physical Integrity Rights Index (Cingranelli, Richards, and Clay 2014). These are both ordinal scales created from content analyses of annual human rights reports issued by Amnesty International and the US State Department. Both scales measure disappearance, extrajudicial killing, political imprisonment, and torture. The CIRI index is the sum of four components that measure each of the abuses in question and range from 0 (frequent abuse) to 2 (no abuse). The resulting scale ranges from 0 to 8 with higher values indicating more respect for physical integrity rights. The PTS is created as a single scale that ranges from 1 to 5 with higher values indicating *more abuse* of physical integrity rights. To avoid confusion, for the analysis that follows we reverse the ordering of the PTS to match that of CIRI, so that higher values indicate *less* state violence.

CIRI and PTS are drawn from the same documents and tend to lead to similar conclusions, though there are differences in some cases (Wood and Gibney 2010). The mean for the reversed PTS across all country years is about 3.5 (out of 5) and the average CIRI score is 4.9 (out of 8), so both indicate that the average state places slightly higher than the middle of the scale. The average PTS and CIRI scores for each country in the data are shown in Figures A2.3 and A2.4. For both scales, countries with higher values (less state violence) tend to be small, wealthy countries with limited to no conflict experience, while countries with low values are typically larger, less wealthy, and more conflict prone countries. The rank correlation (Kendall's τ) between the country averages for these variables is 0.82, indicating strong agreement about which countries experience more state violence than others.

APPENDIX

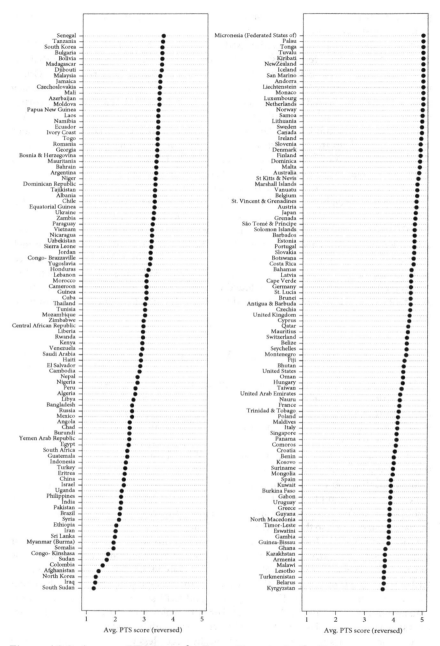

Figure A2.3 Average PTS Score for Every Country in the Data

APPENDIX 223

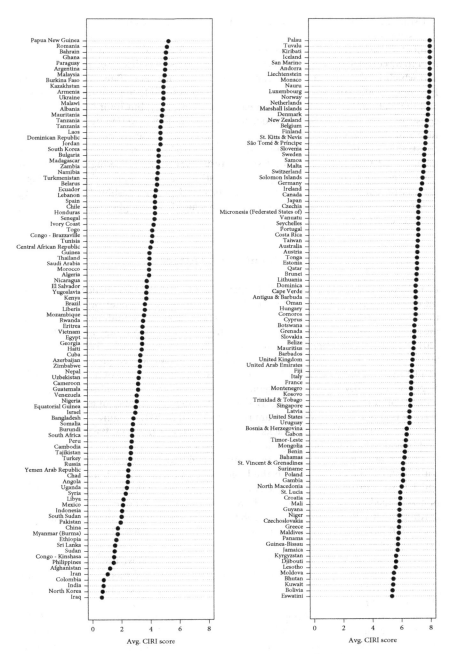

Figure A2.4 Average CIRI Score for Every Country in the Data

224   APPENDIX

Using the CIRI and PTS measures of state violence, we estimate a series of linear regression models. Each of these models includes the UCDP measure of intrastate conflict intensity (coded 0 for no conflict, 1 for conflict, and 2 for war), which we expect to be correlated with women's inclusion for the reasons discussed in this chapter, and which is of course strongly related to state violence (Poe, Tate, and Keith 1999; Davenport 2007; Hill and Jones 2014). These models include the natural logs of GDP and population. We also include a measure of democracy, but limit "democracy" to constraints on the executive in order to avoid operational overlap between democracy and state violence (Hill 2016). For this purpose, we use an indicator of judicial constraints on the executive from V-Dem. This variable is created using a measurement model that combines expert survey responses to the following question: "To what extent does the executive respect the constitution and comply with court rulings, and to what extent is the judiciary able to act in an independent fashion?" The resulting variable is rescaled to take on a value between 0 and 1, with higher values indicating stronger constraints.

Dissident Terror Attacks

In addition to armed internal conflict, external conflict, and state violence, we examine the cross-national incidence of terror attacks. For information on terror attacks we use the Global Terrorism Database (LaFree and Dugan 2007). We limit our focus to domestic terror attacks, using a set of rules outlined in Enders, Sandler, and Gaibulloev (2011) to distinguish between domestic and international attacks. We also remove attacks that target the military, police force, or non-state armed groups as it is difficult to justify their inclusion based on the common definition of a "terror attack" as politically motivated violence against a target with little or no military value.[1] The number of domestic attacks is highly skewed: the median number of attacks is 0, the average is about 9, and the maximum is 955 (for Iraq in 2009). Figure A2.5 shows the median number of domestic attacks for every country in the data. We use the square root to make the graph more legible (the highest median count is 110, for Colombia). It is apparent from the graph that terror attacks, like state violence, coincide strongly with conflict. The countries with the largest counts by far are Colombia and India, which have both experienced decades-long insurgencies. Of the 48 countries that have non-zero median counts, 39 (81.3%) have experienced at least one year of conflict according to UCDP. In contrast, 59 of 108 (52.2%) of the countries that have a median count of 0 have experienced at least one year of conflict (60.8% of all countries have experienced at least one conflict).

For the measure of domestic terror attacks taken from GTD we use count regression models. Preliminary analysis indicated that a negative binomial model provided a substantially better fit to the GTD data than a Poisson model, so we estimate a series of negative binomial regression models which include several control variables. We control for the natural logs of GDP and population size, instrastate conflict intensity, and the CIRI physical integrity scale (Piazza and Walsh 2010; Walsh and Piazza 2010). Population size, conflict, and state violence are all consistently associated with terror attacks in cross-national studies, and we expect they are correlated with women's status for reasons already explained.

APPENDIX 225

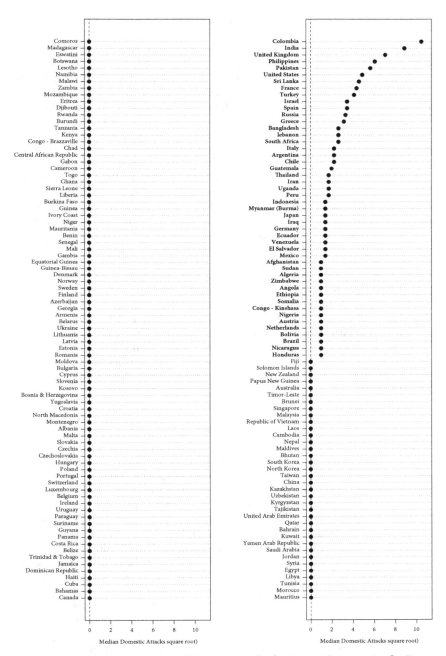

Figure A2.5 Median Number of Terror Attacks for Every Country in the Data

226   APPENDIX

Modeling Strategy

To examine the relationships between our latent variables and the different measures of political violence described earlier, we utilize generalized linear models with random effects (intercepts) for countries to account for the panel structure of our data. The inclusion of random effects means the estimates will be partly based on within-country covariation between the independent and dependent variables, instead of treating each country-year as an independent observation as in the standard "pooled" approach. The random effects are important as they will account for unmeasured, time-invariant factors that may be correlated with both the latent variables and the relevant measure of political violence. The plots shown in Figures A2.1—A2.5 indicate quite a bit of variation in the typical level of political violence from country to country. Failing to account for this can produce biased inferences (Green, Kim, and Yoon 2001). Fixed effects models will eliminate bias that results from failing to model "unit effects" in panel data but can produce unstable estimates, particularly if the independent variables do not vary much over time. Implementing fixed effects also becomes quite complicated in a generalized linear model framework. Random effects provide a good alternative since they effectively pull the estimates away from those in the "pooled" model and closer to those that would be obtained from a fixed effects model while avoiding these problems (Gelman and Hill 2006). Further, once the number of time periods reaches twenty the differences between coefficient estimates from random and fixed effects specifications become negligible (Clark and Linzer 2015). As our data cover a period of several decades the potential problems associated with random effects should be minimal. The main drawback of these models for our study is that if the variation in political violence that is explained by our latent variables is mostly cross-sectional rather than over-time variation, it will be harder to find evidence of such a relationship in our models with the unit effects included.

Another issue we must address is the uncertainty in our latent variable estimates. Recall that our measurement models produce a *distribution* of scores for every observation in the data. To characterize these distributions, we obtain a mean and standard deviation for each observation. The simplest way to include the latent variable in a regression model would be to include the mean score for each observation as an independent variable. The drawback of this approach is that it would overstate the precision of the latent variable estimates, which in turn would lead to coefficient estimates with similarly overstated precision, i.e. the standard errors would be smaller than they should be, and hypothesis tests would be more likely to produce false positives. The alternative approach is to account for the uncertainty in the latent variables by simulating a number of random draws from the posterior distributions and estimating a model using each set of draws as an independent variable. For the analysis below we follow this procedure and take 100 draws from the estimated posterior distributions (1 per observation) of the latent variable. We then estimate the relevant regression model 100 times and pool the estimates using the same formula for pooling estimates from multiply imputed data sets (Rubin 1987).

In the following chapters most of the models we estimate include a single latent variable, meaning we only include one measure of women's status at a time. As can be seen in the analysis that follows, for the measures of political violence we use it is rare that more than one aspect of women's status is found to have a statistically significant association, once control variables are included in the model. This, together with the fact that the latent variables are not highly correlated, suggests that including measures of women's status one at a time is a reasonable strategy.[2] Figure 2.4 indicates that the strongest correlation between the latent variables is between women's inclusion, harm to women, and

APPENDIX 227

women's rights. In cases where more than one of these variables have a statistically significant association with the same measure of political violence, we estimate additional models that include the relevant latent variables.

Appendix for Chapter 3

Measurement Models

In our models each observed indicator is effectively treated as a dependent variable that is influenced or caused by the latent variable. We must specify an appropriate distribution for the observed variables. In the case of a continuous indicator, we assume a normal distribution. This part of the model can be written:

$$Y_{ij} \sim Norm\left(\mu_{ij},\ \sigma_j^{\ 2}\right)$$
$$\mu_{ij} = X_i \beta_j$$

Where i indexes cases (country-years) and j indexes the indicators. Y is an observed indicator. Y_{ij} is read as "the value of observed indicator j for observation i." μ_j is the mean of Y_j, and is modeled as a linear function of X, the latent variable (women's inclusion) and the parameter β_j, which represents the strength of the relationship between the latent variable and the observed indicator j.[3] Continuous variables are all standardized prior to estimation, so we omit the intercept in the equation for μ_j. Because they are standardized, the β parameters for the continuous variables in our inclusion model can be interpreted as "factor loadings" that indicate the linear correlation between the latent and observed variables. Larger absolute values of β indicate a stronger relationship. Since a separate β is estimated for each observed indicator, some indicators may be more strongly related to the latent variable than others. If the estimates for the β_js all have credible intervals that do not contain 0, this would indicate that all of the observed variables have a non-zero correlation with the underlying latent variable.

There are also two binary indicators in our inclusion model: whether the head of government is female, and whether the head of the high court is female. Assuming these indicators follow a continuous distribution (like the normal distribution) is not realistic, so we assign them Bernoulli distributions and use the probit link function. This part of the model can be written:

$$Y_{ij} \sim Bernoulli\left(p_{ij}\right)$$
$$probit\left(p_{ij}\right) = X_i \beta_j - \alpha_j$$

Where Y_j is now a binary indicator and X is the latent variable. p_j represents the probability that $Y_j = 1$, e.g. the probability that the head of state or the high court is female. The parameters that connect the latent variable to the observed binary variable have a similar interpretation to the "discrimination" and "difficulty" parameters from a (two-parameter) IRT model.[4] β_j indicates whether the relationship between the latent variable and p_j is positive or negative, but since p_j is a probability the relationship is not linear, as in a standard probit regression model. β_j for a binary variable is the discrimination parameter and has the same interpretation as a coefficient in a probit regression model: positive values mean that p_j increases as the latent variable increases, and negative values indicate

228 APPENDIX

a negative relationship between p_j and X. Larger absolute values of β_j indicate that the probability changes more quickly as the latent variable increases. α_j is similar to the "difficulty" parameter in an IRT model. It provides some information about the value of the latent variable at which the probability that $Y_j = 1$ is 0.5, meaning the value of the latent variable beyond which the binary variable is more likely than not to equal 1.[5] Here α_j and β_j together can be used to indicate the value of the latent variable at which $\Pr(Y_j = 1) = 0.5$, which is equal to $\dfrac{\alpha_j}{\beta_j}$.

For the measurement model we must assign prior distributions to each β_j, α_j, σ_j^2, and the latent variable X_i. Standard practice is to assign the latent variable a standard normal distribution (mean 0 and variance 1), which we do in every model. This fixes the scale of the latent variable and serves to identify the model. Due to the "rotational invariance" problem inherent to these models, in some models we restrict some of the item parameters (β_j or parameters to make inference easier; see Bollen 1989, 247–48; Jackman 2000, 231). This does not affect the conclusions we draw but simply orients the latent variable so that it correlates with the indicators in an intuitive fashion. For example, in our women's inclusion model all but one indicator (the proportion of family and domestic workers who are women) should correlate positively with women's inclusion in public spaces. If we estimated a model and found a strong, negative relationship between the latent variable and the proportion of legislators who are female, education ratios, etc., this would indicate that they all correlate with a common phenomenon, but we would have to label it something like "women's exclusion."[6] For this reason, in some models some of the β_j parameters are restricted to positive or negative values. This ensures that higher values of the latent variable indicate higher, rather than lower, values of the concept in question.

In the inclusion model it was unnecessary to place such restrictions on any of the item parameters. For β_js associated with continuous variables we used normal prior distributions with mean 0 and variance 5. The σ_j^2 parameters were given inverse gamma prior distributions to restrict them to positive values. For the β_js for binary items, as well as the α_js, we use normal priors with mean 0 and variance 10. For this model we ran 5 Markov chains for 10,000 iterations and stored the last 5,000 to summarize the posterior distributions.

In the political inclusion model, we restricted the β_js for the proportion of ministerial positions occupied by females and the proportion of legislators who are female. These parameters were assigned truncated normal distributions (restricted to positive values) with mean 0 and variance 5. The β parameter for the proportion of high court justices who are women was assigned a normal distribution with mean 0 and variance 10. We again used inverse gamma priors for the σ_j^2 parameters. As in the more general inclusion model, the β_js and α_js for binary items were given normal priors with mean 0 and variance 10. For this model we ran 10 Markov chains for 15,000 iterations and stored every fifth draw from the last 10,000 to summarize the posterior distributions. Convergence for both models was assessed by examining trace and density plots and with a Gelman-Rubin diagnostic test. Visual diagnostics indicated good "mixing" and roughly normal

APPENDIX 229

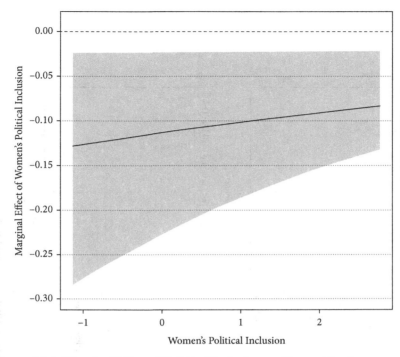

Figure A3.1 Marginal Effect of Political Inclusion on Terror Attacks

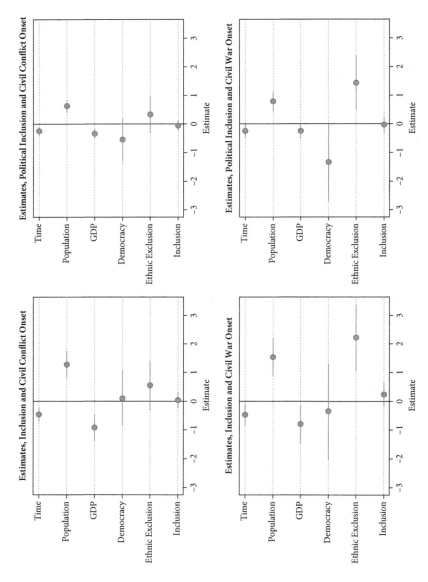

Figure A3.2 Coefficient Estimate from Models of Civil Conflict and War Onset

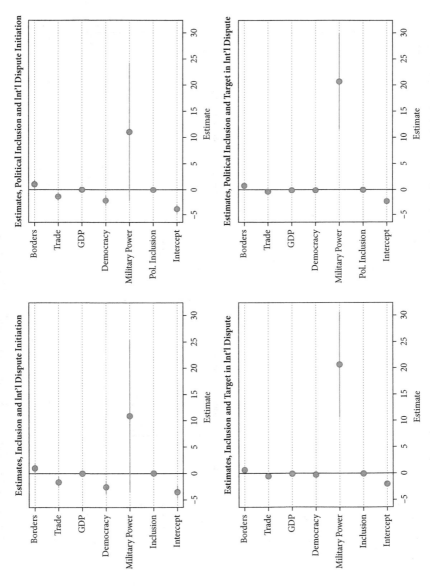

Figure A3.3 Coefficient Estimates from Models of International Disputes

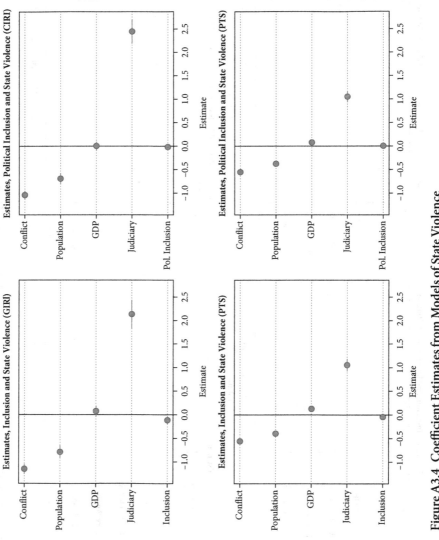

Figure A3.4 Coefficient Estimates from Models of State Violence

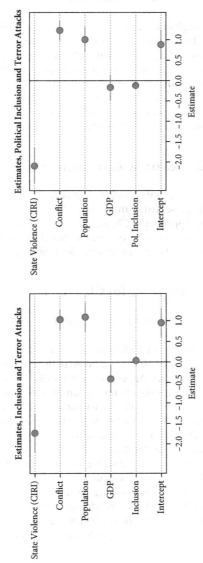

Figure A3.5 Coefficient Estimates from Models of Terror Attacks

234   APPENDIX

(unimodal, symmetric) densities. The upper bound of the interval for the Gelman-Rubin diagnostic was close to 1 (and well below 1.1) for every parameter.

Marginal Effect of Political Inclusion on Terror Attacks

Figure A3.1 displays the marginal effect of women's political inclusion on the expected number of terror attacks. The marginal effect with a 90% confidence interval (based on simulations) is shown across the range of women's political inclusion, with other variables held constant at their in-sample medians. For a given value of political inclusion, the height of the solid line indicates the change in the expected number of attacks for a 1 unit increase in political inclusion. For example, when political inclusion is at its minimum, a 1 unit increase corresponds to a decrease of 0.128 in the expected number of attacks. When political inclusion is 1, a 1 unit increase corresponds to a decrease of 0.08.

Estimates from Regression Models

Here we display estimates for the control variables, in addition to the latent variables, for all of the regression models presented in this chapter. Descriptions for all variables and models can be found in the Appendix to Chapter 2. Sample sizes for each model can be found in Figure 3.6. In the cases of models of state violence (CIRI and PTS) and civil conflict and war onset, the intercepts have been removed for legibility.

Appendix for Chapter 4

Measurement Model

As the variables from V-Dem that we include in our women's rights model are all continuous, they are assigned normal distributions, as were the continuous variables in the models for women's inclusion (see the Appendix to Chapter 3). The relationships between these indicators and the latent variable are thus assumed to be linear. The World Bank indicators are all binary and so, as with the binary variables in the inclusion model, for these indicators we use a Bernoulli distribution with a probit link function to model the relationship between the indicators and latent variable.

We restricted the β_j parameters for the continuous V-Dem variables to positive values. For these we used truncated normal prior distributions with mean 0 and variance 5. The σ_j^2 parameters were given inverse gamma prior distributions. For the β_js for binary items, as well as the α_js, we use normal priors with mean 0 and variance 10. For this model we ran 5 Markov chains for 11,000 iterations and stored every second draw from the last 6,000 to summarize the posterior distributions of the model parameters. Convergence for the model was assessed by examining trace and density plots and with a Gelman-Rubin diagnostic test.

Estimates from Regression Models

Here we display estimates for the control variables, in addition to the latent variables, for all of the regression models presented in this chapter. Descriptions for all variables and models can be found in the Appendix to Chapter 2. Sample sizes for each model can be found in Figure 4.2. In the cases of models of state violence (CIRI and PTS) and civil conflict and war onset, the intercepts have been removed for legibility. Recall that higher values on the CIRI and PTS scales indicate *less* state violence. For these dependent variables, we also show estimates from models that include women's INGOs and the interaction between women's rights and women's INGOs. The scale in Figure A4.4 makes it impossible to tell, but the coefficients for the interaction terms are both positive and statistically significant (90% confidence intervals from about 0.004 to 0.008 in the case of CIRI, and about 0.002 to 0.004 in the case of PTS).

Here we present estimates from models of state violence that include both women's inclusion and women's rights, as these aspects of women's status are moderately correlated with each other and also with the CIRI and PTS scales (see Figures 2.4, 3.6, and 4.2 and Figure A4.3) The estimates indicate that the results for these variables presented in Chapters 3 and 4 are consistent when both are included in a model using CIRI or PTS as the outcome.

Appendix to Chapter 5

Measurement Model

The measurement model in this chapter is essentially the same as in previous chapters but includes three ordinal scales. For the Woman Stats scales, we use an ordered categorical distribution with a probit link function. As with the models for women's inclusion and rights, the continuous indicators are treated as normally distributed and the relationship between these indicators and the latent variable is assumed to be linear.

In the harm to women model the β parameters for adolescent fertility rate, overall fertility rate, and maternal mortality rate are restricted to positive values so that the latent variable is positively correlated with these indicators. For these parameters we used truncated normal priors with mean 0 and variance 5. The rest of the continuous indicators were given normal prior distributions with means of 0 and variances of 5. The σ^2 parameters for the continuous variables were given inverse gamma priors. We also restricted the β parameter for the ordinal Woman Stats Murder Scale to positive values. The scale was assigned a truncated normal prior with mean 0 and variance

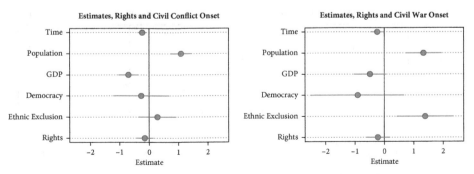

Figure A4.1 Coefficient Estimates from Models of Civil Conflict and War Onset

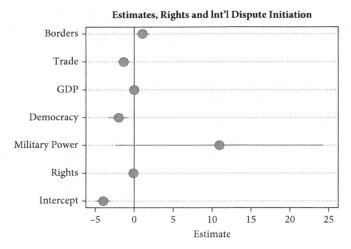

Figure A4.2 Coefficient Estimates from Models of International Disputes

5. The other two ordinal scales were given normal priors with means of 0 and variances of 5. The τ parameters for each ordinal scale were given normal priors with means of 0 and variances of 3. For this model we ran 5 Markov chains for 11,000 iterations and stored every second draw from the last 6,000 to summarize the posterior distributions. Convergence was assessed with visual diagnostics (trace and density plots) and a Gelman-Rubin test.

To illustrate how to interpret the item parameters for the ordinal scales, Figure A5.1 depicts the relationship between our harm to women variable and the Woman Stats Murder Scale, which ranges from 0 to 2 with higher values indicating that the murder of women is more prevalent. The scale has a positive discrimination parameter ($\beta = 0.72$), which means the probability of an observation moving from one category to the next increases as the latent variable increases. It also means the probability that an observation is in the *highest* category of the scale *increases* as the latent variable increases and that the probability that an observation is in the *lowest* category of the scale *decreases* as the latent variable increases.

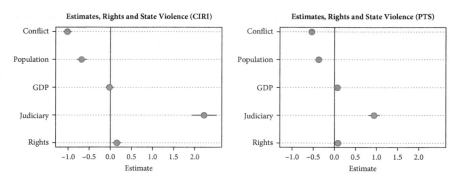

Figure A4.3 Coefficient Estimates from Models of State Violence

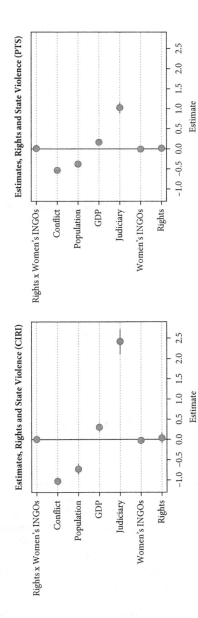

Figure A4.4 Coefficient Estimates from Models of State Violence: Rights Interacted with Women's INGOs

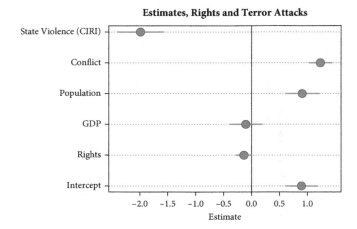

Figure A4.5 Coefficient Estimates from Models of Terror Attacks

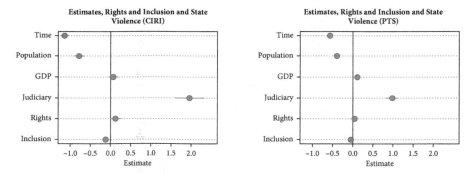

Figure A4.6 Coefficient Estimates from Models of State Violence with Women's Inclusion added

This is clear in Figure A5.1: the most lightly shaded region corresponds to the probability that the scale takes on the lowest value (0), and the more darkly shaded regions correspond to the probabilities for the middle and highest categories (values of 1 and 2, respectively). Moving from left to right, the most lightly shaded region becomes smaller, as does the combined area corresponding to the lowest (0) and middle (1) categories, while the most darkly shaded region becomes larger.

The τ parameters, like the α parameters for the binary variables in previous chapters, can be used with the discrimination parameters to calculate "difficulties" for the item, meaning the values of the latent variable at which the ordered scale changes categories. Difficulty for the 0 to 1 transition is −2.42, which is below the minimum value for the harm to women scale. The minimum observed value for the harm to women scale is −1.38 (shown in Figure A5.1). At the minimum value of the scale, the probabilities for the lowest and middle categories are 0.23 and 0.58, respectively, so that a country-year with a very low latent variable value (less harm to women) is more likely to be in the middle category than in the lowest. For the group of country years that fall into one of these two categories, we cannot say with confidence that 0 indicates less harm to women than 1, since a value of 1 is very likely even at low levels of harm to women. On the other hand, difficulty for the 1 to 2 transition is −0.15, which is slightly below the mean and median values of the latent variable.

This means that the highest category of the Murder Scale does a good job separating cases that lie below the (roughly) mid-point of the latent variable from those that lie above it. Country-years with latent variable values higher than −0.15 are more likely to be in the highest category than in a lower category. We can say with some confidence that a value of 2 indicates more harm to women than a value of 0 or 1, since a value of 2 is only likely at middle-to-high values of the latent variable. Thus, the parameter estimates suggest that the highest category provides more information about the latent variable than the lowest and middle categories. Similarly, the parameters for the Marital Rape Scale indicate that the middle three categories effectively divide country-years that are (roughly) below the thirty-eighth percentile, between the thirty-ninth and sixty-sixth percentile, and above the sixty-seventh

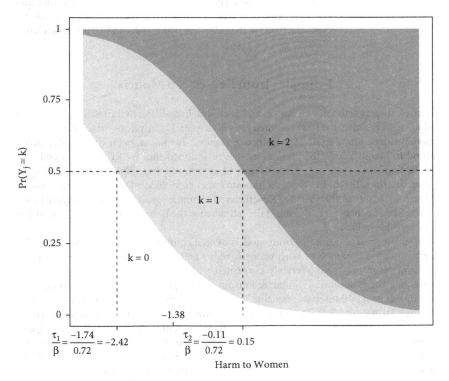

Figure A5.1 The Relationship between Harm to Women and One Ordinal Indicator

240 APPENDIX

percentile on the harm to women scale. This also suggests that, for the Murder Scale, the latent variable does a good job separating cases that fall into the middle or highest categories, and for the Marital Rape Scale, it does a good job separating cases that fall into one of the middle three categories. In this way, the parameter estimates provide some indication that the latent variable gives reasonable predictions for most of the values for these two scales.

Marginal Effect of Harm to Women on Intra- and Interstate Conflict

Figure A5.2 shows the marginal effect of harm to women on intrastate conflict onset as harm to women increases from its in-sample minimum to its maximum, holding all other variables constant at their in-sample medians. The marginal effect changes from 0.004 to 0.01 as harm increases from its minimum to maximum value. This indicates that a 1 unit increase in harm to women corresponds to an increase of 0.004 in the probability of conflict onset when harm to women is at its minimum, and when harm is at its in-sample maximum a 1 unit increase corresponds to an increase of 0.01 in the probability of conflict onset. Figure A5.3 shows the marginal effect of harm on interstate dispute initiation across the range of harm to women, with other variables held constant at their medians. The marginal effect varies from 0.001 at the minimum value of harm to 0.004 when harm is at its maximum.

Estimates from Regression Models

Here we display estimates for the control variables, in addition to the latent variables, for all of the regression models presented in this chapter. Descriptions for all variables and models can be found in the Appendix to Chapter 2. Sample sizes for each model can be found in Figure 5.2. In the cases of models of state violence (CIRI and PTS) and civil conflict and war onset, the intercepts have been removed for legibility. Recall that higher values on the CIRI and PTS scales indicate *less* state violence. Due to the large scale of Figure A5.2 (due to the size of the coefficient for military power), it is impossible to see that the confidence interval around the estimate for the harm does not contain zero, but this is visible in Figure 5.

Here we present estimates from models of civil conflict onset and international dispute initiation that include both women's rights and harm to women, as these aspects of women's status are moderately correlated with each other and also with conflict onset and the initiation of militarized disputes (though rights has a significant association with civil and international conflict only in the absence of control variables—see Figures 2.4, 4.2, and 5.2). These estimates account for the uncertainty in both measures and indicate that the results for harm to women presented in Chapter 5 are consistent when the women's rights measure is also included in the models. The coefficient for women's harm in the civil conflict model is nearly identical to the one in Figure 5.2 and is still statistically significant. The coefficient for women's harm in the dispute initiation model is also nearly identical to the one in Figure 5.2 but falls just short of conventional levels of statistical significance (the lower bound of the 90% confidence interval is −0.01).

APPENDIX 241

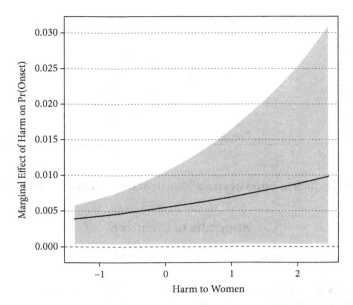

Figure A5.2 Marginal Effect of Harm to Women on Civil Conflict Onset

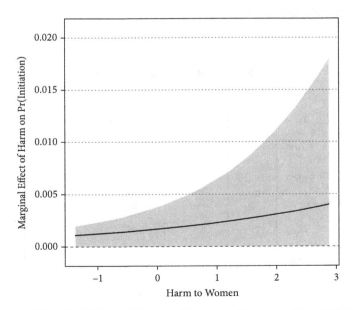

Figure A5.3 Marginal Effect of Harm to Women on Interstate Dispute Initiation

242 APPENDIX

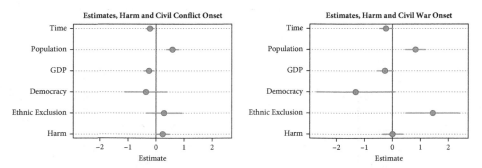

Figure A5.4 Coefficient Estimates from Models of Civil Conflict and War Onset

Appendix to Chapter 6

Social-Psychology Scales on Gender

- Attitudes Toward Women Scale (ATWS) (Spence, Helmreich, and Stapp (1973): This scale includes fifty-five questions that ask about women's appropriate behavior.[7]
- Sex Role Behavior Scale (Orlofsky 1981): includes several hundred items and roles pertaining to (a) leisure and recreational activities and interests, (b) vocational preferences, (c) social and dating behaviors, and (d) marital behaviors (including child-rearing and household responsibilities) that might be more characteristic of males or females.[8] Men and women were then asked to rate the typicality of the item or role to men or women and whether the role was desirable for men or women.

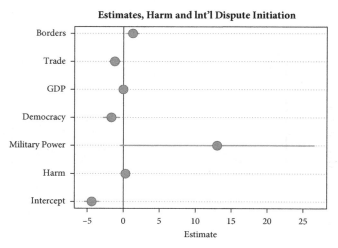

Figure A5.5 Coefficient Estimates from Models of International Disputes

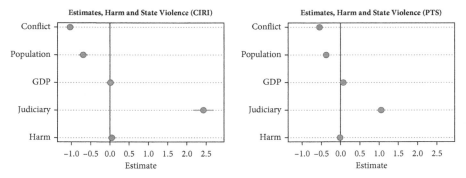

Figure A5.6 Coefficient Estimates from Models of State Violence

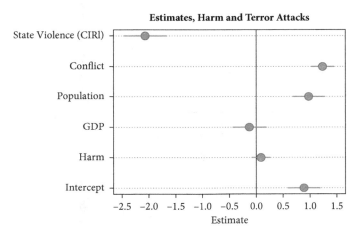

Figure A5.7 Coefficient Estimates from Models of Terror Attacks with Women's Rights Added

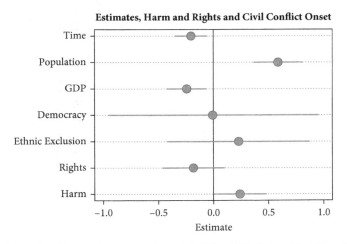

Figure A5.8 Coefficient Estimates from Models of Civil Conflict Onset with Women's Rights Added

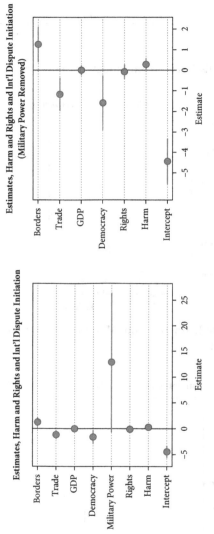

Figure A5.9 Coefficient Estimates from Models of International Disputes with Women's Rights Added

APPENDIX   245

Thus, the scale captures the expectation of what is typical behavior for women and what is deemed desirable behavior for women in any given society.

- Chastity Scale (Mahalingam 2007): measures beliefs about women as pure, self-controlled, and incorruptible.[9]
- Modern Sexism Scale (MSS) (Swim et al. 1995; Swim and Cohen 1997): measures "whether respondents tend to (a) deny the existence of discrimination against women, (b) resent complaints about discrimination, and (c) resent special 'favors' for women." (Swim and Cohen 1997).
- Sexist Attitudes toward Women Scale (Benson and Vincent 1980) measures: the belief that women are genetically inferior (biologically, emotionally, intellectually) to men; support for the premise that men should have greater rights and power than women; support for sex discrimination (antifemale) practices in education, work, and politics; hostility toward women who engage in traditionally masculine roles and behaviors or who fail to fulfill traditional female roles; lack of support and empathy for women's liberation movements and the issues involved in such movements; utilization of derogatory labels and restrictive stereotypes in describing women; evaluation of women on the basis of physical attractiveness information and willingness to treat women as sexual objects.

Models

Using the WVS items, we code responses in the category that corresponds to the most flexible beliefs about women's gender roles as 1 and all other responses as 0. For each country, we then sum the number of responses classified as 1s. The model uses a binomial distribution with a logit link function to model the relationship between the latent variable and the aggregated responses. The binomial distribution models the number of "successes" in N "trials" as a function of N and p, which is the probability of "success" in a single trial. The model we use for the WVS items can be written:

$$Y_{itj} \sim Binomial\left(N_{it}, p_{itj}\right)$$

$$logit\left(p_{itj}\right) = X_{it}\beta_j - \alpha_j$$

Where Y_{itj} is the number of respondents in country i during year t whose answers to item j correspond to a value of 1, which is treated as the number of "successes." N_{it} is the number of respondents in country i during year t, which is the number of "trials." The parameter p_{itj} represents the probability that the response of a randomly selected individual in country i during year t to item j corresponds with the category coded as 1 ("success"). It can also be thought of as the expected proportion of the N_{it} respondents that will indicate a strong positive sentiment toward the belief measured by Y_j. X_{it} is the latent variable, which can be interpreted as aggregate positive beliefs about women's gender roles in country i during year t.

To introduce temporal dependence into the latent variable estimates we specify a random walk prior for the latent variable. We use a standard normal prior for the first year and a normal prior for each subsequent year with mean X_{it-1} (the value of the latent variable in the previous year) and a variance parameter that is estimated from the data.

For this model it was unnecessary to place restrictions on the item parameters. For the α_j and β_j parameters we used normal priors with means of 0 and variances of 5. For the variance of the latent variable beyond the first year we use an inverse gamma prior. We ran 10 Markov chains for 500,000 iterations and stored every hundredth draw from the last 200,000 to summarize the posterior distributions. Convergence was evaluated visually (trace and density plots) and using a Gelman-Rubin diagnostic test.

Marginal Effect of Beliefs about Women's Gender Roles on Terror Attacks

Figure A6.1 shows the marginal effect of beliefs about women's gender roles on the expected number of terror attacks, with a 90% confidence interval. The effect is calculated across the range of the beliefs scale, holding other variables constant at their in-sample medians. The marginal effect is −0.4 at the minimum value of beliefs and becomes smaller in magnitude as beliefs become more flexible, reaching a value of −0.12 at the maximum value of the beliefs scale. This means that the expected reduction in the number of attacks for a 1 unit increase in the beliefs scale is 0.4 when beliefs is at its minimum and is 0.12 when it is at its maximum.

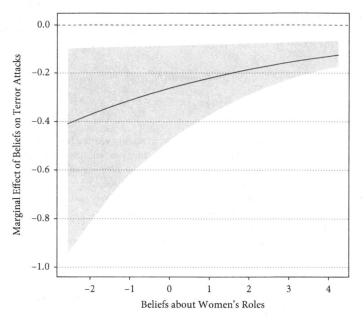

Figure A6.1 Marginal Effect of Beliefs About Women's Gender Roles on Terror Attacks

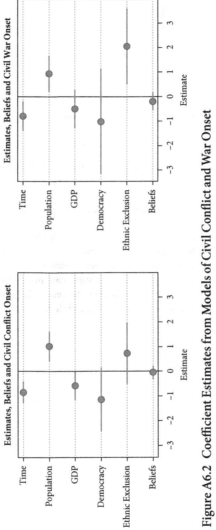

Figure A6.2 Coefficient Estimates from Models of Civil Conflict and War Onset

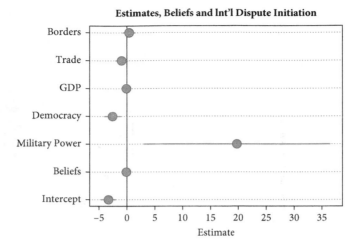

Figure A6.3 Coefficient Estimates from Models of International Disputes

Estimates from Regression Models

Here we display estimates for the control variables, in addition to the latent variables, for all of the regression models presented in this chapter. Descriptions for all variables and models can be found in the Appendix to Chapter 2. Sample sizes for each model can be found in Figure 6.2. In the cases of models of state violence (CIRI and PTS) and civil conflict and war onset, the intercepts have been removed for legibility. Recall that higher values on the CIRI and PTS scales indicate *less* state violence.

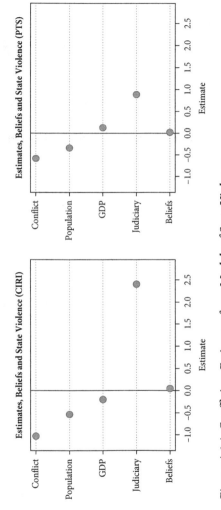

Figure A6.4 Coefficient Estimates from Models of State Violence

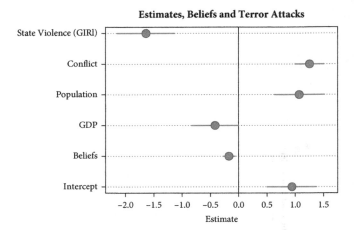

Figure A6.5 Coefficient Estimates from Models of Terror Attacks

Notes

Introduction

1 See also: https://www.nyu.edu/about/news-publications/news/2020/march/movem ent-toward-gender-equality-has-slowed-in-some-areas--stalle.html (accessed June 21, 2023).

2 Amnesty International, "International Women's Day: Dramatic deterioration in respect for women's rights and gender equality must be decisively reversed" March 7, 2022 (accessed January 25, 2024). https://www.amnesty.org/en/latest/news/2022/03/ international-womens-day-dramatic-deterioration-in-respect-for-womens-rights-and-gender-equality-must-be-decisively-reversed/#:~:text=March%207%2C%20 2022-,International%20Women's%20Day%3A%20Dramatic%20deteriora-tion%20in%20respect%20for%20women's%20rights,defenders%20now%20at%20 unprecedented%20risk

3 See footnote 6.

4 The quantitative literature that emerged around this time complemented a wide range of qualitative and theoretical work that had already been published on these topics.

5 For some examples, see: Melander 2005; Hudson et al. 2009. For a useful overview, see also: Väyrynen et al. 2021.

6 We worked with a graduate student to conduct a literature review of all articles that used quantitative methods to study the relationships between gender/sex and conflict for the period 2000–2020. We then coded the dependent variable, whether the article used the terms sex or gender (or both), the measures they used to test the theory, and the sex of the authors.

7 For an overview of this work, see Davies and True 2019. Other authors include, but are not limited to: Tickner 1988, 1992; Enloe 2000, 2014; Pettman 1996; Whitworth 1994; Sylvester 1994; Wibben 2010; Pettman 2005; Cohn 1987; Arat 2015; Ellerby 2017; Sjoberg 2013, 2014; Barkin and Sjoberg 2017; Mohanty, Russo, and Torres 1991; Stiehm 1982; Davis and Barat 2016; Evangelista 2011, among others.

8 Some feminist scholars would argue that concepts cannot necessarily be studied in isolation or assessed separately as this leads to their ahistoricizing; it ignores the histories of the concept construction (Kinsella and Sjoberg 2019; Sjoberg et al. 2018). We argue, however, that both approaches are possible. Not only are both approaches possible, but there are merits to exploring the effect of individual concepts because this allows us to see how they are better interconnected. In short, a close and careful examination of individual concepts and their effects refines our gendered lens. It allows us to see gender more accurately. See Chapter 1.

9 Even when biological sex is used to suggest a binary between men and women, it leaves out those who have ambiguous genitalia: both male and female sex organs or neither.

10 It is important to recognize that the social construction of the feminine does not mean woman and the social construction of masculine does not mean man. Indeed "the conventional trend of valuing (perceived) masculinities over (perceived) femininities does not mean that all symbols of masculinity are male, and women are the only persons who are feminized. Women can be masculine, that is, they can express a social preference for masculinity and subordinate and/or exclude femininity. Correspondingly, men, corporations, and states can be feminized. When this occurs,

252 NOTES

feminized men, corporations, and states take on subordinate positions due to their association with values perceived as feminine" (Sjoberg 2012, 8–9; MacKinnon 1993).

11 The power hierarchy dimension allows for an intersectional understanding of gender (Crenshaw 1989, 139), which is the idea that identity is formed by interlocking and mutually reinforcing vectors of race, gender, class, and sexuality (Nash 2008, 1–15). Hierarchy is created not only by assigning gender to sex, but also by the construction and reinforcement of categorizations such as race, class, ethnicity, etc. For example, feminine identities can also be hegemonic, as with White femininity (hooks 1981; Collins 1991; Mohanty, Russo, and Torres 1991). The ideal of what it means to be a woman is often based on the experiences of White women, thus this form of femininity subordinates the feminine experiences and identities of women of color. The power hierarchy dimension thus allows scholars to interrogate the hierarchy of gender identities based on organizing characteristics other than sex.

12 See also: Wohlforth et al. 2018.

13 We summarize the characteristics in Table 0.1 and develop them in detail in Chapters 3, 4, 5, and 6.

14 Note that we derive two to four characteristics for each concept based on the literature on concept stretching. However, we acknowledge that scholars could come up with more, fewer and different characteristics. Our goal is to show the process that should happen when defining concepts and not to conclude that our definition is definitive.

15 Consider the well-worn example of random measurement error used by many research methods texts of a bathroom scale that is correct on average but is always off by a few kilos or pounds in either direction.

16 Obviously, this is not always the case. For example, lower-class, dark-skinned men might have lower social standing than upper-class, White women.

17 On intersectionality, see: Crenshaw 1991; Al-Faham, Davis, and Ernst 2019; Hancock 2007.

18 See: https://www.v-dem.net (accessed June 21, 2023).

Chapter 1

1 This also includes leaders such as Hillary Clinton and Margot Wallström.

2 As mentioned in the Introduction, we use the language "identify biologically as women" because biological sex can sometimes be constructed. Sex is a dynamic concept, as people can change their sex or may be born without a sex or with both sexes. According to Kinsella and Sjoberg (2019: 265), "Notably, conditions of and responses to intersex, for example, sex chromosome mosaicism, demonstrate that we, in fact, do 'socialize' the 'impossibility' of such against evidence otherwise." They give examples of agentic (XY) males with "inadequate" penises who are categorized "female," as well as the idea that childbearing and ovaries are socialized to be linked (Kinsella and Sjoberg 2019: 265). Going forward, when we use the word "woman," we mean people who biologically identify as women.

3 According to Gerring (1999) "good" concepts are ones that are familiar, parsimonious, differentiable, coherent, deep, that resonate, and that have theoretical utility and field utility. Not all concepts have these characteristics as some of them are contradictory, such as depth and parsimony.

4 For most feminist scholars, the term gender implies a hierarchy among gender identities. To "gender" is to not only ascribe masculine and feminine traits to people and groups, but also to value traits associated with masculinity over those associated with femininity. Adding the qualifier "hierarchy or inequality" would thus be redundant. Yet, the literature includes a number of qualifiers and alternative names such as sexism, gender inequality, gender subordination, or gender discrimination. Tickner (1992) uses the terms gender hierarchy, gender inequality, and gender relations somewhat

interchangeably. While these alternative qualifiers and terms exist, our suggestion is to use the qualifier (in)equality in order to avoid the conceptual stretching described in this chapter. We suggest adding the qualifier "inequality" to refer to the privileging of masculine characteristics over feminine ones, or the practices that sustain hegemonic masculinity. In addition to avoiding conceptual stretching, adding a qualifier such as inequality more clearly signals the power hierarchy inherent in gender.

5 Although Enloe (2004) conceptualizes patriarchy as gender (inequality).

6 See Dotto 2019; Kinsella and Sjoberg 2019. Note that some people have XO, XXY, or XYY chromosomes (Klinefelter, Trisomy X, and Turner Syndrome).

7 See Renshon 2017; Wohlforth; Murray 2018; MacDonald and Parent 2021.

8 See also: Tickner 1988, 1992; Enloe 2000, 2014; Wibben 2010; Whitworth 1994; Pettman 1996, 2005; Sylvester 1994; Cohn 1987; Arat 2015; Ellerby 2017; Sjoberg 2013, 2014; Mohanty, Russo, and Torres 1991; Stiehm 1982; among others.

9 Post-positivist work also challenges the neat categorization of social phenomena. For more on post-positivism, see Lapid 1989 and Peterson 1992.

10 Other concepts that have been theorized about include women's empowerment (Webster, Chen, and Beardsley 2019; Webster et al. 2020) and women's political participation (Forsberg, Erika, and Olsson 2021).

11 They share only the attribute "pertaining to those that biologically identify as girls or women."

Chapter 2

1 Long before the bank scrapped its Doing Business project, Krever (2013) offered a compelling critique of the World Bank's legal scales, which also includes its World Governance Indicators. To sum up the critique, the bank's scales are based on a neoliberal worldview that privileges the property rights of capital over those of labor and through its methodology smuggles in value-laden assumptions that bias the scores.

2 The terms quantify, quantification, etc. can be misleading in that many indicators use ordinal rankings or qualitative categories rather than interval scales with numeric values that can be treated as such. Ordinal rankings could perhaps be described as quantitative in that they are intended to express whether one country is, for example, more or less democratic than another along an unobserved continuum. Of course, ordinal scales cannot indicate exactly how much more or less in a meaningful way, which might be considered necessary for "true" quantification. Although ordinal scales often use numeric values, the values only indicate the ordering of the categories and could be replaced by any numerals or other symbols that preserve this ordering ("agree," "strongly agree," etc.). Qualitative indicators, on the other hand, are just that. They do not indicate the precise locations or even rank order of a set of cases along a continuum, but rather which of a set of mutually exclusive, unordered categories each case belongs in. Even if the different categories are identified by different numerals, the numerals are labels for the purpose of classification rather than an indication of quantity. Nevertheless, for simplicity we will use "quantification" to refer to the creation of any indicator, including those that are ordinal or categorical. For further discussion, see Sartori (1970, 1036–37), and also Ward and Ahlquist (2018, 43).

3 For example, as human rights non-governmental organizations (NGOs) paid increasingly close attention to the practice of torture, many states began to develop "clean" methods of torture, i.e. ways of inflicting harm that leave no scars on victims' bodies, in order to create the impression that they were not engaging in torture (Ron 1997; Rejali 2007). Examining the physical condition of those held in state custody then became an imperfect way of assessing the presence or frequency of torture. Does this mean that NGOs should stop attempting to monitor the behavior of security forces and intelligence services?

254 NOTES

4 Going forward in this section, we put "gender equality" in quotes, because while the measures claim to measure the concept, they are not actually measuring gender equality. See Chapter 1.

5 This visualization is generated from the same data used in Figure 1.1. The plot shows how frequently a particular variable was used across all of the articles surveyed. Most articles used more than one indicator.

6 Sexual violence in conflict stands apart from the other indicators in that it is a characteristic of violent conflict rather than a characteristic of a country/society used to predict violent conflict. Typically, it is treated as an outcome affected by indicators of "gender equality" rather than an indicator of gender equality

7 See Munck and Verkuilen (2002) for a clear discussion of these issues as they relate to measuring democracy.

8 In most cases the concept to be measured by these scales is labeled but not well-defined or even discussed at any length. For example, the GII measures inequality in the three domains mentioned earlier: reproductive health, empowerment, and economic status. Some of the conceptual subcomponents of their concept of "gender equality," for example reproductive health, seem relatively straightforward and may not require lengthy discussions or detailed definitions. In other cases, "empowerment" being a good example, the concept is not as clear and so the measurement exercise would benefit from a precise, or at least explicit, conceptual definition. The GII uses completion of a secondary education and representation in parliament to measure empowerment, but the creators of the scale never define "empowerment," nor do they give a clear definition of gender equality that explains why empowerment and the other two subcomponents are relevant to gender equality.

9 Correlation coefficients using all country-years at once are similar, ranging from about −0.69 in the case of fertility rates and secondary enrollment ratios, to very close to 0 for fertility rates and women in the labor force as well as secondary enrollment ratios and women in the labor force.

10 It is common practice in quantitative IR/comparative politics scholarship to perform "robustness" checks for regression models: using several indicators of the same concept in different regression models to see whether coefficient estimates for different measures are consistent across models. This treats the indicators as substitutable measures. The weak correlations shown in Figure 2.2 suggest that robustness checks using these measures may produce misleading results. It is difficult to know what to make of an analysis if coefficient estimates for the indicators differ substantially across models, which is more likely if the indicators are not highly correlated with each other.

11 For example, the UN's GDI was created as a complement to the well-known HDI, which is composed of a country's average life expectancy, expected years of schooling, average years of schooling, and GDP per capita. Each indicator is first transformed by calculating its value relative to aspirational minimum and maximum values ("goalposts") determined by the UN. The GDI is just the ratio of a country's HDI score for women to that of men. The HDI and GDI use a logarithmic transformation for the income component (i.e. GDP per capita) in order to reflect the theoretically plausible diminishing returns to a person's value capabilities as their income increases (Sen 2001; UN Development Program 2021).

12 One issue is that, if one of the inputs takes on a value of 0, then movement on any other indicator has no effect on the HDI score. Another is that the scale is more sensitive to increases in life expectancy and schooling at higher levels of per capita income, meaning these components contribute more to the scores of wealthy countries than poorer countries. For a broader discussion of threats to validity within HDI measures, see: Ravallion 2012.

13 For a full exposition and description of the formula, see: Permanyer 2013 and Anand 2018.

14 Principal among these is the relationship between the index and the reproductive health inputs: maternal mortality and adolescent fertility. As Permanyer (2013, 7–8) explains, if men and women are equal on all other indicators (for which a direct comparison

NOTES 255

between men and women is possible), the index can only take a value of 0 (no inequality) if the product of maternal mortality (per 100,000 births) and adolescent fertility (births per 1,000 women age 15–19) is exactly 1, which is a knife-edge condition that does not occur in practice. Further, due to the mathematical properties of the aggregation formula, as maternal mortality and adolescent fertility tend toward 0 the GII actually tends toward 1, or the highest possible level of inequality on the scale.

15 See https://www.genderindex.org/sigi (accessed May 25, 2023).

16 See https://www.genderindex.org/building (accessed May 25, 2023).

17 See https://www.genderindex.org/building (accessed May 25, 2023).

18 For example, the World Economic Forum's Gender Gap Index is unusual in that it assigns different weights to the variables used to create the subcomponents that go into the final index (in which the subcomponents receive equal weight). The subcomponents are created using a weighted average that gives more weight to indicators with smaller standard deviations. The reasoning is that if conditions for women relative to men are relatively good and homogenous across countries, countries that deviate should be penalized more, and if conditions are relatively bad and homogenous, countries will be rewarded more for improvements. This weighting scheme is clearly reasoned, but it is not obvious why the conditions in one country should be considered "better" if conditions in many other countries suddenly worsened, or why they would be considered "worse" if conditions in many other countries suddenly improved (Hawken and Munck 2013).

19 See: Crabtree and Fariss 2015 for an illustration of how ignoring uncertainty in an indicator can affect regression estimates.

20 See Chapter 1.

21 Measurement models do require some assumptions about the formula that connects the concept and the indicators, but these are the same kinds of assumptions social scientists typically make in statistical models, e.g. regression models. For example, one must specify particular distributions for the response variables (the observed indicators), which assumes a particular kind of relationship between the concept and indicators (linear in the case of a normal distribution, non-linear in other cases). As another example, these models also require an assumption about whether or not the observations are independent. As with regression models, some measurement models can accommodate dependence between observations while others assume the observations are independent.

22 For example, V-Dem's women's political empowerment scale (Sundström et al. 2017), measures "a process of increasing capacity for women, leading to greater choice, agency, and participation in societal decision making." The index is created from three equally weighted subindices that measure women's civil liberties, women's civil society participation, and women's political participation. The civil liberties subindex is created using a Bayesian factor analysis that combines four sub-subindices that measure women's freedom of movement, forced labor, property rights, and access to justice. These, in turn, are all estimated from Bayesian IRT models that use the expert survey responses as inputs. The other subindices of the empowerment scale are also created by combining sub-subindices using either a Bayesian measurement model or taking the simple average (thus giving equal weight to each component). Most of these other sub-subindices are created by using Bayesian measurement models to combine survey responses, while a measure of the percentage of parliamentary representatives who are women (which is part of the sub-index that measures women's political participation) is coded from secondary sources, and a measure of the percentage of journalists who are women (a component of the civil society participation sub-index) is estimated from survey responses by calculating the bootstrapped mean across respondents.

23 The models we use are more similar to confirmatory factor analysis than exploratory factor analysis. The difference is that the goal of exploratory analysis is to determine *how many* latent variables are needed to most accurately reproduce the covariance structure of the data, while the goal in confirmatory analysis is to determine whether a

256 NOTES

set of indicators correlate (in the way anticipated) with some pre-specified number of latent variables. In each of our models we estimate a single latent variable, meaning we treat each concept as unidimensional. See: Bollen 1989, 227–28.

24 Our models for women's inclusion, harm to women, and women's rights are Bayesian mixed factor analytic models. Our model for beliefs about women's gender roles is a bit different, as we explain in Chapter 6, but can be used for the same purposes that we outline here.

25 For a full formal exposition of Bayesian mixed factor analysis, see: Quinn 2004.

26 Another notable project along these lines is the Sexual Violence in Armed Conflict (SVAC) dataset, which measures reports of the conflict-related sexual violence committed by armed actors during the years 1989–2019. See: Cohen and Nordås 2014.

27 The subsequent chapters present the specific estimates for each model and provide an intuitive interpretation, as well as a visual representation, of the relationships they summarize.

28 As can be seen in Figure 2.4, some of the latent variables cover different time periods. Coverage for harm, political inclusion, and rights estimates begins in 1960, while for inclusion it begins in 1973, and for beliefs in 1982. All variables go through 2015. The figure is useful for examining global changes in each latent variable over time but should not be used to compare variables to each other.

29 We also devote more attention to our measurement models than to our regression models. The appendix to this chapter goes into much more detail about each dependent variable, the control variables, and the models for the regression analysis.

Chapter 3

1 See: "Results from Second Aotearoa New Zealand Gender Attitudes Survey", 2020, https://nzfvc.org.nz/news/white-ribbon-2020-and-16-days-activism-against-gender-based-violence#:~:text=The%20survey%20found%20that%20attitudes,can%20contribute%20to%20gender%20inequality (accessed February 4, 2021).

2 For outcomes that compare women to men (ratios), we cap the indicator at parity. This is because in cases where there is a large imbalance that favors women (which is atypical and only occurs in indicators related to education), the imbalance reflects unusual circumstances that result in the near absence of men rather than more pervasive inclusion of women. Capping at parity gives more sensible estimates for the latent variable but does not affect the conclusions drawn in later chapters about the relationship between inclusion and political violence.

3 The model does not include indicators that capture law or policies related to women's inclusion.

4 Figure 3.1 shows β_j estimates for continuous and binary items, and also the α_j estimates for the two binary items. (See the Appendix to Chapter 3 for an explanation.)

5 This suggests the indicator is not informative about the latent variable, so leaving it in the model will not have much impact on the latent variable estimates themselves (the values will not change). The most obvious negative consequence is that the estimated error may be larger. Overall model fit is difficult to evaluate since some indicators are continuous and some binary. Most of the indicators here are continuous and the factor loadings are, for the most part, moderate to large in magnitude, with just over half being greater than 0.5 (absolute value). This indicates that the latent variable predicts the continuous indicators reasonably well.

6 These include the proportion of wage and salaried workers who are women and the proportion of professional and technical workers who are women. These are both International Labor Organization (ILO) classifications. Wage and salaried workers are

NOTES 257

those who receive regular remuneration in the form of wages or a salary, who are typically considered to have more secure employment. Professional and technical workers encompass a range of occupations in physical and life sciences, health, engineering, and teaching.

7 The six studies include: Tomz and Weeks 2013; Flores-Macías and Kreps 2017; Tago and Ikeda 2015; Grieco et al. 2011; Press, Sagan and Valentino 2013.

8 We might add distributions for other gender identities to this figure but do not for the sake of simplicity.

9 See also: Clayton, Josefsson, and Wang 2017; Mateo Diaz 2005; Lowande, Ritchie, and Lauterbach 2019.

10 See, for example, role congruity theory (Eagly and Karau 2002).

11 For more on how decision-making spaces are gendered and raced, see: Hawkesworth 2003).

12 Note that if women were in fact more peaceful in the sense that they view the costs of war as large, we should still observe larger demands but not necessarily an increase in the probability of conflict as women would be more willing to make larger concessions to avoid conflict (Barnhart et al. 2020, Appendix 49–50).

13 The estimates are shown as dots, and 90% confidence intervals are shown as horizontal lines. Where the lines do not cross zero the estimate is significant at the $\alpha = 0.10$ level for a two-tailed test (or, significant at the $\alpha = 0.05$ level for a one-tailed test where the alternative hypothesis is that the coefficient is less than/greater than zero, which is a more appropriate test for our hypotheses since we have expectations about the directions of the relationships).

14 See the appendix to this chapter for estimates for the other variables in the models.

15 To give some context to this result, we picked the country with the lowest political inclusion score in the estimation sample, which is the Solomon Islands, and calculated the expected change in terror attacks when political inclusion increases to its in-sample maximum, holding the other variables in the model constant at typical values for the Solomon Islands. The expected number of attacks decreases from 0.17 to 0.11. The expected change is −0.06, with a 90% confidence interval (based on simulations) from −0.11 to −0.1. A plot showing the typical marginal effect of women's political inclusion on terror attacks is included in the appendix to this chapter.

16 Recall that higher values on these scales indicate fewer violent abuses of civil and political rights. The estimates for the women's inclusion variable are negative and statistically significant in the PTS and CIRI models. The results thus indicate a positive relationship between women's inclusion and state violence. Since these are linear models, the coefficients can be interpreted as marginal effects, or a change in the dependent variable for a 1 unit increase in the independent variable. A 1 unit increase in the women's inclusion scale corresponds to a reduction of 0.11 in the CIRI scale and 0.04 in the PTS.

17 The authors find that in the Israeli-Palestinian conflict, Jewish women are no less supportive than Jewish men of violence against politicians and public officials and express more support for social segregation and the formal exclusion of Palestinian citizens.

18 For further discussion of this point, see Basu 2016; Folke et al. 2020; Labonne, Parsa, and Querubin 2021.

19 See the Women's Rights After War (WRAW) project headed by Marie Berry and Milli Lake: https://www.wrawproject.org/about-project (accessed June 14 2023).

20 For more on critical mass theory, see Kanter 1977; Dahlerup 2006, 2017, 2018; Beckwith and Cowell-Meyers 2007. For a critique of critical mass theory, see Childs and Krook (2009).

21 The same could be true for men who increase their representation in private spaces. Men who assume the "stay at home" father role, for example, may have little power in discussions and forums related to parenting when compared to mothers.

22 Women often become political leaders during a crisis. When they cannot fix the crisis (usually created by men), they are deemed unworthy of those positions of power. For example, in 2016 Theresa May became only the second female prime minister of the UK,

258 NOTES

just in time to preside over the country's economically perilous break from the European Union. She only lasted three years. In 2022, in the aftermath of the UK's withdrawal, Liz Truss succeeded Boris Johnson to become the third female prime minister. She lasted less than two months after her proposed economic policies, which were not terribly different from typical conservative Reagan-Thatcherite "trickle-down" policies, caused strong negative reactions in public opinion and financial markets.

23 Recall that our measure of inclusion increases with the number of women in school, including in higher education, with the number of women in the workforce, but especially in positions that require more education and training, with the number of women in positions of political leadership, and decreases with the number of women performing unpaid household labor. Our measure of political inclusion increases only with the number of women in positions of leadership. The stereotype hypothesis implies that the latter would be more strongly correlated with state violence than the former, but we find the opposite.

24 Similar to the "upholding the status quo "argument in Chapter 6.

25 See Corlett and McClure (2022).

Chapter 4

1 Only six UN member states have not ratified CEDAW: Iran, Palau, Somalia, Sudan, Tonga, and the United States.

2 See the CIRI coding guide: http://www.humanrightsdata.com/p/data-documentation.html (accessed May 31, 2023).

3 In their book, Htun and Weldon use women's rights, gender equality policies, sex equality policies, and gender issues as synonymous (2018, 7), but they suggest that women's rights and sex equality issues are a subset of a larger group of "gender equality issues" and "gender issues."

4 See the Appendix to this chapter.

5 Rather, 2 of the 3 estimates, which are the Bayesian equivalent of factor loadings, are larger than 0.85, indicating a change of at least 0.85 standard deviations in the V-Dem scale for a 1 standard deviation increase for the latent variable or, alternatively, a linear correlation of at least 0.85. This indicates the latent variable predicts these indicators well.

6 A common way to assess the fit of the model for binary items is to calculate classification errors based on predicted probabilities. Using a cutoff of 0.5 to define a prediction of 1, the percent of cases correctly classified is 78% when averaging across the items. It correctly classifies more than 50% of cases for 57 of 62 items (92%), and more than 80% of cases for 37 of 62 (60%).

7 Note that the parameter for laws that require women to obey their husbands is large and positive. Since the estimate is negative, this item has negative difficulty as well, indicating that this kind of law is likely to exist when legal protection for women is relatively *low*. Difficulty for this item is $\frac{\alpha}{\beta} = \frac{1.69}{-2.10} = -0.80$, which is around the eighteenth or nineteenth percentile of the women's rights variable. Because the slope of the item curve is negative, once women's rights increases beyond −0.80 this kind of law is unlikely to exist.

8 For example, between 1912 and 1914, suffragettes in Great Britain and Ireland orchestrated a bombing and arson campaign between the years. The campaign was instigated by the Women's Social and Political Union (WSPU). See: Bearman 2005, 365–97; Rosen 2013; Teele 2019.

NOTES 259

9 As values for this variable are only recorded every five years, we impute the missing values using linear interpolation.

10 See: "Russian Federation Violated Woman's Rights by Failing to Provide Gender-Sensitive Drug Dependence Treatment, UN Committee Finds," ONCHR, March 26, 2023. https://www.ohchr.org/en/press-releases/2023/03/russian-federation-violated-womans-rights-failing-provide-gender-sensitive (accessed June 15, 2023).

11 These null findings are partly consistent with the expansive literature on liberalism, democracy, and violent political conflict. In general, countries with more democratic institutions have a relatively low risk of civil conflict, but the relationship between democracy and conflict is not entirely straightforward. Research on the topic consistently finds that partial democracies/autocracies are more likely to experience conflicts than strongly autocratic countries, though strongly democratic countries are least likely to experience a conflict. Similarly, states in political transition, whether moving away from or toward a more democratic form of government, are more prone to conflict than stable democracies or dictatorships (see Hegre et al 2001; Cederman, Hug, and Krebs 2010; Lupu and Jones 2018).

12 See "Jo Becker: Hillary Clinton, Foreign Policy and the Question of U.S. Military Intervention," April 5, 2016, Harvard Kennedy School Shorenstein Center, (https://shorensteincenter.org/jo-becker/) (accessed July 15, 2023).

13 Despite global funding on women's rights, only a small portion goes to women's groups. See "How the U.S. Gender Equality Funding Increase Can Actually Be Effective," Carnegie Endowment for International Peace, March 22, 2022, (https://carnegieendowment.org/2022/03/22/how-u.s.-gender-equality-funding-increase-can-actually-be-effective-pub-86686) (accessed June 15, 2023).

Chapter 5

1 See: Marsden 2018. "International Women's Day: What are Matriarchies, and Where Are They Now?," *Independent*, March 8, 2018. https://www.independent.co.uk/news/long_reads/international-womens-day-matriarchy-matriarchal-society-women-feminism-culture-matrilineal-elephant-bonobo-a8243046.html (accessed June 15, 2023).

2 For a concise list of examples, see "6 Matriarchal Societies That Have Been Thriving with Women at the Helm for Centuries," *Town & Country*, August 5, 2019, https://www.townandcountrymag.com/society/tradition/g28565280/matriarchal-societies-list/ (accessed June 15, 2023).

3 It is possible that even the categorization of people into the categories of man and women based on physical traits creates a system of structural violence against (trans) people. A definition of women based on physical traits, whether genitalia or chromosomes, excludes individuals who identify as women, but who do not possess the physical traits associated with the social category "woman." Such women are often marginalized and treated in ways that cause psychological harm, and they are often subject to physical harm because they identify as women though they do not have two X chromosomes and a vagina (Greenberg 2012; Hoewer 2014; Lee 2014).

4 For more information, see "WomanStats": http://www.womanstats.org/new/codebook (accessed June 15, 2023).

5 The idea being that one could use student's letter grades (which are ordered scales where 90–100 = A, 80–89 = B, etc.) on assignments to determine if they are in fact measuring students' aptitude.

260 NOTES

6 Most (15 of 27) of the factor loadings are large (greater than 0.7), indicating that the latent variable predicts the continuous indicators well. Fit is more difficult to assess for the ordered items, but we discuss this some in the Appendix to Chapter 5.

7 These variables are coded from survey responses and indicate the proportion of women who gave a particular response, e.g. answered "yes" when asked if they are responsible for making household purchase decisions.

8 See the Appendix to Chapter 5 for more details.

9 As in regression models for ordered responses, the relationship between the latent variable (here the "independent variable") and the probability that an observation is in a middling category cannot be inferred from the sign of the estimate.

10 See also: Caprioli 2000, 2003.

11 For further discussion, see: Forsberg and Olsson 2021, 8.

12 The flip side, of course, is that societies with relatively low levels of structural violence against women may be more peaceful because respect for human life is universalized and applied in decision-making (Bjarnegård and Melander 2011).

13 They cite social psychological research, which supports this claim. The first notion of difference that babies learn, for example, is the difference between boys and girls. Studies in that field have consistently found three basic differences that individuals notice immediately when they encounter a new person almost from infancy, age, sex, and race, with the sex difference the only distinction that is never disabled. Alice Eagly and co-authors assert that, "gender stereotypes trump race stereotypes in every social science test" (Eagly and Chin 2010; Eagly and Mladinic 1989; Eagly and Steffen 1984). In this way, sex, more so than age and race, becomes a basic social category of identification and a profound marker of difference.

14 Kinsella and Sjoberg (2019) point out that this framing has racial implications as well.

15 See: Krystalli and Schulz 2022.

16 The Russian invasion of Ukraine in 2022 may be an example of this dynamic. President Vladimir Putin justified the invasion in part by claiming that Ukrainian autonomy was a historical mistake and an aberration that needed to be forcefully corrected. According to Putin, Ukraine is "rightfully" part of Russia's national territory. Subsequently he has portrayed the conflict as part of a larger struggle between Russia and its enemies, in which Russia is protecting traditional religious and conservative values, including values related to family relations and gender identity. See https://web.archive.org/web/20230227195023/en.kremlin.ru/events/president/news/70565, (accessed June 15, 2023).

17 The flip side, of course, is that non-violence in the household leads to children learning other ways to resolve conflicts. Saiya, Zaihra and Fidler (2017), for example, suggest if women are treated in a manner that is fair and nonviolent, it instills in children the importance of dialogue, discussion, and reasoning as legitimate means of resolving conflict.

18 There is a surprising dearth of recent scholarly literature on norms of marriage payment in the West. Despite its coverage in media and op-eds, academia has yet to examine this worthwhile topic in greater detail. For more on this discussion, see: https://www.washingtonpost.com/news/soloish/wp/2017/05/18/parents-of-the-bride-are-still-getting-stuck-with-the-majority-of-wedding-costs/ (accessed June 15, 2023).

19 See also: https://www.lbc.co.uk/radio/special-shows/the-mystery-hour/culture/why-do-the-brides-family-pay-for-the-wedding/ (accessed June 15, 2023).

20 Younas and Sandler (2017) find that high female to male ratios in developing countries lead to an increase in domestic terror attacks. They attribute this increase to a relative lack of men available to staff agencies responsible for combating terrorism and point out that in developing countries these agencies are typically male dominated. They argue that "developing countries with both a female gender imbalance and weak bureaucracies to administer and foster the rules of law should be particularly vulnerable to terrorism" (485). The empirical record on the connections between bride price and conflict is also mixed. Hudson and Matfess (2017) examine case studies and find evidence that it can

NOTES   261

aid rebel groups' recruitment efforts, however a quantitative analysis by Thies and Cook (2019) finds no relationship between bride price and political violence.

21 See: "Iran: A really simple guide to the protests," BBC, September 15, 2022, https://www.bbc.com/news/world-middle-east-63240911 (accessed October 5, 2023).

22 For a literature review, see: Bauer et al. 2016.

23 To examine the relationship between harm to women and conflict in substantive terms, we followed the same procedure as in Chapter 3: we identified the country with the highest harm to women score in the sample, which is Sierra Leone, and calculated the expected changes in the probabilities of intrastate conflict onset and interstate dispute initiation when harm to women moves to its minimum from its maximum value, holding other variables constant at typical values for Sierra Leone. The expected probability of interstate conflict decreases from 0.013 to 0.004. The difference is −0.009, with a (simulated) 90% confidence interval from −0.026 to −0.001. For intrastate conflict onset, the expected probability decreases from 0.057 to 0.023. The difference is −0.034 (90% confidence interval from −0.68 to −0.003). The latter change is relatively large considering the (unconditional) probability of conflict in the sample is 0.036. A plot showing the typical marginal effects of harm to women on interstate dispute initiation and intrastate conflict onset are included in the Appendix to this chapter.

Chapter 6

1   John Doe is a pseudonym we will use for the purposes of this chapter. Terrorists such as Doe crave infamy and notoriety and using a pseudonym is one way of denying them this.

2   Though this attack was not anti-state terror, it had key characteristics of a terror attack: it was an act of violence that targeted civilians for the purpose of intimidating and influencing a broader audience. In this case, the "audience" was all women.

3   Since these are direct quotations from Doe's manifesto, we have elected to forgo a citation to mitigate the ethical hazards of legitimizing and circulating the source materials.

4   See: Barnes and Karim 2024.

5   Ibid.

6   Ibid

7   See https://www.washingtonpost.com/sports/redskins/donald-trumps-idea-of-locker-room-talk-is-as-demeaning-to-men-as-it-is-to-women/2016/10/10/7e34718a-8eee-11e6-a6a3-d50061aa9fae_story.html (accessed June 16, 2023).

8   See also: https://politicalviolenceataglance.org/2016/12/14/prospects-for-state-violence-in-trumps-america/ (accessed June 16, 2023).

9   See the Appendix to Chapter 6 for more details about these scales.

10 We considered using opinion data from other surveys, particularly the regional "barometers," but ultimately chose to use the WVS alone. Other large survey projects are more limited in their temporal coverage since their data begin in the relatively recent past. Regional surveys also tend to cover fewer countries than the WVS. Unless there is an item for which the wording is nearly identical to one of the questions in WVS, adding a question from another survey amounts to adding another item to the model that would contain information for only a handful of countries and years. While this could add more countries to the data, if those countries do not correspond to countries in the WVS we would be estimating the beliefs variable from different survey sources for different countries. For these reasons we use only WVS to create our measure, but the possibility of combining survey data for different countries to measure beliefs about gender roles is something that should be explored in the future.

11 This last question is a bit different than the others but has clear implications for the respondent's beliefs about women's gender roles. Democracy can be defined in

262   NOTES

many ways, but the concept is commonly understood to entail responsiveness to the demands of the populace and equal opportunities for political participation. A belief that equal rights for men and women is not necessary for democracy suggests either that women's preferences are inherently less important or that women's participation in political decision making is not necessary for their interests to be protected. Both of these beliefs imply inherently different social roles for women and men: women's interests are either of secondary importance to men's or are necessarily served by whatever men happen to decide, and so it is unnecessary for them to participate in the process of governance.

12 See Caughey and Warshaw (2015), for an example of a more complex version of the model we use. They use their model to create estimates of public opinion (in the United States) at the group level from individual level survey data. We use a similar model to create estimates at the country level.

13 See the Appendix to Chapter 6 for more details.

14 While there is no widely accepted way to evaluate the overall fit of this kind of model, a good approach is to compare the observed and predicted proportions of respondents who answer the question "correctly." The correlations between observed and predicted proportions for our model vary from 0.69 to 0.93, and average to 0.8, indicating that the latent variable predicts the observed proportions with reasonable accuracy.

15 Of course, despite the gendered title of Gurr's book (originally published in 1970), the argument is intended to apply to women as well as men.

16 See: Pratto, Sidanius, and Levin 2006.

17 These terms are used interchangeably in the literature on social dominance.

18 While we focus primarily on insights from social dominance theory that dovetail with those from the literature on gender and conflict, there are at least two points of considerable divergence between these bodies of research. First, social psychologists assert that the boundaries of ethnic identities are more permeable than those based on sex and gender. This is potentially in tension with the feminist view of gender (and sex-based) identities as more or less fluid, and with the view among scholars of ethnic politics that "passing" as a member of another social group is more difficult when group membership is based on ethnic identity (Chandra 2006). Second, social dominance theory claims that distinctions based on ethnicity (or other arbitrary set groupings) are characterized by more violence than those based on sex or age. The occurrence of genocide and lack of any equivalent episode of mass killing between male and female or adult and child groups is treated as *prima facie* evidence of this claim. However, conflict between distinct ethnic groups is exceedingly rare compared to the number of opportunities for such conflict (Fearon and Laitin 1996), whereas violence against women by men and against children by adults seem to be universal phenomena, which is consistent with the view of social dominance theorists that hierarchies based on age and sex are universal, unlike those based on arbitrary set groupings.

19 See also: https://blogs.lse.ac.uk/gender/2018/01/15/traditional-values-for-the-99-the-new-gender-ideology-in-russia/ (assessed June 16, 2023).

20 The governments of Canada and New Zealand have gone so far as to designate Proud Boys a terrorist organization.

21 See: Kattelman and Burnes 2022.

22 To illustrate the substantive relationship between beliefs about women's gender roles and terror attacks, we locate the country in our sample with the lowest value on the beliefs indicator, which is Bangladesh. We calculate the expected number of attacks when the beliefs scale is at its lowest value, holding the other variables in the model constant at

NOTES 263

values typical for Bangladesh. We then calculate the expected number of attacks when the beliefs variable is at its highest in-sample value, holding the other variables constant at the same values. The expected number of attacks decreases from 22 to 7. The expected change is −15, with a (simulated) 90% confidence interval from −30 to −5. A plot showing the typical marginal effect of beliefs on terror attacks can be found in the Appendix to Chapter 6.

23 Note that we do not empirically test whether right-wing groups are more likely to rely on the recruitment of people with rigid beliefs about women.

24 See Chapter 2, Figure 2.4.

Chapter 7

1 The largest limitation of our analysis of interstate conflict is that it is "monadic" rather than "dyadic," meaning it uses single countries rather than pairs of countries as the unit of analysis. It is possible that pairs of states with similar degrees of women's inclusion, rights, or beliefs about women's roles are less likely to become involved in conflict. However, previous analyses of women's inclusion, harm to women, and international conflict is not exclusively dyadic. For examples, see: Barnhart et al. 2020, Caprioli 2000; Caprioli and Boyer 2001; Hudson et al. 2009.

2 As another example, one of the rights that women's rights activists champion is private property for women. Yet, ownership of land means that collective (feminine) means of living become obsolete. These collective forms of living often benefit women who rely on "the village" for collectively taking care of children. Additionally, it means the possible destruction of public land that is important for women's livelihoods (Ryan 2018). Thus, women's rights can benefit some women at the expense of others while pushing out women-friendly ways of living.

3 See, for example: Manne 2018; Matfess, Kishi, and Berry 2022.

4 We note that while some of the indicators in our women's rights model, for example protections for property rights, are consistent with the principal concerns of liberal feminism, other indicators, for example laws concerning violence and harassment, are not.

5 See: Doyle 2018; Arat 2022.

6 These are the three Woman Stats scales and an indicator that records the proportion of women who report having been subjected to physical violence within the past year.

7 Not to mention that male and female specific bathrooms also could create structural harm as this affects trans and intersex people, among others. See: Herman 2013; Jones and Slater 2020.

8 See also: "Covid 19: Rebuilding for Resilience," UN, https://www.unwomen.org/en/hq-complex-page/covid-19-rebuilding-for-resilience?gclid=Cj0KCQjw4NujBhC5ARIsAF4Iv6chh9LEMhO73XODzzkH69N4KXxMcMUWq3TXz8znpwDz0whcgV2zJu4aAnkdEALw_wcB (accessed June 20, 2023).

9 See work by Betsy Paluck, for example. See also: Mousa 2020.

10 https://www.equimundo.org/about/ (accessed June 20, 2023).

11 Other work on women's status and conflict has also turned micro. See, for example: Bjarnegård, Brounéus, and Melander 2017; Bjarnegård et al. 2023.

12 See Kattleman and Burns (2022) for an example of an analysis that disaggregates groups by ideology.

264 NOTES

13 Forsberg and Olsson (2021) analyze women's status and conflict using sub-national data from India.
14 This argument also suggests an indirect relationship whereby harm influences sex imbalances, which influences recruitment practices; a structural equation approach may be useful for better examining it.
15 See, for instance: Paris 2001; Kaldor 2010.

Appendix 1

1 Note that we do not exclude attacks against *government* targets as long as they are not part of the military or police.
2 There is also the complication of accounting for measurement error to consider. When taking many draws from the posterior distributions of one of the latent variables and estimating many (non-linear) regression models that include random effects for countries along with the control variables, ensuring that all of the models converge and produce sensible estimates is challenging. This becomes more challenging when including additional latent variables with measurement error that must be accounted for.
3 σ_j^2s the model variance (analogous to mean squared error in a linear regression model) of the observed indicator Y_j.
4 IRT models developed mostly in the fields of education and psychology and are used to evaluate whether a set of test questions (answers to which are marked as binary, either correct or incorrect) is able to assess the underlying ability or trait (e.g. intelligence) they are supposed to assess. For an overview of IRT models, see: DeMars 2010.
5 The name "difficulty parameter" reflects the common application of these models to educational settings. A question with a high difficulty parameter is less likely to be answered correctly ($Y_j = 1$) than a question with a low difficulty parameter, holding the latent trait constant.
6 In applications of these models to roll call votes in national legislatures, for example, it is common to restrict some of the parameters so that ideology score estimates for more liberal politicians are to the left of estimates for more conservative ones. "Rotating" the estimates would not change any substantive conclusions but would result in latent trait (ideology) estimates where movement up/to the right side of the scale indicates more liberal ideology.
7 Some examples of survey questions asked are: "Swearing and obscenity are more repulsive in the speech of a woman than of a man"; "Women should take increasing responsibility for leadership in solving the intellectual and social problems of the day"; "Both husband and wife should be allowed the same grounds for divorce"; "Telling dirty jokes should be mostly a masculine prerogative"; "Intoxication among women is worse than intoxication among men"; "Under modern economic conditions with women being active outside the home" (Spence, Helmreich, and Stapp 1973, 219–20).
8 Examples of items range from sailing, hiking, gardening, to taking special care with one's appearance, to deciding where to go on a first date, to being faithful in a marriage (Orlofsky 1981, 931).
9 Questions include: 1. Only a virtuous woman can be a good woman. 2. Sacrificing her needs in life is the hallmark of good woman. 3. A good woman always puts other people's needs before her own. 4. A virtuous woman has sacred powers. 5. The power

of a woman comes from her capacity to be patient. 6. Only a virtuous woman can be a good mother. 7. A good woman never loses her temper. 8. A virtuous woman has the capacity to endure any sufferings in life without complaining. 9. A virtuous woman will be greatly rewarded in her next life. 10. A curse from a virtuous woman could be harmful. 11. Other than her husband, a virtuous woman will never even think of another man even in her thoughts. 12. Only good women can give birth to a son. 13. A virtuous woman will never have sex with anyone other than her husband. 14. A good woman always obeys her husband. 15. Only a virtuous woman can uphold the honor of the family. 16. A good woman will always adjust with her husband. 17. A virtuous woman will never divorce her husband. 18. A woman should be a virgin at the time of her marriage. 19. A good woman will die as a sumangali (an auspicious woman). 20. A virtuous woman is a sacred woman. 21. A virtuous woman has divine powers. 22. A virtuous woman is like a goddess. 23. A virtuous woman will never even look at other men.

References

Adcock, Robert, and David Collier. 2001. "Measurement Validity: A Shared Standard for Qualitative and Quantitative Research." *The American Political Science Review* 95 (3): 529.

Adjei, Maxwell. 2021. "Ending Civil War through Nonviolent Resistance: The Women of Liberia Mass Action for Peace Movement." *Journal of International Women's Studies* 22 (9): 19–35.

Aggestam, Karin, and Annika Bergman-Rosamond. 2016. "Swedish Feminist Foreign Policy in the Making: Ethics, Politics, and Gender." *Ethics & International Affairs* 30 (3): 323–34. https://doi.org/10.1017/S0892679416000241.

Al-Faham, Hajer, Angelique M. Davis, and Rose Ernst. 2019. "Intersectionality: From Theory to Practice." *Annual Review of Law and Social Science* 15: 247–65.

Anand, Sudhir. 2018. "Recasting Human Development Measures." United Nations Development Programme. https://hdr.undp.org/system/files/documents/anandrecasting humandevelopmentmeasurespdf.pdf.

Anderson, Siwan. 2007. "The Economics of Dowry and Brideprice." *Journal of Economic Perspectives* 21 (4): 151–74. https://doi.org/10.1257/jep.21.4.151.

Apodaca, Clair. 2000. "The Effects of Foreign Aid on Women's Attainment of Their Economic and Social Human Rights." *Journal of Third World Studies* 17 (2): 205–19. https://doi.org/10.2307/45198200.

Arat, Zehra F. Kabasakal. 2015. "Feminisms, Women's Rights, and the UN: Would Achieving Gender Equality Empower Women?" *American Political Science Review* 109 (4): 674–89. https://doi.org/10.1017/S0003055415000386.

Arat, Zehra F. Kabasakal. 2022. "Democratic Backsliding and the Instrumentalization of Women's Rights in Turkey." *Politics & Gender* 18 (4): 911–41.

Armstrong, David A. 2011. "Stability and Change in the Freedom House Political Rights and Civil Liberties Measures." *Journal of Peace Research* 48 (5): 653–62. https://doi. org/10.1177/0022343311411744.

Asal, Victor, Richard Legault, Ora Szekely, and Jonathan Wilkenfeld. 2013. "Gender Ideologies and Forms of Contentious Mobilization in the Middle East." *Journal of Peace Research* 50 (3): 305–18. https://doi.org/10.1177/0022343313476528.

Autesserre, Séverine. 2014. *Peaceland: Conflict Resolution and the Everyday Politics of International Intervention*. Cambridge University Press.

Autesserre, Séverine. 2021. *The Frontlines of Peace: An Insider's Guide to Changing the World*. Oxford University Press.

Bacarisse, Bonnie. 2017. "The Republican Lawmaker Who Secretly Created Reddit's Women-Hating 'Red Pill.'" https://www.thedailybeast.com/the-republican-lawmaker-who-secretly-created-reddits-women-hating-red-pill.

Bacchus, Loraine J., Meghna Ranganathan, Charlotte Watts, and Karen Devries. 2018. "Recent Intimate Partner Violence against Women and Health: A Systematic Review and Meta-Analysis of Cohort Studies." *BMJ Open* 8 (7).

Baines, Erin. 2014. "Forced Marriage as a Political Project: Sexual Rules and Relations in the Lord's Resistance Army." *Journal of Peace Research* 51 (3): 405–17.

Baldez, Lisa. 2011. "The UN Convention to Eliminate All Forms of Discrimination Against Women (CEDAW): A New Way to Measure Women's Interests." *Politics & Gender* 7 (3): 419–23.

268 REFERENCES

Baldez, Lisa. 2014. *Defying Convention: US Resistance to the UN Treaty on Women's Rights*. Problems of International Politics. Cambridge University Press. https://doi.org/10.1017/CBO9781107775565.

Banerjee, Sikata. 2006. "Armed Masculinity, Hindu Nationalism and Female Political Participation in India: Heroic Mothers, Chaste Wives and Celibate Warriors." *International Feminist Journal of Politics* 8 (1): 62–83.

Barkin, J. Samuel, and Laura Sjoberg, eds. 2017. *Interpretive Quantification: Methodological Explorations for Critical and Constructivist IR*. University of Michigan Press.

Barnes, Collin D., Ryan P. Brown, and Lindsey L. Osterman. 2012. "Don't Tread on Me: Masculine Honor Ideology in the US and Militant Responses to Terrorism." *Personality and Social Psychology Bulletin* 38 (8): 1018–29.

Barnes, Mariel J. 2020. "Divining Disposition: The Role of Elite Beliefs and Gender Narratives in Women's Suffrage." *Comparative Politics* 52 (4): 581–601. https://doi.org/10.5129/001041520X15794417475850.

Barnes, Mariel, and Sabrina Karim. 2024. "The Manosphere and Politics." Madison, wisconsin.

Barnhart, Joslyn N., Robert F. Trager, Elizabeth N. Saunders, and Allan Dafoe. 2020. "The Suffragist Peace." *International Organization* 74 (4): 633–70. https://doi.org/10.1017/S0020818320000508.

Barnhart, Joslyn, and Robert F. Trager. 2023. The Suffragist Peace: How Women Shape the Politics of War. Oxford University Press.

Barry, Colin M., K. Chad Clay, and Michael E. Flynn. 2013 "Avoiding the spotlight: Human rights shaming and foreign direct investment." *International Studies Quarterly* 57 (3): 532–44.

Basu, A. 2016. Women, Dynasties, and Democracy in India. In Democratic dynasties: State, Party and Family in Contemporary Indian politics, ed. Kanchan Chandra. Cambridge Press.

Bauer, Michal, Christopher Blattman, Julie Chytilová, Joseph Henrich, Edward Miguel, and Tamar Mitts. "Can War Foster Cooperation?" 2016. *Journal of Economic Perspectives* 30 (3): 249–74.

BBC News. 2023 "Jacinda Ardern: New Zealand's prime." Accessed January 31, 2024. ministerhttps://www.bbc.com/news/world-asia-54565381.

Bearman, Christopher J. 2005. "An Examination of Suffragette Violence." *The English Historical Review* 120 (486): 365–97.

Beath, Andrew, Fotini Christia, and Ruben Enikolopov. 2013 "Empowering Women Through Development Aid: Evidence from a Field Experiment in Afghanistan." *American Political Science Review* 107 (3): 540–57.

Becerra, D., Lechuga-Peña, S., Castillo, J., González, R. P., Ciriello, N., Cervantes, F., and Porchas, F. 2022. "Esto no se lo deseo a nadie": the Impact of Immigration Detention on Latina/o Immigrants. *Journal of Human Rights and Social Work*, 7(4): 361–72.

Beck, Nathaniel, Jonathan N. Katz, and Richard Tucker. 1998. "Taking Time Seriously: Time- Series-Cross-Section Analysis with a Binary Dependent Variable." *American Journal of Political Science* 42 (4): 1260–88. https://doi.org/10.2307/2991857.

Beckwith, Karen, and Kimberly Cowell-Meyers. 2007. "Sheer Numbers: Critical representation thresholds and women's political representation." *Perspectives on politics* 5 (3): 553–65.

Ben Shitrit, Lihi, Julia Elad-Strenger, and Sivan Hirsch-Hoefler. 2017. "Gender Differences in Support for Direct and Indirect Political Aggression in the Context of Protracted Conflict." *Journal of Peace Research* 54 (6): 733–47.

Benson, Peter L., and Steven Vincent. 1980. "Development and Validation of the Sexist Attitudes Toward Women Scale (SATWS)." Psychology of Women Quarterly 5 (2): 276–91.

Beger, Andreas, and Daniel Hill Jr. 2019. "Examining repressive and oppressive state violence using the Ill-Treatment and Torture data." *Conflict Management and Peace Science* 36 (6): 626–44.

REFERENCES 269

Berger, Joseph, Cecilia L. Ridgeway, and Morris Zelditch. 2002 "Construction of status and referential structures." *Sociological Theory* 20 (2): 157–79.

Berry, Marie E. 2018. *War, Women, and Power: From Violence to Mobilization in Rwanda and Bosnia-Herzegovina.* New York, NY: Cambridge University Press.

Berry, Marie E., and Milli Lake. 2021. "Women's Rights after War: On Gender Interventions and Enduring Hierarchies." *Annual Review of Law and Social Science* 17: 459–81.

Besley, Olle Folke, Torsten Persson, and Johanna Rickne. 2017. "Gender Quotas and the Crisis of the Mediocre Man: Theory and Evidence from Sweden." *The American Economic Review* 107 (8): 2204.

Best, Rebecca H., Sarah Shair-Rosenfield, and Reed Wood. 2019. "Legislative Gender Diversity and the Resolution of Civil Conflict." *Political Research Quarterly* 72 (1): 215–28. https://doi.org/10.1177/1065912918785459.

Bhalotra, Sonia, Abhishek Chakravarty, and Selim Gulesci. 2020. "The Price of Gold: Dowry and Death in India." *Journal of Development Economics* 143 (March): 102413. https://doi.org/10.1016/j.jdeveco.2019.102413.

Biroli, Flávia. 2019. "The Crisis of Democracy and the Backlash against Gender." UN Women Paper, Beijing 25.

Bjarnegård, E., A. Engvall, S. Jitpiromsri, and E. Melander. 2023. "Armed Violence and Patriarchal Values: A Survey of Young Men in Thailand and Their Military Experiences." *American Political Science Review* 117 (2): 439–53.

Bjarnegård, Elin, Karen Brounéus, and Erik Melander. 2017. "Honor and Political Violence: Micro-Level Findings from a Survey in Thailand." *Journal of Peace Research* 54 (6): 748–61. https://doi.org/10.1177/0022343317711241.

Bjarnegård, Elin, and Erik Melander. 2011. "Disentangling Gender, Peace and Democratization: The Negative Effects of Militarized Masculinity." *Journal of Gender Studies* 20 (2): 139–54. https://doi.org/10.1080/09589236.2011.565194.

Bjarnegård, Elin, and Pär Zetterberg. 2022. "How Autocrats Weaponize Women's Rights." *Journal of Democracy* 33 (2): 60–75.

Blazak, Randy. 2001. "White Boys to Terrorist Men: Target Recruitment of Nazi Skinheads." *American Behavioral Scientist* 44 (6): 982–1000.

Bogers, Marcel, Nicolai J. Foss, and Jacob Lyngsie. 2018. "The 'Human Side' of Open Innovation: The Role of Employee Diversity in Firm-Level Openness." *Research Policy* 47 (1): 218–31. https://doi.org/10.1016/j.respol.2017.10.012.

Bollen, Kenneth A. 1989. *Structural Equations with Latent Variables.* Vol. 210. New York: John Wiley & Sons.

Bonnet, Florence, Joann Vanek, and Martha Chen. 2019. "Women and Men in the Informal Economy: A Statistical Brief." 20. Geneva: International Labour Office.

Boyce, James K. 2013. *Investing in Peace: Aid and Conditionality after Civil Wars.* New York, NY: Routledge.

Boyden, Jo. 2007. "Children, War and World Disorder in the 21st Century: A Review of the Theories and the Literature on Children's Contributions to Armed Violence." *Conflict, Security & Development* 7 (2): 255–79. https://doi.org/10.1080/14678800701333051.

Boyer, Mark A., Brian Urlacher, Natalie Florea Hudson, Anat Niv-Solomon, Laura L. Janik, Michael J. Butler, Scott W. Brown, and Andri Ioannou. 2009. "Gender and Negotiation: Some Experimental Findings from an International Negotiation Simulation." *International Studies Quarterly* 53 (1): 23–47.

Brambor, Thomas, William Roberts Clark, and Matt Golder. 2006. "Understanding Interaction Models: Improving Empirical Analyses." *Political Analysis* 14 (1): 63–82.

Bratton, Kathleen A. 2005. "Critical Mass Theory Revisited: The Behavior and Success of Token Women in State Legislatures." *Politics & Gender* 1 (1): 97–125.

Brechenmacher, Saskia, and Nikhita Salgame. 2022. "How the U.S. Gender Equality Funding Increase Can Actually Be Effective." Carnegie Endowment for International Peace. March. https://carnegieendowment.org/2022/03/22/how-u.s.-gender-equality-funding-increase-can-actually-be-effective-pub-86686.

270 REFERENCES

Brooks, Deborah Jordan, and Benjamin A. Valentino. 2011. "A War of One's Own: Understanding the Gender Gap in Support for War." *The Public Opinion Quarterly* 75 (2): 270–86.

Broughton, Sharon, and Sonia Palmieri. 1999. "Gendered Contributions to [Australian] Parliamentary Debates: The Case of Euthanasia." *Australian Journal of Political Science* 34 (1): 29–45.

Buhaug, H., Cederman, L. E., & Gleditsch, K. S. (2014). Square pegs in round holes: Inequalities, grievances, and civil war. *International Studies Quarterly*, 58(2), 418–31.

Bunch, Charlotte. 1990. "Women's Rights as Human Rights: Toward a Re-Vision of Human Rights." *Human Rights Quarterly* 12 (4): 486–98. https://doi.org/10.2307/762496.

Bunch, Charlotte, and Susana Fried. 1996. "Beijing '95: Moving Women's Human Rights from Margin to Center." *Signs: Journal of Women in Culture and Society* 22 (1): 200–204.

Bush, Laura. 2001. "The Weekly Address Delivered by the First Lady." The American Presidency Project. http://www.presidency.ucsb.edu.

Butler, Christopher K., Tali Gluch, and Neil J. Mitchell. 2007. "Security Forces and Sexual Violence: A Cross-National Analysis of a Principal—Agent Argument." Journal of Peace Research 44 (6): 669–87.

Butler, Judith. 2004. *Undoing Gender.* New York, NY: Psychology Press.

Byman, Daniel L. 2023. "Countering Organized Violence in the United States." Brookings Institution. May 16, 2023. https://www.brookings.edu/testimonies/countering-organized-violence-in-the-united-states/.

Byman, Daniel L. 2023. "The Risk of Election Violence in the United States 2024." Brookings Institution. February 17, 2024. https://www.brooking.edu/articles/the-risk-of-electionviolence-in-the-united-states-in-2024/

Caprioli, M., Valerie M. Hudson, Rose McDermott, Bonnie Ballif-Spanvill, Chad F. Emmett, and Matthew Stearmer. 2009. "The WomanStats Project Database: Advancing an Empirical Research Agenda." *Journal of Peace Research* (September). http://journals.sagepub.com/doi/10.1177/0022343309342947.

Caprioli, Mary. 2000. "Gendered Conflict." *Journal of Peace Research* 37 (1): 51–68.

Caprioli, Mary. 2003. "Gender Equality and State Aggression: The Impact of Domestic Gender Equality on State First Use of Force." *International Interactions* 29 (3): 195–214. https://doi.org/10.1080/03050620304595.

Caprioli, Mary. 2005. "Primed for Violence: The Role of Gender Inequality in Predicting Internal Conflict." *International Studies Quarterly* 49 (2): 161–78.

Caprioli, Mary, and Mark A. Boyer. 2001. "Gender, Violence, and International Crisis." *Journal of Conflict Resolution* 45 (4): 503–18. https://doi.org/10.1177/0022002701045004005.

Carpenter, R. Charli. 2003. "'Women and Children First': Gender, Norms, and Humanitarian Evacuation in the Balkans 1991–95." *International Organization* 57 (4): 661–94. https://doi.org/10.1017/S002081830357401X.

Carpenter, R. Charli. 2007. "Setting the Advocacy Agenda: Theorizing Issue Emergence and Nonemergence in Transnational Advocacy Networks." *International Studies Quarterly* 51 (1): 99–120.

Carter, David B., and Curtis S. Signorino. 2010. "Back to the Future: Modeling Time Dependence in Binary Data." *Political Analysis* 18 (3): 271–92. https://doi.org/10.1093/pan/mpq013.

Caughey, Devin, and Christopher Warshaw. 2015. "Dynamic Estimation of Latent Opinion Using a Hierarchical Group-Level IRT Model." *Political Analysis* 23 (2): 197–211.

Cederman, Lars-Erik, Kristian Skrede Gleditsch, and Halvard Buhaug. 2013. *Inequality, Grievances, and Civil War.* Cambridge Studies in Contentious Politics. Cambridge University Press. https://doi.org/10.1017/CBO9781139084161.

Cederman, Lars-Erik, Simon Hug, and Lutz F. Krebs. 2010. "Democratization and Civil War: Empirical Evidence." New York, NY: *Journal of Peace Research* 47 (4): 377–94.

Chandra, Kanchan. 2006. "What Is Ethnic Identity and Does It Matter?" *Annu. Rev. Polit. Sci.* 9: 397–424.

REFERENCES   271

Chappell, Louise. 2002. "The 'Femocrat' Strategy: Expanding the Repertoire of Feminist Activists." *Parliamentary Affairs* 55 (1): 85–98. https://doi.org/10.1093/parlij/55.1.85.

Chaudhry, Suparna. 2022. "The Assault on Civil Society: Explaining State Crackdown on NGOs." *International Organization* 76 (3): 549–90.

Chayes, Abram, and Antonia Handler Chayes. 1993. "On Compliance." *International Organization* 47 (2): 175–205. https://doi.org/10.1017/S0020818300027910.

Chenoweth, Erica. 2021. *Civil Resistance: What Everyone Needs to Know®*. New York, NY: Oxford University Press.

Chenoweth, Erica, and Zoe Marks. 2022. "Revenge of the Patriarchs: Why Autocrats Fear Women." *Foreign Affairs*. 101: 103.

Chenoweth, Erica, and Maria Stephan. 2011. *Why Civil Resistance Works: The Strategic Logic of Nonviolent Conflict*. New York, NY: Columbia University Press.

Childs, Sarah, and Mona Lena Krook. 2009. "Analysing Women's Substantive Representation: From Critical Mass to Critical Actors." *Government and Opposition* 44 (2): 125–45. https://doi.org/10.1111/j.1477-7053.2009.01279.x.

Chuck, Elizabeth. 2023. "U.S. Ranks 43rd on Gender Parity Index This Year, Sliding 16 Slots from Last Year." https://www.nbcnews.com/news/us-ranks-43rd-gender-parity-index-year-sliding-16-slots-last-year-rcna90189.

Cingranelli, David L., and David L. Richards. 2010. "The Cingranelli and Richards (CIRI) Human Rights Data Project." *Human Rights Quarterly* 32: 401.

Cingranelli, David L., David L. Richards, and K. Chad Clay. 2014. "The Cingranelli and Richards (CIRI) Human Rights Data Project." http://www.humanrightsdata.com/

Cingranelli, David L., David L. Richards, and K. Chad Clay. 2014. "The Cingranelli and Richards (CIRI) Human Rights Data Project." *Human Rights Quarterly* 32 (2): 401–24.

Clark, Richard, Roza Khoban, and Noah Zucker. 2022. "Breadwinner Backlash: The Gendered Effects of Industrial Decline."

Clark, Tom S., and Drew A. Linzer. 2015. "Should I Use Fixed or Random Effects?" *Political Science Research and Methods* 3 (2): 399–408. https://doi.org/10.1017/psrm.2014.32.

Clay, K Chad. 2018. "Threat by Example: Economic Sanctions and Global Respect for Human Rights." *Journal of Global Security Studies* 3 (2): 133–49. https://doi.org/10.1093/jogss/ogy006.

Clay, K. Chad, Ryan Bakker, Anne-Marie Brook, Daniel Hill, and Amanda Murdie. 2018. "HRMI Civil and Political Rights Metrics: 2018 Technical Note." https://doi.org/10.2139/ssrn.3164046.

Clayton, A., C. Josefsson, and V. Wang. 2017. "Quotas and Women's Substantive Representation: Evidence from a Content Analysis of Ugandan Plenary Debates." *Politics and Gender* 13 (2): 276–304. https://doi.org/10.1017/S1743923X16000453.

Clearinghouse, The New Zealand Family Violence. 2021. "Results from Second Aotearoa New Zealand Gender Attitudes Survey." https://nzfvc.org.nz/news/results-second-aotearoa-new-zealand-gender-attitudes-survey.

Clinton, Hillary Rodham. 1995. "Remarks by First Lady Hillary Rodham Clinton: United Nations Fourth World Conference on Women, September 5-6, 1995, China." https://clintonwhitehouse3.archives.gov/WH/EOP/First_Lady/html/China/plenary.html

Cohen, Dara Kay, and Sabrina M. Karim. 2022. "Does More Equality for Women Mean Less War? Rethinking Sex and Gender Inequality and Political Violence." *International Organization* 76 (2): 414–44.

Cohen, Dara Kay, and Ragnhild Nordås. 2014. "Sexual Violence in Armed Conflict: Introducing the SVAC Dataset, 1989–2009." *Journal of Peace Research* 51 (3): 418–28. https://doi.org/10.1177/0022343314523028.

Cohn, Carol. 1987. "Sex and Death in the Rational World of Defense Intellectuals." *Signs: Journal of Women in Culture and Society* 12 (4): 687–718.

272 REFERENCES

Cohn, Carol. 2013. *Women and Wars: Contested Histories, Uncertain Futures*. Maldon, MA: John Wiley & Sons.

Cohn, Carol, and Cynthia Enloe. 2003. "A Conversation with Cynthia Enloe: Feminists Look at Masculinity and the Men Who Wage War." *Signs: Journal of Women in Culture and Society* 28 (4): 1187–1207.

Cole, Wade M. 2013. "Government Respect for Gendered Rights: The Effect of the Convention on the Elimination of Discrimination against Women on Women's Rights Outcomes, 1981–2004." *International Studies Quarterly* 57 (2): 233–49.

Collier, David, and Steven Levitsky. 1997. "Democracy with Adjectives: Conceptual Innovation in Comparative Research." SSRN Scholarly Paper, no. ID 1540876. https://papers.ssrn.com/abstract=1540876.

Collier, David, and Steven Levitsky. 2009. "Conceptual Hierarchies in Comparative Research: The Case of Democracy." SSRN Scholarly Paper, no. ID 1750505. https://papers.ssrn.com/abstract=1750505.

Collier, David, and James E. Mahon. 1993. "Conceptual 'Stretching' Revisited: Adapting Categories in Comparative Analysis." SSRN Scholarly Paper, no. ID 1747306. https://papers.ssrn.com/abstract=1747306.

Collins, Patricia Hill. 1991. *Black Feminist Thought: Knowledge, Consciousness, and the Politics of Empowerment*. https://www.routledge.com/Black-Feminist-Thought-Knowledge-Consciousness-and-the-Politics-of-Empowerment/Collins/p/book/9780415964722.

Committee, International Rescue. 2014. *Preventing Violence against Women and Girls: Engaging Men through Accountable Practice (Implementation Guide)*. New York.

Conover, Pamela Johnston. 1988. "Feminists and the Gender Gap." *The Journal of Politics* 50 (4): 985–1010. https://doi.org/10.2307/2131388.

Conover, Pamela Johnston, and Virginia Sapiro. 1993. "Gender, Feminist Consciousness, and War." *American Journal of Political Science* 37 (4): 1079–99. https://doi.org/10.2307/2111544.

Conrad, Courtenay Ryals, and Will H. Moore. 2010. "What stops the torture?." *American Journal of Political Science* 54 (2): 459–76.

Conrad, Courtenay R., Jillienne Haglund, and Will H. Moore. 2013. "Disaggregating Torture Allegations: Introducing the Ill-Treatment and Torture (ITT) Country-Year Data." *International Studies Perspectives* 14 (2): 199–220. https://doi.org/10.1111/j.1528-3585.2012.00471.x.

Conrad, Courtenay R., Jillienne Haglund, and Will H. Moore. 2014. "Torture Allegations as Events Data: Introducing the Ill-Treatment and Torture (ITT) Specific Allegation Data." *Journal of Peace Research* 51 (3): 429–38. https://doi.org/10.1177/0022343314524427.

Conrad, Courtenay R., Daniel W. Hill, and Will H. Moore. 2018. "Torture and the Limits of Democratic Institutions." *Journal of Peace Research* 55 (1): 3–17. https://doi.org/10.1177/0022343317711240.

Coppedge, Michael, Amanda B. Edgell, Carl Henrik Knutsen, and Staffan I. Lindberg, eds. 2022. *Why Democracies Develop and Decline*. New York, NY: Cambridge University Press.

Coppedge, Michael, John Gerring, David Altman, Michael Bernhard, Steven Fish, Allen Hicken, Matthew Kroenig, et al. 2011. "Conceptualizing and Measuring Democracy: A New Approach." *Perspectives on Politics* 9 (2): 247–67. https://doi.org/10.1017/S1537592711000880.

Coppedge, Michael, John Gerring, Carl Henrik Knutsen, Staffan I. Lindberg, Svend-Erik Skaaning, Jan Teorell, David Altman, et al. 2017. "V-Dem Country-Year Dataset v7.1." SSRN Scholarly Paper. Rochester, NY: Social Science Research Network. https://doi.org/10.2139/ssrn.3172791.

Coppedge, Michael, John Gerring, Carl Henrik Knutsen, Staffan I. Lindberg, Jan Teorell, Naz- ifa Alizada, David Altman, Michael Bernhard, Agnes Cornell, M. Steven Fish, Lisa Gastaldi, Haakon Gjerløw, Adam Glynn, Allen Hicken, Garry Hindle, Nina Ilchenko, Joshua Krusell, Anna Lührmann, Seraphine F. Maerz, Kyle L. Marquardt,

Kelly McMann, Valeriya Mechkova, Juraj Medzihorsky, Pamela Paxton, Daniel Pemstein, Josefine Pernes, Johannes von Römer, Brigitte Seim, Rachel Sigman, Svend-Erik Skaaning, Jeffrey Staton, Aksel Sundström, Eitan Tzelgov, Yi-ting Wang, Tore Wig, Steven Wilson and Daniel Ziblatt. 2021. "V-Dem [Country– Year/Country–Date] Dataset v11.1" Varieties of Democracy (V-Dem) Project. https://doi. org/10.23696/vdemds21.

Corlett, Eva, and Tess McClure. 2022. "'This Is a Moment': New Zealand Reckons with Aftermath as Smoke Clears on Violent Protests." *The Guardian*. March 2. https://www.theguardian.com/world/2022/mar/03/this-is-a-moment-new-zealand-reckons-with-aftermath-as-smoke-clears-on-violent-protests.

Corredor, Elizabeth S. 2021. "On the Strategic Uses of Women's Rights: Backlash, Rights-Based Framing, and Anti-Gender Campaigns in Colombia's 2016 Peace Agreement." *Latin American Politics and Society* 63 (3): 46–68.

Crabtree, C. D., & Fariss, C. J. 2015. Uncovering patterns among latent variables: human rights and de facto judicial independence. Research & Politics, 2(3).

Crandall, Christian S., Jason M. Miller, and Mark H. White. 2018. "Changing Norms Following the 2016 US Presidential Election: The Trump Effect on Prejudice." *Social Psychological and Personality Science* 9 (2): 186–92.

Crenshaw, Kimberle. 1989. "Demarginalizing the Intersection of Race and Sex: A Black Feminist Critique of Antidiscrimination Doctrine, Feminist Theory and Antiracist Politics." *University of Chicago Legal Forum* 139–68.

Crenshaw, Kimberle. 1991. "Mapping the Margins: Intersectionality, Identity Politics, and Violence against Women of Color." *Stanford Law Review* 43 (6): 1241. https://doi.org/10.2307/1229039.

Dahl, Robert A. Polyarchy: Participation and opposition. New Haven, NY: Yale University Press, 2008.

Dahlerup, Drude. 2006. "The Story of the Theory of Critical Mass." *Politics & Gender* 2 (4): 511–22. https://doi.org/10.1017/S1743923X0624114X.

Dahlerup, Drude. 2017. *Has Democracy Failed Women?* 1st ed. Cambridge, UK; Malden, MA: Polity.

Dahlerup, Drude. 2018. "Gender Equality as a Closed Case: A Survey among the Members of the 2015 Danish Parliament." *Scandinavian Political Studies* 41 (2): 188–209. https://doi.org/10.1111/1467-9477.12116.

Danneman, Nathan, and Emily Hencken Ritter. 2014. "Contagious Rebellion and Preemptive Repression." *Journal of Conflict Resolution* 58 (2): 254–79.

Darden, Jessica Trisko, Alexis Henshaw, and Ora Szekely. 2019. *Insurgent Women: Female Combatants in Civil Wars*. Georgetown University Press.

Davenport, Christian. 2007. *State Repression and the Domestic Democratic Peace*. Cambridge Studies in Comparative Politics. New York, NY: Cambridge University Press. https://doi.org/10.1017/CBO9780511510021.

Davenport, Christian, and Benjamin Appel. 2022. *The Death and Life of State Repression: Understanding Onset, Escalation, Termination, and Recurrence*. Oxford University Press.

Davies, Sara E., and Jacqui True. 2019. "Women, Peace, and Security." In *The Oxford Handbook of Women, Peace, and Security*. New York, NY: Oxford University Press. https://doi.org/10.1093/oxfordhb/9780190638276.013.1.

Davis, Angela Yvonne, and Frank Barat. 2016. *Freedom Is a Constant Struggle: Ferguson, Palestine, and the Foundations of a Movement*. Chicago: Haymarket Books.

Dayal, Anjali Kaushlesh, and Agathe Christien. 2020. "Women's Participation in Informal Peace Processes." *Global Governance: A Review of Multilateralism and International Organizations* 26 (1): 69–98.

DeMars, Christine. 2010. Item Response Theory. New York, NY: Oxford University Press.

DeMeritt, Jacqueline H. R., and Courtenay R. Conrad. 2019. "Repression Substitution: Shifting Human Rights Violations in Response to UN Naming and Shaming." *Civil Wars* 21 (1): 128–52.

274 REFERENCES

Dilts, Andrew. 2012. "Revisiting Johan Galtung's Concept of Structural Violence." *New Political Science* 34 (2): 191–94. https://doi.org/10.1080/07393148.2012.676396.

Donnelly, Phoebe Grace. 2019. "Wedded to Warfare: Forced Marriage in Rebel Groups." Ann Harbor, MA: Tufts University.

Donner, Francesca, and Alisha Haridasani Gupta. 2020. "António Guterres Wants Gender Parity at the U.N. It May Take Time." *The New York Times*, March 5. https://www.nyti mes.com/2020/03/05/world/antonio-guterres-un.html.

Dotto, Gian-Paolo. 2019. "Gender and Sex—Time to Bridge the Gap." *EMBO Molecular Medicine* 11 (5): e10668. https://doi.org/10.15252/emmm.201910668.

Dowless, Mason Robert. 2022. "Proud Boys: The Rising Threat of the Militant Right During 2020–2021." PhD diss. The University of Texas at Austin.

Downs, George W., David M. Rocke, and Peter N. Barsoom. 1996. "Is the Good News about Compliance Good News about Cooperation?" *International Organization* 50 (3): 379–406.

Doyle, Jessica Leigh. 2018. "Government Co-option of Civil Society: Exploring the AKP's Role within Turkish Women's CSOs." *Democratization* 25 (3): 445–63.

Doyle, Michael W. 2005. "Three Pillars of the Liberal Peace." *The American Political Science Review* 99 (3): 463–66.

Dube, Oeindrila, and S. P. Harish. 2020. "Queens." Journal of Political Economy 128.7 2579–652.

Eagly, Alice H., and Jean Lau Chin. 2010. "Are Memberships in Race, Ethnicity, and Gender Categories Merely Surface Characteristics?" *The American Psychologist* 65 (9): 934–35. https://doi.org/10.1037/a0021830.

Eagly, Alice H., and Antonio Mladinic. 1989. "Gender Stereotypes and Attitudes toward Women and Men." *Personality and Social Psychology Bulletin* 15 (4): 543–58. https://doi.org/10.1177/01461672289154008.

Eagly, Alice H., and Valerie J. Steffen. 1984. "Gender Stereotypes Stem from the Distribution of Women and Men into Social Roles." *Journal of Personality and Social Psychology* 46 (4): 735–54. https://doi.org/10.1037/0022-3514.46.4.735.

Eagly, Alice, and Steven Karau. 2002. "Role Congruity Theory of Prejudice toward Female Leaders." *Psychological Review* 109 (3). https://doi.org/10.1037/0033-295x.109.3.573.

Edlund, Lena, Hongbin Li, Junjian Yi, and Junsen Zhang. 2013. "Sex Ratios and Crime: Evidence from China." *Review of Economics and Statistics* 95 (December): 1520–34. https://doi.org/10.1162/REST_a_00356.

Eichenberg, Richard C. 2016. "Gender Difference in American Public Opinion on the Use of Military Force, 1982–2013." *International Studies Quarterly* 60 (1): 138–48. https://doi.org/10.1093/isq/sqv019.

Eichenberg, Richard C. 2019. *Gender, War, and World Order*. Ithaca, NY: Cornell University Press. https://www.cornellpress.cornell.edu/book/9781501738142/gender-war-and-world-order/.

Eichenberg, Richard C., and Richard J. Stoll. 2012. "Gender Difference or Parallel Publics? The Dynamics of Defense Spending Opinions in the United States, 1965–2007." https://journals-sagepub-com.proxy.library.cornell.edu/doi/10.1177/0022002711420983.

Eisenstein, Hester. 1983. "Contemporary Feminist Thought." *Science and Society* 48 (3): 364–66.

Ellerby, Kara. 2017. *No Shortcut to Change: An Unlikely Path to a More Gender-Equitable World*. New York: New York University Press.

Enders, Walter, Todd Sandler, and Khusrav Gaibulloev. 2011. "Domestic versus Transnational Terrorism: Data, Decomposition, and Dynamics." *Journal of Peace Research* 48 (3): 319–37.

England, Paula, Andrew Levine, and Emma Mishel. 2020a. "Is the Gender Revolution Stalled? An Update." *Proceedings of the National Academy of Sciences*, forthcoming, 1–37.

England, Paula, Andrew Levine, and Emma Mishel. 2020b. "Progress toward Gender Equality in the United States Has Slowed or Stalled." *Proceedings of the National Academy of Sciences* 117 (13): 6990–97.

REFERENCES 275

Engle, Karen. 2007. "Calling in the Troops: The Uneasy Relationship among Women's Rights, Human Rights, and Humanitarian Intervention." *Harvard Human Rights Journal* 20: 189.

Englehart, Neil A., and Melissa K. Miller. 2014. "The CEDAW Effect: International Law's Impact on Women's Rights." *Journal of Human Rights* 13 (1): 22–47. https://doi.org/ 10.1080/14754835.2013.824274.

Enloe, Cynthia. 2000. *Maneuvers: The International Politics of Militarizing Women's Lives*. 1st ed. University of California Press. https://www.jstor.org/stable/10.1525/j.ctt14qrzb1.

Enloe, Cynthia. 2004. *The Curious Feminist: Searching for Women in a New Age of Empire*. 1st ed. University of California Press. https://www.jstor.org/stable/10.1525/j.ctt1pnb63.

Enloe, Cynthia. 2014. *Bananas, Beaches & Bases: Making Feminist Sense of International Politics*. Pandora.

Enloe, Cynthia H. 1983. *Does Khaki Become You?: The Militarisation of Women's Lives*. South End Press.

Erikson, Robert S., and Kent L. Tedin. 2015. *American Public Opinion: Its Origins, Content and Impact*. New York, NY: Routledge.

Escobar, Martha D. 2016. *Captivity beyond Prisons: Criminalization Experiences of Latina (Im)migrants*. Austin, TX: University of Texas Press.

European Institute for Gender Equality. 2023. "Gender Equality." https://eige.europa.eu/ publications-resources/thesaurus/terms/1059.

Evangelista, Matthew. 2011. *Gender, Nationalism, and War: Conflict on the Movie Screen*. Cambridge University Press.

Fariss, Christopher J. 2014. "Respect for Human Rights Has Improved over Time: Modeling the Changing Standard of Accountability." *American Political Science Review* 108 (2): 297–318. https://doi.org/10.1017/S0003055414000070.

Fearon, James D. 1994. Domestic Political Audiences and the scalation of International Disputes. *American Political Science Review*, 88 (3): 577–92.

Fearon, James D, and David D Laitin. 1996. "Explaining Interethnic Cooperation." *American Political Science Review* 90 (4): 715–35.

Fearon, J. D., & Laitin, D. D. (2003). Ethnicity, insurgency, and civil war. *American political science review*, 97(1), 75–90.

Ferree, Myra Marx, and Aili Mari Tripp, eds. 2006. *Global Feminism: Transnational Women's Activism, Organizing, and Human Rights*. New York, NY: NYU Press.

Filipovic, Jill. 2021. "America Has Abandoned the Women of Afghanistan." https://www. cnn.com/2021/08/18/opinions/america-abandoning-afghanistan-women-filipovic/ index.html.

Flores-Macías, Gustavo A., and Sarah E. Kreps. 2017. "Borrowing Support for War: The Effect of War Finance on Public Attitudes toward Conflict." *Journal of Conflict Resolution* 61 (5): 997–1020.

Fodor, Eva. 2021. *The Gender Regime of Anti-Liberal Hungary*. Cham, Switzerland: Springer Nature.

Forsberg, Erika, and Louise Olsson. 2021. "Examining Gender Inequality and Armed Conflict at the Subnational Level." *Journal of Global Security Studies* 6 (2). https://doi. org/10.1093/jogss/ogaa023.

Fraser, Nancy. 2007. "Feminist Politics in the Age of Recognition: A Two-Dimensional Approach to Gender Justice." *Studies in Social Justice* 1 (1): 23–35. https://doi.org/ 10.26522/ssj.v1i1.979.

Friedman, Elisabeth. 1995. "Women's Human Rights: The Emergence of a Movement." In *Women's Rights, Human Rights: International Feminist Perspectives*, edited by Roger Peters. New York, NY: Routledge.

Galtung, Johan. 1969. "Violence, Peace, and Peace Research." *Journal of Peace Research* 6 (3): 167–91.

Galtung, Johan. 1990. "Cultural Violence." *Journal of Peace Research* 27 (3): 291–305. https://doi.org/10.1177/0022343390027003005.

276 REFERENCES

Gates, Scott. 2002. "Recruitment and Allegiance: The Microfoundations of Rebellion." *Journal of Conflict Resolution* 46 (1): 111–30.

Gaye, Amie, Jeni Klugman, Milorad Kovacevic, Sarah Twigg, and Eduardo Zambrano. 2010. "Measuring Key Disparities in Human Development: The Gender Inequality Index." United Nations Development Programme.

Gelman, Andrew, and Jennifer Hill. 2006. *Data Analysis Using Regression and Multilevel/ Hierarchical Models*. Analytical Methods for Social Research. New York, NY: Cambridge University Press. https://doi.org/10.1017/CBO9780511790942.

Gerring, John. 1999. "What Makes a Concept Good? A Criterial Framework for Understanding Concept Formation in the Social Sciences." *Polity* 31 (3): 357–93. https://doi.org/10.2307/3235246.

Gerring, John. 2001. *Social Science Methodology: A Criterial Framework*. New York, NY: Cambridge University Press.

Giani, Marco, and Pierre-Guillaume Méon. 2021. "Global Racist Contagion Following Donald Trump's Election." *British Journal of Political Science* 51 (3): 1332–39.

Gibney, Mark, Linda Cornett, Reed Wood, Peter Haschke, Daniel Arnon, Attilio Pisanó, and Gray Barrett. 2019. "The Political Terror Scale 1976–2018." http://www.political terrorscale.org/.

Gilligan, Carol. 1982. *In a Different Voice: Psychological Theory and Women's Development*. Cambridge, MA: Harvard University Press.

Ging, Debbie. 2019. "Alphas, Betas, and Incels: Theorizing the Masculinities of the Manosphere." *Men and Masculinities* 22 (4): 638–57.

Gizelis, Theodora-Ismene. 2009. "Gender Empowerment and United Nations Peacebuilding." *Journal of Peace Research* (June). http://journals.sagepub.com/doi/10.1177/0022343309334576.

Gizelis, Theodora-Ismene. 2011. "A Country of Their Own: Women and Peacebuilding." *Conflict Management and Peace Science* 28 (5): 522–42. https://doi.org/10.1177/07388 94211418412.

"Global Issues: Gender Equality and Women's Empowerment." n.d. Peace Corps. Accessed June 16, 2023. www.peacecorps.gov/educators/resources/global-issues-gen der-equality-and-womens-empowerment/.

Glynn, Carroll J., and Michael E. Huge. 2008. "Public Opinion." In *The International Encyclopedia of Communication*, edited by W. Donsbach. Hoboken, NJ: Wiley and Sons. Published Online. https://doi.org/10.1002/9781405186407.wbiecp124.

Goertz, Gary. 2006. *Social Science Concepts: A User's Guide*. Princeton, NJ: Princeton University Press.

Goettner-Abendroth, Heide. 2012. *Matriarchal Societies: Studies on Indigenous Cultures across the Globe*. New York, NY: Lang.

Goldsmith, B. E., Semenovich, D., Sowmya, A., & Grgic, G. 2017. Political Competition and the Initiation of International Conflict: A New Perspective on the Institutional Foundations of Democratic Peace. *World Politics*, 69 (3): 493–531.

Goldstein, Joshua S. 2001. *War and Gender: How Gender Shapes the War System and Vice Versa*. New York, NY: Cambridge University Press.

Goldstein, Robert Justin. 1986. "The Limitations of Using Quantitative Data in Studying Human Rights Abuses." *Human Rights Quarterly* 8 (4): 607–27. https://doi.org/10.2307/762195.

Government Offices of Sweden. 2014. "Feminist Foreign Policy—Government.Se." https://www.government.se/government-policy/feminist-foreign-policy/.

Green, Donald P., Soo Yeon Kim, and David H. Yoon. 2001. "Dirty Pool." *International Organization* 55 (2): 441–68. https://doi.org/10.1162/00208180151140630.

Greenberg, Kae. 2012. "Still Hidden in the Closet: Trans Women and Domestic Violence." *Berkeley Journal of Gender, Law & Justice* 27 (2). https://lawcat.berkeley.edu/record/1124982.

REFERENCES 277

Grieco, Joseph M., Christopher Gelpi, Jason Reifler, and Peter D. Feaver. 2011. "Let's Get a Second Opinion: International Institutions and American Public Support for War." *International Studies Quarterly* 55 (2): 563–83. https://doi.org/10.1111/j.1468-2478.2011.00660.x.

Gurr, Ted Robert. 2015. *Why Men Rebel*. Routledge.

Guterres, António. 2023. "Remarks to the Commission on the Status of Women." United Nations Meeting Coverage and Press Releases. March. https://press.un.org/en/2023/sgsm21713.doc.htm.

Hafner-Burton, Emilie M. 2005. Trading Human Rights: How Preferential Trade Agreements Influence Government Repression. *International Organization* 59(3): 593–629.

Hafner-Burton, Emilie M. 2008. "Sticks and Stones: Naming and Shaming the Human Rights Enforcement Problem." *International Organization* 62 (4): 689–716.

Hafner-Burton, Emilie M., and Kiyoteru Tsutsui. 2005. "Human Rights in a Globalizing World: The Paradox of Empty Promises." *American Journal of Sociology* 110 (5): 1373–1411. https://doi.org/10.1086/428442.

Hafner-Burton, Emilie M., and Kiyoteru Tsutsui. 2007. "Justice Lost! The Failure of International Human Rights Law to Matter Where Needed Most." *Journal of Peace Research* 44 (4): 407–25. https://doi.org/10.1177/0022343307078942.

Hafner-Burton, Emilie M., Kiyoteru Tsutsui, and John W. Meyer. 2008. "International Human Rights Law and the Politics of Legitimation: Repressive States and Human Rights Treaties." *International Sociology* 23 (1): 115–41. https://doi.org/10.1177/0268580907084388.

Haglund, Jillienne, and David L Richards. 2018. "Enforcement of Sexual Violence Law in Post-Civil Conflict Societies." *Conflict Management and Peace Science* 35 (3): 280–95. https://doi.org/10.1177/0738894217695536.

Halton, Mary. 2018. "Climate Change 'Impacts Women More Than Men.'" BBC. March. https://www.bbc.com/news/science-environment-43294221.

Hancock, Ange-Marie. 2007. "Intersectionality as a Normative and Empirical Paradigm." *Politics & Gender* 3 (2): 248–54.

Harris, Cameron, and Daniel James Milton. 2016. "Is Standing for Women a Stand against Terrorism? Exploring the Connection between Women's Rights and Terrorism." *Journal of Human Rights* 15 (1): 60–78. https://doi.org/10.1080/14754835.2015.1062722.

Haschke, Peter. *Human Rights in Democracies*. New York, New York: Routledge, 2019.

Hathaway, Oona A. 2007. "Why Do Countries Commit to Human Rights Treaties?" *Journal of Conflict Resolution* 51 (4): 588–621.

Hawken, Angela, and Gerardo L. Munck. 2013. "Cross-National Indices with Gender-Differentiated Data: What Do They Measure? How Valid Are They?" *Social Indicators Research* 111 (3): 801–38. https://doi.org/10.1007/s11205-012-0035-7.

Hawkesworth, Mary. 2003. "Congressional Enactments of Race-Gender: Toward a Theory of Raced-Gendered Institutions." *The American Political Science Review* 97 (4): 529–50.

Hayes, Eden-Reneé, and Janet K. Swim. 2013. "African, Asian, Latina/o, and European Americans' Responses to Popular Measures of Sexist Beliefs: Some Cautionary Notes." *Psychology of Women Quarterly* (April). http://journals.sagepub.com/doi/10.1177/0361684313480044.

Hegre, Håvard, Tanja Ellingsen, Scott Gates, and Nils Petter Gleditsch. 2001. "Toward a Democratic Civil Peace? Democracy, Political Change, and Civil War, 1816–1992." *The American Political Science Review* 95 (1): 33–48. https://www-jstor-org.proxy.library.cornell.edu/stable/3117627?seq=1#metadata_info_tab_contents.

Hendrix, Cullen S., and Wendy H. Wong. 2013. "When Is the Pen Truly Mighty? Regime Type and the Efficacy of Naming and Shaming in Curbing Human Rights Abuses." *British Journal of Political Science* 43 (3): 651–72. https://doi.org/10.1017/S0007123412000488.

278 REFERENCES

Henshaw, A.L. 2016. *Why Women Rebel: Understanding Women's Participation in Armed Rebel Groups.* New York, NY: Taylor & Francis.

Herman, Jody L. 2013. "Gendered Restrooms and Minority Stress: The Public Regulation of Gender and Its Impact on Transgender People's Lives." *Journal of Public Management & Social Policy* 19 (1): 65.

Hill, Daniel W. 2010. "Estimating the Effects of Human Rights Treaties on State Behavior." *The Journal of Politics* 72 (4): 1161–74. https://doi.org/10.1017/s0022381610000599.

Hill, Daniel W. 2016. "Democracy and the Concept of Personal Integrity Rights." *The Journal of Politics* 78 (3): 822–35. https://doi.org/10.1086/685450.

Hill, Daniel W., Jr., and Jennifer Inglett. 2016. "New Measures of Women's Social, Political, and Economic Rights with an Application to Studies of Intrastate Conflict." Unpublished Manuscript.

Hill, Daniel W., Jr., and Zachary M. Jones. 2014. "An Empirical Evaluation of Explanations for State Repression." *American Political Science Review* 108 (3): 661–87. https://doi.org/10.1017/S0003055414000306.

Hoewer, M. 2014. *Crossing Boundaries during Peace and Conflict: Transforming Identity in Chiapas and in Northern Ireland.* The Politics of Intersectionality. New York, NY: Palgrave Macmillan US. https://doi.org/10.1057/9781137468741.

Hofmann, Katharina, Sarah Koch, Alexandra Tschacher, and Claudia Ulferts. 2023. *Spannungsfeld Männlichkeit: So Ticken Junge Männer Zwischen 18 Und 35 Jahren in Deutschland.* Haburg, Deutschland: Plan International Deutschland. https://www.plan.de/fileadmin/website/04._Aktuelles/Umfragen_und_Berichte/Spannungsfeld_Maennlichkeit/Plan-Umfrage_Maennlichkeit-A4-2023-NEU-online_2.pdf.

Hooghe, Liesbet, Ryan Bakker, Anna Brigevich, Catherine De Vries, Erica Edwards, Gary Marks, Jan Rovny, Marco Steenbergen, and Milada Vachudova. 2010. "Reliability and Validity of the 2002 and 2006 Chapel Hill Expert Surveys on Party Positioning." *European Journal of Political Research* 49 (5): 687–703. https://doi.org/10.1111/j.1475-6765.2009.01912.x.

Hooks, Bell. 1981. *Ain't I a Woman: Black Women and Feminism.* Boston, MA: South End Press.

Htun, Mala, and S. Laurel Weldon. 2010. "When Do Governments Promote Women's Rights? A Framework for the Comparative Analysis of Sex Equality Policy." *Perspectives on Politics* 8 (1): 207–16.

Htun, Mala, and S. Laurel Weldon. 2012. "The Civic Origins of Progressive Policy Change: Combating Violence against Women in Global Perspective, 1975–2005." *American Political Science Review* 106 (3): 548–69. https://doi.org/10.1017/S0003055412000226.

Htun, Mala, and S. Laurel Weldon. 2018. *The Logics of Gender Justice: State Action on Women's Rights Around the World.* Cambridge Studies in Gender and Politics. New York, NY: Cambridge University Press. https://doi.org/10.1017/9781108277891.

Huber, Laura. 2019. "When Civilians Are Attacked: Gender Equality and Terrorist Targeting." *Journal of Conflict Resolution* 63 (10): 2289–2318. https://doi.org/10.1177/0022002719835601.

Hudson, Valerie M. 2010. "Sex, War, and Peace: Rank, and Winter on Rank." *Political Psychology* 31 (1): 33–39.

Hudson, Valerie M., Bonnie Ballif-Spanvill, Mary Caprioli, and Chad F. Emmett. 2012. *Sex and World Peace.* New York, NY: Columbia University Press.

Hudson, Valerie M., Donna Lee Bowen, and Perpetua Lynne Nielsen. 2020. *The First Political Order: How Sex Shapes Governance and National Security Worldwide.* New York, NY: Columbia University Press.

Hudson, Valerie M., Mary Caprioli, Bonnie Ballif-Spanvill, Rose McDermott, and Chad F. Emmett. 2009. "The Heart of the Matter: The Security of Women and the Security of States." *International Security* 33 (3): 7–45. https://doi.org/10.1162/isec.2009.33.3.7.

REFERENCES 279

Hudson, Valerie M., and Andrea Den Boer. 2002. "A Surplus of Men, a Deficit of Peace: Security and Sex Ratios in Asia's Largest States." *International Security* 26 (4): 5–38.

Hudson, Valerie M., and Kaylee B. Hodgson. 2020. "Sex and Terror: Is the Subordination of Women Associated with the Use of Terror?" *Terrorism and Political Violence* (February): 1–28. https://doi.org/10.1080/09546553.2020.1724968.

Hudson, Valerie M., and Patricia Leidl. 2015. *The Hillary Doctrine: Sex and American Foreign Policy*. New York, NY: Columbia University Press.

Hudson, Valerie M., and Hilary Matfess. 2017. "In Plain Sight: The Neglected Linkage between Brideprice and Violent Conflict." *International Security* 42 (1): 7–40. https://doi.org/10.1162/ISEC_a_00289.

Hughes, Diane Owen. 1978. "From Brideprice to Dowry in Mediterranean Europe." *Journal of Family History* 3 (3): 262–96.

Hughes, Melanie, Pamela Paxton, Sharon Quinsaat, and Nicholas Reith. 2017. "Women's International Nongovernmental Organizations, 1950–2013." Inter-University Consortium for Political and Social Research (ICPSR). https://doi.org/10.3886/E100514V1.

Ikenberry, G. John. 2009. "Liberal Internationalism 3.0: America and the Dilemmas of Liberal World Order." *Perspectives on Politics* 7 (1): 71–87.

Ikenberry, G. John. 2011. "The Future of the Liberal World Order: Internationalism after America." *Foreign Affairs* 90 (3): 56–68.

Ikenberry, G. John. 2012. *Liberal Leviathan: The Origins, Crisis, and Transformation of the American World Order*. Princeton, NJ: Princeton University Press.

Inglehart, Ronald, and Pippa Norris. 2003. *Rising Tide: Gender Equality and Cultural Change Around the World*. Cambridge University Press.

International Covenant on Civil and Political Rights, Dec. 16, 1966, 999 U.N.T.S. 171.

International Covenant on Economic, Social, and Cultural Rights, Dec. 16, 1966, 993 U.N.T.S. 3.

International Rescue Committee. 2014. Implementation guide: Preventing violence against women and girls: Engaging men through accountable practice. New York: IRC.

Jackman, Simon. 2000. "Estimation and Inference Are Missing Data Problems: Unifying Social Science Statistics via Bayesian Simulation." *Political Analysis* 8 (4): 307–32. https://doi.org/10.1093/oxfordjournals.pan.a029818.

Jehn, Karen A., Gregory B. Northcraft, and Margaret A. Neale. 1999. "Why Differences Make a Difference: A Field Study of Diversity, Conflict and Performance in Workgroups." *Administrative Science Quarterly* 44 (4): 741–63.

Jensen, Michael, Elizabeth Yates, and Sheehan Kane. 2022. "Proud Boys Crimes and Characteristics." College Park, MD: START.

Jo, Hyeran. 2015. *Compliant Rebels: Rebel Groups and International Law in World Politics*. Problems of International Politics. New York, NY: Cambridge University Press. https://doi.org/10.1017/CBO9781316273142.

Joachim, Jutta. 2003. "Framing Issues and Seizing Opportunities: The UN, NGOs, and Women's Rights." *International Studies Quarterly* 47 (2): 247–74.

Johnson, Dominic D.P., Rose McDermott, Emily S. Barrett, Jonathan Cowden, Richard Wrangham, Matthew H. McIntyre, and Stephen Peter Rosen. 2006. "Overconfidence in Wargames: Experimental Evidence on Expectations, Aggression, Gender and Testosterone." *Proceedings of the Royal Society B: Biological Sciences* 273 (1600): 2513–20. https://doi.org/10.1098/rspb.2006.3606.

Jones, Charlotte, and Jen Slater. 2020. "The Toilet Debate: Stalling Trans Possibilities and Defending 'Women's Protected Spaces.'" *The Sociological Review* 68 (4): 834–51.

Jones, Owen. 2022. "This Terrifying Backslide on LGBTQ Rights Is a Threat to Women's Rights Too." *The Guardian*, Tue Jul 5, 2022. https://www.theguardian.com/commentisfree/2022/jul/05/lgbtq-womens-rights-abortion-unite.

280 REFERENCES

Jones, Zachary M., and Yonatan Lupu. 2018. "Is There More Violence in the Middle?" *American Journal of Political Science* 62 (3): 652–67. https://doi.org/10.1111/ajps.12373.

Kaldor, Mary. 2010. "Inconclusive Wars: Is Clausewitz Still Relevant in These Global Times?" *Global Policy* 1 (3): 271–81. https://doi.org/10.1111/j.1758-5899.2010.00041.x.

Kanter, Rosabeth Moss. 1977. "Some Effects of Proportions on Group Life: Skewed Sex Ratios and Responses to Token Women." *American Journal of Sociology* 82 (5): 965–90.

Karim, Sabrina. 2019. "Restoring Confidence in Post-Conflict Security Sectors: Survey Evidence from Liberia on Female Ratio Balancing Reforms." *British Journal of Political Science* 49 (3): 799–821. https://doi.org/10.1017/S0007123417000035.

Karpowitz, Christopher F., Tali Mendelberg, and Lee Shaker. 2012. "Gender Inequality in Deliberative Participation." *American Political Science Review* 106 (3): 533–47. https://doi.org/10.1017/S0003055412000329.

Kattelman, K., and C. Burns. 2022. "Unpacking the Concepts: Examining the Link between Women's Status and Terrorism." *Journal of Peace Research.* 60 (5): 792–806. https://doi.org/10.1177/0022343322109588.

Katzenstein, Mary Fainsod. 1989. "Organizing against Violence: Strategies of the Indian Women's Movement." *Pacific Affairs* 62 (1): 53–71. https://doi.org/10.2307/2760264.

Katzenstein, Mary Fainsod. 1998. *Faithful and Fearless: Moving Feminist Protest inside the Church and Military.* Princeton, NJ: Princeton University Press.

Keith, Linda Camp, C. Neal Tate, and Steven C. Poe. 2009. "Is the Law a Mere Parchment Barrier to Human Rights Abuse?" *The Journal of Politics* 71 (2): 644–60. https://doi.org/10.1017/S0022381609090513.

Keohane, Robert O. 1998. "Beyond Dichotomy: Conversations between International Relations and Feminist Theory." *International Studies Quarterly* 42 (1): 193–97.

Kerr, Joanna. 1993. *Ours by Right: Women's Rights as Human Rights.* Zed Books; Ottowa, Canada: North-South Institute.

Kinsella, Helen M., and Laura Sjoberg. 2019. "Family Values? Sexism and Heteronormativity in Feminist Evolutionary Analytic (FEA) Research." *Review of International Studies* 45 (2): 260–79. https://doi.org/10.1017/S026021051800044X.

Kirton, Michael J. 2003. *Adaption-Innovation: In the Context of Diversity and Change.* New York, NY: Psychology Press.

Koch, Michael T., and Sarah A. Fulton. 2011. "In the Defense of Women: Gender, Office Holding, and National Security Policy in Established Democracies." *The Journal of Politics* 73 (1): 1–16. https://doi.org/10.1017/S0022381610000824.

Kolb, Deborah M., and Gloria G. Coolidge. 1988. "Her Place at the Table: A Consideration of Gender Issue in Negotiation." Working Paper No. 88-5. Cambridge, MA: Harvard Law School, Program on Negotiation.

Korolczuk, Elżbieta, and Agnieszka Graff. 2018. "Gender as 'Ebola from Brussels': The Anticolonial Frame and the Rise of Illiberal Populism." *Signs: Journal of Women in Culture and Society* 43 (4): 797–821.

Krever, Tor. 2013. "Quantifying Law: Legal Indicator Projects and the Reproduction of Neoliberal Common Sense." *Third World Quarterly* 34 (1): 131–50. https://doi.org/10.1080/01436597.2012.755014.

Krystalli, Roxanne, and Philipp Schulz. 2022. "Taking Love and Care Seriously: An Emergent Research Agenda for Remaking Worlds in the Wake of Violence." *International Studies Review* 24 (1): viac003.

Kunst, Jonas R., Ronald Fischer, Jim Sidanius, and Lotte Thomsen. 2017. "Preferences for Group Dominance Track and Mediate the Effects of Macro-Level Social Inequality and Violence across Societies." *Proceedings of the National Academy of Sciences* 114 (21): 5407–12. https://doi.org/10.1073/pnas.1616572114.

Kutner, Samantha. 2020. "Swiping Right: The Allure of Hyper Masculinity and Cryptofascism for Men Who Join the Proud Boys," ICCT Research Paper, https://www.jstor.org/stable/resrep25259?seq=1, DOI: 10.19165/2020.1.03 ISSN: 2468-0486

REFERENCES 281

Kydd, Andrew H., and Barbara F. Walter. 2006. "The Strategies of Terrorism." *International Security* 31 (1): 49–80.

Labonne, Julien, Sahar Parsa, and Pablo Querubin. 2021. "Political Dynasties, Term Limits and Female Political Representation: Evidence from the Philippines." *Journal of Economic Behavior & Organization* 182: 212–28.

LaFree, Gary, and Laura Dugan. 2007. "Introducing the Global Terrorism Database." *Terrorism and Political Violence* 19 (2): 181–204. https://doi.org/10.1080/0954655070 1246817.

Lai, Brian, and Dan Slater. 2006. "Institutions of the Offensive: Domestic Sources of Dispute Initiation in Authoritarian Regimes, 1950–1992." *American Journal of Political Science* 50 (1): 113–26. https://doi.org/10.1111/j.1540-5907.2006.00173.x.

Lake, Milli. 2018. *Strong NGOs and Weak States: Pursuing Gender Justice in the Democratic Republic of Congo and South Africa*. New York, NY: Cambridge University Press. https://doi.org/10.1017/9781108297745.

Lapid, Yosef. 1989. "The Third Debate: On the Prospects of International Theory in a Post-Positivist Era." *International Studies Quarterly* 33 (3): 235–54. https://doi.org/ 10.2307/2600457.

Leader Maynard, Jonathan. 2019. "Ideology and Armed Conflict." *Journal of Peace Research* 56 (5): 635–49.

Lebovic, James H., and Erik Voeten. 2009. "The Cost of Shame: International Organizations and Foreign Aid in the Punishing of Human Rights Violators." *Journal of Peace Research* 46 (1): 79–97.

Lee, Cynthia. 2014. "The Trans Panic Defense: Masculinity, Heteronormativity, and the Murder of Transgender Women." *Hastings Law Journal* 66 (1): 77.

Li, Quan. 2005. "Does Democracy Promote or Reduce Transnational Terrorist Incidents?" *The Journal of Conflict Resolution* 49 (2): 278–97.

Liebowitz, Debra J., and Susanne Zwingel. 2014. "Gender Equality Oversimplified: Using CEDAW to Counter the Measurement Obsession." *International Studies Review* 16 (3): 362–89. https://doi.org/10.1111/misr.12139.

Linzer, Drew, and Jeffrey K. Staton. 2012. "A Measurement Model for Synthesizing Multiple Comparative Indicators: The Case of Judicial Independence." Emory University.

Liou, Ryan Yu-Lin, Amanda Murdie, and Dursun Peksen. 2020. "Revisiting the Causal Links between Economic Sanctions and Human Rights Violations." *Political Research Quarterly* 1065912920941596. https://doi.org/10.1177/1065912920941596.

Lopez, Vera, and Lisa Pasko, eds. 2021. *Latinas in the Criminal Justice System: Victims, Targets, and Offenders*. Vol. 18. New York, NY: NYU Press.

Lowande, Kenneth, Melinda Ritchie, and Erinn Lauterbach. 2019. "Descriptive and Substantive Representation in Congress: Evidence from 80,000 Congressional Inquiries." *American Journal of Political Science* 63 (3): 644–59. https://doi.org/10.1111/ajps.12443.

Loxton, Deborah, Xenia Dolja-Gore, Amy E. Anderson, and Natalie Townsend. 2017. "Intimate Partner Violence Adversely Impacts Health over 16 Years and Across Generations: A Longitudinal Cohort Study." *PLoS One* 12 (6).

Lupu, Yonatan. 2013. "The Informative Power of Treaty Commitment: Using the Spatial Model to Address Selection Effects." *American Journal of Political Science* 57 (4): 912–25. https://doi.org/10.1111/ajps.12033.

MacDonald, Paul K., and Joseph M. Parent. 2021. "The Status of Status in World Politics." *World Politics* 73 (2): 358–91.

MacKinnon, Catharine A. 1993. *Only Words*. Cambridge, MA: Harvard University Press.

Mahalingam, Ramaswami. 2007. "Culture, Ecology, and Beliefs about Gender in Son Preference Caste Groups." *Evolution and Human Behavior* 28: 319–29.

Manne, Kate. 2018. *Down Girl: The Logic of Misogyny*. New York, NY: Oxford University Press.

282 REFERENCES

Marks, Zoe. 2014. "Sexual Violence in Sierra Leone's Civil War: 'Virgination,' Rape, and Marriage." *African Affairs* 113 (450): 67–87. https://doi.org/10.1093/afraf/adt070.

Marsden, Harriet. 2018. "International Women's Day: What Are Matriarchies, and Where Are They Now?" *The Independent*, March 8. https://www.independent.co.uk/news/lon g_reads/international-womens-day-matriarchy-matriarchal-society-women-femin ism-culture-matrilineal-elephant-bonobo-a8243046.html.

Martín de Almagro Iniesta, María. 2015. "(Un) Globalizing Civil Society: When the Boomerang Rebounds. Transnational Advocacy Networks and Women Groups in Post-Conflict Burundi and Liberia." PhD diss. LUISS Guido Carli of Rome.

Masih, Niha. 2023. "Need Time Off Work for Period Pain? These Countries Offer 'Menstrual Leave.'" *The Washington Post*, February 17. https://www.washingtonpost. com/world/2023/02/17/spain-paid-menstrual-leave-countries/.

Mateo Diaz, Mercedes Mateo. 2005. *Representing Women?: Female Legislators in West European Parliaments*. Colchester, United Kingdom: ECPR Press.

Matfess, Hilary, Roudabeh Kishi, and Marie E. Berry. 2022. "No Safety in Numbers: Political Representation and Political Violence Targeting Women in Kenya." *International Feminist Journal of Politics*, 25 (3): 1–23.

May, Elaine Tyler. 2008. *Homeward Bound: American Families in the Cold War Era*. New York, NY: Basic Books.

Mayka, Lindsey. n.d. "Civil Society Mobilization against Equal Citizenship in Latin America."

McClure, Tess. 2023. "Jacinda Ardern: Political Figures Believe Abuse and Threats Contributed to PM's Resignation." *The Guardian*, January 19. https://www.theguard ian.com/world/2023/jan/20/jacinda-ardern-speculation-that-abuse-and-threats-cont ributed-to-resignation.

McDermott, Rose. 2015. "Sex and Death: Gender Differences in Aggression and Motivations for Violence." *International Organization* 69 (3): 753–75. https://doi.org/ 10.1017/S0020818315000065.

McDermott, Rose, Dominic Johnson, Jonathan Cowden, and Stephen Rosen. 2007. "Testosterone and Aggression in a Simulated Crisis Game." *The ANNALS of the American Academy of Political and Social Science*. https://doi.org/10.1177/0002716207305268.

McIntyre, Matthew H., Emily S. Barrett, Rose McDermott, Dominic D. P. Johnson, Jonathan Cowden, and Stephen P. Rosen. 2007. "Finger Length Ratio (2D:4D) and Sex Differences in Aggression during a Simulated War Game." *Personality and Individual Differences* 42 (4): 755–64. https://doi.org/10.1016/j.paid.2006.08.009.

Mechkova, Valeriya, Anna Luhrmann, and Staffan I. Lindberg. 2017. "How Much Democratic Backsliding?" *Journal of Democracy* 28: 162.

Meernik, James, Rosa Aloisi, Marsha Sowell, and Angela Nichols. 2012. "The Impact of Human Rights Organizations on Naming and Shaming Campaigns." *Journal of Conflict Resolution* 56 (2): 233–56.

Melander, Erik. 2005a. "Gender Equality and Intrastate Armed Conflict." *International Studies Quarterly* 49 (4): 695–714.

Melander, Erik. 2005b. "Political Gender Equality and State Human Rights Abuse." *Journal of Peace Research* 42 (2): 149–66. https://doi.org/10.1177/0022343305050688.

Merry, Sally Engle. 2011. "Measuring the World: Indicators, Human Rights, and Global Governance: With CA Comment by John M. Conley." *Current Anthropology* 52 (S3): S83–95. https://doi.org/10.1086/657241.

Merry, Sally Engle. 2016. *The Seductions of Quantification: Measuring Human Rights, Gender Violence, and Sex Trafficking*. Chicago, IL: University of Chicago Press. https:// press.uchicago.edu/ucp/books/book/chicago/S/bo23044232.html.

Mesquita, Bruce Bueno de, James D. Morrow, Randolph M. Siverson, and Alastair Smith. 2004. "Testing Novel Implications from the Selectorate Theory of War." *World Politics* 56 (3): 363–88. https://doi.org/10.1353/wp.2004.0017.

Meyer, David S., and Nancy Whittier. 1994. "Social Movement Spillover." *Social Problems* 41 (2): 277–98. https://doi.org/10.2307/3096934.

REFERENCES   283

Mohanty, Chandra Talpade, Ann Russo, and Lourdes Torres. 1991. *Third World Women and the Politics of Feminism*. Bloomington, IN: Indiana University Press.

Moller, Herbert. 1968. "Youth as a Force in the Modern World." *Comparative Studies in Society and History* 10 (3): 237–60.

Mousa, Salma. 2020. "Building Social Cohesion between Christians and Muslims through Soccer in Post-ISIS Iraq." *Science* 369 (6505): 866–70.

Moyer, Cheryl A., and Jenny Birchall. 2023. "Stalled Progress in Reducing Maternal Mortality Globally: What Next?" *The Lancet* 401 (10382): 1060–62.

Mueller, John. 2000. "The Banality of 'Ethnic War.'" *International Security* 25 (1): 42–70. https://doi.org/10.1162/016228800560381.

Munck, Gerardo L., and Jay Verkuilen. 2002. "Conceptualizing and Measuring Democracy: Evaluating Alternative Indices." *Comparative Political Studies* 35 (1): 5–34. https://doi.org/10.1177/001041400203500101.

Murdie, Amanda, and David Davis. 2012. "Shaming and blaming: Using Events Data to Assess the Impact of Human Rights INGOs." International Studies Quarterly 56 (1): 1–16.

Murdie, Amanda, and Dursun Peksen. 2015. "Women's Rights INGO Shaming and the Government Respect for Women's Rights." *The Review of International Organizations* 10 (1): 1–22. https://doi.org/10.1007/s11558-014-9200-x.

Murray, Michelle. 2018. *The Struggle for Recognition in International Relations: Status, Revisionism, and Rising Powers*. New York, NY: Oxford University Press.

Muscati, Samer. 2014. "Women's Rights." Human Rights Watch. www.hrw.org/topic/womens-rights.

Mutz, Diana C. 2018. "Status Threat, Not Economic Hardship, Explains the 2016 Presidential Vote." *Proceedings of the National Academy of Sciences* 115 (19): E4330–39.

Myrttinen, Henri. 2019. *Security Sector Governance, Security Sector Reform and Gender*. Geneva, Switzerland: DCAF.

Nash, Jennifer C. 2008. "Re-Thinking Intersectionality." *Feminist Review* 89 (1): 1–15. https://doi.org/10.1057/fr.2008.4.

Ní Aoláin, Fionnuala, Dina Francesca Haynes, and Naomi Cahn. 2011. *On the Frontlines: Gender, War, and the Post-Conflict Process*. New York, NY: Oxford University Press.

Nincic, Miroslav, and Donna J. Nincic. 2002. "Race, Gender, and War." *Journal of Peace Research* 39 (5): 547–68.

Nordås, Ragnhild, and Christian Davenport. 2013. "Fight the Youth: Youth Bulges and State Repression." *American Journal of Political Science* 57 (4): 926–40.

O'Neal, John R., and Bruce Russett. 1999. "Assessing the Liberal Peace with Alternative Specifications: Trade Still Reduces Conflict." *Journal of Peace Research* 36 (4): 423–42.

O'Neal, John R., and Bruce M. Russett. 2015. "The Kantian Peace: The Pacific Benefits of Democracy, Interdependence, and International Organizations, 1885–1992." In *Bruce M. Russett: Pioneer in the Scientific and Normative Study of War, Peace, and Policy*, Cambridge University Press 52 (1):74–108.

Orlofsky, Jacob L. 1981. "Relationship between Sex Role Attitudes and Personality Traits and the Sex Role Behavior Scale-1: A New Measure of Masculine and Feminine Role Behaviors and Interests." *Journal of Personality and Social Psychology* 40 (5): 927–40. https://doi.org/10.1037/0022-3514.40.5.927.

Orlova, Alexandra V. 2018. "Russian Politics of Masculinity and the Decay of Feminism: The Role of Dissent in Creating New Local Norms." *William & Mary Journal of Race Gender & Social Justice* 25: 59.

Østergaard, Christian R., Bram Timmermans, and Kari Kristinsson. 2011. "Does a Different View Create Something New? The Effect of Employee Diversity on Innovation." *Research Policy* 40 (3): 500–509. https://doi.org/10.1016/j.respol.2010.11.004.

Otto, Herbert A., and Robert B. Andersen. 1967. "The Hope Chest and Dowry: American Custom?" *The Family Life Coordinator* 16 (1/2): 15–19.

284 REFERENCES

Page, Benjamin I., and Robert Y. Shapiro. 1983. "Effects of Public Opinion on Policy." *The American Political Science Review* 77 (1): 175–90. https://doi.org/10.2307/1956018.

Palmer, Glenn, Vito D'Orazio, Michael R. Kenwick, and Roseanne W. McManus. 2020. "Updating the Militarized Interstate Dispute Data: A Response to Gibler, Miller, and Little." *International Studies Quarterly* 64 (2): 469–75.

Paluck, Elizabeth Levy. 2009. "Reducing Intergroup Prejudice and Conflict Using the Media: A Field Experiment in Rwanda." *Journal of Personality and Social Psychology* 96 (3): 574–87. https://doi.org/10.1037/a0011989.

Paluck, Elizabeth Levy, and Donald P. Green. 2009. "Prejudice Reduction: What Works? A Review and Assessment of Research and Practice." *Annual Review of Psychology* 60: 339–67.

Paris, Roland. 2001. "Human Security: Paradigm Shift or Hot Air?" *International Security* 26 (2): 87–102.

Parkinson, Sarah Elisabeth. 2021. "Practical Ideology in Militant Organizations." *World Politics* 73 (1): 52–81.

Parrotta, Pierpaolo, Dario Pozzoli, and Mariola Pytlikova. 2014. "The Nexus between Labor Diversity and Firm's Innovation." *Journal of Population Economics* 27 (2): 303–64. https://doi.org/10.1007/s00148-013-0491-7.

Pateman, Carole. 1988. *The Sexual Contract*. Cambridge, United Kingdom: Polity Press.

Paxton, Pamela, Melanie M. Hughes, and Jennifer L. Green. 2006. "The International Women's Movement and Women's Political Representation, 1893-2003." *American Sociological Review* 71 (6): 898–920.

PeaceWomen. 2014. "UN Resolutions on Women, Peace and Security. 2014. 'The Resolutions.'" http://www.peacewomen.org/why-WPS/solutions/resolutions.

Peksen, Dursun. 2009. "Better or Worse? The Effect of Economic Sanctions on Human Rights." *Journal of Peace Research* 46 (1): 59–77.

Pemstein, Daniel, Stephen A. Meserve, and James Melton. 2010. "Democratic Compromise: A Latent Variable Analysis of Ten Measures of Regime Type." *Political Analysis* 18 (4): 426–49.

Pemstein, Daniel, Kyle L. Marquardt, Eitan Tzelgov, Yi-ting Wang, Juraj Medzihorsky, Joshua Krusell, Farhad Miri, and Johannes von Römer. 2021. "The V-Dem Measurement Model: La- tent Variable Analysis for Cross-National and Cross-Temporal Expert-Coded Data". V-Dem Working Paper No. 21. 6th edition. University of Gothenburg: Varieties of Democracy Institute.

Permanyer, Iñaki. 2013. "A Critical Assessment of the UNDP's Gender Inequality Index." *Feminist Economics* 19 (2): 1–32. https://doi.org/10.1080/13545701.2013.769687.

Peterson, V. Spike. 1992. "Transgressing Boundaries: Theories of Knowledge, Gender and International Relations." *Millennium-Journal of International Studies* 21 (2): 183–206. https://doi.org/10.1177/03058298920210020401.

Pettman, Jan. 1996. *Worlding Women: A Feminist International Politics*. New York, NY: Routledge.

Pettman, Jan Jindy. 2005. *Worlding Women: A Feminist International Politics*. New York, NY: Routledge.

Phillips, Anne. 1995. *The Politics of Presence*. Oxford: Clarendon Press. https://hdl.handle.net/2027/mdp.39015034897721?urlappend=%3Bsignon=swle:https://shibidp.cit.corn ell.edu/idp/shibboleth.

Piazza, James A., and James Igoe Walsh. 2010. "Physical Integrity Rights and Terrorism." *PS: Political Science and Politics* 43 (3): 411–14.

Pitkin, Hanna Fenichel. 1967. *The Concept of Representation*. Berkeley: University of California Press. https://hdl.handle.net/2027/uc1.b3950977?urlappend=%3Bsignon=swle:https://shibidp.cit.cornell.edu/idp/shibboleth.

Poe, Steven C., C. Neal Tate, and Linda Camp Keith. 1999. "Repression of the Human Right to Personal Integrity Revisited: A Global Cross-National Study Covering the Years 1976-1993." *International Studies Quarterly* 43 (2): 291–313.

REFERENCES   285

Post, Abigail S., and Paromita Sen. 2020. "Why Can't a Woman Be More like a Man? Female Leaders in Crisis Bargaining." *International Interactions* 46 (1): 1–27. https://doi.org/10.1080/03050629.2019.1683008.

Powell, Emilia Justyna, and Jeffrey K. Staton. 2009. "Domestic Judicial Institutions and Human Rights Treaty Violation." *International Studies Quarterly* 53 (1): 149–74. https://doi.org/10.1111/j.1468-2478.2008.01527.x.

Powell, Jonathan, and Karina Mukazhanova-Powell. 2019. "Demonstrating Credentials? Female Executives, Women's Status, and the Use of Force." *Journal of Women, Politics & Policy* 40 (2): 241–62. https://doi.org/10.1080/1554477X.2019.1535107.

Power, Margaret. 2008. "The Engendering of Anticommunism and Fear in Chile's 1964 Presidential Election." *Diplomatic History* 32 (5): 931–53.

Power, Margaret. 2015. "Who but a Woman? The Transnational Diffusion of Anti-Communism among Conservative Women in Brazil, Chile and the United States during the Cold War." *Journal of Latin American Studies* 47 (1): 93–119.

Prakash, G. 2019. Emergency chronicles: Indira Gandhi and Democracy's Turning Point. Princeton University Press.

Prasch, Allison M. 2015. "Maternal Bodies in Militant Protest: Leymah Gbowee and the Rhetorical Agency of African motherhood." *Women's Studies in Communication* 38 (2): 187–205.

Pratto, Felicia, Jim Sidanius, and Shana Levin. 2006. "Social Dominance Theory and the Dynamics of Intergroup Relations: Taking Stock and Looking Forward." *European Review of Social Psychology* 17 (1): 271–320. https://doi.org/10.1080/10463280601055772.

Press, Daryl G., Scott D. Sagan, and Benjamin A. Valentino. 2013. "Atomic Aversion: Experimental Evidence on Taboos, Traditions, and the Non-Use of Nuclear Weapons." *American Political Science Review* 107 (1): 188–206. https://doi.org/10.1017/S0003055412000597.

Quinn, Kevin M. 2004. "Bayesian Factor Analysis for Mixed Ordinal and Continuous Responses." *Political Analysis* 12 (4): 338–53. https://doi.org/10.1093/pan/mph022.

Rabe-Hemp, Cara E. 2009. "POLICEwomen or PoliceWOMEN?: Doing Gender and Police Work." *Feminist Criminology* 4 (2): 114–29. https://doi.org/10.1177/1557085108327659.

Ravallion, Martin. 2012. "Troubling Tradeoffs in the Human Development Index." *Journal of Development Economics* 99 (2): 201–9.

Regan, Patrick M., and Aida Paskeviciute. 2003. "Women's Access to Politics and Peaceful States." *Journal of Peace Research* 40 (3): 287–302.

Reingold, Beth. 2003. *Representing Women: Sex, Gender, and Legislative Behavior in Arizona and California*. Chapel Hill, NC: University of North Carolina Press.

Reingold, Beth. 2008. "Women as Officeholders: Linking Descriptive and Substantive Representation." In *Political Women and American Democracy*, edited by Christina Wolbrecht, Karen Beckwith, and Lisa Baldez, 128–47. New York, NY: Cambridge University Press. https://doi.org/10.1017/CBO9780511790621.011.

Reiter, Dan, and Scott Wolford. 2022. "Gender, Sexism, and War." *Journal of Theoretical Politics* 34 (1): 59–77.

Rejali, Darius. 2007. *Torture and Democracy*. Princeton, NJ: Princeton University Press.

Renshon, Jonathan. 2017. *Fighting for Status*. Princeton, NJ: Princeton University Press.

Reynolds, Adam Z., Katherine Wander, Chun-Yi Sum, Mingjie Su, Melissa Emery Thompson, Paul L. Hooper, Hui Li, et al. 2020. "Matriliny Reverses Gender Disparities in Inflammation and Hypertension among the Mosuo of China." *Proceedings of the National Academy of Sciences* 117 (48): 30324–27.

Richards, David L., Ronald D. Gelleny, and David H. Sacko. 2001. "Money with a Mean Streak? Foreign Economic Penetration and Government Respect for Human Rights in Developing Countries." *International Studies Quarterly* 45 (2): 219–39.

Ritter, Emily Hencken. 2014. "Policy Disputes, Political Survival, and the Onset and Severity of State Repression." *Journal of Conflict Resolution* 58.1: 143–68.

286 REFERENCES

Ritter, Emily Hencken, and Courtenay R. Conrad. 2016. "Human Rights Treaties and Mobilized Dissent against the State." *The Review of International Organizations* 11: 449–75.

Ron, James. 1997. "Varying Methods of State Violence." *International Organization* 51 (2): 275–300.

Rosen, Andrew. 2013. Rise up, women!: The Militant Campaign of the Women's Social and Political Union, 1903–14. New York, New York: Routledge.

Rosga, Ann Janette, and Margaret L. Satterthwaie. 2009. "The Trust in Indicators: Measuring Human Rights." *Berkeley Journal of International Law* 27 (2): 253.

Rousseau, Stephanie. 2020 "Antigender Activism in Peru and its Impact on State Policy." Politics & Gender 16 (1).

Rovito, M. J., Leonard, B., Llamas, R., Leone, J. E., Talton, W., Fadich, A., & Baker, P. 2017. A Call for Gender-inclusive Global Health Strategies. *American Journal of Men's Health*, 11 (6): 1804–08.

Rubin, Donald B. 1987. Multiple Imputation for Nonresponse in Surveys. John Wiley & Sons.

Ryan, Caitlin. 2018. "Large-Scale Land Deals in Sierra Leone at the Intersection of Gender and Lineage." *Third World Quarterly* 39 (1): 189–206. https://doi.org/10.1080/01436 597.2017.1350099.

Saiya, Nilay, Tasneem Zaihra, and Joshua Fidler. 2017. "Testing the Hillary Doctrine: Women's Rights and Anti-American Terrorism." *Political Research Quarterly* 70 (2): 421–32.

Salehyan, Idean. 2007. "Transnational Rebels: Neighboring States as Sanctuary for Rebel Groups." *World Politics* 59 (2): 217–42.

Sanín, Francisco Gutiérrez, and Elisabeth Jean Wood. 2014. "Ideology in Civil War: Instrumental Adoption and Beyond." *Journal of Peace Research* 51 (2): 213–26. https://www.jstor.org/stable/24557417.

Sartori, Giovanni. 1970. "Concept Misformation in Comparative Politics." *The American Political Science Review* 64 (4): 1033–53. https://doi.org/10.2307/1958356.

Sartori, Giovanni. 1984. *Social Science Concepts: A Systematic Analysis*. Beverly Hills, CA: Sage Publications.

Scharff, Xanthe. 2023. "America Is Again Failing Afghanistan's Women—and Itself." March. https://foreignpolicy.com/2023/03/08/united-states-afghanistan-taliban-women/.

Schedler, Andreas. 2012. "Judgment and Measurement in Political Science." *Perspectives on Politics* 10 (1): 21–36. https://doi.org/10.1017/S1537592711004889.

Schnakenberg, Keith E., and Christopher J. Fariss. 2014. "Dynamic Patterns of Human Rights Practices." *Political Science Research and Methods* 2 (1): 1–31.

Schramm, Madison, and Alexandra Stark. 2020. "Peacemakers or Iron Ladies? A Cross-National Study of Gender and International Conflict." *Security Studies* 29 (3): 515–48. https://doi.org/10.1080/09636412.2020.1763450.

Schultz, Kenneth A. 1998. Domestic Opposition and Signaling in International Crises. *American Political Science Review* 92 (4): 829–44.

Schultz, Kenneth A. 1999. Do democratic institutions constrain or inform? Contrasting Two Institutional Perspectives on Democracy and War. *International Organization* 53 (2): 233–66.

Schwartz, Joshua A., and Christopher W. Blair. 2020. "Do Women Make More Credible Threats? Gender Stereotypes, Audience Costs, and Crisis Bargaining." *International Organization* 74 (4): 872–95. https://doi.org/10.1017/S0020818320000223.

Scott, Joan Wallach. 1999. *Gender and the Politics of History*. New York, NY: Columbia University Press.

Sell, Aaron, John Tooby, and Leda Cosmides. 2009. "Formidability and the Logic of Human Anger." *Proceedings of the National Academy of Sciences* 106 (35): 15073–78. https://doi.org/10.1073/pnas.0904312106.

REFERENCES 287

Sen, A. 1992. "Missing Women." *British Medical Journal* 304 (6827): 587–88. https://doi.org/10.1136/bmj.304.6827.587.

Sen, Amartya. 2001. *Development as Freedom*. Oxford: Oxford University Press.

Shair-Rosenfield, Sarah, and Reed M. Wood. 2017. "Governing Well after War: How Improving Female Representation Prolongs Post-Conflict Peace." *The Journal of Politics* 79 (3): 995–1009. https://doi.org/10.1086/691056.

Shalal, Andrea. 2023. "World Bank launches more robust, transparent business climate rankings." Reuters. May. https://www.reuters.com/markets/world-bank-set-launch-more-robust-transparent-business-climate-rankings-2023-05-01/.

Sharpe, Tanya Telfair. 2000. "The Identity Christian Movement: Ideology of Domestic Terrorism." *Journal of Black Studies* 30 (4): 604–23.

Shea, Patrick E., and Charlotte Christian. 2017. "The Impact of Women Legislators on Humanitarian Military Interventions." *Journal of Conflict Resolution* 61 (10): 2043–73.

Simmons, Beth A. 2009. *Mobilizing for Human Rights: International Law in Domestic Politics*. New York, NY: Cambridge University Press.

Sjoberg, Laura. 2006. *Gender, Justice, and the Wars in Iraq: A Feminist Reformulation of Just War Theory*. Oxford, United Kingdoom: Lexington Books.

Sjoberg, Laura. 2010. *Gender and International Security: Feminist Perspectives*. New York, NY: Routledge.

Sjoberg, Laura. 2011. *Women, Gender, and Terrorism*. Athens, Georgia: University of Georgia Press.

Sjoberg, Laura. 2012. "Toward Trans-Gendering International Relations?" *International Political Sociology* 6 (4): 337–54.

Sjoberg, Laura. 2013. *Gendering Global Conflict: Toward a Feminist Theory of War*. New York, NY: Columbia University Press.

Sjoberg, Laura. 2014. *Gender, War, and Conflict*. Cambridge, United Kingdom: John Wiley & Sons.

Sjoberg, Laura. 2018. "Reevaluating Gender and IR Scholarship: Moving beyond Reiter's Dichotomies toward Effective Synergies." *Journal of Conflict Resolution* 62 (4): 848–70. https://doi.org/10.1177/0022002716669207.

Sjoberg, Laura, and Caron E. Gentry. 2007. *Mothers, Monsters, Whores: Women's Violence in Global Politics*. New York, NY: Zed Books.

Sjoberg, Laura, and Caron E. Gentry, eds. 2011. *Women, Gender, and Terrorism*. University of Georgia Press.

Sjoberg, Laura, Kelly Kadera, and Cameron G. Thies. 2018. "Reevaluating Gender and IR Scholarship: Moving beyond Reiter's Dichotomies toward Effective Synergies." *Journal of Conflict Resolution* (September). https://doi.org/10.1177/0022002716669207.

Sjoberg, Laura, and Sandra Via, eds. 2010. *Gender, War, and Militarism: Feminist Perspectives*. Santa Barbara, CA: Praeger Security International.

Slattery, Gram. 2023, "Americans Broadly Support Military Strikes in Mexico, Reuters/Ipsos poll finds," Accessed January 25, 2024. Reuters, https://www.reuters.com/world/americans-broadly-support-military-strikes-mexico-reutersipsos-poll-finds-2023-09-14/.

Souva, Mark, and Brandon Prins. 2006. "The Liberal Peace Revisited: The Role of Democracy, Dependence, and Development in Militarized Interstate Dispute Initiation, 1950–1999." *International Interactions* 32 (2): 183–200.

Speckhard, A., and M. Ellenberg. 2021. "ISIS and the Allure of Traditional Gender Roles." *Women & Criminal Justice*, 33 (2): 1–21.

Spence, Janet T., Robert Helmreich, and Joy Stapp. 1973. "A Short Version of the Attitudes Toward Women Scale (AWS)." *Bulletin of the Psychonomic Society* 2 (4). https://doi.org/10.3758/BF03329252.

288 REFERENCES

Sprinzak, Ehud. 1995. "Right-wing Terrorism in a Comparative Perspective: The Case of Split Delegitimization." *Terrorism and Political Violence* 7 (1): 17–43. https://doi.org/10.1080/09546559508427284.

Stetson, Dorothy M., Amy Mazur, and Dorothy E. Mcbride. 1995. *Comparative State Feminism*. Beverly Hills, CA: SAGE Publications.

Stiehm, Judith Hicks. 1982. "The Protected, the Protector, the Defender." *Women's Studies International Forum* 5 (3–4): 367–76.

Strolovitch, Dara Z. 2006. "Do Interest Groups Represent the Disadvantaged? Advocacy at the Intersections of Race, Class, and Gender." *The Journal of Politics* 68 (4): 894–910.

Sundström, Aksel, Pamela Paxton, Yi-Ting Wang, and Staffan I. Lindberg. 2017. "Women's Political Empowerment: A New Global Index, 1900–2012." *World Development* 94: 321–35. https://doi.org/10.1016/j.worlddev.2017.01.016.

Sundström, Malena Rosén, and Ole Elgström. 2020. "Praise or Critique? Sweden's Feminist Foreign Policy in the Eyes of Its Fellow EU Members." *European Politics and Society* 21 (4): 418–33. https://doi.org/10.1080/23745118.2019.1661940.

Sweetman, Caroline, and Louise Medland. 2017. "Introduction: Gender and Water, Sanitation and Hygiene." *Gender & Development* 25 (2): 153–66. https://doi.org/10.1080/13552074.2017.1349867.

Swim, Janet, Kathryn Aikin, Wayne Hall, and Barbara Hunter. 1995. "Sexism and Racism: Old-Fashioned and Modern Prejudices." *Journal of Personality and Social Psychology* 68 (2): 199–214. https://doi.org/10.1037/0022-3514.68.2.199.

Swim, Janet, and Laurie Cohen. 1997. "Overt, Covert, and Subtle Sexism: A Comparison between the Attitudes Toward Women and Modern Sexism Scales." https://journals-sagepub-com.proxy.library.cornell.edu/doi/10.1111/j.1471-6402.1997.tb00103.x.

Sylvester, Christine. 1994. *Feminist Theory and International Relations in a Postmodern Era*. New York, NY: Cabridge University Press. https://www.google.com/books/edition/Feminist_Theory_and_International_Relati/CZO4EQumX4sC?hl=en&gbpv=0.

Ta-Johnson, Vivian P., Eric Keels, and A. Burcu Bayram. 2022. "How Women Promote Peace: Gender Composition, Duration, and Frames in Conflict Resolution." *International Interactions* 48 (6): 1089–1120.

Tago, Atsushi, and Maki Ikeda. 2015. "An 'A' for Effort: Experimental Evidence on UN Security Council Engagement and Support for US Military Action in Japan." *British Journal of Political Science* 45 (2): 391–410. https://doi.org/10.1017/S0007123413000343.

Teele, Dawn Langan. 2019. *Forging the Franchise: The Political Origins of the Women's Vote*. Princeton, NJ: Princeton University Press.

Tessler, Mark, Jodi Nachtwey, and Audra Grant. 1999. "Further Tests of the Women and Peace Hypothesis: Evidence from Cross-National Survey Research in the Middle East." *International Studies Quarterly* 43 (3): 519–31. https://doi.org/10.1111/0020-8833.00133.

Tessler, Mark, and Ina Warriner. 1997. "Gender, Feminism, and Attitudes toward International Conflict: Exploring Relationships with Survey Data from the Middle East." *World Politics* 49 (2): 250–81. https://doi.org/10.1353/wp.1997.0005.

Themnér, Lotta, and Peter Wallensteen. 2014. "Armed Conflicts, 1946–2013." *Journal of Peace Research* 51 (4): 541–54. https://doi.org/10.1177/0022343314542076.

Thies, Scott J, and Cameron G Cook. 2019. "In Plain Sight? Reconsidering the Linkage between Brideprice and Violent Conflict." *Conflict Management and Peace Science* (August). http://journals.sagepub.com/doi/10.1177/0738894219863254.

Thomas, Gwynn, and Melinda Adams. 2010. "Breaking the Final Glass Ceiling: The Influence of Gender in the Elections of Ellen Johnson-Sirleaf and Michelle Bachelet." *Journal of Women, Politics & Policy* 31 (2): 105–31. https://doi.org/10.1080/15544771003697270.

Thomas, J. L., and K. D. Bond. 2015. "Women's Participation in Violent Political Organizations." *American Political Science Review* 109 (3): 488–506.

Thomas, Sue. 1994. *How Women Legislate*. Oxford, United Kingdom: Oxford University Press.

REFERENCES 289

Thyne, Clayton L. 2012. "Information, Commitment, and Intra-War Bargaining: The Effect of Governmental Constraints on Civil War Duration." *International Studies Quarterly* 56 (2): 307–21.

Tickner, J. Ann. 1988. "Hans Morgenthau's Principles of Political Realism: A Feminist Reformulation." https://eds-b-ebscohost-com.proxy.library.cornell.edu/eds/detail/det ail?vid=0&sid=1415edf9-369e-4d39-a471-e554100cb508%40sessionmgr103&bdata= JnNpdGU9ZWRzLWxpdmUmc2NvcGU9c2l0ZQ%3d%3d#AN=edselc.2-52.0-8497 0744435&db=edselc.

Tickner, J. Ann. 1992. *Gender in International Relations: Feminist Perspectives on Achieving Global Security.* New York, NY: Columbia University Press.

Tokdemir, Efe, Evgeny Sedashov, Sema Hande Ogutcu-Fu, Carlos E. Moreno Leon, Jeremy Berkowitz, and Seden Akcinaroglu. 2021. "Rebel Rivalry and the Strategic Nature of Rebel Group Ideology and Demands." *Journal of Conflict Resolution* 65 (4): 729–58.

Tomz, Michael R., and Jessica L. P. Weeks. 2013. "Public Opinion and the Democratic Peace." *American Political Science Review* 107 (4): 849–65. https://doi.org/10.1017/ S0003055413000488.

Treier, Shawn, and Simon Jackman. 2008. "Democracy as a Latent Variable." *American Journal of Political Science* 52 (1): 201–17. https://doi.org/10.1111/j.1540-5907.2007.00308.x.

Tripp, Aili Mari. 2015. *Women and Power in Post-Conflict Africa.* New York, NY: Cambridge University Press.

Tripp, Aili Mari. 2019. *Seeking Legitimacy: Why Arab Autocracies Adopt Women's Rights.* New York, NY: Cambridge University Press. https://doi.org/10.1017/9781108348621.

UN Women. 2013. "UN Women: The United Nations Entity for Gender Equality and the Empowerment of Women—Office of the Secretary-General's Envoy on Youth." www. un.org/youthenvoy/2013/07/un-women-the-united-nations-entity-for-gender-equal ity-and-the-empowerment-of-women/.

UNDP. 2018. "Gender Equality Strategy 2018–2021." https://www.undp.org/publicati ons/undp-gender-equality-strategy-2018-2021.

UNICEF. 2017. "Gender Equality: Glossary of Terms and Concepts." www.unicef.org/rosa/ media/1761/file/Gender%20glossary%20of%20terms%20and%20concepts%20.pdf.

United Nations. 2022. "Closing Gender Pay Gaps Is More Important Than Ever." https:// news.un.org/en/story/2022/09/1126901.

United Nations Population Fund. 2005. "Frequently Asked Questions about Gender Equality." www.unfpa.org/resources/frequently-asked-questions-about-gender-equality.

United Nations Secretary General. 2019. "Secretary-General's remarks to High-level event on Women in Power." https://www.un.org/sg/en/content/sg/statement/2019-03-12/ secretary-generals-remarks-high-level-event-women-power-delivered.

United Nations Secretary General. 2020. "Secretary-General's Remarks at High-Level Meeting on Gender Equality and Women's Empowerment." https://www.un.org/sg/en/ content/sg/statement/2020-02-08/secretary-generals-remarks-high-level-meeting-gender-equality-and-womens-empowerment.

Urdal, Henrik. 2004. "The Devil in the Demographics: The Effect of Youth Bulges on Domestic Armed Conflict, 1950–2000." *Social Development Papers* 14: 1–25.

Väyrynen, Tarja, Swati Parashar, Élise Féron, and Catia Cecilia Confortini, eds. 2021. *Routledge Handbook of Feminist Peace Research.* New York, NY: Routledge.

Vogt, Manuel, Nils-Christian Bormann, Seraina Rüegger, Lars-Erik Cederman, Philipp Hunziker, and Luc Girardin. 2015. "Integrating Data on Ethnicity, Geography, and Conflict: The Ethnic Power Relations Data Set Family." *Journal of Conflict Resolution* 59 (7): 1327–42. https://doi.org/10.1177/0022002715591215.

Von Stein, Jana. 2005. "Do Treaties Constrain or Screen? Selection Bias and Treaty Compliance." *The American Political Science Review* 99 (4): 611–22.

Vucetic, Srdjan. 2018. "The Uneasy Co-Existence of Arms Exports and Feminist Foreign Policy." April 8. http://theconversation.com/the-uneasy-co-existence-of-arms-expo rts-and-feminist-foreign-policy-93930.

290 REFERENCES

Walby, Sylvia. 1989. "Theorising Patriarchy." *Sociology* 23 (2): 213–34. https://doi.org/10.1177/0038038589023002004.

Walfridsson, Hanna. 2022. "Sweden's New Government Abandons Feminist Foreign Policy." October 31. https://www.hrw.org/news/2022/10/31/swedens-new-government-abandons-feminist-foreign-policy.

Walsh, J. I., & Piazza, J. A. (2010). Why respecting physical integrity rights reduces terrorism. Comparative Political Studies, 43(5), 551–77.

Walter, Barbara F. 1997. "The Critical Barrier to Civil War Settlement." *International Organization* 51 (3): 335–64.

Walter, Barbara F. 2009. "Bargaining Failures and Civil War." *Annual Review of Political Science* 12: 243–61.

Walter, Barbara F. 2023. *How Civil Wars Start: And How to Stop Them.* New York, NY: Crown.

Wang, Yi-Ting, Patrik Lindenfors, Aksel Sundström, Fredrik Jansson, Pamela Paxton, and Staffan I. Lindberg. 2017. "Women's Rights in Democratic Transitions: A Global Sequence Analysis, 1900–2012." *European Journal of Political Research* 56 (4): 735–56.

Ward, M. D., and J. S. Ahlquist. 2018. *Maximum Likelihood for Social Science: Strategies for Analysis.* New York, NY: Cambridge University Press.

Ward, Michael D., Randolph M. Siverson, and Xun Cao. 2007. "Disputes, Democracies, and Dependencies: A Reexamination of the Kantian Peace." *American Journal of Political Science* 51 (3): 583–601.

Webster, Kaitlyn, Chong Chen, and Kyle Beardsley. 2019. "Conflict, Peace, and the Evolution of Women's Empowerment." *International Organization* 73 (2): 255–89. https://doi.org/10.1017/S0020818319000055.

Webster, Kaitlyn, Priscilla Torres, Chong Chen, and Kyle Beardsley. 2020. "Ethnic and Gender Hierarchies in the Crucible of War." *International Studies Quarterly* 64 (3): 710–22. https://doi.org/10.1093/isq/sqaa031.

Wegner, Nicole. 2021. "Helpful Heroes and the Political Utility of Militarized Masculinities." *International Feminist Journal of Politics* 23 (1): 5–26.

Weinstein, Jeremy M. 2005. "Resources and the Information Problem in Rebel Recruitment." *Journal of Conflict Resolution* 49 (4): 598–624.

Weinstein, Jeremy M. 2006. *Inside Rebellion: The Politics of Insurgent Violence.* New York, NY: Cambridge University Press.

Weldon, S. Laurel. 2002. "Beyond Bodies: Institutional Sources of Representation for Women in Democratic Policymaking." *The Journal of Politics* 64 (4): 1153–74.

Weldon, S. Laurel. 2011. *When Protest Makes Policy: How Social Movements Represent Disadvantaged Groups.* Ann Harbor, MI: University of Michigan Press.

Wenar, Leif. 2020. "Rights." In *The Stanford Encyclopedia of Philosophy*, edited by Edward N. Zalta. Stanford, GA: Metaphysics Research Lab, Stanford University. Online. https://plato.stanford.edu/archives/spr2020/entries/rights/.

Westen, Drew, and Robert Rosenthal. 2003. "Quantifying Construct Validity: Two Simple Measures." *Journal of Personality and Social Psychology* 84 (3): 608–18.

Whitfield, Charles L., Robert F. Anda, Shanta R. Dube, and Vincent J. Felitti. 2003. "Violent Childhood Experiences and the Risk of Intimate Partner Violence in Adults: Assessment in a Large Health Maintenance Organization." *Journal of Interpersonal Violence* 18 (2): 166–85. https://doi.org/10.1177/0886260502238733.

Whitworth, Sandra. 1994. *Feminism and International Relations: Towards a Political Economy of Gender.*

Wibben, Annick T. R. 2010. *Feminist Security Studies: A Narrative Approach.* New York, NY: Routledge.

Winkler, Inga T. 2019. "Human Rights Shine a Light on Unmet Menstrual Health Needs and Menstruation at the Margins." *Obstetrics and Gynecology* 133 (2): 235–37. https://doi.org/10.1097/AOG.0000000000003098.

REFERENCES 291

Wirtz, Andrea L., Tonia C. Poteat, Mannat Malik, and Nancy Glass. 2020. "Gender-Based Violence against Transgender People in the United States: A Call for Research and Programming." *Trauma, Violence, & Abuse* 21 (2): 227–41.

Wohlforth, William C., Benjamin De Carvalho, Halvard Leira, and Iver B. Neumann. 2018. "Moral Authority and Status in International Relations: Good States and the Social Dimension of Status Seeking." *Review of International Studies* 44 (3): 526–46.

Wood, Reed M. 2008. "'A Hand upon the Throat of the Nation': Economic Sanctions and State Repression, 1976–2001." *International Studies Quarterly* 52 (3): 489–513.

Wood, Reed M. 2019. *Female Fighters: Why Rebel Groups Recruit Women for War.* New York, NY: Columbia University Press.

Wood, Reed M., and Mark Gibney. 2010. "The Political Terror Scale (PTS): A Re-Introduction and a Comparison to CIRI." *Human Rights Quarterly* 32 (2): 367–400.

Wood, Reed, and Mark D. Ramirez. 2018. "Exploring the Microfoundations of the Gender Equality Peace Hypothesis." *International Studies Review* 20 (3): 345–67.

Wood, Reed M., and J. L. Thomas. 2017. "Women on the Frontline: Rebel Group Ideology and Women's Participation in Violent Rebellion." *Journal of Peace Research* 54 (1): 31–46.

World Health Organization. 2023. "Gender and Health." https://www.who.int/health-top ics/gender#tab=tab_1.

Yair, Omer, and Dan Miodownik. 2016. "Youth Bulge and Civil War: Why a Country's Share of Young Adults Explains Only Non-Ethnic Wars." *Conflict Management and Peace Science* 33 (1): 25–44. https://doi.org/10.1177/0738894214544613.

Yoon, Mi Yung. 2001. "Democratization and Women's Legislative Representation in Sub-Saharan Africa." *Democratization* 8 (2): 169–90. https://doi.org/10.1080/714000199.

Younas, Javed, and Todd Sandler. 2017. "Gender Imbalance and Terrorism in Developing Countries." *The Journal of Conflict Resolution* 61 (3): 483–510. https://doi.org/10.1177/0022002715603102.

Yount, Kathryn M., Yuk Fai Cheong, Rose Grace Grose, and Sarah R. Hayford. 2020. "Community Gender Systems and a Daughter's Risk of Female Genital Mutilation/Cutting: Multilevel Findings from Egypt." *PLOS ONE* 15 (3): e0229917. https://doi.org/10.1371/journal.pone.0229917.

Zenko, Micah. 2015. "Book Review—'The Hillary Doctrine: Sex & American Foreign Policy.'" Council on Foreign Relations. https://www.cfr.org/blog/book-review-hillary-doctrine-sex-american-foreign-policy.

Zlotnick, Caron, Dawn M. Johnson, and Robert Kohn. "Intimate Partner Violence and Long-term Psychosocial Functioning in a National Sample of American Women." 2006. *Journal of Interpersonal Violence* 21 (2): 262–75.

Index

For the benefit of digital users, indexed terms that span two pages (e.g., 52–53) may, on occasion, appear on only one of those pages.

Tables, figures, and boxes are indicated by *t*, *f*, and *b* following the page number

Afghanistan
  Afghanistan War, 93, 143–44
  backsliding on women's rights in, 1–2, 145–46
  Taliban, 1–2, 116
ahistoricization, 7n.7
Akan people, 147–48
Alapine Village, 147–48
Amini, Mahsa (Zhina), 138, 166
Anand, Sudhir, 63–64
Arat, Zehra F. Kabasakal, 5–7, 43, 112
Ardern, Jacinda, 81, 117, 118
Asal, Victor, 134–35
Attitudes Toward Women Scale (ATWS), 177, 242
Autesserre, Séverine, 207

Baines, Erin, 165
Bayesian measurement models
  advantages of, 68–69
  assumptions, 255n.21
  beliefs about women's roles, for, 69–76, 245–46
  correlations between latent variables, 72–73, 73*f*
  harm to women, for, 69–76, 235–40
  latent variables over time, 72*f*, 72–73
  modeling strategy, 226–27
  women's inclusion, for, 69–76, 227–34
  women's rights, for, 69–76, 234
Beijing Conference (Fourth UN Conference on Women), 72–73, 123, 130
Beijing Declaration, 123
beliefs about women's roles
  characteristics of, 175*b*, 175–76
  conceptualizing, 174–76

contribution of study, 22–23
definition, 15–16
delineation of, 19
democracy and, 178, 261–62n.11
estimates of, 74–75, 75*f*, 180*f*, 189*f*, 247*f*, 248*f*, 249*f*, 250*f*
measurement of
  Bayesian measurement models, 69–76, 245–46
  existing measures, 176–77
  present study measure, 177–80
overview, 13–14, 14*t*, 24–25, 173–74, 191–92
perceptions, 174–75
policy recommendations, 208
political violence and
  armed groups, gateway for recruitment into, 185–88, 190
  civil conflict, 190–91, 243*f*, 247*f*
  dissident groups, 190
  gendered institutions, 202–3
  grievance-based, 181–82
  hypotheses, 184–85
  interstate conflict, 189, 191, 242*f*, 244*f*, 248*f*
  male backlash, 200
  null findings, 193–96, 194*t*
  overview, 180–81
  social dominance theory and, 182, 262n.18
  state violence, 189–90, 243*f*, 249*f*
  status quo, upholding, 181–85, 200
  terror attacks, 173–74, 188–89, 190, 197, 211, 243*f*, 246, 250*f*, 262–63n.22
  testing hypotheses, 189–91
regression models, 248

294 INDEX

beliefs about women's roles (*cont.*)
  women, peace and security (WPS)
    agenda and, 30
  World Values Survey (WVS), 177–78,
    179*t*, 245, 261n.10
Berry, Marie E., 115–16, 199–200
Best, Rebecca H., 99–100
Bjarnegård, Elin, 186
Boebert, Lauren, 210–11
Bowen, Donna Lee, 18–19, 129–30, 156,
    157–58, 163–64
Boyer, Mark A., 95–96
Bribri people, 147–48
Bush, Laura, 143–44
Butler, Judith, 10–11

Caprioli, Mary, 3–4, 18–19, 39, 91, 155–56
causal identification, 204–5
CEDAW. *See* Convention on the
    Elimination of All Forms of
    Discrimination Against Women
    (CEDAW)
Chastity Scale, 177, 245
China
  crime rate in, 163–64
  Cultural Revolution, 147
  matriarchal communities in, 147
  Mosuo people, 147
  shortages of women in, 163–64
Christian, Charlotte, 97–98
Cingranelli–Richards (CIRI) Physical
    Integrity Rights Index, 60–61, 75–
    76, 124–25, 139–40, 168
CIRI. *See* Cingranelli–Richards (CIRI)
    Physical Integrity Rights Index
civil conflict
  beliefs about women's roles and, 190–
    91, 243*f*, 247*f*
  dependent variable, as, 217–19, 218*f*
  harm to women and, 168, 169–71, 198–
    99, 235*f*, 240, 241*f*
  women's inclusion and, 102–3, 108, 230*f*
  women's rights and, 139, 142–43
civil society organizations, 207
Clinton, Hillary, 120, 143–44, 145
Cohen, Dara Kay, 209–10
Cold War, 183, 185
Collier, David, 41

concept stretching
  generally, 2
  contribution of study to problem of,
    21–22
  gender equality and
    delineation as solution to problem
      of, 48–49
    differentiation as solution to problem
      of, 48–49
    gender equality as concept stretched,
      31–38
    missing theory, problem of, 38–41
    problems with stretching concept of,
      38–48
  overview, 24, 29–31, 49–50
  scholarly literature, in, 41–48, 42*f*
Conover, Pamela Johnston, 93
Convention on the Elimination of All
    Forms of Discrimination Against
    Women (CEDAW), 60, 123–25,
    130–31, 132–33, 141–42
Correlates of War, 75–76
Costa Rica, matriarchal communities in,
    147–48
Covid-19 pandemic
  New Zealand, in, 81, 118
  role in backsliding on women's rights, 1
crime rate, 163–64

delineation
  beliefs about women's roles, of, 19 (*see
    also* beliefs about women's roles)
  concept stretching, as solution to
    problem of, 48–49
  harm to women, of, 18 (*see also* harm
    to women)
  limitations of, 19–21
  measurement, through, 14–17
  overview, 2–3, 8, 193–96
  specific theory, through, 17–21
  women's inclusion, of, 18 (*see also*
    women's inclusion)
  women's rights, of, 18 (*see also* women's
    rights)
Den Boer, Andrea, 164–65
differentiation
  concept stretching, as solution to
    problem of, 48–49

INDEX 295

definition, through, 9–14
limitations of, 19–21
overview, 2–3, 8, 193–96
domestic violence, 161–63. *See also* harm
to women
Donnelly, Phoebe Grace, 165
dowries, 164, 260n.18
Dube, Oeindrila, 106–7

Eagly, Alice H., 260n.13
Eichenberg, Richard C., 93
Ellerby, Kara, 5–7, 42, 43
Enloe, Cynthia, 47–48, 167–68
Equimundo, 208
Ethiopia, beliefs about women's roles in,
74–75, 75f
evolutionary perspective of structural
violence, 157–59
extremism, 187–88

feminism, 5–7, 23–24, 39, 42, 43, 71, 201–
2, 203
feminist foreign policy, 2, 120–21,
142, 145–46
feminist theory
Ferree, Myra Marx, 18
Fidler, Joshua, 39–40, 98–99, 260n.17
Forsberg, Erika, 112, 155–56
Fraser, Nancy, 11
Fulton, Sarah A., 105–6
future research
gender equality, 212–14
less aggregated data, 209–12
overview, 209

Galtung, Johan, 148–49, 155–56
Gandhi, Indira, 81, 117–18
Gaye, Amie, 64
gender
conflation with sex, 5–8, 30–31,
48, 193
fluidity of, 10–11, 31–32
identification and, 30, 252n.2
power hierarchy and, 9n.10, 9–
10, 31–32
relational nature of, 10, 31–32
social construction, as, 9n.9, 9, 31–32
violence, masculinity and, 46–48

Gender Development Index (GDI), 62,
63–66, 254n.11
gender equality
aggregation and, 16
classical subtypes of, 32–35, 33b
concept stretching and
delineation as solution to problem
of, 48–49
differentiation as solution to problem
of, 48–49
gender equality as concept stretched,
31–38
missing theory, problem of, 38–41
problems with stretching concept of,
38–48
definitions, 5–8, 15, 43, 44t
diminished subtypes of, 35–38
future research, 212–14
gender hierarchy as subtype, 36b, 36
human rights and, 43
indicators of
connecting concepts and, 55–58
lack of agreement between, 59–61
scholarly studies, 57f
measurement, problems in, 8
misogyny as subtype, 34–35, 35b
overview, 13–14, 14t
patriarchy as subtype, 34b, 34
scholarly studies, 3–4, 4f, 5f, 6f
social inequality as subtype, 35–36, 36b
status hierarchy and, 11
women's status distinguished, 11–12, 30
Gender Equality Index (GII), 56, 64, 65–
66, 254n.8
Gender Gap Index, 255n.18
gender hierarchy, 36b, 36, 252–53n.4
Gentry, Caron E., 212–13
Gerring, John, 252n.3
Ghana, matriarchal communities in,
147–48
Gizelis, Theodora-Ismene, 100
Global Terrorism Database (GTD), 75–76
Goldstein, Jushua S., 92
Gulf War, 93
Guterres, António, 1, 29–30

Hafner-Burton, Emilie M., 131–32, 137
Haglund, Jillienne, 97–98, 131

296   INDEX

Harish, S.P., 106–7
harm to women
   characteristics of, 149*b*, 149
   conceptualizing, 148–50
   contribution of study, 22–23
   definition, 15–16
   delineation of, 18–19
   domestic violence, 161–63
   estimates of, 154*f*, 169*f*, 235*f*
   indicators of, 150–53, 152*t*, 239*f*
   intersectional analysis and, 20
   measurement of
      Bayesian measurement models, 69–76, 235–40
      overview, 150–53
   overview, 13–14, 14*t*, 24–25, 147–48, 171–72
   physical violence, 148–49, 150–51, 153, 156
   policy recommendations, 207–8
   political violence and
      armed groups, 164–65, 211–12
      civil conflict, 168, 169–71, 198–99, 235*f*, 240, 241*f*
      crime rate, 163–64
      dowries, 164
      early exposure to violence as normalizing violence at individual level, 161–63
      evolutionary perspective of structural violence, 157–59
      hypotheses, 157, 163
      INGOs, presence of, 237*f*
      interstate conflict, 168, 236*f*, 240, 241*f*
      "marriage market," 164–65
      normative constraints on violence, weakening of, 155–57
      null findings, 193–96, 194*t*
      overview, 153–55
      physical violence, 156
      shortages of women, creating, 163–65, 198–99, 211–12
      social hierarchy, sustaining, 159–61
      state violence, 156–57, 168, 170–71, 236*f*
      structural violence, 155–56, 203–4, 211
      terror attacks, 162, 168, 170–71, 238*f*, 260–61n.20

      testing hypotheses, 168–71
      women's political mobilization, as strategy to prevent, 165–68, 199, 211–12
      "youth bulges," 164–65
   regression models, 240
   structural violence
      evolutionary perspective of, 157–59
      measuring, 151
      normative constraints on violence, weakening of, 155–56
      overview, 149, 203–4, 211
      patrilineal/fraternal syndrome and, 157–59
   women, peace and security (WPS) agenda and, 30

Hathaway, Oona A., 131–32
Hawken, Angela, 66
Hindu nationalism, 187–88
Htun, Mala, 12–13, 18, 125–26, 129–30, 131, 137, 258n.3
Huber, Laura, 102
Hudson, Valerie M., 18–19, 129–30, 156, 157–58, 163–65, 260–61n.20
Human Development Index (HDI), 51, 52, 63–65
Hungary, beliefs about women's roles in, 185

Ikenberry, G. John, 129
India, matriarchal communities in, 147–48
indicators. *See also specific indicator*
   benefits of, 53–55
   connecting concepts and, 55–58
   correlation coefficients, 59–60, 60*f*, 254n.9
   gender equality, of
      connecting concepts and, 55–58
      lack of agreement between, 59–61
      scholarly studies, 57*f*
   harm to women, of, 150–53, 152*t*, 239*f*
   lack of agreement between, 59–61
   limitations of, 53
   robustness checks, 254n.10
   UN using, 51, 52
   "usual suspect" indicators, 60*f*, 61*f*
   women's inclusion, of, 85*t*, 87*f*, 88*f*

women's rights, of, 126, 127*t*
World Bank using, 51–52
Indonesia, matriarchal communities in,
147–48
Inglehart, Ronald, 71–72, 129–30, 177, 178
INGOs, 141
International Covenant on Civil and
Political Rights (CCPR), 122
International Covenant on Economic,
Social, and Cultural Rights
(CESCR), 122
intersectional analysis, harm to women
and, 20
interstate conflict
beliefs about women's roles and, 189,
191, 242*f*, 244*f*, 248*f*
dependent variable, as, 219–21, 220*f*
harm to women and, 168, 236*f*,
240, 241*f*
monadic versus dyadic
analysis, 195n.1
women's inclusion and, 114, 231*f*
women's rights and, 141–42, 143
Iran
mobilization of women in, 166
Morality Police, 138
women's rights in, 138
Iraq War, 93, 138
Islamic State, 187–88
Isla Vista attack, 173–74, 191–92

Joachim, Jutta, 135–36

Kadera, Kelly, 5–7, 41–42
Karim, Sabrina M., 209–10
Keith, Linda Camp, 131
Kenya, matriarchal communities in,
147–48
Keohane, Robert, 3–4
Khasi people, 147–48
Kinsella, Helen M., 11, 30, 159, 201–2
Kishi, Roudabeh, 199–200
Koch, Michael T., 105–6

left-wing extremism, 188
Levitsky, Steven, 41
liberalism, 129–33
Liberia
mobilization of women in, 166

Women of Liberia Mass Movement for
Peace, 138, 166
women's rights in, 138
Libya, military intervention in, 143–44

male backlash, 200, 202
"marriage market," 164–65
masculinity
structural violence and, 157–59
violence against women and, 46–48
Matfess, Hilary, 199–200, 260–61n.20
matriarchal communities, 147–48
May, Theresa, 257–58n.22
McDermott, Rose, 92–93
McInnes, Gavin, 186–87
measurement
beliefs about women's roles, of
Bayesian measurement models, 69–
76, 245–46
existing measures, 176–77
present study measure, 177–80
harm to women, of
Bayesian measurement models, 69–
76, 235–40
overview, 150–53
invalidity (*see* measurement invalidity)
structural violence against women, of,
151
women's inclusion, of
Bayesian measurement models, 69–
76, 227–34
overview, 84–88
politics, in, 89–90
women's rights, of
Bayesian measurement models, 69–
76, 234
overview, 126
measurement invalidity
generally, 2
aggregate scales, problems with, 62
aggregation methods, 63–66
agreement between indicators, lack of,
59–61
Bayesian measurement models as
solution to problem of (*see*
Bayesian measurement models)
causal identification, lack of, 204–6
connecting concepts and indicators,
55–58

298 INDEX

measurement invalidity (*cont.*)
  contribution of study to problem of, 21–22
  measurement error, 66–67
  missing data, 62–63, 204–6
  overview, 24, 51–52, 76–77
  "usual suspect" indicators, 60*f*, 61*f*
measurement models. *See* Bayesian measurement models
Meir, Golda, 81, 117–18
Melander, Erik, 91, 103–4
Merry, Sally Engle, 20–21, 53, 76–77
Militarized Interstate Dispute (MID), 75–76
Mill, John Stuart, 162
Milton, Daniel James, 102–3
Minangkabau people, 147–48
misogyny, 34–35, 35*b*
Modern Sexism Scale (MSS), 177, 245
Moore, Will H., 97–98
Mosuo people, 147, 171–72
Mukazhanova-Powell, Karina, 106, 107
Munck, Gerardo L., 66

"naming and shaming," 136, 145
New Zealand
  Covid-19 pandemic in, 81, 118
  health policy in, 207–8
Nielsen, Perpetua Lynne, 18–19, 129–30, 156, 157–58, 163–64
Nincic, Donna J., 95
Nincic, Miroslav, 95
Norris, Pippa, 71–72, 129–30, 177, 178
Norway, beliefs about women's roles in, 74–75, 75*f*
null findings, 23, 111–13, 208–9, 259n.11

Ocasio-Cortez, Alexandria, 210–11
Olsson, Louise, 112, 155–56
Organisation for Economic Co-operation and Development (OECD) Social Institutions and Gender Index (SIGI), 62, 64, 65–66

patriarchy, 34*b*, 34
patrilineal/fraternal syndrome
  social hierarchy, sustaining, 159–61
  structural violence and, 157–59

Permanyer, Iñaki, 64, 254–55n.14
Peru, male backlash in, 200
physical violence against women, 148–49, 150–51, 153, 156. *See also* harm to women
Poe, Steven C., 131
Poland
  backsliding on women's rights in, 1–2
  beliefs about women's roles in, 185
policy recommendations
  beliefs about women's roles, 208
  civil society organizations, regarding, 207
  harm to women, 207–8
  health, regarding, 207–8
  overview, 23–24
  women's inclusion, 23–24, 206–7
  women's rights, 207
  workplace equality, regarding, 206–7
Political Terror Scale (PTS), 75–76
political violence
  beliefs about women's roles (*see* beliefs about women's roles)
  harm to women and (*see* harm to women)
  women's inclusion and (*see* women's inclusion)
  women's rights and (*see* women's rights)
  women's status and, 214–15
Post, Abigail S., 107
Powell, Jonathan, 106, 107
private property, 263n.2, 263n.4
Proud Boys, 173–74, 186–88
public opinion surveys, 13
Putin, Vladimir, 260n.16

regression models
  dependent variables
    civil conflict, 217–19, 218*f*
    interstate conflict, 219–21, 220*f*
    state violence, 221–24, 222*f*, 223*f*
    terror attacks, 224, 225*f*
  marginal effect of beliefs, 246*f*, 246
  marginal effect of harm, 240, 241*f*, 241*f*
  modeling strategy, 226–27
Richards, David L., 97–98, 131
right-wing extremism, 188

INDEX   299

Risse, Thomas, 137
Ropp, Stephen C., 137
Russia
   backsliding on women's rights in, 1–2, 145–46
   beliefs about women's roles in, 185
   CEDAW and, 141–42
   Ukraine, invasion of, 260n.16

Saiya, Nilay, 39–40, 98–99, 260n.17
Sandler, Todd, 260–61n.20
Sanin, Francisco Gutiérrez, 185–86
Sapiro, Virginia, 93
Schramm, Madison, 106
Scott, Jacqueline, 10
Security Council Resolution 1325, 12–13, 23–24, 29, 124, 130
Sen, Paromita, 107
Sexist Attitudes toward Women Scale, 177, 245
Sex Role Behavior Scale, 177, 242–45
Sexual Violence in Armed Conflict (SVAC), 256n.26
Shair-Rosenfield, Sarah, 95–96, 99–100, 105
Shea, Patrick E., 97–98
Sierra Leone
   armed groups in, 165
   harm to women in, 261n.23
   The Revolutionary United Front (RUF), 165
   signaling, 134–35
Sikkink, Kathryn, 137
Sjoberg, Laura, 5–7, 11, 30, 41–42, 159, 201–2, 212–13, 214
social dominance theory, 182, 262n.18
social hierarchy, harm to women and, 159–61
social inequality, 35–36, 36b
Social Institutions and Gender Index (SIGI), 62, 64, 65–66
South Korea, backsliding on women's rights in, 1–2
Stark, Alexandra, 106
state repression, 199–200
state violence
   beliefs about women's roles and, 189–90, 243f, 249f

dependent variable, ad, 221–24, 222f, 223f
   harm to women and, 156–57, 168, 170–71, 236f
   women's inclusion and, 103–4, 109–11, 115–16, 212, 232f
   women's rights and, 139–41, 143, 145, 197–98
structural violence against women
   evolutionary perspective of, 157–59
   measurement of, 151
   normative constraints on violence, weakening of, 155–56
   overview, 149, 203–4, 211
   patrilineal/fraternal syndrome and, 157–58
Sweden
   backtracking on women's rights in, 1–2, 145–46
   feminist foreign policy in, 120–21
Syrian crisis, 93

Tate, C. Neal, 131
terror attacks
   beliefs about women's roles and, 173–74, 188–89, 190, 197, 211, 243f, 246, 250f, 262–63n.22
   concept stretching and, 39–40
   dependent variable, as, 224, 225f
   harm to women and, 162, 168, 170–71, 238f, 260–61n.20
   women's inclusion and, 102–3, 109–11, 114–15, 197, 210–11, 229f, 233f, 234
   women's rights and, 142–43
Thatcher, Margaret, 81, 117–18
Thies, Scott J., 5–7, 41–42, 260–61n.20
Tickner, J. Ann, 252–53n.4
Tripp, Aili Mari, 12–13, 18, 123
Trump, Donald, 81, 173–74, 186–87
Tsutsui, Kiyoteru, 131–32, 137
Turkey, backsliding on women's rights in, 1–2

UCDP/PRIO, 75–76
Uganda
   armed groups in, 165
   Lord's Resistance Army, 165

300 INDEX

Ukraine, Russian invasion of, 260n.16
Umoja people, 147–48
United Kingdom
　health policy in, 207–8
　Women's Social and Political Union
　　(WSPU), 133n.8
United Nations
　Beijing Conference, 72–73, 123, 130
　Convention on the Elimination of All
　　Forms of Discrimination Against
　　Women (CEDAW), 60, 123–25,
　　130–31, 132–33, 141–42
　Gender Development Index (GDI), 62,
　　63–66, 254n.11
　Gender Equality Index (GII), 56, 64,
　　65–66, 254n.8
　Human Development Index (HDI), 51,
　　52, 63–65
　indicators, use of, 51, 52
　Security Council Resolution 1325, 12–
　　13, 23–24, 29, 124, 130
　Statistics Division, 150–51
　UNICEF, 42
　UN Women, 42
　women, peace and security (WPS)
　　agenda, 29–30
　women's rights and, 123
　World Women's Conferences, 123
United States
　Ambassador-at-Large for Global
　　Women's Issues, 120
　backsliding on women's rights in, 1–
　　2, 145–46
　beliefs about women's roles in, 173–74,
　　183, 185
　feminist foreign policy in, 120
　Isla Vista attack, 173–74, 191–92
　January 6 Capitol attack, 174
　matriarchal communities in, 147–48
　National Action Plan for UN Security
　　Council Resolution 1325, 120
　Proud Boys, 173–74, 186–88
　reproductive rights in, 1–2
　State Department, 120
　USAID, 120
　Universal Declaration of Human Rights
　　(UDHR), 122–23

Valentino, Banjamin A., 93
Varieties of Democracy (V-Dem) Project,
　21–22, 69–70, 126
Vietnam War, 138
violence against women. *See also* harm
　to women
　domestic violence, 161–63
　masculinity and, 46–48
　physical violence, 148–49, 150–51,
　　153, 156
　structural violence
　　evolutionary perspective of, 157–59
　　measurement of, 151
　　normative constraints on violence,
　　　weakening of, 155–56
　　overview, 149
　　patrilineal/fraternal syndrome and,
　　　157–58
　women's caregiving and relationships,
　　effect of, 47–48
　women's rights, correlation with, 2

Wallström, Margot, 120–21
Walter, Barbara F., 181–82
Warshaw, Christopher, 262n.12
watchdogs, 135–37
Weldon, S. Laurel, 12–13, 18, 125–26,
　129–30, 131, 137, 258n.3
Whitfield, Charles L., 161–62
Wibben, Annick T.R., 214
Woman Stats, 71, 150–51, 153, 263n.6
　women, peace, and security agenda, 12,
　　29–30, 49–50
women's inclusion
　characteristics of, 83, 84*b*
　conceptualizing, 82–83
　contribution of study, 22–23
　definition, 15–16
　delineation of, 17–18
　estimates of, 86*f*, 89*f*, 110*f*
　exclusion versus, 83
　feminist critiques, 201–2
　indicators of, 85*t*, 87*f*, 88*f*
　measurement of
　　Bayesian measurement models, 69–
　　　76, 227–34
　　overview, 84–88

politics, in, 89–90
overview, 13–14, 14*t*, 24–25, 81–82, 117–19
"parity" and, 82–83, 256n.2
policy recommendations, 23–24, 206–7
political violence and
  civil conflict, 102–3, 108, 230*f*
  conditions for peace, women creating, 98–100
  hypotheses, 102, 103, 104, 108–9
  interstate conflict, 114, 231*f*
  more disposed toward peace, women as, 82, 91–96
  null findings, 111–13, 193–96, 194*t*
  overview, 90–91
  perceptional stereotypes of women and, 104–9
  political decisions, affecting, 96–98
  regression models, 234
  state repression, 199–200
  state violence, 103–4, 109–11, 115–16, 212, 232*f*
  terror attacks, 102–3, 109–11, 114–15, 197, 210–11, 229*f*, 233*f*, 234
  testing hypotheses, 109–16
  variations in preferences and experiences as shaping, 100–4
  women versus men, 94*f*, 94–95
  women, peace and security (WPS) agenda and, 30
women's rights
  backtracking on, 1–2, 24
  characteristics of, 124*b*, 124
  conceptualizing, 121–26
  contribution of study, 22–23
  definition, 15–16
  delineation of, 18
  enforcement of, 125–26
  estimates of, 130*f*
  feminist critiques, 201–2
  freedom to act, 121–22
  gender justice and sex equality and, 125
  indicators of, 126, 127*t*
  marginal effect of, 140*f*
  measurement of

Bayesian measurement models, 69–76, 234
  overview, 126
overview, 12–14, 14*t*, 24–25, 120–21, 144–46
policy recommendations, 207
political violence and
  civil conflict, 139, 142–43
  formal protections, effect of, 203, 211
  hypotheses, 133, 135, 137
  INGOs, presence of, 141
  interstate conflict, 141–42, 143
  liberal democratic states, in, 140–41
  liberalism, women's rights signaling, 129–33
  military intervention, 143–44
  NGOs, presence of, 143
  non-violent advocacy, transitioning to, 137–38
  null findings, 193–96, 194*t*, 259n.11
  overview, 128–29
  state openness to claim making, women's rights signaling, 134–35
  state violence, 139–41, 143, 145, 197–98
  terror attacks, 142–43
  testing hypotheses, 138–44
  watchdogs, increasing number of, 135–37
private property, 263n.2, 263n.4
regression models, 234–35
women's risk, 13
women's status
  aspects of, 12
  characteristics of, 37*b*, 37–38
  contribution of study, 22
  gender equality distinguished, 11–12, 30
  "gender lens" and, 201
  overview, 13–14, 14*t*
  political violence and, 214–15
  women, peace and security (WPS) agenda and, 30
women's vulnerability, 13
Wood, Elisabeth Jean, 185–86
Wood, Reed, 95–96, 99–100, 105

302 INDEX

World Bank
    Business Ready (B-READY), 51–52
    Doing Business, 51–52
    Gender Stats, 150–51
    indicators, use of, 51–52
    World Governance Indicators, 253n.1
World Economic Forum, 255n.18
World Governance Indicators, 253n.1

World Values Survey (WVS), 71–72, 177–78, 179t, 245, 261n.10

Yemen, conflict in, 120–21
Younas, Javed, 260–61n.20
"youth bulges," 164–65

Zaihra, Tasneem, 39–40, 98–99, 260n.17

The manufacturer's authorised representative in the EU for product safety is Oxford University Press España S.A. of El Parque Empresarial San Fernando de Henares, Avenida de Castilla, 2 – 28830 Madrid (www.oup.es/en or product.safety@oup.com). OUP España S.A. also acts as importer into Spain of products made by the manufacturer.

Printed in the USA/Agawam, MA
March 28, 2025

885041.016